American Music

A PANORAMA

The Concise Edition

American Music

A PANORAMA

DANIEL KINGMAN

SCHIRMER BOOKS
AN IMPRINT OF SIMON & SCHUSTER MACMILLAN
New York

PRENTICE HALL INTERNATIONAL
London • Mexico City • New Delhi • Singapore • Sydney • Toronto

Acknowledgements for quoted material are found on p. 434, which should be considered an extension of the copyright page.

Schirmer Books
An Imprint of Simon & Schuster Macmillan
1633 Broadway
New York, NY 10019

Book design by Charles B. Hames

Library of Congress Catalog Card Number: 97–29048

Printed in the United States of America

Printing Number
 2 3 4 5 6 7 8 9 10

Library of Congress Cataloging-in-Publication Data

Kingman, Daniel.
    American music : a panorama / Daniel Kingman. — Concise ed.
      p. cm.
    Includes index.
      ISBN 0–02–864614–2 (alk. paper)
      1. Music—United States—History and criticism. I. Title.
ML200.K55 1998
780'.973—dc21   97–29048
                                                        CIP
                                                        MN

This paper meets the requirements of ANSI/NISO Z.39.48–1992 (Permanence of Paper).

To Louise

The *panorama* was a popular form of didactic art in the larger frontier cities of America in the mid-1800s. It was an exhibition of the painter's art done on a mammoth scale. A huge canvas, twenty feet high or more, would slowly pass before the assembled audience, moving, scroll-like, from one large roll to another. The paying spectators would see vast scenes unrolling before their eyes in a sort of primitive motion picture—battle scenes, or the course of the Mississippi River between two points. Often this was done to the accompaniment of music.

CONTENTS

Author's Guide to the Concise Edition

It is my hope to have placed in your hands an inviting and reliable guide to the boisterous, teeming panorama of American music. Some of you may have been using this guide in one, or even both, of its earlier versions. What is being offered here is an updated and concise edition, as being more affordable than a new full edition, and having less reading material, a feature that will make the book more appropriate for some users. A full edition (currently the second) will be kept in print as long as there is sufficient demand for it; it is a resource for more comprehensive information and background, as well as for more complete reading lists and lists of projects.

This edition offers something many of you have awaited with anticipation: an audio supplement of musical examples, coordinated with each chapter.

The fundamental organization of the book has not been altered. Rejecting a traditional chronological–historical approach to the subject as a whole, I have maintained an ordering that reflects my view of American music as a number of more or less distinct but parallel streams. The metaphor still remains, for me, a sufficiently useful and compelling one; furthermore, it gives the book a flexibility that can be useful in designing a course. Added to the six sections devoted to these streams I have kept a brief seventh, to call attention to what is still an important characteristic of American music—a regionalism that defies absorption and homogenization, and a diversity that calls into question the concept of the "melting pot."

A Word to Teachers about Mapping Your Own Tour of the Terrain

A frequent objection to *American Music: A Panorama* when used as a text has been that it is difficult to cover all that it presents in a single term of ten, twelve, or even fifteen weeks. In putting this edition in your hands, a word of warning, together with some respectful advice, is in order. A concise edition can shrink the number of pages in a guide to the panorama of American music, but it cannot shrink the panorama itself. It is simply too richly and gloriously vast! What I do most earnestly advise is that you map your own tour of the terrain. The organization of the topography into streams makes it possible to begin wherever you like—with whichever stream you feel most comfortable, or are the most enthusiastic about at the time, or you feel would interest your students the most at the time. This flexibility is easily affordable, since a course does not always have to consist of the same ingredients in the same order. The interconnectedness of the subject can lead to an easy transition to other streams, in almost any order you like. And if some streams have to be neglected by the group as a whole, the book is there to entice its readers into following other streams, and to guide them in their exploration. The most that organized courses can do in any case is simply to open doors. After many years of teaching, I find myself more than ever convinced that what education is all about is equipping and encouraging us *all* to pursue knowledge, and with it increased appreciation, on our own, as a lifetime joy whose rewards never diminish.

A Word about Listening to Music

The supplement is meant to offer a sampling of the wide variety of musical genres and styles that constitute American music, past and present. In order to accommodate even a rudimentary sampling of genres within a reasonable number of compact discs, it has been necessary to use excerpts in most cases. What has been presented with each example is enough, it is hoped, to convey the *essence* of a particular kind of music. For convenience, the title of every item in the Audio Supplement is printed in bold type wherever it is mentioned in the body of the text itself.

Readers will naturally want to pursue their listening further in many cases. For the benefit of those wishing to hear the entire work that is sampled, or other works of the same type, the source of nearly every item in the Audio Supplement is given in the annotations to the Supplement. In as many cases as possible the sources are recorded anthologies that are recognized as being authentic, representative, and apt to be readily available.

Longer works such as symphonies require, and reward, special consideration. Because it is impossible to convey the essence of a longer work in a short excerpt, such works have not been included in the Audio Supplement. But more extended compositions have their place in any study, and the experiencing of these works in their entirety has its unique rewards, and should not be neglected. Therefore suggestions of longer pieces to be listened to are included in the body of the text. Their durations have been given in the text in most cases as an aid to teachers in planning for their inclusion in class sessions. For longer works readers and teachers will have to rely, as they have in the past, on separate recordings from libraries, from borrowed recordings, or from their own collections.

A Word about Musical Examples in the Text

For reasons of space, the number of notated examples has been reduced considerably. The songs that appear in the concise edition are intended to be *sung* whenever possible, and have been pitched with this in mind. There is hardly any substitute for this experience. An easy beginning would be "Amazing Grace" (chapter 8), "De Colores" (chapter 4), or the cowboy songs in chapter 16. From there it is an easy step to "Simple Gifts" (chapter 8), or the stirring Revolutionary War song "Chester" in the same chapter. The revival spiritual is hardly better experienced than in the sturdy "On Jordan's Stormy Banks" in both of its versions (chapter 8). William Billings's beautiful canon "When Jesus Wept" (chapter 8) can be sung in four parts by the entire group. They may enjoy singing from shape notes the folk hymn "Wondrous Love," first the melody, then all the parts (chapter 8). Having gone this far, the class would be ready to enjoy singing such Americana as "The Wabash Cannonball" (chapter 5) or "De Boatman's Dance" (chapter 11). The notation of the blues scale (chapter 2) and of blues harmony (at its simplest in chapter 2 and in its more elaborate form in chapter 14) is included with the idea that the teacher can play these for the class, thereby recreating them as aural experiences for those who do not read music. Other instrumental examples, such as the excerpts from Copland's *Billy the Kid* or the Third Symphony by Roy Harris (chapter 16), are intended to be played for the class. This adds an important dimension even if the complete recordings are being played.

A Word about Biography

We can never deny the fact that it is *individuals* who make all the difference in music, and that their lives are part of its history, and are therefore never wholly irrelevant and are often fascinating. But the panorama is so vast, and the number of musicians, even quite important ones, is so great, that space could not be given to biography as such. The incidental biographical material in the book, beyond what is necessary to place the individual in time and place, is included only where it sheds light either on the nature of the music itself, on the life experience or ambience from which it came, or on some aspect of American music that goes beyond the career of a single individual. Readers who wish to satisfy an understandable curiosity about a particular American musician can make a good start by consulting the four-volume *The New Grove Dictionary of American Music* (1986), which covers all periods and genres.

A Word about the Lists for Further Reading and the Projects

The reading lists have been substantially reduced from those in the full edition, which should be consulted for additional items. The suggestions for projects at the end of each chapter are intended to give the student an opportunity to investigate further, on her or his own, many different aspects of American music. Even a tiny scrap of knowledge that one discovers, with a little effort, for oneself becomes a cherished corner of the whole subject—forever one's own. The number of projects has been considerably reduced in the concise edition; the full edition may be consulted for suggestions for more detailed and specialized projects. The projects are merely sample suggestions; the imaginative teacher and the inventive student can come up with many more, along similar or different lines.

Acknowledgements

It is been my good fortune to have had the help of very knowledgeable and willing colleagues in the revising of certain areas. My able research assistant in rock music has been Larry Worster, an unabashed fan who is also a thoroughly trained musician and scholar. His work in digging out details of texts and recorded sources was tireless, but even more appreciated was his breadth of perspective. Fred Hess, able performer and arranger as well as scholar and teacher, was a great help in jazz, especially putting into perspective recent developments. John Koegel, an eminent young authority on many aspects of Latino music, was generously forthcoming with material and suggestions. Philip Sonnichsen also willingly shared some of his vast knowledge and experience in this area, as did William John Summers, an eminent authority on California mission music. Tara Browner gave valuable advice on bibliography in American Indian music. My good friend Toshiye Kawamura, a practicing expert on Japanese music and dance as cultivated in this country, loaned material and gave invaluable advice for this part of the final chapter. Justin Bishop put into perspective for me the modern folk scene he knows so well. Yuriy and Ola Oliynyk were generous with material and information on Ukrainian music in Sacramento. Lisa Salyer some years ago did a graduate course project on local Portuguese music; her work made it possible to include some details on this music in the last chapter. My colleague Susan Willoughby, an experienced teacher of the subject who has used this book over a period of years, has given me many useful suggestions. Finally, I wish to express my appreciation to my wife, Louise, for her careful reading of the manuscript, and for months and months of patience.

Part One

Folk and Ethnic Musics

"Willie Thomas." Photo by David Gahr

A scanning of the vast panorama of American music can begin nowhere more logically than with our folk and ethnic musics. America's music, throughout its broad spectrum, is so relatively new as to have remained closer to folk sources than is the case in almost any other country. The professional sector of our musical life has never gone very long without returning to refresh and revitalize itself at the fount of folk culture. Masterpieces as diverse as *Porgy and Bess* and *Appalachian Spring* bear witness to this, as do large amounts of music in popular culture, from Dan Emmett to Bob Dylan and Paul Simon.

Yet this very closeness of our music to its roots is attended by a paradox. There is probably no other country in the world in which the soil of folk culture has been so thoroughly broken up, and either eroded away or rendered sterile. Not only have the all-pervasive media spread commercial urban music exhaustively, they have put music largely in the hands of the professional entertainer. Continuous and extensive migration has broken down isolation and emasculated regional character. And affluence, spectacular in comparison to the rest of the world, has put applicances and products of the media into the hands of virtually everyone, so that the need or desire to make one's own music has lessened, where it has not actually disappeared.

So it would appear that the rich humus of folklore has provided us with nourishment but proved to be fragile as well. Yet the realization of fragility has made us more aware of its value and encouraged us to make efforts to conserve it. And our folk and ethnic musics do live on in the space age—perhaps because, faced with the formidable challenge to human values and human scale posed by technology, and with the disorientations of an unstable world, we have come to realize both our need for the sense of community that a living connection with the past provides, and the benefits of keeping alive, through adaptation to the world we live in, an oral tradition that is simple, direct, and unflinchingly honest in its expression.

Chapter 1

The Anglo-American Tradition

The Anglo-American tradition of folk music, its origins traceable to England, Scotland, and Ireland, is best epitomized in the ballad, that venerable story-telling convergence of poetry and music. We begin with one of the most widespread and popular of these.

"Barbara Allen" as a Prototype of the Anglo-American Ballad

It might seem unlikely that the tale of a man who, spurned by a coldhearted woman, actually dies of his love for her, should have so enduringly engaged ballad singers and listeners from the seventeenth century in Scotland (its first recorded emergence) to the twentieth century in America. Yet this has been the history of "**Barbara Allen.**" Oliver Goldsmith wrote in 1765, "The music of the finest singer is dissonance to what I felt when an old dairy-maid sung me into tears with . . . 'The Cruelty of Barbara Allen.'"[1] It had the same effect in 1938 in east Texas on the singer Bob Brown, an old-timer who lived at the edge of the Big Thicket. When Brown came to the line "Young man, I think you're dying," folk-song collector William Owens reports that "tears filled his eyes and he brushed at his wrinkled cheek with the back of his hand."

Owens writes, "If I were asked to name the ballad most deeply ingrained in the heart and thinking of the American folk, 'Barbara Allen' would be my choice. I have heard it up and down the country against backgrounds ranging from expensive nightclubs to sharecroppers' shacks."[2]

Dispersion and Variation with the Passage of Time

"Barbara Allen" has traveled far and wide. The Library of Congress Archive of American Folk Song contained, as of 1962, 243 transcribed versions of this ballad, picked up from twenty-seven states, from Maine to Florida to California. The essence of the story, sometimes referred to as the *emotional core*, endures in all versions. But less vital elements are subject to considerable variation, as is the case with any tale passed on by word of mouth. The subsequent death from remorse of Barbara herself is the usual ending in most versions that we encounter today, but this was not a part of older versions of the ballad. Other accretions are

1. the rose and briar motif: the two are buried side by side; a rose grows out of William's grave, and a briar out of Barbara's. The plants grow up to become entwined in a lovers' knot. This sentimental device, rooted in old beliefs that the soul, upon death, either passes into or becomes a plant expressing the character of the dead person, occurs in other ballads as well.[3]
2. Barbara's viewing of William's corpse as it passes, a sight that moves her in some versions to heartless laughter, in others to remorse.
3. Barbara's attempt to excuse her cruelty and coldness by accusing William of having drunk a toast "to the ladies round" but slighting Barbara.
4. William's bequests to Barbara on his deathbed of a gold watch and a gold ring, or, on a somewhat grimmer note, a basin full of tears, and a blood-soaked shirt.

Traditional folksingers do not intentionally alter a song. But there are many things about oral transmission that make changes inevitable. Simple forgetting is a constant factor. Another source of change is a misunderstanding of elements of language as the ballad ages. Difficult or ambiguous words, or words and phrases no longer in current usage, are very vulnerable to change. "The Gypsy Laddie" is a Scottish ballad in which the lady of the castle, in her lord's absence, is abducted by a band of gypsies who appear at the castle, cast a spell on her (or give her nutmeg and ginger, considered to be aphrodisiacs), and abduct her. One old version of the ballad, still retaining aspects of the supernatural, says of the gypsy band that as they saw the lady, "They coost their glamourie owre her." A later garbled version says of the gypsies at this point that "They called their grandmother over!" Not only has the word *glamourie* ("glamour") been misunderstood, but its older meaning as an actual spell to be cast over someone has been lost, to the impoverishment of the ballad.

Old ballads, transplanted in time and place, usually retain their emotional core, but become "naturalized" in their details. Changes in place names are common; the "Oxford girl" easily becomes the "Knoxville girl," for example. Other details that surround us in daily life are adapted as well. Nowhere is this more strikingly illustrated than in Woody Guthrie's version of "The Gypsie Laddie," known as "Gypsy Davey."[4] At the core of the story is the fact that the lord, on returning to the castle, rides after the gypsies. In some versions he is successful in retrieving his wife; in others he is not. (The ballad has been viewed as a parody on the Greek myth of Orpheus and his attempt to bring Eurydice back from the underworld.) In Guthrie's version the "lord" becomes the "boss"; his black steed becomes the "buckskin horse with the hundred-dollar saddle"; instead of riding east and riding west in search of the abducted lady, "till they cam' to yonder boggie," there are, as would be expected on the Western plains, wagon tracks to be followed, and they lead to a gypsy encampment and a campfire with gypsies singing to the "sound of a big guitar." Also noteworthy is the presence of a child, the "blue-eyed babe," a typically American addition not in the original Scottish version.

Interpreting the Ballads

The early attention given to ballads was directed almost exclusively to their texts, and indeed "the ballad as literature" is a prominent branch of study. There are many ways to approach the interpretation of ballads. Using "Barbara Allen" as an example, one could pursue the *historical* context. Was Barbara a real person? One theory is that the ballad was a popular libel on Barbara Villiers, the famous mistress of Charles II of England (1630–85). Or, to take another road (admittedly less traveled by), one could explore the *social-psychoanalytical* dimensions of the ballad, as Alan Lomax, noted folklorist, has done, viewing Barbara Allen as "frigid western woman humbling and destroying the man whom she sees as her enemy and antagonist."[5]*

Print and the Ballad

Oral tradition—human memory as the conservator and the human voice as the "publisher"—still retains among folklorists its preeminence as the *ideal* medium of folk song, and whether a ballad can be found to be in oral tradition is still regarded as a valid test of its "folkness," regardless of its origins. But print has long had a hand in ballad conservation and dissemination, and more recently so have other media such as recordings. The older a ballad is, the more likely it is to have been in and out of print over the course of its history. Furthermore, it is likely that its printed versions have had an influence both on the state in which it exists today and on its geographical distribution.

The "broadside" (a cheap printed version on a single sheet of paper giving the words only) and the "songster" (a small collection of such texts, also cheaply printed, for popular sale) have long figured in ballad history, both here and in the British Isles. Broadside ballads were usually hastily written (using preexisting material liberally) by hack writers for quick sale to capitalize on current public events, such as hangings. James W. Day, a blind Kentucky musician who used

*For a more recent interpretation of this ballad, reinventing Barbara's character in quite a different way, see *Sing Out!* magazine (May–July 1996).

the pseudonym Jilson Setters, told of writing a ballad about a convicted murderer named Simpson Bush. He took it to the hanging and recalled: "I had my pockets plum full of my song-ballet [*sic*] that I had made up about Bush and that a printer had run off for me on a little hand press at the county seat. I sold every one I had."[6] The "broadside'" was brought up to date during the famous Scopes trial of 1925, when sixty thousand phonograph recordings of a ballad on the subject were sold on the steps of the courthouse in Dayton, Tennessee, while the trial was going on.[7]

One example of the interaction between print and sound media on the one hand and oral tradition on the other will close our brief consideration of this complex and fascinating subject. In 1925 Polk Brockman, an early country-music talent scout, heard of a cave death in Kentucky and wired the Reverend Andrew Jenkins in Atlanta, in effect "ordering" a song on the subject. Brockman paid Jenkins $25, plus another $25 to make a recording of it, which became popular. This was the origin of the ballad "Floyd Collins," which was later collected from oral tradition in Virginia, North Carolina, Tennessee, Kentucky, New York, and Utah.[8]

Imported versus Native Ballads

Many of the immigrant ballads have, after generations here, become so thoroughly naturalized, and evolved such distinctively American variants, that they seem very much at home in our culture. There are in addition, however, a great number of younger ballads that have originated in America, most of them from the latter part of the nineteenth century.

Whereas the older English and Scottish ballads, even in adaptation, have not entirely concealed their archaic style and medieval atmosphere (part of their charm for twentieth-century singers, no doubt), the native ballads have more realistic immediacy. They have known authors in many cases, and they are much more apt to be based on actual occurrences, even though assigning an exact time and place to the events may present fascinating and nearly insoluble problems.* In contrast to the older British ballads, American ballads tend to be more about occupations—buffalo hunters ("**The Buffalo Skinners**"),[9] cowboys ("Little Joe the Wrangler"), railroading ("The Wreck of Old 97"), lumberjacks ("The Jam on Gerry's Rock"), sailors ("The Bigler's Crew"), and criminals ("Jesse James"). They frequently involve fatal physical disasters ("The Avondale Disaster," "The Titanic") or a more or less journalistic recounting of murders and executions ("Pearl Bryan," "Little Omie Wise," "John Hardy") rather than dwelling on more psychic, introverted, or pathological themes such as supernatural phenomena,

*The search for the factual basis of the railroad ballad "Casey Jones" and the lumberjack ballad "The Jam on Gerry's Rock" is a case in point.

fatal jealousy, or incest. Malcolm Laws finds in native ballads a more subjective, sympathetic approach to their heroes or heroines—evidence of a "tender humanity toward all who are faced with tragedy"—and concludes that native balladry "may be rugged and colorful or commonplace and sentimental; much of it may be inept, some even illiterate, but above all it shows compassion, neighborliness, and concern for other men's misfortunes."[10]

Ballad-making does not belong solely to the past. The folk movement has many active performers who are not only collectors and compilers, but poets and composers as well. To cite one example, "**South Coast**" is a gambler's tale of love and death written in the 1920s by Lillian Bos-Ross, its setting not the Hebrides but the wild coast of California in the colonial days of the *vaquero*.[11]

The Music of the Ballads
Ballad Form and Tune Variants

Ballads typically consist of four-line stanzas, with the number of *feet* (or stressed syllables) per line alternating 4 + 3 + 4 + 3 —a metric arrangement known as "ballad meter." There are as many stanzas as it takes to tell the story, or as many as the singer can remember or cares to sing. All the stanzas are sung to the same tune.

Tunes are subject to the same organic processes of change wrought by oral tradition that operate on the words, and these also produce tune variants—sometimes in great numbers. How does the tune of "Barbara Allen" go?* It all depends on who is singing it. Examples 1-1 and 1-2 are two versions recovered from traditional singing. They are quite different. Each is representative of a large group of tunes that has dozens of variants. Example 1-1 was recorded in West Liberty, Kentucky, in 1937.

Example 1–1. "Barbara Allen" I

> *It was early in the month of May,*
> *When the May-buds they were a-swelling,*
> *Sweet William on his death-bed lay*
> *For the love of Barbara Allen.*

*A sampling of the rich variety of versions of "Barbara Allen" can be gained from the following archival releases from the Library of Congress: AFS L1 (*Anglo-American Ballads*), L14 (*Anglo-American Songs and Ballads*), L54 (*Versions and Variants of Barbara Allen*), as well as from many versions by professional folksingers.

Example 1-2 is from Tennessee, as sung for the Library of Congress Archive collection in 1936.

Example 1–2. "Barbara Allen" II

'Twas in the lovely month of May
The flowers all were bloomin'.
Sweet William on his death-bed lay
For the love of Barbry Allen.

This second example is fairly closely related to the tune most commonly printed in popular collections, and thus the one most frequently encountered in commercial arrangements and professional performances (Ex. 1-3).

Example 1–3. "Barbara Allen" III

In Scarlet town where I was born,
There was a fair maid dwelling,
Made every youth cry, Well away,
And her name was Barb'ra Allen.

Time, memory, and geography operate on music as well as on words, and no ballad is apt to have only a single tune indissolubly wedded to it. Neither is any given tune always exclusively associated with only one ballad. Charles Seeger puts it both accurately and colorfully when he writes that "both spouses are frequently unfaithful to their common-law kind of union."[12]

Tune Sources and Scales

Many ballad tunes exhibit characteristics of antiquity, particularly those coming from the Appalachians. Much of this antique flavor can be attributed to the scales on which they are based. One scale frequently encountered is the *pentatonic*, a scale of five (rather than the more familiar seven) notes to the octave. (You can hear the sound of the pentatonic scale by playing only the black keys of the piano.) This scale is the basic building material of much folk and ethnic music worldwide; we hear it in American Indian music, and in the music of Africa, the Orient, and central Europe. It occurs in our popular music as well; the first two phrases of two of Stephen Foster's best known songs, "Old Folks at Home" and "Oh, Susannah," are pure pentatonic. The first two versions of "Barbara Allen" given above are (with the exception of one unstressed neighbor note) also pentatonic. Certain *modal* scales (scales using six or seven tones to the octave, but not in the usual major or minor configuration) are also found in the tunes inherited from the Anglo-Celtic tradition. The use of these modes also imparts a certain archaic flavor to the music.

Other Aspects of Folk Music

Two other aspects of folk music are indispensable to an adequate understanding of it. The first is *singing style* as an integral part of folk song. This includes tone quality, vocal inflection and embellishment, and subtle variations in rhythm and pitch—all of which are practically impossible to put into printed notation. The second aspect is the distinction between the traditional and the professional singer; it is important to understand and distinguish the role of each. Traditional singers are themselves part of the tradition, and their memory constitutes the reservoir of this tradition. Professionals must reach a larger audience and must please and entertain that audience. In doing so they may find it necessary to make changes, large or small, that compromise the tradition somewhat. But professionals have positive contributions to make as well. They may stimulate interest in, and thus help to preserve, traditional music that would otherwise be lost. They bring to their performances a proven degree of musical talent inherently greater than that of the average "carrier" of the tradition. Further, their renditions are not going to be marred by the lapses of memory that mutilate many a ballad in the hands of traditional singers.

Fiddle Tunes

There is probably no form of rural homespun music so indelibly associated in the popular mind with the American folk scene as the familiar *hoedown*. The fiddle and its tunes provided music to dance to, and the fiddle was long the dominant

Country fiddler and banjo player. *From the collections of the Library of Congress.*

instrument in rural America.* A product of situations where prejudice on religious grounds against the fiddle forebade its use for dancing was a genre of Anglo-American folk music that occupied a niche somewhere between the ballad and the fiddle tune—the *play-party song*, used to accompany movement games.

Fiddle Tune Types and Sources

The most typical kinds of tunes found in the repertory of the country fiddler are the *hoedowns*, or *breakdowns*—rapid dance tunes in duple meter, relatives of the reels and hornpipes of the British Isles. The names and tunes of the most popular breakdowns are well known to any square-dance enthusiast or frequenter of fiddlers' contests: "Lost Indian," "Soldier's Joy," "Devil's Dream," "Leather Britches," "Wag'ner" ("Wagoner"), "Old Joe Clark," "Give the Fiddler a Dram,"

---

*"Violin" and "fiddle" are usually used as contrasting terms to describe the contrasting uses to which the same instrument is put in the fine-art and folk traditions, respectively. Interestingly enough, both words come from the same root.

"Natchez Under the Hill," "Sourwood Mountain,"* and so on. The term *break-down* is but one illustration of the frequent exchange between the often-parallel musical traditions of blacks and whites. *Breakdown* was used in the nineteenth century to designate any dance in African-American style, but especially those popular with white boatmen on the Ohio and the Mississippi.[13]

The jigs are there, too—lively tunes in 6/8 time like "The Irish Washerwoman." The waltz, a seemingly unlikely transplant from central Europe, has wide currency among country fiddlers. Less surprising are the occasional schottisches, with their characteristic dotted rhythms like those of the Scottish strathspey. The fiddler's repertory, especially in the lowlands and in the West, has come to include rags and blues. The bulk of Anglo-American fiddle tunes, how-ever, has come more or less directly from the thriving body of reels and hornpipes used for dancing in the British Isles, especially in Scotland and Ireland.

Some individual tunes not in any of these categories have interesting histories. Both "Jordan Is a Hard Road to Travel" and "Old Dan Tucker" were written by Dan Emmett for the professional minstrel stage. And the famous "Bonaparte's Retreat" is a kind of reminiscence of the Battle of Waterloo—possibly, as the solemn drone indicates, having reached the fiddle repertory by way of a bagpipe air.

Print and the Fiddle Tune

The complex intertwining of print and oral tradition that we have observed in the case of the ballad has also been at work with the fiddle tune. Despite many fiddlers' independence of, or honest aversion to, notated music ("Girl, they ain't no music to them tunes. You jes' play 'em"),[14] the fact is that fiddle tunes have been collected in written form, at first in manuscript and later to appear in pub-lished collections, since at least as far back as the early nineteenth century. Elias Howe, a New England fiddler, published in 1840 *The Musician's Companion*, a collection of fiddle tunes that he sold from door to door. He published numerous and ever-larger collections over the next half-century, culminating in a joint ven-ture with Sydney Ryan in 1883—*Ryan's Mammoth Collection of 1050 Jigs and Reels*. This was reissued by M. M. Cole in 1940 as *1000 Fiddle Tunes*. Sold ini-tially through the Sears Roebuck stores across the nation, it has since become firmly established as the "fiddler's bible."

The Instruments

The fiddler's instrument may be "store-bought," possibly from a mail-order house. (An old catalog lists "Our Amati Model Violin" for $7.25, while the

*The first two are well represented in a performance recorded in Hazard, Kentucky on *Mountain Music of Kentucky*, Smithsonian/Folkways 40077.

"Special Stradivarius Model" sells for $9.25, the latter including bow, case, an extra set of strings, an instruction book, and a fingerboard chart.[15]) But fiddles were often homemade as well.

The standard violin tuning in perfect fifths was used, but so were a number of variants as well, and for various reasons. To secure a low "drone" string, the G string was sometimes tuned down to an E or even a D; open strings were sometimes duplicated for resonance in a given key (the standard tuning for "Bonaparte's Retreat," for example, uses D strings!).

Folk Music as an Instrument of Persuasion in the Twentieth Century

The 1920s saw the irreversible onset of change for American folk music. Through radio and recordings, urban popular music began to reach the "folk," which then still clearly meant the rural people. And the rural people's own folk music was being recorded, thus making it available, not only to the folk themselves, but to city people as well.* One effect of this was to foster a "nonfolk" intellectual awareness of folk music, in contrast to the "folk" view of it as something wholly integrated into daily life. With this nonfolk awareness came an increased tendency to *use* folk music for nonmusical ends.

The use of converted folk tunes in the service of a cause is nothing new. The Populist movement in the 1890s produced songs like "**The Farmer Is the Man Who Feeds Them All**," and "Hayseed Like Me," the latter to the popular folk tune "Old Rosin the Beau." In the early years of this century, militant unionist Joe Hill wrote "The Preacher and the Slave," a stinging parody on the gospel hymn "Sweet By-and-By."

The Urban Folk-Song Movement of the 1930s and 1940s

The Depression period of the 1930s brought changes that went beyond simply adapting folk tunes, to the appropriating of an entire folk *tradition* in the service of social and political causes. R. Serge Denisoff refers to the mystique of the term "folk" as Folk Consciousness, which includes "the emulation of rural attire, and the idealization of folk singers as 'people's artists'. . . ."[16] The ensuing urban folk-song movement involved such interesting and diverse figures as Aunt Molly Jackson from the Kentucky coal mines, Leadbelly (Huddie Ledbetter), discovered in a Louisiana prison by folklorists John and Alan Lomax, Harvard dropout Pete Seeger, son of a distinguished ethnomusicologist, and Woody Guthrie.

---

*It is significant that one of the most important collections of recordings documenting our folk music, the Smithsonian/Folkways *Anthology of American Folk Music*, consists entirely of commercial recordings made in the 1920s and 1930s.

Woody Guthrie. *Courtesy New York Public Library.*

Woody Guthrie

Woody Guthrie (1912–67) was a highly individual and somewhat enigmatic figure. His Oklahoma background was certainly folk in any sense of the term, and his absorption of this heritage is evident in his early recordings of traditional ballads, including "**Gypsy Davy**." The broad and varied experiences of his life, the first thirty years of which are so colorfully set forth in his autobiography, *Bound for Glory*, gave him abundant contact with the common people. His identification with them, and his sympathies for them, resulted in a spontaneous flood of songs (only a small proportion of which have been preserved), and of poems and sketches. Many of the songs, even those that became broadly popular, had a hard and determined edge of protest to them, though this edge was concealed or censored in popular versions. "**So Long, It's Been Good to Know Ya**," for example, reveals its original context only in its spontaneous, rambling, talking-and-singing version by Woody himself.

A man of shrewd intelligence and diverse talents (Guthrie read voluminously and was a very prolific writer apart from his songs, a painter, and the confidant of a president of the United States), he was no simple "man of the soil"; yet he often found himself having to deny his own acute perceptions and to conceal his intellect behind a mask of simplistic doggerel in trying to fulfill his most difficult job of all—which was largely thrust upon him—that of being a kind of universal "folk poet" of the common man.

Protest and Folk Song in the 1960s
Bob Dylan

When the protest folk-song movement reemerged in the 1960s it presented a marked contrast to the movement of the thirties and forties. The career of Bob Dylan (Robert Zimmerman, b. 1941) is illustrative. Dylan emerged into prominence from the same Greenwich Village milieu that had launched his idol Woody Guthrie before him into the role of protester and "folk poet." But the men, their backgrounds, and their times were different. As a folk musician Guthrie never had consciously to adopt a style and never felt it necessary to change his style—in fact there is no indication that he was ever much *aware* of such a thing as style. Dylan, coming along at a later and more self-conscious period for folk music, had already gone from rock 'n' roll to acoustic folk by the time he went to New York; he was to change his style, his sound, and his type of material many times thereafter. Because of Dylan's popularity and the force of his talent, each of his changes from the 1960s on sent waves of influence, and alienation, through the folk and rock worlds. As Wayne Hampton has put it, Dylan, the "self-proclaimed 'song and dance man,'. . . has continued to seek new audiences and to alienate old ones."[17]

Dylan created some memorable songs and ballads of protest, especially in his early career. Some are explicit as to the issues "The Lonesome Death of Hattie Carroll" and "Seven Curses" (the corruption of justice); "Only a Pawn in Their Game" and "Oxford Town" (the machinations of racial prejudice); "Masters of War" and "With God on Our Side" (war); "Let Me Die in My Footsteps" (bomb shelters). He also produced some very realistic ballads that are not overt protest songs, in that the target, as a defiantly general human condition, is less readily assailable, as in "The Ballad of Hollis Brown" and "North Country Blues" (poverty). Others are more highly distilled and convey more generalized feelings about the future: "Blowin' in the Wind" and "The Times They Are A-Changin'."

Some songs display that surrealistic kind of private imagery that marks much of the poetry of the sixties and seventies, and is a sign of a distinct departure from the old tradition in the direction of the esoteric ("A Hard Rain's A-Gonna Fall" and "Subterranean Homesick Blues").

Dylan has absorbed many influences. His debt to African-American blues is readily apparent. Less obvious is his relationship to the Anglo-American ballad tradition and to the cultural milieu (including the religious) that nourished it. His "Girl of the North Country" is an offshoot of a perennial ballad. The tune of "Masters of War" is basically that of the haunting "Nottamun Town," a song from the Appalachians.[18] The question-and-answer incipits to the stanzas of "A Hard Rain's A-Gonna Fall" are an adaptation from the Scottish ballad "Lord Randall." "Who Killed Davy Moore?" is a modern version of "Cock Robin"; "When the Ship Comes In" draws on the imagery of the revival spiritual, and "I Pity the Poor Immigrant" has the parallel construction of the Old Testament canticles.

Wayne Hampton, writing in the mid-1980s a perceptive summation of Dylan's work, sees "a congruence underneath the chaos of Dylan's public images," which he identifies as "two interpenetrating themes." The first is that of "the outcast, the rolling-stone drifter . . . fleeing conformity and convention." The second is that of "the seer in quest of visions" whose roots "seem to be an eclectic brand of Christianized mysticism." These two themes are combined in characterizations of the "real Bob Dylan" as "Bible-toting hobo," "mystery tramp," and "mystical drifter."[19]

Freedom Songs and the Civil Rights Movement in the South

For all the differences between the 1930s and the 1960s, there was an interesting parallel. In the thirties, labor sympathizers who went into the South to help organize the miners found a sturdy singing tradition already at work furnishing songs for the workers. In the early 1960s, protest folksingers from the North who went into the South at the time of the early Civil Rights struggle also found a Southern tradition, in this case based on African-American religious singing, already furnishing songs for those engaged in marches, mass meetings, sit-ins, and prayer vigils, and for those in jails. Of these songs from an indigenous tradition "We Shall Overcome," based on the African-American church song "I'll Overcome Some Day," with words by the gospel hymnodist C. Albert Tindley, is the best known, and it is sung today all over the world.[20]

Continuity and Change in the Folk Style
of Persuasion from the 1970s to the 1990s

Although the writing and singing of protest songs has not attracted the attention in the last quarter of the century that it did in the 1960s, it continues to exist, though in changed form. The single big issues, such as civil rights and the Vietnam War, with the capacity to galvanize a significant portion of the public, have been replaced by issues that are far more diverse and complex, including racism in its more subtle forms, the many manifestations of environmental degradation, the unimaginably long-term problems associated with nuclear energy, women's rights, help for the aging and the disabled, and the widespread malaise of overconsumption and preoccupation with "lifestyle" that exists among the more affluent members of our society. Among singer/composers active in the 1970s and 1980s, protest has been expressed in ways more subtle and indirect, often achieving impact through understatement and satire. To name a few examples, in the early 1970s John Prine, in a Dylan style and approach, produced an unsurpassed classic protest against the degradation of the Appalachians by strip mining in his "Paradise." Racism is treated with a sadder, gentler touch by Pierce Pettis in "Legacy." Humor is evident in the anecdotal treatment of the immigrant problem in David Massengill's "My Name Joe."

Although protest is now more sophisticated, it is interesting to note that releases of recordings from an earlier era—songs by Woody Guthrie, Pete Seeger and the Almanacs, and so on—occupy a considerable position in the market. This may represent either a nostalgia for the days when the issues, the supposed solutions, and the songs themselves were clearer and more straightforward, or simply an affection for what happened when you just put Woody Guthrie and his guitar in front of a microphone any place that was handy, and recorded whatever came out.

In conclusion, protest songs, granted that their messages are often exaggerated, crudely expressed, and simplistic, can express the gut concerns of the many. In that sense they are part of a long and healthy tradition of dissent that has contributed to the character of American culture and its music. And there is gold in the songs themselves, as the ephemeral dross is discarded: "We Shall Overcome" (from black hymnody), "So Long, It's Been Good to Know Ya" (Woody Guthrie), "Where Have All the Flowers Gone" (Pete Seeger), and "Blowin' in the Wind" (Bob Dylan) are as much a part now of our oral tradition as the songs of Stephen Foster or the favorites of Tin Pan Alley.

FURTHER READING

General song collections, with expository notes

Bronson, Bertrand Harris. *The Singing Tradition of Child's Popular Ballads*. Princeton: Princeton University Press, 1976.

A single volume abridgement of Bronson's 4-volume work *The Traditional Tunes of the Child Ballads*. The extensive introduction includes a description of the modes used in the tunes. There is a monumental bibliography.

Lomax, Alan. *The Folk Songs of North America*. Garden City, NY: Doubleday, 1960.

This excellent broad collection surveys the entire field of American folk songs in the English language. The introduction and notes are especially valuable.

Sandburg, Carl. *The American Songbag*. New York: Harcourt Brace, 1927.

An early landmark collection by an American writer famous for his enthusiasm for folklore, song, and poetry. The notes have the Sandburg touch, and make good reading.

Selective list of specialized or regional song collections, mostly with expository notes. For the sake of brevity, many fine and even classic collections have been omitted. Consult any good library for these.

Carawan, Guy, and Candie Carawan, comp. *We Shall Overcome: Songs of the Southern Freedom Movement*. New York: Oak, 1963.

Fife, Austin and Alta. *Cowboy and Western Songs: A Comprehensive Anthology*. New York: Clarkson N. Potter, 1969.

Greenway, John. *American Folksongs of Protest*. Philadelphia: University of Pennsylvania Press, 1953. Paperback reprint. New York: Barnes, 1960.

> A rather detailed account of protest songs, especially those used in the labor movement. Many examples, including music.

Lomax, Alan, comp. *Hard-Hitting Songs for Hard-Hit People*. With notes by Woody Guthrie; music transcribed and edited by Pete Seeger. New York: Oak, 1967.

> Probably the best collection concentrating on the period of the 1930s. Illustrated with fine photographs made under the auspices of the Farm Security Administration by Walker Evans and others.

Randolph, Vance. *Ozark Folksongs*. Ed. and abr. Norm Cohen. Urbana: University of Illinois Press, 1982.

> A single-volume abridgement of a classic collection.

Sharp, Cecil. *English Folk-Songs from the Southern Appalachians*. Ed. Maud Karpeles. London: Oxford University Press, 1932. 2 vols. Reprinted in 1, 1966.

> Not only is the collection a rich source of ballads and their variants in pure form from oral tradition, but the introduction is a valuable essay on both the folk and their songs.

Studies, with no music

Cantwell, Robert S. *When We Were Good: The Folk Revival*. Cambridge, MA: Harvard University Press, 1976.

Coffin, Tristram. *The British Traditional Ballad in North America*. Philadelphia: American Folklore Society, 1950.

Hampton, Wayne. *Guerrilla Minstrels: John Lennon, Joe Hill, Woody Guthrie, Bob Dylan*. Knoxville: University of Tennessee Press, 1986.

Jackson, Bruce, ed. *Folklore and Society*. Hatboro, PA: Folklore Associates, 1966.

> This collection includes excellent articles by Charles Seeger, Willard Rhodes, Richard Dorson, and Ellen Stekert.

Laws, G. Malcolm, Jr. *American Balladry from British Broadsides*. Philadelphia: American Folklore Society, 1957.

———. *Native American Balladry*. Philadelphia: American Folklore Society, 1964.

> A significant study of native balladry outside the Child canon, dealing with an area of American folk song indispensable to a comprehensive picture.

Lomax, Alan, ed. *Folk Song Style and Culture*. New Brunswick, NJ: Transaction, Rutgers, The State University, 1994.

> Extensive, basic reference works on the ballads

Child, Francis James. *The English and Scottish Popular Ballads*. 5 vols. Boston, 1882–98. Paperback reprint. New York: Dover, 1965.

Bronson, Bertrand Harris. *The Traditional Tunes of the Child Ballads*. 4 vols. Princeton, NJ: Princeton University Press, 1959–72.

Periodicals

Broadside (New York) (1962–1988)

> The leading publication for topical songs, its editorial policy was to include songs by a variety of writers, thus giving new writers a chance to be published. It was started in 1962 by Pete Seeger, Malvina Reynolds, and Agnes Cunningham to serve this purpose, and to include more topical songs than the earlier *Sing Out!*

Sing Out! (Bethlehem, PA).

> Founded in 1950, *Sing Out!* tends toward more traditional folk songs than did *Broadside*, and includes articles.

Articles

Yurchenko, Henrietta. "The Beginning of an Urban Folk-Song Movement in New York: A Memoir." *Sonneck Society Bulletin* 8, no. 2 (Summer 1987): 39.

> A brief, vivid account of this movement in New York in the 1930s, including firsthand impressions of Woody Guthrie, by one who participated in it.

Projects

1. Find an example of a traditional ballad sung by a present-day professional singer and compare it with a version in a printed collection (either words or music or both).

2. Find examples of popular music, especially folk-rock, which in your opinion show the influence of the ballad, and define this influence.

3. Find some traditional ballads in collections of folk music from your own region. (A few outstanding regional collections are listed in the "Further Reading" section accompanying this chapter. Libraries in your region will emphasize local collections.)

4. Make a collection and comparison of ballad refrains, noting the presence or absence of meaningless syllables, words, or phrases.

5. Find and record some piece of folklore (song, poem, story) that your family, friends, or acquaintances know from oral tradition.

6. Investigate the *localization* of names and places that occurs when ballads travel. If you have access to the services of a large library you might consult a doctoral thesis by W. Edson Richmond, "Place Names in the English and Scottish Popular Ballads and Their American Variants" (Ohio State University, 1947).

7. If you are familiar with another language and its culture, find an example of one of the traditional ballads (many of which are international) in this other language.

8. Read Charles Seeger's thought-provoking article "The Folkness of the Non-Folk vs. the Non-Folkness of the Folk," in Jackson, *Folklore and Society*. Write a brief essay setting forth *your* interpretation of "folkness" and "nonfolkness," drawing examples from the life and culture you see around you.

9. Try to document a local example of a topical song or a protest song being used at a meeting, rally, or other gathering. Analyze the song itself (trying to determine its source) and as much of the context of its usage as you can. Consider, for example: How well did the people seem to know it? Was it sung primarily to sway the uncommitted or to promote solidarity and raise morale among the cause's adherents?

Notes

1. See Francis James Child, *The English and Scottish Popular Ballads*, vol. 2, 276.

2. William A. Owens, *Texas Folk Songs*, 23.

3. Charles Wimberly, *Folklore in the English and Scottish Ballads*, 39–43.

4. An excellent Scottish version of "The Gypsie Laddie," sung by Ewan MacColl and including interesting notes, is included in *The Long Harvest* (Argo Records), now out of print.

5. Alan Lomax, *The Folk Songs of North America*, 171.

6. See Jean Thomas, *Ballad Makin' in the Mountains of Kentucky*, 136–38, and G. Malcolm Laws, Jr., *Native American Balladry*, 44–45.

7. See John Cohen and Mike Seeger, *Old-Time String Band Song Book*.

8. See Laws, *Native American Balladry*, 51 and 223–24.

9. "The Buffalo Skinners" is one of the earliest ballads of the West, predating the advent of the cowboy. Several versions are available. One sung by an actual cowboy is included in *Slim Critchlow: Cowboy*

Songs, Arhoolie 5007; one sung by a famous collector, John Lomax, is on AFS L28 (Library of Congress); one sung by a famous professional, Pete Seeger, is on *Industrial Ballads*, Smithsonian Folkways 40058.

10. Laws, op. cit., 111.

11. "South Coast" can be heard on *Horse Sense: Songs of the Western Soil*, Kicking Mule 329.

12. Charles Seeger, "Versions and Variants of the Tunes of Barbara Allen," *Selected Reports*, no. 1 (Los Angeles: Institute of Ethnomusicology, University of California, 1966), 122. Reprinted as notes to *Versions and Variants of Barbara Allen* (AAFS: L–54).

13. See Hans Nathan, *Dan Emmett and the Rise of Early Negro Minstrelsy* (Norman: University of Oklahoma Press, 1962), 92, and Mark Twain, *Life on the Mississippi*, chapter 3.

14. Quote from Marion Thede, *Fiddle Book*, 11.

15. See the endpaper of R. P. Christeson's excellently printed collection *The Old-Time Fiddler's Repertory* (Columbia: University of Missouri Press, 1973).

16. R. Serge Denisoff, *Sing Me a Song of Social Significance*, 99.

17. Wayne Hampton, *Guerrilla Minstrels*, 194 and 199. "Song and dance man" is a reference to Michael Gray, *Song and Dance Man: The Art of Bob Dylan*.

18. Bob Dylan's source for the tune of "Nottamun Town," which he used for "Master's of War," was Appalachian folksinger Jean Ritchie and her family, which source he at first failed to credit. Woody Guthrie similarly borrowed tunes from the Carter Family's recordings.

19. Wayne Hampton, op. cit., 194–95.

20. "We Shall Overcome" has been adapted from the religious song as early as 1945 by union workers in Charleston, South Carolina. It was the "theme song" of Highlander Folk School, from whence it was introduced into the Civil Rights movement.

Chapter 2

The African-American Tradition

African Music and Its Relation to Black Music in America

In beginning our study of African-American music, two questions occur immediately: To what extent is it African, and what evidence do we have of its African-ness?*

In the Western Hemisphere, African survivals are strongest on the north and east coasts of South America, and in the islands of the Caribbean (the latter including, culturally, French-dominated Louisiana until this century). In what is now the United States, African traits survived less vigorously, for a variety of reasons. Nevertheless, African culture certainly did persist and there were early opportunities to observe its survival in the customary celebrations on special occasions. In the South under slavery Christmas and Easter were traditionally occasions for "jubilees," and before the mid-nineteenth century colorful public festivities such as 'Lection Day in New England (in May or June), Pinkster (which immediately followed Pentecost, or *Pinksteren* in Dutch) in New York, and the Sunday afternoon dancing in Congo Square in New Orleans furnished ample evidence of the survival of African music and dance in antebellum America.[1]

One geographical area in the United States noted for its exceptional preservation of African music, language, and customs is that of the sea islands off the coast of Georgia and South Carolina. Here, in relative isolation, numbers of black people, often living in extreme poverty, retained Africanisms in music, speech, and customs well into this century. This area has been a rich mine for folklorists and anthropologists.[2]

African music is vast and complex. Continentwide it is far from homogeneous. The greatest influence on African-American music has come from West Africa. We can here only note certain outstanding traits that have marked

---

*This question is not new. A title such as "The Survival of African Music" has a contemporary ring; actually, it is the title of an article published in 1899.

correspondences with black music in America. Most obvious is the dominance of *rhythm*, manifested in a number of ways: (1) a highly developed *metronome sense*—the sense of an inexorably steady pulse governing the music; (2) a high degree of rhythmic complexity and diversity; (3) the perception of music as largely a *kinetic* experience, practically inseparable from some form of bodily movement such as dancing; and (4) the corresponding dominance of percussion instruments. Other traits, having to do with musical form, are the use of short vocal phrases, repeated and varied, against a continuous rhythmic background, and the often-cited use of the call-and-response pattern. The spiritual **"Sheep, Sheep, Don't You Know the Road"** illustrates beautifully both metronome sense and call-and-response.

Since only actual sounds are convincing, it is suggested that in order to *hear* the relationship of African to African-American music, you listen first to a recording of some West African music (such as Music in Praise of a Yoruban Chief, recorded in Nigeria), followed by a *ring-shout* such as "Run, Old Jeremiah."*

Religious Folk Music: The Spiritual

The term *spiritual* has been applied to two related bodies of folk music that began to flourish notably in the nineteenth century—one black and the other white, with a great deal of interchange between them. The African-American spiritual came into being following the conversion of significant numbers of slaves to Christianity. The religious singing of blacks in Colonial times is reported in a few contemporary observations, of which the often-quoted one by Rev. Samuel Davies in the mid-1700s is representative:

> I can hardly express the pleasure it affords me to turn to that part of the Gallery where they sit, and see so many of them with their Psalm or Hymn Books, turn-ing to the part then sung, and assisting their fellows who are beginners, to find the place; and then all breaking out in a torrent of sacred harmony, enough to bear away the whole congregation to heaven.

This describes the singing of blacks in the context of a formal religious ser-vice. But the spiritual itself was born under far less formal circumstances. The real spiritual represents not so much an *adaptation* of the Methodist and Baptist hymns and formal services, as a thoroughly African *response* to them.

Many accounts confirm the fact that the "sperichils" were not at first a part of the formal services, but belonged to the *shout* that took place *after* these services,

*The first is on *African and Afro-American Drums*, Smithsonian/Folkways 4502, and the second on *Afro-American Spirituals, Work Songs, and Ballads*, Library of Congress AFS L3.

The Fisk Jubilee Singers. *Courtesy Frank Driggs Collection.*

when the benches were pushed back to the wall, and the worshipers stood in the middle of the floor. The shouters were really in a sense dancers, forming a *ring* in which they circled in a kind of shuffling movement to the sound of singing and hand clapping. The ring itself was significant as a distinctly African heritage. The shout could last well into the night. "Run, Old Jeremiah" is a vivid example. The shout was viewed with disapproval by pious whites, and even by the African Methodist Episcopal Church itself, which tried to curb the shout (called by some the "Voodoo Dance") and the spirituals themselves, which were labeled "cornfield ditties."

The Discovery, Publication, and Adaptation of the Spirituals

The Civil War and its aftermath brought whites from the North, many of them abolitionists, into direct contact with black people for the first time. Even before the war's end, events such as the formation of black regiments fighting for the Union cause, and the famous "Port Royal experiment,"* began the process of acquainting northerners with the songs of the slaves. Written accounts appeared in northern periodicals, some with texts of spirituals. In 1867 there was published the first collection of African-American spirituals in book form, *Slave Songs of the United States*. This justly famous collection includes a number of spirituals well known today, although some are more familiar in later variants. These

---

*In the Port Royal experiment, teachers and missionaries from the North were recruited to teach and supervise thousands of African Americans on Carolina sea island plantations abandoned by white owners and overseers as a result of the Union blockade of the coast.

include "Roll, Jordan, Roll," "Michael, Row the Boat Ashore," "Nobody Knows the Trouble I've Had," and "Good News, Member." There were also a number of secular songs, among them work songs ("Heave away, Heave away! I'd rather court a yellow gal than work for Henry Clay") and a number of Louisiana Creole songs in patois French. Altogether a rather broad collection!

After the Civil War a number of schools and colleges were established in the South, under the auspices of the Freedmen's Bureau and various church and missionary groups, to begin the great task of educating the newly freed slaves. The Fisk Jubilee Singers, from Fisk University, were first formed to help raise money for the fledgling school. They had an important role in letting the spirituals be heard, first in their Nashville community, then throughout the northern states, and finally in Europe. Their moving story, with its trials and triumphs, is too long to be dwelt on, but their success inspired other colleges and choral groups.

Solo singers also performed spirituals. Although white soloists began including them in their programs in the 1920s, it was great black concert artists such as Roland Hayes, Paul Robeson, and Marian Anderson who sang them with the greatest effectiveness and meaning, and established their stature in the repertoire of solo song.

Thus the spiritual, in what might be termed its concert phase—written down, harmonized, arranged, and provided with a piano accompaniment—was launched. Though valid and highly moving music, it should not be confused with African-American religious folk song as it originally existed, or as it has continued to exist down to our own time in the backwoods churches and camp meetings of the South.

The Words of the Spiritual

Not all African-American folk music is religious. Many black people regard the blues as sinful music, and even if we view their condemnation as the product of a particular tradition of religious orthodoxy, we can also recognize that between the broad epic and moral connotations of "Go Down, Moses" and the self-centered eroticism of "The Black Snake Moan" there is indeed a great gulf fixed. Nevertheless, the lines of demarcation between sacred and secular are far from rigid. Thus, the biblical imagery so pervasive in the spiritual may also appear in the work song:

> *Well, God told Norah.*
> *Hammer, ring . . .*
> *You is a-goin' in the timber.*
> *Hammer, ring . . .*

It may even occasionally crop up in the blues:

I went down in Death valley, nothin' but the tombstones and dry bones, {repeated}
That's where a poor man be, Lord, when I'm dead and gone.

No image was either too humble or too intimately connected with daily life to be used.

Cryin' what kind o' shoes am dose you wear, . . .
Cryin' dese shoes I wear am de Gospel shoes, . . .

I know my robe's gwinter fit me well,
I'm gwinter lay down my heavy load.
I tried it on at de gates of hell,
I'm gwinter lay down my heavy load.

Spirituals have drawn deeply upon a thorough acquaintance with biblical narrative and symbol, as dramatized through the generations by many a gifted and anonymous backwoods preacher. So immense is their number and range that they constitute in toto an epic re-creation, in folk fashion, of virtually the entire Bible, from Genesis:

He made the sun an' moon an' stars,
To rule both day an' night;
He placed them in the firmament,
An' told them to give light.

to Revelation:

De Lord spoke to Gabriel,
Fare you well, Fare you well;
Go look behin' de altar,
Fare you well, Fare you well.
Take down de silvah trumpet,
Fare you well, Fare you well.
Blow yo' trumpet Gabriel;
Fare you well, Fare you well.

Instances abound of the vivid pictorial imagery brought to their subjects by anonymous black poets:

> *Dark clouds a-risin'!*
> *Thunder-bolts a-bustin'!*
> *Master Jesus comes a-ridin' by*
> *With a rainbow on his shoulder.*

It should be noted that the generally assumed anonymity of the authors was not universal; the existence of individual African-American "bards" in the late nineteenth century has been documented. James Weldon Johnson describes "Singing" Johnson, who went from church to church making up, singing, and teaching new songs to the congregations.[3]

It was once commonly believed that spirituals represented solely an other-worldly view; that they expressed the consolation that African Americans found in religion for their intolerable worldly conditions, and that the promises and hopes referred only to life in the hereafter. Evidence for a contrasting view, however—a view of spirituals' concrete relationship to contemporary conditions—began to be put forward in the nineteenth century by abolitionist writers and others. In this view spirituals express (or cloak) in biblical terms not only the wretchedness of slavery, but hopes and plans for an escape from its bondage in this life. This could come about either through Northern intervention (thus "de Lord" could stand for a collective embodiment of "de Yankees") or through escape ("Steal away") to the North ("heab'n") or to Canada ("Canaan"). The secret meetings to which the faithful were called ("Go down in de lonesome valley") kept hope and morale alive, spread news, and laid plans. The yearning for a "home" encouraged by the colonization projects could be expressed as a reliance on the "old ship of Zion" that would "take us all home"—or even as the hope for a Moses who would smite and divide the broad waters ("Deep river") so that the slaves could miraculously pass over—back to Africa.

The figure of Moses was quite naturally a very central one. The Israelites were the slaves, longing for deliverance; Pharaoh represented the slaveowners; Egypt (or alternatively Babylon) was the South and slavery. The famous "Go Down, Moses" hardly needs "translation" to see its relevance to the black people in slavery.

> *When Israel was in Egypt's land,*
> *Let my people go.*
> *Oppressed so hard they could not stand,*
> *Let my people go.*

Go down, Moses,
'Way down in Egypt's land;
Tell ole Pharaoh,
Let my people go.

The Music of the Spiritual

As with all folk music, what we see in print cannot convey anything like the full effect of the music as sung. As William Francis Allen wrote in 1867,

> The best we can do, however, with paper and types, or even with voices, will convey but a faint shadow of the original. The voices of the colored people have a peculiar quality that nothing can imitate; and the intonations and delicate variations of even one singer cannot be reproduced on paper. And I despair of conveying any notion of the effect of a number singing together, especially in a complicated shout, like "I can't stay behind, my Lord," or "Turn, sinner, turn O!" There is no singing in *parts*, as we understand it, and yet no two appear to be singing the same thing—the leading singer starts the words of each verse, often improvising, and the others, who "base" him, as it is called, strike in with the refrain, or even join in the solo, when the words are familiar. When the "base" begins, the leader often stops, leaving the rest of his words to be guessed at, or it may be they are taken up by one of the other singers. And the "basers" themselves seem to follow their own whims, beginning when they please and leaving off when they please, striking an octave above or below . . . . or hitting some other note that chords, so as to produce the effect of a marvelous complication and variety, and yet with the most perfect time, and rarely with any discord. And what makes it all the harder to unravel a thread of melody out of this strange network is that, like birds, they seem not infrequently to strike sounds that cannot be precisely represented by the gamut, and abound in "slides from one note to another, and turns and cadences not in articulated notes."[4]

This description confirms at least four distinct points about the singing. First, the subtlety and variety of vocal delivery is noted: the "intonations and delicate variations," the "sounds that cannot be precisely represented by the gamut," the "slides from one note to another." Second, we are definitely reminded that this is communal singing; unlike the more solitary blues, it calls for the participation and interaction of a closely knit society of singers, all feeling the same impulse to break into song. Third, though it is choral singing, there is usually a leader to whom the rest of the group responds, although not with the drilled rhythmic precision of trained choirs. And fourth, we are reminded of the important role of improvisation—the spur-of-the-moment variations wrought spontaneously by the singers. This is a trait particularly associated with black music. "No two African performances are identical," says A. M. Jones, and the description applies equally to blues, jazz, and the African-American spiritual.

One further observation, implicit in early descriptions, must be added; there was in most cases no accompaniment by instruments. The use of piano, guitar, tambourine—even in some cases trumpet or trombone—was a later addition belonging more to gospel songs.

The Survival of the Folk Spiritual

Folk spirituals have survived in popular culture, and Allen's observation of 1867 may be reviewed as a quite accurate description of rural spiritual singing as it has survived into our own time. Fortunately, some of this old-style singing was recorded in the 1930s and 1940s. It is probably best epitomized in the spirituals sung by Dock Reed and Vera Hall of Alabama. In "Look How They Done My Lord," "Handwriting on the Wall," and "Low Down the Chariot and Let Me Ride"[5] we hear traditional spirituals sung in a living folk context. Call-and-response is beautifully illustrated, as is the rhythmic impulse or "metronome sense." We also hear in their singing the use of the variable, or ambiguous, third and seventh degrees of the scale—a practice that does not belong exclusively to the blues. **My Name Has Been Written Down**," sung by a family of singers, furnishes a fine example of communal singing in the old style, with hand-clapping emphasizing the rhythmic pulse and drive of the music.*

The spiritual has provided material and inspiration for many subsequent forms. Though it is still cultivated to some extent in the old style as a folk form, it was inevitable that African-American religious music would over time reflect changing social and cultural patterns. The story is continued in chapter 9, which deals with the emergence of gospel music.

Secular Folk Music
Cries, Calls, and Hollers

A kind of musical expression among black people that is at once primitive and evocative is found in the cries, calls, and hollers. Early observers described these occasionally. Frederick Olmsted, reporting on a journey through the South in 1853, tells of being awakened in his railroad car in the middle of the night by a gang of black workmen enjoying a brief break around a fire: "Suddenly one raised

---

*The first and third of these are on *Spirituals with Dock Reed and Vera Hall Ward*, Smithsonian/Folkways 2038, the second on *Afro-American Spirituals, Work Songs, and Ballads*, Library of Congress AFS L4, and the fourth on *Negro Folk Music of Africa and America*, Smithsonian/Folkways 4500.

such a sound as I had never heard before, a long, loud, musical shout, rising, and falling, and breaking into falsetto, his voice ringing through the woods in the clear, frosty night air, like a bugle call. As he finished, the melody was caught up by another, then by several in chorus."[6]

These cries and calls—of the field, the levee, the track—were highly individualized expressions, for communication, for relieving loneliness, for giving vent to feelings, or simply for expressing the fact of one's existence. Their city counterparts, the street cries, were more utilitarian: they advertised goods and services. Both types have all but disappeared from their original setting. A few have been recorded.[7] Musically, they are florid, melismatic vocalizations, based on a single interval, a single chord, or a pentatonic or modal scale, with embellishing tones and often certain "blue" notes of variable pitch.

In fact, the embryonic blues scale is so apparent in some of these calls that it will be well to introduce its main features here. This underscores the close relation between some of these solitary, highly individualized calls and hollers and the primitive rural blues. For this purpose, we shall examine one call in some detail. It is a cornfield holler, or *arwhoolie*, specifically a "Quittin' Time Song." It may be notated (though only approximately!) as shown in Example 2-1 (facing page). It will be noted that there are only three essential pitch areas; a high one (which may be called the *dominant*) on which nearly all the phrases begin; a low one (which may be called the *final*) on which they all end; and an important area a third above the final, a *mediant*. The first two are relatively stable in pitch, but the mediant is variable. It sometimes gives a definite impression of major (marked with a sharp); sometimes it sounds minor; and sometimes ambiguous (indeterminately in between major and minor).

If we were to add to this scale a second area of variable pitch a third above the dominant, we would have the bare bones of the traditional blues scale (Ex. 2-2, p. 30).*

Folk Blues

African-American cries, calls, and hollers were intensely personal expressions, and this is also one of the most important characteristics of the blues. When we listen to "I Don't Mind the Weather" we realize how this kind of elemental song gradually approaches the rural blues in proportions, range, and explicitness of expression. In a more tightly knit stanza form of four repeated lines, still unaccompanied, is the rather haunting "Another Man Done Gone." Both songs are

---

* Playing this music on an instrument of fixed and equal temperament such as the piano gives a highly conventionalized and falsified impression of its subtly inflected and extremely fluid nature as performed by the voice, whether in spirituals, hollers, or blues.

The music notation shows the following lyrics:

Oh,_____ the sun go - in' down and I won't be here long.

Oh, the sun go - in' down and I won't be here long.

Oh,____ then____ I____ be go - in' home.

Oh, I can't let this dark cloud catch me here.

Oh,_____ I can't__ stay__ here long.

Oh,_____ I be__ at home.

Scale

Dominant / Auxiliary tone area / Mediant area / Final

variable 3rd

Example 2–1. "Quittin' Time Song"

about prison life—the first from a man who looks forward to getting out of jail and leaving the South, the second reporting in enigmatic language about the escape of a man from a county chain gang.*

Social Changes and the Blues

The spiritual began life in slavery; the blues could only have evolved afterward, with the profound changes that affected the lives of African Americans in the South after the Civil War. These changes had to do with the new, albeit severely circumscribed, dimension of leisure; with a new degree of solitude; with the

*Both are on *Afro-American Blues and Game Songs*, Library of Congress AFS L3.

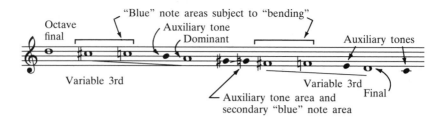

Example 2–2. Complete blues scale

confrontation with an entirely new set of social and economic problems, not the least being the need for money; with broader contacts and experiences; with a much greater fluency in the American language; and finally with a new mobility.* This mobility was forced in most cases by the relentless (and new) necessity of finding employment—much harder for the men than for the women. Among these were the blind street musicians who had gravitated to the larger cities; making street music was the prime means of livelihood and independence available to those with even a modicum of talent. Thus it happened that the blues were propagated by a class of musicians who were to a degree outcasts, even among their own race—rejected at least by its more settled and established members, especially the most devoutly religious, to whom the blues were "devil songs." The black author Richard Wright writes in his preface to Paul Oliver's *The Meaning of the Blues*:

> All American Negroes do not sing the blues. These songs are not the expression of the Negro people in America as a whole. I'd surmise that the spirituals . . . came from those slaves who were closest to the Big Houses of the plantations where they caught vestiges of Christianity whiffed to them from the Southern Whites' cruder forms of Baptist or Methodist religions. If the plantations' house slaves were somewhat remote from Christianity, the field slaves were almost completely beyond the pale. And it was from them and their descendants that the devil songs called the blues came—that confounding triptych of the convict, the migrant, the rambler, the steel driver, the ditch digger, the roustabout, the pimp, the prostitute, the urban or rural illiterate outsider.

---

*These changes are dealt with extensively by Amiri Baraka (Le Roi Jones) in *Blues People*, chapter 6.

Jimmie Strothers (guitar) and Joe Lee (vocal) perform "Do Lord Remember Me" at the Virginia State Convict Farm, 1936. *From the collections of the Library of Congress.*

Blues Texts and Subjects

The subjects treated in the blues encompass a wide range. No area of commonly shared human experience is excluded. Some blues speak of a nameless depression:

Early this morning the blues came walking in my room.

Some are about work—

I worked all summer, yes, and all the fall
Going to spend Christmas in my overalls.

or the lack of it—

>*I'm goin' to Detroit, get myself a good job,*
>*Tried to stay around here on this starvation farm.*

Some sing of gambling—

>*Jack of Diamonds, you appear to be my friend*
>*But gamblin' gonna be our end.*

of crime, of the law, of prisons—

>*Judge gave me life this mornin' down on Parchman Farm;*

of prostitution, of enslaving addiction, or of the necessity or the irresistible urge to move on:

>*When a woman gets the blues, she hangs her head and cries.*
>*But when a man gets the blues, he flags a freight train and rides.*

But the greatest number are in some way about the fundamental man-woman relationship. As the blues singer Robert Pete Williams said, "Love makes the blues. That's where it comes from."[8] The man-woman relationship is displayed in the blues in a great variety of aspects—from a comment on the power of a woman's attraction—

>*Well, a long, tall woman will make a preacher lay his Bible down*

or the exhilaration of being in love—

>*Well, I feel all right and everything is okay.*
>*Yes, I feel all right, everything is okay.*
>*It's the love of my baby, oh, makes me feel this way.*

to a scornful comment on infidelity—

>*High yeller, she'll kick you, that ain't all,*
>*When you step out at night 'nother mule in your stall.*

or the painful fact of separation—

> *My man left this morning, jest about half past four,*
> *He left a note on his pillow, sayin' he couldn't use me no more—*

or the most bitter rejection:

> *If I was cold and hungry, I wouldn't even ask you for bread,*
> *I don't want you no more, if I'm on my dying bed.*

Blues language is keen, apt, and colorful, and is given to the use of irony, metaphor, and double entendre. No subject is off limits, and although broad social comment is foreign to such a personal medium, the blues poet finds a way to relate the most topical subject to an earthy metaphor with a telling phrase:

> *Uncle Sam ain't no woman, but he sure can take your man away.*

Blues Form

The form of the blues is often described as though it were invariably convention-alized. Actually the rural blues is often quite free in form. The sung portions do not always arrange themselves into three-line stanzas, but many consist of a vary-ing number of lines, often unequal in length. The standard form—a line, repeated, followed by a different concluding line—should be considered, in the country blues, as a tendency only:

> *My mama told me before I left home,*
> *My mama told me before I left home,*
> *You better let them Jacksonville women alone.*

The three-line form was perhaps first crystallized in the published blues that began appearing as early as 1912, and that certainly influenced subsequent blues performers.

The standard musical phrase is four bars long—hence the standard "12-bar blues" form. But in the case of the blues in its folk phase, single phrases could be four and a half, five, or seven bars long. When there is instrumental accompani-ment, which is nearly always, the sung line never takes up the whole musical "space," so to speak. The voice comes to its cadence about halfway through, and the phrase is always completed by an instrumental *break*. This paces the song, gives the singer time to think of the next line, and provides the opportunity for some more or less fancy and often highly individual instrumental playing.

The Music of the Blues

The melodic material of the blues has already been set forth in Example 2-2, with the areas of variable pitch noted. But a sense of clearly defined pitch may be further obscured by a wide variety of highly personalized vocal techniques. In the blues the words themselves are not as important as they are in the ballad. Thus blues may be shouted (a manner of delivery related to the primitive field holler, which has been taken over successively by rhythm-and-blues and rock 'n' roll). They may be hummed; they may be sung in falsetto, or with falsetto breaks; they may be sung with the gravelly tone of the false bass voice; they may be chanted in the manner of a recitative; they may even be spoken. In the folk blues, words and even lines may be left unfinished. As for melodic contour, there are many individual variations, but the general tendency is to start the phrase high and proceed downward, ending with a dropping inflection, as in the field holler previously transcribed.

Blues harmony may consist simply of a single chord with embellishments, as we hear in "Levee Camp Moan," and "Special Rider Blues." The more usual practice involves the use of the three principal chords of the key in a pattern that *tends* toward the standard blues plan:

1st phrase	I	—	—	I^7
2d phrase	IV$^{(7)}$	—	I	—
3d phrase	V^7	(IV)	I	—

"Weary Worried Blues" shows this standard blues pattern, with a full 12-bar warm-up before the voice starts. Later, more sophisticated embellishing harmonies are sometimes used, especially at the end of the second phrase and the beginning of the last. This practice shows the influence of European harmony, probably by way of ragtime, and is typical of blues harmony as used in jazz.*

The elemental blues, related to field calls and hollers, were sung unaccompanied. But at some undefined early date, the guitar was adopted as the natural instrument for accompanying the sung laments and comments that were the

---

*"Levee Camp Moan" and Weary Worried Blues" are in *The Country Blues*, vol. 2, Smithsonian/Folkways RF9, and "Special Rider Blues" is on *Negro Blues and Hollers*, Library of Congress AFS L59.

blues. It could provide harmony, rhythm, and, in the hands of an adept player, melody as well, for the warm-ups and the breaks, such as is heard in Blind Lemon Jefferson's famous "Matchbox Blues."

Skillful players developed their own individual sounds and techniques, some of which passed into general currency. Sliding between tones, for example, was made possible by running the back of a knife blade over the strings, or the broken top of a bottle (with the jagged edge annealed) worn on the little finger. This "bottleneck" style, perhaps suggested by the Hawaiian guitar, overrode the rigid tuning imposed by the frets and provided a flexibility that made it possible for a skillful performer to match the sliding and wailing of the voice. The playing of Robert Johnson (in "**Preachin' Blues**") illustrates this.

Other instruments were used as auxiliaries to the ubiquitous guitar. The harmonica was fairly cheap and very portable, and this "blues harp" became, in the hands of virtuosos such as Sonny Terry, a very flexible and expressive instrument, capable of shadings and bendings that approached the subtlety of the voice. "Weary Worried Blues," from 1934, shows the harmonica as a full-fledged "partnering" instrument, sharing the 12-bar warm-up, and after two verses, taking a complete chorus, as the tenor saxophone did later in the blues bands.

Improvised instruments were common. The jug served as a kind of substitute tuba. The washboard, fitted out with auxiliary metal pans and lids attached, was a whole rhythm section. The inverted washtub, with a piece of rope stretched between a hole through its center and a broom handle, was a substitute bass (and was a relative of the African earth bow). Jug bands and washboard bands incorporating these instruments were sometimes recorded commercially, so that their sounds have come down to us.

The blues story is continued in chapter 6 as the story of a popular music evolving from folk roots. Admittedly it is difficult to draw a very precise line between the blues as folk music and the blues as essentially popular music, with professional entertainers catering to a "public" instead of casual music-makers performing within a closely knit community. But the distinction exists, nonetheless. Amiri Baraka has written:

> Socially, classic blues and the instrumental styles that went with it represented the Negro's entrance into the world of professional entertainment and the assumption of the psychological imperatives that must accompany such a phenomenon. . . . It was no longer strictly the group singing to ease their labors or the casual expression of personal deliberations on the world. It became a music that could be used to entertain others *formally*. The artisan,

the professional blues singer, appeared; blues-singing no longer had to be merely a passionately felt avocation, it could now become a way of making a living. An external and sophisticated idea of performance had come to the blues, moving it past the casualness of the "folk" to the conditioned emotional gesture of the "public."[9]

It is at this real, if difficult to define, boundary that we take leave of the blues for the present.

Work Songs and Ballads

The use of singing to coordinate and lighten physical work, acting as both a coordinator of effort and a lifter of spirits, is practically universal among men who must engage in hard communal labor, on land or sea. Work songs were prevalent among black laborers during slavery; even spirituals could be used in this way, and some of the earliest collected songs (such as "Michael, Row the Boat Ashore") had this duality of function about them. After the Civil War, work songs were needed wherever gang labor was used, especially in the work of building railroads. There had to be a leader, of course; this called for not only a first-hand knowledge of the work and its pacing and a gift for timing, but the ability to infuse into the work the balm of rhythm and song. A few of the recordings we possess of genuine work songs communicate this sense of rhythm and spirit. With increased mechanization the work song almost disappeared. The only conditions under which it survived were those that closely duplicated conditions under slavery—that is, in the prisons and on the work farms, where, indeed, practically all the field recordings of work songs were made.

The ballad and the work song are dissimilar in function. However, the leader's need to prolong the work song to fit the task at hand often led to the adoption of the ballad, or storytelling, method, with its possibilities for improvisation and its indefinite proliferation of stanzas. "**Hammer, Ring**," a work song used in railroad building to coordinate the driving of spikes to fasten the long steel rails to the ties, is a long-drawn-out ballad-like song that recounts the story of "Norah" and the building of the ark.

The ballad of "John Henry," the steel driver, is probably the best known of all African-American ballads. A hero-ballad, it deals with the once well-known occupation of hand-driving a steel drill to make a deep hole in solid rock for a blasting charge. The competition between mechanization and the "natural man" is an important feature in most versions of the ballad that have not been severely truncated.* The ballad has been transmuted into both a work song and a blues.[10] Students of the African-American ballad such as Malcolm Laws have pointed out the fecundity of invention that manifests itself in improvisation, and also (in contrast with white balladry) the greater emphasis on character, situation, and empathy with the subject, rather than on events as such.[11]

FURTHER READING

Collections, with some expository notes

Allen, William Francis, Charles Pickard Ware, and Lucy McKim Garrison, eds. *Slave Songs of the United States*. New York, 1867. (There have been many reprints.)
> A classic, of permanent importance as the first such collection published.

Johnson, James Weldon, and J. Rosamund, eds. *The Books of American Negro Spirituals*. 2 vols. in 1. New York: Viking, 1940.
> Originally issued as two books, the first in 1925, this is a standard collection. James Weldon Johnson was a novelist and poet, author of *God's Trombones (Seven Negro Sermons in Verse)*. His brother, J. Rosamund Johnson, made the piano arrangements.

Primarily studies, which include some complete songs

Charters, Samuel. *The Bluesmen and Sweet as the Showers of Rain*. New York: Oak, 1967 and 1977.
> These two titles constitute a two-volume expansion of the author's earlier *The Country Blues* (New York: Rinehart, 1959).

Courlander, Harold. *Negro Folk Music, U.S.A.* New York: Columbia University Press, 1963.
> Includes forty-three complete songs.

Epstein, Dena J. *Sinful Tunes and Spirituals: Black Folk Music to the Civil War*. Urbana: University of Illinois Press, 1977.
> A valuable study, with extensive citations from contemporary sources.

Katz, Bernard, ed. *The Social Implications of Early Negro Music in the United States*. New York: Arno, 1969.
> A collection of important articles and excerpts from books, dating from 1862 to 1939, most of which include a generous number of examples.

Studies and background reading

Baraka, Amiri. *Blues People*. New York: Morrow, 1963.
> A perceptive social study of African-American music by a prominent black writer (known as LeRoi Jones when the book was first published). The first six chapters are applicable to folk music.

Lovell, John, Jr. *Black Song: The Forge and the Flame*. New York: Macmillan, 1972.
> A major comprehensive survey (686 pages long) of the spiritual. While no aspect is excluded, Lovell, a literary scholar, devotes his major attention to the texts and to their social background and implications.

---

* "John Henry" is one of the few ballads that legend has attached to an actual event: the construction of the Big Band Tunnel on the Chesapeake & Ohio Railroad near Hilton, West Virginia, in 1870–72. A fairly complete version recorded in Arkansas in 1939 is on *Afro-American Spirituals, Work Songs, and Ballads*, Library of Congress AFS L3.

Oliver, Paul. *The Meaning of the Blues*. New York: Macmillan, 1960.

> An exhaustive and perceptive study of blues subjects and the milieu of its people, in the form of extensive commentary on 350 blues texts arranged according to subject. Most of the blues used as examples in this chapter are quoted in Oliver's work.

Southern, Eileen. *The Music of Black Americans*. 3d ed. New York: Norton, 1996.

> A comprehensive, indispensable study of the entire field.

———, ed. *Readings in Black American Music*. 2d ed. New York: Norton, 1983.

> Excerpts from important source material ranging over the entire field.

Projects

1. Write a short paper on the South Carolina and Georgia sea islands as repositories of black folklore, speech, and song. Include whatever you can find out about conditions there today.

2. Review some of the significant studies that have been made of African survivals in American black music. Some of these are by Melville Herskovits, Alan Merriam, Harold Courlander, Richard Waterman, and Paul Oliver (*Savannah Syncopators*).

3. Write a short paper on the work and significance of the Fisk Jubilee Singers. (Locate if possible nineteenth-century works by Marsh and Pike in the bibliography of Katz, *Social Implications of Early Negro Music in the United States*.)

4. Write a short paper on textual themes in African-American spirituals, including the double meanings they contain. (John Lovell's *Black Song: The Forge and the Flame*, his article in Katz, *The Social Implications of Early Negro Music in the United States*, and Sterling Brown, *Negro Poetry and Drama*, could serve as points of departure.)

5. Compare a traditional version of a spiritual (as found in an early collection such as Allen et al., *Slave Songs of the United States*) with a concert version as sung by a recitalist or a trained concert choir. Discuss the advantages and disadvantages of such concert arrangements.

6. Collect recorded examples of at least three different blues guitarist-singers. Describe and compare their original guitar techniques and styles, especially their treatment of the "breaks."

7. Collect recorded examples of blues illustrating at least four of the textual themes identified and treated in Paul Oliver, *The Meaning of the Blues*.

Notes

1. For further information on African survivals see Eileen Southern, *The Music of Black Americans* (3d ed.), and *Readings in Black American Music* (2d ed.), especially Readings 7, 8, and 9. See also Dena J. Epstein, *Sinful Tunes and Spirituals: Black Folk Music to the Civil War*, especially chapters 1 and 7; and Portia K. Maultsby, "West African Influences and Retentions in U. S. Black Music" in Irene Jackson, ed., *More Than Dancing: Essays on Afro-American Music and Musicians*.

2. Two permanently valuable documents to come out of this area are the *Slave Songs of the Georgia Sea Islands* by Lydia Parrish, and the recordings of *Animal Tales in the Gullah Dialect* by Albert Stoddard (AAFS: L–44, 45, 46). The Gullah dialect contains a high percentage of West African words, as was revealed in Lorenzo Turner's study *Africanisms in the Gullah Dialect*. A fine recording illustrating both the sacred and the secular music of the islands is *Georgia Sea Island Songs* (New World 88278–2), recorded in 1960–61 by Alan Lomax, who also provided notes for the album.

3. See James Weldon Johnson, *The Books of American Negro Spirituals*, preface.

4. William Francis Allen, in his preface to Allen et al., *Slave Songs of the United States*.

5. "Look How They Done My Lord" and "Handwriting on the Wall" appear in printed versions in James Weldon Johnson and J. Rosamund Johnson's *The Books of Negro Spirituals*, an important publication of the 1920s.

6. Quoted in Harold Courlander, *Negro Folk Music, U. S. A.*, 81–82.

7. *Negro Work Songs and Calls* (AAFS: L–8), *Negro Music of Alabama*, vol. 1 (Smithsonian/Folkways 4417). For transcriptions of some of the calls in this latter album, and an excellent treatment of the subject, see Courlander, *Negro Folk Music, U. S. A.,* chapter 4.

8. As quoted in Bruce Cook, *Listen to the Blues*, 40.

9. Amiri Baraki (LeRoi Jones), *Blues People*, 81–82.

10. "John Henry" can be found as a work song in Library of Congress AFS L3. Printed versions appear in a great number of collections. As for recordings by traditional singers, there are greatly truncated versions sung by Leadbelly (*History of Jazz*, vol. 1, Smithsonian/Folkways 2951). A derivative blues ("Spike Driver Blues"), as sung by Mississippi John Hurt, is in *Anthology of American Folk Music*, vol. 3 (Smithsonian/Folkways 2953).

11. This is splendidly illustrated in the ballad "The Titanic," on *Georgia Sea Island Songs* (New World 80278).

Chapter 3

The American Indian Tradition

At the time of the first European exploration and colonization, it is estimated that some three million native people lived in North America, between one and two million of them north of what is now Mexico. The population consisted of a thousand different tribal units, each generally having its own language, belonging to one of approximately sixty language families.* The music of the North American Indians has many characteristics shared by all; this fact has given a limited validity to the concept of *generic*, or pan-Indian, music. But there are significant distinctions as well—characteristics that can be identified more or less successfully with some eight roughly defined *culture areas*: Southeast, Northeast (both east of the Mississippi), Plains, Southwest (including most of California), Great Basin, Northwest Coast (from northern coastal California to and including coastal Alaska), Plateau (north of the Great Basin, between the Northwest Coast area and the Rocky Mountains), and North (Arctic and Subarctic, including the Athapaskan and Inuit, or Eskimo, peoples).[1]

When we study Indian music we are dealing with the music of native societies that once were aboriginal cultures but are so no longer. In the 300-odd years during which the whites completed their westward advance across the continent, aboriginal Indian life was thoroughly disrupted. Native societies were dispossessed and decimated by disease and warfare, some tribal groups were totally destroyed, and most others were relocated or confined on reservations, where they were first treated as a conquered, subject population. As a consequence, large elements of indigenous cultural ways, including some musical elements, disappeared—destroyed, discarded, lost, or altered beyond modern recognition. One of the most remarkable things about American Indian musical culture is that a

---

* The cultural complexity resulting from the 25,000-year history of the original inhabitants of North America is illustrated by the fact that the language families are not necessarily identified or coincident with the cultural areas, as defined below. The Navajo and Apache of the desert Southwest, for example, have a language related to that of the tribes of the far north of Canada and Alaska.

significant remnant of it has not only survived, but has entered a new phase of cultivation. It will therefore be necessary to treat native American music in two distinct, though related, aspects: first, what can be learned of it as an integral part of the culture of an aboriginal people; and second, Indian music as it exists today.

Music in Aboriginal Indian Life

There are two ways to view an artistic artifact. The first is as a thing of interest and beauty in and of itself. The second is as something to be viewed in the complete context of the society that brought it forth, having essential meaning only in this context. The two are never absolutely separate; we experience every art object with some mixture of both. But the closer we get to art in the folk or primitive state, the more necessary it becomes to take into account the second view. While never abandoning the study and apprehension of a work of art intrinsically, we must give a much greater proportion of our effort to understanding what the lives of those who made the art were like, and what place and meaning it had for them. This is in no case more imperative than with the music of the Indian people.

Whatever one's immediate reaction to Indian music, it must be realized that it was never created to be experienced in the essentially passive way in which we listen to music in the concert hall or on recordings. Its ambience determines its essence. As Willard Rhodes has said: "Primitive music is so inextricably bound up in a larger complex, ceremonial or social, that it is practically non-existent out of its functional context."

Here is a condensation of a description of a Hopi ceremony that included music, as in fact do most Indian ceremonies:

> With a Hopi acquaintance I drove one July morning to Bakabi, to see the final ritual of the *Niman*. When I arrived in the village, I found that most of the Hopis had ascended to the line of roof tops, from which they could watch the ceremony in the plaza below. . . . The sky was cloudless and intensely blue. Sunshine flooded everything, illuminating the white walls of the houses along the plaza's farther side. . . . Soon a file of fifteen or twenty men came slowly into the plaza. . . . Each man's body, bare above the waist, was painted brown and marked with white symbols. Behind his right knee was fastened a rattle, made of a turtle shell. With each step that he took, the rattle gave out a hollow, muffled sound. In his right hand he carried a gourd rattle. . . . But the striking feature was the mask that each man wore. This covered his head completely and came down to his shoulders. The front was white and was inscribed with block-like figures, which suggested eyes, nose, and mouth. . . . Immediately, the ceremony

began. With measured, rhythmic step the long single file moved slowly forward, in time with a subdued chant. . . . With every step the turtle-shell rattle fastened behind the right knee contributed its hollow accent, sometimes suddenly magnified when all the dancers in unison struck the right foot sharply against the ground. Now and then the gourd rattles were shaken for two or three seconds, giving a curious accompaniment of elevated sound in contrast to the low, chanting voices. . . . When it was all over, I came away with the feeling that I had witnessed an ancient rite that was rich in symbolism and impressive in its significance.[2]

Even if a recording of this music had been made, how much could it convey to us, abstracted from its context?

Music in Indian life had also a *concreteness* unknown to sophisticated societies. The abstraction *music* would have been an unfamiliar and useless concept; it was only *this* song that had meaning. The important thing about a song is not its *beauty* but its *efficacy*. Frances Densmore, one of the pioneering authorities on Indian music, wrote: "The radical difference between the musical custom of the Indian and our own race is that, primarily, the Indians used song as a means of accomplishing definite results."[3] This view of music is by no means dead. For a recent recording of gambling songs by the Yurok and Tolowa tribes of northern California, translations of the words could not be made because "to do so would put the songs' luck in jeopardy."[4]

The degree of concreteness with which Indian songs are viewed is further illustrated by the fact that in many cases they are treated as strictly personal possessions, which may be transmitted to others only by being sold or given away. One old man, after being persuaded to record a noted war song, said that he would not live long now that he had given away his most valuable possession. There is a sense of tangible reality, of magical power, of "presence" in *all* manifestations of what we would term "art" among primitive peoples. In the nineteenth century, after an eastern artist had been among the Plains Indians sketching the buffalo, an old Indian complained to a white friend that there were no longer so many buffalo on their range—a white man had put a great number of them in a book and taken them away with him. Is this not indeed an expression of the same magic-imbued worldview that inscribed on rocks and in caves those often remarkably impressionistic likenesses of beasts the hunters needed to kill? It is this world we must be prepared to enter if we would understand what music originally meant to our first people.

Songs of great power, sung chiefly by medicine men or women, would be used in communal ceremonies, and would be very carefully passed on in oral tradition. In the songs of the Navajo, for example, the need for extreme accuracy was (and is) crucial to their efficacy. There could also be new songs, belonging to men who had acquired them in the course of "vision quests"—self-imposed ordeals of courage and self-denial that were known among virtually all tribes. Lonely fasts, often carried out in locations and conditions of extreme discomfort and danger, and lasting as long as four days, would, when successful, result in what appeared as tangible communication with the spirit dwelling in some animal or natural phenomenon. With the imparting of the vision (which identified the seeker forever afterward with the particular animal, if that were the apparent source) would often come what was received as a new song. These, then, were the "real" songs—the property either of individuals or of the tribe. A clear distinction was made in most tribes between these songs, which had inherent power, and other songs that were either borrowed from other tribes or were made up— consciously composed—and used to enhance various forms of recreation. In recent years, under the pressures of acculturation, the old songs have decreased in importance in the repertory of most tribes. Many that are known to have existed have been lost altogether.

The older ceremonial songs are heard in their purer form on the early recordings, sung often by old men whose memories stretch back to a time on the Plains and farther west when little acculturation had taken place. A very important class of songs were those used for healing the sick. One example is from the Menominee, an Algonquian tribe that, at the time this song was collected in the late 1920s, was still living along the Menominee River in Wisconsin, an area they had inhabited for at least three centuries. Example 3-1, "Pigeon's Dream Song," was sung by Louis Pigeon, who had secured it as a boy. After fasting for two days, he saw two birds, a crow and a raven, who gave him the song.

Example 3–1. "Pigeon's Dream Song"

Ceremonial dances could also be used for the curing of the sick. The Ribbon Dance of the Navajo, a dance of the Mountain Way, although now adapted for public demonstration, is an example.

Navajo fire dance from the Mountain Way ceremony. Like the Menominee dream song transcribed as Example 3-1, this dance was performed to help a sick person recover. *Courtesy of Library Services, American Museum of Natural History.*

Example 3–2. "Menominee Moccasin Game Song"

Dances for celebratory purposes have always been important, in spite of the fact that many have been used in public displays. "The Butterfly Dance" of San

Juan Pueblo, New Mexico, constitutes just one part (the war priest's song) of an extended ceremony based on a sacred narrative.

Gambling songs are present from the earliest recorded collections. Gambling was mostly restricted to men, and the stakes could be very high. The gambling usually takes the form of a guessing game between two opposing teams. A guesser from one team must choose the location of a marked object (a stick, a bullet, a prune pit, etc.) that has been hidden by the opposing team among like unmarked objects concealed in the hands, under overturned moccasins, and so forth. Songs were sung to bring luck; the singer might have assistants, or "seconds," to sing with him if he wished. Example 3-2 is a "Menominee Moccasin Game Song" recorded seventy or eighty years ago.

There were love songs as well—not, as in our popular culture, for the expression of sentimental feelings, but as "lucky" songs, to secure success in love through the invocation of magical power. **"Sioux Love Song"** (Ex. 3-3) is an example. The flute, as heard here, is almost uniquely associated with love songs, and these songs constitute almost the only use of purely instrumental music. These love songs could also be sung, as in this example.

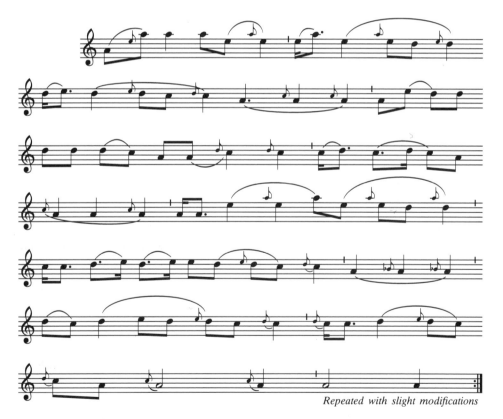

Repeated with slight modifications

Example 3–3. "Sioux Love Song"

The "Yurok Love Song," from northwest California, is a more recently recorded example.

Songs related to women's work exist, as in the corn-grinding songs, though these are not work songs in the sense of those in the African-American tradition. Among the Navajo these are sung by the men while the women grind the corn, to imbue the grain with spiritual quality so that it can be used in ceremonies. A similar invocational use of song is seen in the "Basket Song" of the Yurok of northwest California, who are superb basket makers. Here the song is sung to invoke aid in getting a good buyer for the basket.

Songs for other social functions exist: to welcome and bid farewell to guests (very elaborate along the northwestern coast); to honor warriors and chieftains; and to use in contests and other purely social ceremonies. Social dancing, with its own music, was originally relatively unimportant, though it has now become much more prevalent—one manifestation of the changes that have come over Indian life.

Characteristics of Indian Music

Through listening to these examples you will have acquired a practical introduction to the characteristics of Indian music. Though it is predominantly vocal, the singing is usually accompanied by a drum or some sort of rattle, or both. The basic unit of the music is the song, which may last anywhere from less than a minute to several minutes. When the song accompanies dancing, as it very often does, there is a good deal of repetition; it is common to sing a song four times.

The scales used in Indian music are found generally to correspond to our familiar diatonic scale—that is, the basic scale structure available on the white keys of the piano. Some form of the pentatonic scale (that obtainable on the black keys) is also very common. Singing in other than the unison (or octave, if the women sing also) is extremely rare, though not unknown.

Indian instruments include drums, whistles, flutes, hand-shaken rattles, and ornaments worn by dancers (made of shell, bone, or some kind of metal), which produce a rhythmic kind of rattling during the dance. The drums range in size from small handheld ones to quite large ones resting on the ground, or suspended between posts in the ground, and played by several people at once. They are made in a variety of ways, and are even improvised from inverted baskets, washtubs, kettles covered with skin, or wooden boxes. Flutes are usually fashioned from some straight-grained wood or cane, but in the Southwest they can be made of clay. Rattles are nearly universal, are of many types, and usually have (or had) ritual significance. The use of drums alone, without singing, is virtually unknown; this is in distinct contrast to African, and hence to West Indian, tradition. The rhythms of drum and rattle are simple, the impulses usually grouped in pairs in a relation that ranges from perfectly even pulses to those that alternate long-short, or heavy-light. Longer songs may be divided into clearly defined sections, with definite tempo changes. The tempo of the drum is sometimes independent of that of the voice.

The songs are very often not in the language of speech. *Vocables*—simple vocal sounds—are often either interpolated between actual words or replace them altogether.* To call these syllables meaningless is not quite correct; they may have private or ritual significance, or they may be sounds whose original meaning has been lost, either through changes in the language or because they were borrowed from other tribes. Whatever their origin, the vocables are not improvised, but belong to the given song and are reproduced with complete consistency.

Indian Music and Acculturation

Acculturation has gone on continuously since the first contacts with the white man. The French Huguenots were teaching the Florida Indians to sing psalms in the sixteenth century, and the Franciscans who traveled to the Rio Grande Valley with the settlers and their military escorts brought Spanish religious festivals and music to New Mexico in the seventeenth century. At the Zuñi pueblo of Hawikuh, in western New Mexico, Fray Roque de Figueredo in 1630 was teaching not only Gregorian chant and counterpoint, but also bassoon, cornett, and organ (portable organs were brought on expeditions by the Franciscans). Indian music has assimilated certain aspects of non-Indian music. On occasion, the tunes of Christian hymns and white secular songs have been adopted.[5] English words have been used, with either Indian tunes or disguised white tunes. A Hopi version of "Dixie" (perhaps sung as some kind of satire) is an amusing example of this phenomenon.**

The length of time that the indigenous Americans have been exposed to the white man's culture varies widely from area to area. We know the least about aboriginal Indian music in the eastern United States, where the cultural pressures, and the dispossessions and dispersions, began earliest and were most severe. As a single example of a major uprooting, Indians from five tribes (the Choctaw, the Creek, the Cherokee, the Chickasaw, and the Seminole) were forced to move between 1830 and 1842 (in an episode known as the Trail of Tears) from the southeastern states to an area west of the Mississippi known as the Indian Territory—and formally so designated until its admission to the Union as the

---

* The *fa-la-la* refrains of Anglo-American ballads are an interesting parallel.
**The Hopi version of "Dixie" is on *Pueblo: Taos, San Ildefonson, Zuni, Hopi*, Library of Congress AFS L43.

state of Oklahoma in 1907.[6] After the Civil War, the western portion of the Indian Territory became home for many Indians from the northern and central Plains as well. This dislocation brought tribes from greatly separated regions into contact, marking the beginnings of the pan-Indian movement.

The Ghost Dance and the Peyote Cult

Two singular developments in Indian culture since the encroachment of white civilization grew out of that cataclysm, directly or indirectly. The first of these was the spread of the Ghost Dance, with its accompanying music. Originating in the Great Basin area, the Ghost Dance cult represented a kind of messianic religious belief in the appearance of a savior and the expulsion of the white man, accompanied by the resurrection of dead Indian leaders and the return of the buffalo and of the old ways. In the 1880s the Ghost Dance spread rapidly, especially among Plains tribes. It was outlawed by the Bureau of Indian Affairs, and its repression by the United States Army culminated in the tragic massacre of Sioux Ghost Dance devotees at Wounded Knee in South Dakota in 1890. As an active cult and ritual, a vehicle of a fanatical hope, the Ghost Dance died out as rapidly as it had spread. Its songs persisted, however, and were recorded among Plains tribes as late as the 1940s. It was a pan-Indian cultural phenomenon; Ghost Dance songs of various tribes show similar characteristics, of Great Basin origin, that are often markedly different from those of their own indigenous tribal music.[7]

A second, and not unrelated, development has been the spread of the peyote cult (the Native American Church), based on the use of the hallucinogenic buttons of the peyote cactus. Originating apparently in pre-Columbian Mexico, it had spread northward into the Rio Grande and Gila River basins by the eighteenth century, where it was known among the Apache. The cult reached the Plains about 1870. Taking on there a somewhat different form, it became a group or community rite, with a well-defined ceremonial that incorporated some elements of Christian theology and symbolism. (In a Sioux **Peyote Song** the singer spells out JESUS ONLY.) Its spread since then has been carefully documented, and is still going on; it reached some groups of the Navajo, and the Indians of Canada and Florida, in the mid-twentieth century. Singing is an integral part of the meetings at which the peyote buttons are consumed, and while any songs, including Christian hymns, may be used, special peyote songs have evolved.[8] The relation of the peyote cult to the vanished Ghost Dance, and to the severe upheaval to which the American Indians and their aboriginal culture generally have been subjected in the modern world, is summed up by David McAllester:

The wide spread of the Ghost Dance must have contributed to the receptivity of the Indians to peyote. After the brief currency of the former the Indians were left with little sense of spiritual direction, although the conditions of radical change and insecurity that fostered the Ghost Dance were intensified after its collapse. . . . In place of resistance a philosophy of peaceful conciliation and escape rose. . . . The vision, all-important on the Plains, was made easily available by the use of the cactus.[9]

Outside Influences on Music Made by Native Americans

Indians themselves have absorbed and adopted outside influences in their music, including the use of the English language, often in a satirical way. A "forty-nine song" is a particular kind of humorous, often derisive, song with English words. A recent rendition of the **Rabbit Dance**, a social dance of the northern Plains Indians, contains the following lines, in a parody of a white cowboy song.

> *Hey, sweetheart, I always think of you.*
> *I wonder if you are alone tonight.*
> *I wonder if you are thinking of me.*[10]

The greatest degree of integration of Indian and non-Indian elements in music and dance has taken place in the Southwest. Hispanic influence is evident in the *matachines* of New Mexico—pageants of dance and drama derived from quite old Spanish fiestas (possibly introduced by the Franciscans as early as the seventeenth century) that are associated with the Christian observances of Easter and Christmas.[11]

A more recent absorption, wholly in the secular domain, is represented by the popular dance music among the Papago, Pima, and Yaqui tribes in southern Arizona known as *waila*, or more popularly as "chicken scratch." Chicken scratch bands use combinations of such instruments as guitar, accordion, saxophone, and drum set (non-Indian) to play waltzes, two-steps, and polkas that show resemblances to Mexican *mariachi* music, Texas-Mexican *norteña* music, German band music, and even Louisiana *zydeco*.

The State of Indian Music Today

American Indian music today can best be described as a *renovated* art—that is, an art renewed in a way that consciously preserves tradition while adapting it in a manner that allows it to survive, and even thrive, in the conditions under which Indians live in the modern world. Twentieth-century influence is seen in an altered view of the *function* of music. While its religious function has by no means disappeared altogether, it coexists with both a recreational and an entertainment function. There exist sizable communities of native Americans not only in virtually every small city in the West, but in and around large urban areas, particularly Chicago, Denver, Los Angeles, and the San Francisco Bay area, especially Oakland. These urban Indian communities regularly enjoy large social gatherings, at which Indian songs and dances are performed—in Los Angeles, for example, by such groups as the Los Angeles Northern Singers, made up of members of the Sioux, Arikara, Hidatsa, and Northern Arapaho tribes.

At these gatherings not only are the tribal songs and dances found to be flourishing, but unmistakable traces of the older attitude toward music are preserved. These can be seen, for example, in the custom of "sponsoring" an entertainment in honor of a person or event (which had its aboriginal counterpart in customs such as the *potlatch*), and in surviving manifestations of the concepts that certain songs are private possessions and bring luck. Another aspect of Indian music today is the fact that Indian musicians with a creative bent have the opportunity to function as composers, using Indian culture as a basis for the creation of individual works within, and with meaning for, the Indian community—an opportunity that did not exist in the older tribal society.

In spite of the pressures of professionalism and commercialization, music has been part of a serious movement of cultural *revival* since the 1950s. The intertribal *powwows* held annually on the Plains (especially in Oklahoma) are today great social events, but they are also important cultural events as well. They include contests, both for "straight dancers," and for "fancy dancers," the latter giving an opportunity for the display of prodigious virtuosity in dancing, and elaborateness of costume. A live recording of a "Contest Song for Fancy Dancers" conveys some of the excitement and spirit of this event. The "Flag Parade" that ends the powwow is convincing evidence of the energy of present-day revivalism in American Indian culture.*

Another approach to revivalism seeks to emphasize not the *externals* of indigenous American culture, but its *inner, esoteric*, meaning for the members of a tribe today—that is, instead of trying to recreate their musical past, "to create their musical present." This kind of musical *revitalization*, as it has been called, has taken place among the Choctaw in the Ardmore, Oklahoma, area. As Victoria Lindsay Levine, who has studied this revival extensively, has put it: "In revitalizing their musical culture, the Ardmore Choctaw did not attempt to reproduce their historic dance events as such, but they did seek to recreate the spirit of early dances in contemporary performance contexts." These contexts

*"Contest Song for Fancy Dancers" is on *Powwow Songs*, New World 80343.

involve a "de-emphasis on the more external aspects of performance," including dance costumes—a de-emphasis that allows for a high degree of individuality. This would seem a promising "Native American strategy for cultural survival."[12]

FURTHER READING

General

Curtis, Natalie (Natalie Curtis Burlin). *The Indians' Book*. New York: Harper Bros., 1907. Reprint. New York: Dover, 1968.

> An important early work, illustrated with paintings and drawings by Indians. Includes a considerable number of song transcriptions.

Densmore, Frances. *The American Indians and Their Music*. New York: Women's Press, 1926.

> An early comprehensive work by a pioneer researcher. It is supplemented by numerous tribal studies published between 1910 and 1939, and reprinted by Da Capo Press. More than mere transcriptions, they treat the customs, ceremonies, and legends of the tribes.

Heth, Charlotte. "Update on Indian Music: Contemporary Trends." In *Sharing a Heritage*. Los Angeles: UCLA American Indian Studies Center, 1984, 89–100.

Nettl, Bruno. *North American Indian Musical Styles*. Philadelphia: American Folklore Society, 1954.

> An important brief study, somewhat technical, of regional characteristics. Includes some musical examples.

Representative regional studies, or works on special topics

Kurath, Gertrude P. *Music and Dance of the Tewa Pueblos*. Santa Fe: Museum of New Mexico Press, 1970.

> This modern study includes extensive transcriptions of music, diagrams of dance, and some photos.

Merriam, Alan P. *Ethnomusicology of the Flathead Indians*. Chicago: Aldine, 1967.

> The jacket description is accurate: "The first complete survey of the entire musical output of a people in its cultural context, exemplifying a new technique of musical analysis." This important work has helped to set new standards for research and writing in the field.

Smythe, Willie, ed. *The Songs of the Indian Territory*. Oklahoma City: The Center for the American Indian, 1989.

> Comes with cassette tape.

Weibel-Orlando, Joan. *Indian Country L. A.: Maintaining Ethnic Community in a Complex Society*. Urbana: University of Illinois Press, 1991.

Projects

1. Select one American Indian tribe and listen to as much of its music as is available. (Try to work from a sample of at least fifteen songs.) Note the musical characteristics, and see to what extent they conform to, or differ from, the description of the area characteristics as given by Nettl in *North American Indian Musical Styles*, or in his article in the *New Grove Dictionary of American Music*, vol. 2, pp. 460ff.

2. If there is one in your vicinity, attend a powwow or other Indian gathering that includes singing, dancing, and games. In a paper assess the degree to which what you observed either reinforces or contradicts the impressions you have gotten of Indian music and culture from reading this chapter. Assess also the ways in which acculturation has taken place, and those areas in which it has *not* taken place.

3. Talk with some persons of Indian descent—at least two, if possible—about the current state of Indian culture from their point of view. Should it be preserved, and if so for what reasons? In what ways should the preservation of traditional ways compromise and adapt to modern society, and in what ways should it retain its distinctness and integrity?

4. Write an essay discussing what you, or what non-Indians in general, might have to learn from the way Indians traditionally used and regarded music.

5. Do some research into the curriculum of one or more Indian colleges (Navajo Community College, for example); try to determine the extent to which traditional Indian music is being studied and taught there.

Notes

1. To learn more about the characteristics of the music of the various cultural areas, consult *North American Indian Musical Styles* by Bruno Nettl (Philadelphia: American Folklore Society, 1954), and the article in *The New Grove Dictionary of American Music* by the same author (vol. 2, 460–68).

2. Walter Collins O'Kane, *Sun in the Sky* (Norman: University of Oklahoma Press, 1950), 186–91.

3. Frances Densmore, *The American Indians and Their Music* (New York: Women's Press, 1926), 63.

4. See *Songs of Love, Luck, Animals, and Magic*, New World 80297.

5. A Chinook version of "Jesus Loves Me" can be heard on *Music of the American Indian: Northwest (Puget Sound)* (AAFS: L-34).

6. Thus we have songs and dances of "eastern Indians" (Cherokee and Creek) being recorded in Sequoyah County, Oklahoma: see *Songs of the Allegany and Seneca Indians*, New World 80337.

7. Ghost Dance songs recorded among Great Basin and Plains tribes may be heard on the following recordings in the Library of Congress *Music of the American Indian* series (AAFS): *Songs of the Pawnee and Northern Ute* (L-25), *Plains: Comanche, Cheyenne, Kiowa, Caddo, Wichita, Pawnee* (L-39), *Kiowa* (L-35), *Great Basin: Paiute, Washo, Ute, Bannock, Shoshone* (L-38), and *Sioux* (L-40).

8. There is no doubt about the acculturational influence on the peyote cult and music. Called the Native American Church, the cult has Christian overtones, and has adopted Christian symbols and words, which appear in many of the songs. Other peyote songs can be heard on AAFS: L-35 and L-38 (cited above), and on *Delaware, Cherokee, Choctaw, Creek* (AFFS: L-37) and *Navajo* (AAFS: L-41).

9. David P. McAllester, *Peyote Music*, Viking Fund Publications in Anthropology, no. 13 (New York: Viking, 1949), 85.

10. Willard Rhodes regarded this category of songs as "a passing fad or fashion which flourished because of novelty in uniting an Indian melody with English words" (Rhodes, "Acculturation in North American Indian Music" in *Acculturation in the Americas* [Chicago: University of Chicago Press, 1952]), but he may well not have been in a position to grasp the cultural significance of this special type of song.

11. For more information on the *matachines* dance, see "Matachines: A Midwinter Drama from Iberia" in *Music and Drama of the Tewa Pueblos* by Gertrude Prokosch Kurath (Santa Fe: Museum of New Mexico Press, 1970), and portions of her article in *The New Grove Dictionary of American Music* (vol. 2, 477–78). See also "The Matachines Dance—A Ritual Folk Dance" by J. Donald Robb in *Western Folklore* 20, no. 2 (1961): 87–101, as well as many references and examples of the music from the same author's *Hispanic Folk Music of New Mexico* (FE-4426), with notes by J. Donald Robb. Robb points out that at times these dances appear in two distinct versions: "a Spanish version with fiddle and guitar imported from a nearby Spanish village and an Indian version with Indian music, chorus, drums, and costuming, which nevertheless follows generally the plot, the dance evolutions, and other aspects of the traditional *matachine* dance" (*Hispanic Folk Music of New Mexico and the Southwest*, 6).

12. See Victoria Lindsay Levine "Musical Revitalization Among the Choctaw," *American Music* 11, no. 4 (Winter 1993), and the same author's Ph.D. dissertation, "Choctaw Indian Musical Cultures in the Twentieth Century," University of Illinois at Urbana-Champaign, 1990.

Chapter 4

The Latino Tradition

The complexities confronting anyone investigating music coming from "south of the border" can be traced to the fact that this music represents a complicated overlaying and blending of cultures from four continents: North and Central America, South America, Europe (specifically the Iberian peninsula), and West Africa. We begin our exploration of this complex subject with the impact of Spanish conquest and colonization in the Western Hemisphere.

The Legacy of the Spanish Conquest

The first persistent European presence in America was that of the Spaniards. In the generation following Columbus's voyages, Spain, the foremost European power of the time, entered upon a period of phenomenal exploration and conquest. By the mid-sixteenth century the Spanish had begun extensive exploration by land and by sea from Florida to the northern California coast, and by 1565 (at St. Augustine, Florida) the first attempts at colonization in what is the present area of the United States (many of which proved to be disastrous) had begun. Although Florida was the first point of contact, Spanish influence along the eastern coast of the Gulf of Mexico was not destined to be significant in the long term. In the Southwest, on the other hand, it was decisive. Beginning with the earliest missions and small colonial settlements in the upper Rio Grande Valley of New Mexico as early as 1598, and culminating with the high-water mark of Spanish penetration in the California mission period of the late eighteenth and early nineteenth centuries, the foundation was laid for Hispanic influence, which is still of the greatest importance culturally in that part of the country, and which has been reinforced in all periods by almost continuous migrations from Mexico.

Sacred Music from Mexico

The first musical influences were religious. Spanish sacred music reached the highest point of its development in the prosperous sixteenth century, rivaling in its excellence and in the intensity of its cultivation that of Rome itself. It was Spanish sacred music from that era that traveled with the *conquistadores*, and music was found to be one of the priests' most powerful tools for converting and teaching the Indians.* Before the end of the sixteenth century, vocal and instrumental music were intensively cultivated in Mexico by both Indians and Spanish, accompanied by the manufacture of musical instruments and the printing of music.

New Mexico

Because of its early penetration by soldiers, settlers, and missionaries beginning in the 1540s, New Mexico is the area of the oldest sustained Hispanic influence in the United States. And because of its subsequent relative isolation (from the Re-conquest after the Pueblo Revolt of the 1680s to the testing of the atomic bomb in the 1940s), especially in the valleys of the upper Rio Grande and Pecos Rivers, this influence has until recently persisted with little interference. The opening of the Santa Fe Trail in 1821, and the conquest and annexation of the area by the United States in 1846–48 had little effect on life in the remote villages, much of which centered on their churches.

During the seventeenth century Spanish religious music, coming by way of Mexico, almost certainly was performed in the missions of New Mexico. However, during the Pueblo Revolt nearly all records from the missions were destroyed. As a result, the religious music of New Mexico that we know the most about today is the relatively simple folklike music cultivated and preserved by a devout people worshiping for generations in relative isolation. Of particular antiquity and interest is the music of *La Fraternidad Piadosa de Nuestro Padre Jesús Nazareno*, more familiarly known as *Los Hermanos Penitentes*, or simply *Los Penitentes*.

The most characteristic form of music cultivated by the Penitentes was the *alabado*, a religious folk song in free meter sung in unison. The alabado currency is not limited to the Brotherhood, has been called the "backbone of congregational singing since the 16th century," and has been and still is sung in Hispanic Catholic churches throughout the Southwest.[1] Its forebears are the medieval plainchant of the Catholic Church, and the cantillations of the Sephardic Jews of Spain and Portugal. Most of the alabados sung by the Penitentes are lengthy strophic songs commemorating aspects of the Passion of Christ, such as the Stations of the Cross, which are reenacted in pageant form. They are unaccompanied except by the florid improvised interjections of the *pito* (a homemade flute played only during Holy Week), which are said to represent the lamenting cries of the

---

* A survival of this influence into the twentieth century has been cited in chapter 3, in the matachines dance-drama among Indians of New Mexico.

Virgin Mary. Many of the alabados have been preserved, having been recorded around 1950 in their many variants from village to village.[2]

A more widespread form of religious folk song is that associated with the Christmas play *Los Pastores* (The Shepherds), and its prelude, *Las Posadas* (The Lodgings). They are related to the mystery plays, liturgical dramas prevalent in Europe from the ninth through the sixteenth centuries. Possibly written by the Franciscans in Mexico, they made their ways by separate routes to California, New Mexico, and Texas. *Las Posadas* and *Los Pastores* commemorate first Mary and Joseph seeking lodging, and then the shepherds coming to pay homage to the infant Jesus. Many versions of *Los Pastores* were also recorded in New Mexico around the middle of this century, and some have been painstakingly transcribed.[3] Today *Las Posadas*, partially because of the interest it has aroused among non-Hispanics, is more frequently cultivated than the longer and more involved *Los Pastores*.

California

An echo of the greatness of Spanish church music belatedly reached California in the late eighteenth and early nineteenth centuries. During the brief flourishing of the Franciscan missions in California from 1769 to their secularization beginning in 1834, there was a rather considerable musical culture, and that music was integral to mission life.[4] Both vocal and instrumental music were taught to the Indians, who made up the choirs and small orchestras. The range of music extended from folklike hymns and *alabados* to elaborate settings of the Mass for chorus with instrumental accompaniment. At least nine of the missions had collections of instruments; Santa Barbara, possibly the most prosperous, had forty-three instruments in 1834, including a fairly large organ. The presence of these instruments, the training and dedication to music of *padres* Juan Sancho, Narciso Durán, Arroyo de la Cuesta, and Junipero Serra himself, and the fact that visitors reported the existence of orchestras and choruses of over thirty musicians and were much impressed by the quality of their music make it reasonably certain that at some of the missions, on special occasions, elaborate polyphonic music such as the recently discovered Mass in D Major by Ignacio de Jerúsalem was performed.*

Spanish California was not a cultural backwater. The Franciscan missions and their attendant *presidios* and secular communities, while remote, were for the most part very prosperous centers—even compared with towns in Spain and in the United States of the time. They were situated in a naturally fertile land with

---

* de Jerúsalem was a prolific composer who was chapel master of the Mexico City Cathedral from 1749 to 1769.

a mild climate, and with abundant livestock and food supplies, and abundant labor supplied by a captive population. It was only after Mexican independence, and with it the secularization of the missions and the departure of the Franciscan priests, that mission music declined and virtually disappeared. Such manuscripts as existed (consisting wholly of liturgical music) were destroyed or forgotten, and what little was preserved of a musical culture went over into oral tradition. Under the circumstances, it is remarkable that any survived; it is therefore rather surprising to come upon a photograph of the last Indian choir of Mission San Buenaventura, taken in 1860, with each of the Indians holding what appears to be a homemade instrument—a flute, for example, fashioned from an old gun barrel. That the singing of the Indian choirs survived even longer in some cases, without losing its intensity or meaning, is attested to by Robert Louis Stevenson's account of a festival at Mission San Carlos Borromeo (Carmel) in 1879: "I have never seen faces more vividly lit up with joy than the faces of these Indian singers. It was to them not only the worship of God, nor an act by which they recalled and commemorated better days, but was besides an exercise of culture, where all they knew of art and letters was united and expressed."[5]

Secular Music from Mexico

Secular folk music from Latin America has been far more widespread and influential in the culture of the United States than has sacred music. To begin to understand the nature and sources of this music, it is important to realize that the *mestizo* folk culture of Latin America is everywhere a blend of Spanish, Indian, and African elements, the mix varying from region to region. African influence is strongest in the Caribbean (especially Cuba, Jamaica, and Hispaniola) and in the Caribbean and Brazilian coastal areas of South America, though it is not to be discounted in Mexico itself.[6] The music from south of our borders has reached the United States in two strains and by two routes. Music that has come from Mexico is obviously of the greatest importance in the Southwest—in Texas, New Mexico, Colorado, Arizona, and California—but has penetrated farther north as well. The other strain, from the Caribbean and South America, will be treated later.

In the secular music from Mexico (as indeed from the rest of Latin America as well) dance and song are closely associated.[7] Many kinds of music can be used for either. For example, the *corrido* (or ballad) can be danced as well as sung, and the *huapango*, originally a dance from Veracruz, can also be sung. Dancing was a very important pastime from the earliest times in rural Hispanic communities, and there are numerous accounts of *bailes* or *fandangos* in the *salas* of the towns or villages of New Mexico and California, to the accompaniment of fiddle and guitar.

Popular Mexican dances were the *el jarabe*, *la jota*, and *la bamba*. European dances, arriving either from Mexico itself, or, in California, from Anglo-American sailors, were *el valse* (the waltz), *la polca* (the polka), *el chotís* (the schottische), and *el cutilio* (the cotillion or square dance).[8]

A second point about this music is the marks that other cultures have made on it, either here or in Mexico itself.[9] The mixture of Austrian, German, Czech, and Anglo-American influences can be seen in the types of dances cited above and in their names. In the border region the German influence (its chief contributions being the polka and the button accordion) proved to be decisive.

While genuine regional musics, as enjoyed by the mostly rural people in the highly differentiated parts of Mexico, have existed and continue to exist, they have been overshadowed by a kind of "generic" Mexican music, perpetuated as part of a professionalized "cultural front." This development is similar to, but much older than, that of the pan-Indian music described in chapter 3. In the 1880s, for example, during the Díaz regime, *orquestas típicas*, made up of professional musicians dressed in *charro*[10] costumes, were formed, and were supported by the government as a means of promoting Mexican culture abroad. Orquestas típicas, led by directors such as Carlos Curtí, toured the United States and Europe before the turn of the century. Since then, such ensembles have been important, both as tourist attractions in the large Mexican cities and as exporters of "typical" Mexican music, as have the more recent trumpet mariachi ensembles. With the advent of broadcasting and recording, the production of popular music based on folk styles but performed by professional musicians began in Mexico City, in the same kind of development that produced "country music" from regional folk styles here.

The Mariachi

The result of this popularization and consequent standardization of Mexican music has been the emergence of two dominant types of instrumental ensemble, used to accompany either dancing or singing. One is the *mariachi*, which in its current popular form consists of trumpets, violins, a vihuela (a smaller 5-string, guitar-like instrument), a guitar, a guitarrón, or bass guitar, and optionally a harp of a particular design from the state of Jalisco. The musical form most characteristic of the mariachi is the *son*, with its intriguing rhythmic surprises, flip-flopping deftly back and forth between 3/4 and 6/8 meters. Of these *sones*, none is more well known than the highly characteristic La Negra.

Mariachi music attained considerable popularity north of the border after trumpets were added to the ensemble in the 1930s and 1940s. With its rhythms, its trumpets playing in parallel thirds, and not least the typical costumes of its

Mariachi musicians in Sinaloa Territory, Mexico, 1944. *Photo by Betty Volk. Courtesy Arizona Historical Society Library.*

musicians, it has become a kind of convenient symbol of "Mexicanness." Professonal mariachis in the United States have become highly skilled and versatile show and recording bands, with as many as fourteen musicians who both sing and play. While they have broadened both their repertory and their musical styles to reach a larger musical public, they have never abandoned their musical roots, to which they consistently pay homage. Mariachi Cobre of Tucson, for example, recently recorded **"Las Abajeñas" (The Lowland Women)**, a *son* that can be traced as far back as a recording made in Mexico prior to 1908.

Musica norteña

The other dominant Mexican-American instrumental ensemble is the *conjunto* of the *musica norteña*. This distinctively regional ensemble, coming from the lower Rio Grande Valley shared by Texas and the far northeastern part of Mexico (hence the adjective *norteña*, "northern"), consisted in its early stages of only the highly characteristic button accordion with an accompaniment of guitar or *bajo sexto* (a form of 12-string guitar). Beginning in the 1950s, a saxophone was frequently added (often doubling the accordion in thirds, a typically Mexican device also used with voices and with mariachi trumpets), as well as a jazz-type drum set and a bass—more recently an electric one. The differences between mariachi music and musica norteña are not so much distinctions in repertory—they may perform the same songs or dances—but in their instrumentation and style of performance. Musica norteña most often has as its rhythmic basis either the "oom-pa oom-pa" of the adopted polka or the "oom-pa-pa oom-pa-pa" of the adopted waltz, while the mariachi ensemble is more apt to retain the complex rhythms and cross-rhythms of the Mexican *son*.

Conjunto music is probably the more widely popular of the two styles among Mexican-Americans themselves, especially the younger generation. It evolved into a distinctive and regionally very influential style at the hands of accordionists, most notably in the beginning by Narciso Martinez ("El Huracán del Valle") and Santo Jiménez, and later by his son, Flaco. "Que me gano con llorar" (What's the Use of Crying) by the Conjunto Trio San Antonio, with the German-born accordionist Fred Zimmerle, shows the lively staccato style of accordion playing associated with norteño music.[11] The music was spread throughout the Southwest by a more recent generation of performers, including Flaco Jiménez and the guitarist-singers Freddy Fender (Baldemar Huerta), Doug Sahm (an Anglo with the acquired name of Doug Saldaña), and José Maria De Leon ("Little Joe") Hernández. Acquiring political overtones to some degree, and associated with the ethnic pride and aspirations of Chicanos, musica norteña has become identified throughout the West as Chicano music.

Those who identify themselves as Chicanos are only one part of the Mexican-American populace. Making up an increasingly large percentage of the population of the United States, especially in the Southwest, people of Mexican descent constitute a rather complex cluster of three or four fairly distinct groups. *Mexican-Americans* are those who were born or have lived here for a long time, identify themselves most strongly as Americans, and have become thoroughly assimilated into mainstream American business, political, and social life. Sometimes identified as a separate, and much smaller, group are *Hispanic-Americans*, whose ancestors settled in Texas, New Mexico, or California (the "californios") before Anglo settlement and domination came to those areas. They may even regard their cultural heritage as coming more from Spain than from Mexico, especially the Hispanic New Mexicans (*"Spanish-Americans"*). A third group are *Chicanos*, whose identity as a cultural group was born in the 1960s. These tend to be young Mexican-Americans who have rediscovered and are celebrating their ethnic identity. In varying degrees activist and militant, they are impatient with what they see as discrimination against their race (La Raza) and may, in the extreme, look upon the United States as a country of oppression and racism. The overt extreme was expressed in the dress (the zoot suit) and stance of the *pachuco*, the young Mexican "gang" member. As Steven Loza has said: "The Los Angeles Chicano movement reflected the general spirit of young people who rejected the term *Mexican American* in favor of *Chicano*, a word that symbolized defiance of the notions of cultural assimilation and represented an expression of pride . . . ."[12] Their cultural focus tends to be definitely not Spanish (except in language), and not so much Mexican as pre-Columbian Indian, and even pre-Aztec. (The mythical Aztlán, placed somewhere in the American Southwest, is regarded as the birthplace of all native American races. According to this view, the migrations northward from Mexico in historical times are regarded as a *return* to a legendary homeland.) A fourth group are *Mexicanos*, or Mexican immigrants, both documented and undocumented. They form a large and mobile population. Although many, if not most, of them do not intend to stay in this country and resist assimilation, they account for a significant part of the constant replenishment of Mexican culture that comes through the continuous immigration from Mexico.[13]

The Corrido

Of all the popular folk forms, none is more distinctive or more interesting than the *corrido*. The Hispanic love of poetry, and especially the commemoration of people and events in poetry, finds expression in this vital tradition. The corrido is the equivalent of the folk ballad—a narrative strophic song. As distinguished from the older *romance*, of Spanish origin, it deals with actual people and events, often of immediate and topical concern, in an earthy, frank, and unembellished way. It had its origins in Mexico in the turbulent mid-nineteenth century, when it was often political and satirical. Before the advent of recordings and radio, corridos were circulated by itinerant *corridistas* or *trovadores* (troubadours), going from hacienda to hacienda, or singing in marketplaces and on street corners. As with the Anglo-American ballad, corridos were cheaply printed as broadsides, with words only.

The corrido of the southwestern United States is nearly as old as its Mexican forebear. An area rich in the production of corridos has been the valley of the lower Rio Grande, from the two Laredos to the Gulf. A fertile valley in the midst of an arid plain, overlooked in early exploration and colonialization, largely ignored by Spain and Mexico, and spurned by the United States, it was inhabited by people of a fiercely independent spirit. When in 1836 Texas declared its independence of Mexico, the valley suddenly became a border area, and a period of unrest, oppression, and bloodshed began that was to last intermittently for nearly a century. Like many strife-torn border areas—that between England and Scotland, for example—it bred its heroes and its villains, and ballads to commemorate them. An early corrido was "El Corrido de Kiansis," known in the border area by 1870. It describes the experiences and hardships of the Mexican *vaqueros* in the cattle drives of the late 1860s and early 1870s from Texas to the western terminus of the railroad in Kansas.

One of the most famous corridos, still sung today, is **"El Corrido de Gregorio Cortez"** (Ex. 4-1), based on an incident that took place in Cameron County, Texas, in 1901. The hero was a young Mexican who, having been falsely accused of horse stealing, shot and killed in self-defense the sheriff who had fatally wounded his brother. The corrido, in some twenty to thirty stanzas, goes on to trace Cortez's flight and capture, ending with the customary *despedida* "Now with this I say farewell."[14]

Example 4–1. "El Corrido de Gregorio Cortez"

This corrido shows the typical form of four-line rhymed stanzas, or *coplas*, each line customarily having eight syllables. The musical rhythm is simple, but rather characteristically irregular in its metrical structure.

In the corrido we encounter a ballad tradition still very much alive. In the days of the 45-rpm single local radio stations could be playing a newly composed and recorded corrido within twenty-four hours of the event (often a violent crime or scandal) it commemorated. The almost journalistic immediacy of the corrido resulted in some lawsuits against record companies. Corridos of protest were, and are, common. Many are *homenajes*, lamenting the deaths of popular heros.[15] Since the 1970s there have been many corridos written about César Chávez and Dolores Huerta and the farm labor movement in California. Example 4-2 is a typical modern corrido with words by Arnoldo Ramirez and music by his brother, Rafaél Ramirez, entitled **"La Muerte de Martin Luther King"** (The Death of Martin Luther King).

Example 4–2. "La Muerte de Martin Luther King"

The early corridos were performed and recorded as *duetos*—two singers with guitar. Later, by the mid-1940s, they were performed by *conjuntos*, with their distinctive addition of accordion and sometimes saxophone, and thus became part of the *norteño* repertoire.

The Canción

The *canción* is lyrical and often sentimental, in contrast to the narrative and even epic quality of the corrido. The term *canción* is used to cover a broad range of songs, of which songs about love are only one type. In the category of folk songs in oral tradition, a noted folk music collector has printed ninety-two canciones from New Mexico alone, including such traditional songs as "Cielito Lindo" and "La Golondrina."[16] Two soldiers' songs are "La Cucaracha," of which there are many satirical parodies, and "La Adelita," both extremely popular during the revolutionary period of 1910–20. Belonging to a large and variously defined category of songs are the *canciones rancheras*—part of the "country music revival" glorifying the peasantry after the Revolution. The best-known survivor, probably written for a film by the same name, is "Allá en el Rancho Grande."

Corresponding roughly to the romantic *ballad* of American popular music is the *bolero*, usually a lament about lost love. Lydia Mendoza (b. 1916), "La Alondra de la Frontera" (the Meadowlark of the Border) and "La Cancionera de los Pobres" (the Songstress of the Poor), sang many of these, accompanying herself on the 12-string guitar. Her story gives some insight into Mexican-American music throughout the Southwest, and *Tejano* (Texas) border music in particular, and the lives of those who made, and still make, this music. She was a member of a musical family that, in the 1920s, was traveling from town to town in the lower Rio Grande Valley, trying to make a living from their singing and playing. Like many Mexican families, they had fled the violence and turmoil of the prolonged Mexican Revolution. Lydia was only twelve when La Familia Mendoza made their first recording in 1928, at a time when record companies were first beginning to realize the potential market that existed for recordings of regional folk music. (There are many parallels with the Carter Family of Virginia, who began recording what eventually became "country music" at about the same time; see chapter 5.*) The hardship and discrimination the Mendozas endured was typical of the experience of most immigrant musicians and their families. Lydia Mendoza's first success was the recording of a canción, "**Mal hombre**" (translated "Cold-hearted Man"), in 1934.[17] Recordings brought increased personal appearances, and eventually she became what has been described as "perhaps the single most important and historic pioneer recording artist not only in Tejano music but in the entire field of Mexican-American music." Her recorded repertoire is certainly representative of this field; it includes mostly canciones, but also corridos, rancheras, boleros, valses, and tangos, recorded not only "con su guitarra," but also with leading conjuntos in Texas, and Mariachi Vargas de Tecalitlan, the most famous mariachi in Mexico.[18]

A *canción* of powerful significance to Chicanos in recent years, especially those in the farm worker movement in California, is "De Colores." It was originally an old Spanish folk song. Most of the five verses that are extant, including

---

* The music of the Carter Family, who actually did some of their recording in San Antonio, was being broadcast over powerful radio stations in Texas, and later in northern Mexico, at about the same time that La Familia Mendoza was popular. See "The Carter Family on Border Radio" in *American Music* 14, no. 2 (Summer 1996).

De co-lo-res,_____ de co-lo-res se vis-ten los cam-pos en

la pri-ma-ve-ra;_____ de co-lo-res,_____ de co-

-lo-res son los pa-ja-ri-llos que vie-nen de fue-ra._____

De co-lo-res,_____ de co-lo-res es el ar-co i-ris qu

ve-mos lu-cir,_____ y por e-so los gran-des a-mo-res de

mu-chos co-lo-res me gus-tan a mi,_____ y por e-so los

gran-des a-mo-res de mu-chos co-lo-res me gus-tan a mi.

Example 4–3. "De Colores"

the two that are widely known and sung, express an appreciation of nature. Other verses introduce a religious dimension, with special reference to the *cursillos*, intensive three-day "courses" sponsored by the Catholic Church that have been particularly popular in the Spanish-speaking Southwest. "De Colores" became associated with the farm labor movement under the leadership of César Chávez, and it was certainly sung during the historic march from Delano to Sacramento in 1966. Although its theme of harmony and unity has been effective in organizing workers, it is not a militant song. Literal translation fails to convey the essence of the simple words, which invoke light, color, and the harmony of nature, using the images of the colors of the fields in spring, the colors of birds that come from afar, and the colors that are seen in the rainbow. It has assumed the character of a deeply meaningful hymn.

Los Lobos. *Courtesy New York Public Library.*

Los Angeles

Los Angeles, with a Mexican population exceeded in number only by that of Mexico City itself, has its own distinctive Mexican musical history and culture. A part of Mexico until 1848, El Pueblo de Nuestra Señora la Reina de Los Angeles, founded in 1781, had a lively tradition of *bailes*, *fandangos*, feasts, and processions, all accompanied by music. Among the *californios* of all classes, music was an important part of life, and there were few who could not sing or play an instrument. After annexation by the United States, immigration from Mexico decreased while that from the rest of the States increased dramatically. Mexican cultural and political influence declined overall, but did not by any means disappear. Records of the period show a flourishing musical life for the Spanish-speaking public in southern California in the last half of the nineteenth century. For the cultivated society there were the *bailes*, in homes or hotels, for which there were printed invitations. Less formal were the *fandangos* of the cantinas and the saloons. There were many open-air band concerts, and touring virtuosi and opera and theatrical companies came from Mexico City, and even from Spain.[19]

The demographics of Southern California started to change early in the twentieth century, as immigration from Mexico began the inexorable, if uneven, rise that continues to this day. This was due to the increased industrialization of southern California, and in the early years of the century to the turmoil associated with the Mexican Revolution. Mexican settlement tended to concentrate around the oldest part of the city, much of it on the lowlands along the river that gave the city its name. Out of this *barrio* (literally *district*, or *neighborhood*) emerged in the 1930s numerous *corridos* in the Hispanic tradition, not only about tragedies such as the suicide in prison of Juan Reyna, but satirical corridos such as "El lavaplatos" (The Dishwasher), "Consejos al maje" (Advice to the Naive), and "Se acabó el WPA" (The WPA Has Ended) commenting on social and economic conditions affecting Mexicans. These began to be recorded, at about the same time that local Spanish-speaking radio stations began to flourish. (A popular ensemble of singers and guitarists, Los Madrugadores [The Early Risers], performed on the radio between 4 and 6 A.M. beginning in the 1930s.) The World War II years saw the emergence among young Mexican-Americans, partly as a defensive reaction to the rising prejudice against them, of a sense of pride and uniqueness in their race—*La Raza*.

Many musicians and groups emerged to celebrate this identity— this "Chicano experience," as documented by *La Opinión*, a venerable Spanish-language newspaper published in Los Angeles. Probably the most influential group of the last twenty years is Los Lobos (The Wolves). Referring to his extensive documentation of groups and individuals in the Los Angeles scene, Loza says: "More than any of the other [groups], Los Lobos reflect the musical diversity and processes of change, maintenance, and adaptation among the Mexican/Chicano people of Los Angeles."[20] Their range of styles and subjects has included Spanish-language *rancheras*, *conciones*, *corridos*, and *boleros* in more or less traditional style, as heard in their albums, *Just Another Band from East L.A.* and *La Pistola y El Corazón*. Their songs in the 1980s and 1990s have been mostly in English, and use an adapted rock 'n' roll style, but with consistently interesting use of instrumental color. An effective piece of social commentary, on the plight of the illegal immigrant, is "Will the Wolf Survive." An excellently crafted traditional song in Spanish by Los Lobos is "La pistola y el corazón," recorded in 1988.

Nueva canción

In the 1970s and 1980s, at a time when protest music in the United States had gone off in many directions, a movement called *nueva canción* ("new song") in Latin American countries reached a degree of intensity and focus comparable to that of the civil rights movement or the Depression and its aftermath in this country. Political in its nature and its message, it was spawned in various Latin countries, spontaneously and sometimes simultaneously, to oppose by means of song oppression and murder, and to better the lives of the common people. It emerged in Chile in the 1960s, with Violetta Parra and Victor Jara (who was murdered in 1973); in Argentina with Mercedes Sosa (exiled in 1978); in Cuba (where it is called *nueva trova*) with Silvio Rogríguez and Pablo Milanés; and in Nicaragua and El Salvador. As the movement grew there were festivals in Nicaragua, Peru, Argentina, and Brazil. Its relation to folk song in the United States has been peripheral but not negligible. It certainly had its antecedents in the Peoples Song movement here in the 1930s and 1940s. It has engaged the redoubtable Pete Seeger, and, on an occasional basis, younger singers such as Holly Near. In keeping with its democratic ideals, *nueva canción* has placed its emphasis not on folk "stars," but on groups, chief of which, in its greatest area of influence in the Southwest, have been Los Peludos (The Hairy Ones) in San Francisco, Los Perros (The Dogs) in Los Angeles, and Los Alacranes Mojados (The Wet Scorpions) in San Diego. Its guiding tenets have been (1) the eschewing of commercialism, and (2) the use of native acoustic instruments indigenous to all areas of the Western Hemisphere.[21]

Music from the Caribbean and South America

Music from the Caribbean and South America reached the United States by sea, the chief ports of entry having been New Orleans in the nineteenth century and New York City in the twentieth. It has come from areas as far away as Argentina and as close as Cuba, and from cultures reflecting individually unique mixtures of Spanish, Portuguese, and African influences. (All are in the final analysis importations, as the influence of native Indian musics from these regions has been, until recently, negligible.)

In contrast with the music of Mexico, this music, and especially that from Cuba and Hispaniola, shows much more African influence. This influence is apparent in the greater role of percussion, and the vast array of percussion instruments. The drums are of primary importance, and there are several families of them: the *congas* (consisting, from small to large, of the *quinto*, the *segunda*, and the *tumba* or *tumbadora*), the *seguidoras*, the *requintos*, the *timbales* (usually used in pairs), and the *bongos* (also a pair of drums, joined together). Associated with the Yoruban *lucumí* religion, the Spanish name for which is *santería*, are the *batá* drums (consisting, from small to large, of the *okónkolo*, the *itótele*, and the largest, or "mother" drum, the *iyá*, which communicates directly with the *orishas*, or spirits). Each of these families of drums is associated with its own particular kind of Latin music. In addition to the drums are the smaller handheld percussion instruments, including the *claves* (two hardwood sticks struck together), the *maracas* (gourd-shaped, with seeds or shot in them), the *güiro* (a slotted gourd scraped with a piece of metal), and the *campanas* (cowbells). This partial list of

Latin percussion instruments is given simply to convey the importance of rhythm in this music—an importance that is readily confirmed on hearing it.

Latin-Derived Fashions in American Popular Music

There are two aspects to these importations from the Caribbean and South America. The first has been their impact on American popular music by way of popular dance. The *habanera* around the turn of the century was followed in the 1910s and 1920s by the *tango* (related rhythmically to the habanera), which arrived from Argentina by way of Paris! In the 1930s came the *rumba*, from the Cuban *son*, and after this the *samba* (Afro-Brazilian), the *mambo* (Afro-Cuban), the *chachachá* (Cuban), the *merengue* (Dominican), and in the 1960s the *bossa nova* (Brazilian). These successive waves of popular Latin genres have been initiated mostly as professional musicians, steeped in their own traditions, moved into the arenas of American jazz or popular music, bringing their traditional styles with them but adapting them to cater to broad popular taste. The term "salsa," so commonly heard in relation to the Latin music of New York City, is basically a marketing label (much like "soul" in African-American popular music) that includes under its umbrella a variety of Latin-flavored popular music.

Indigenous Music of the Caribbean Immigrants

The second aspect of the importation of Latin music to the United States is its meaning to the Latin immigrants, in their own lives and communities. As John Storm Roberts has explained: "The presence of a large Latin community in New York—and later in other U.S. cities—provided a demand for authenticity, a place for musicians to play undiluted Latin styles, and, perhaps most important, a doorway for innovations from Cuba and other Latin countries."[22]

Roberts's point about the "demand for authenticity" deserves attention. Just as Chicano music has become a symbol and focus of ethnic pride for those of Mexican descent in the Southwest, so has Afro-Cuban, Afro-Puerto Rican, and Afro-Dominican music performed the same function for those of Cuban, Puerto Rican, and Dominican origin in New York City. They illustrate, in the words of one writer, "the proclivity of people to seize on traditional cultural symbols as a definition of their own identity."[23]

But Latino musicians are no different from other musicians in that they do not *automatically* "seize on traditional cultural symbols" in making their music; these must usually be learned, in one way or another. The Afro-Caribbean music played in New York is essentially a music played by ear and therefore aurally transmitted. But the personal contact between musicians that is traditionally associated with aural transmission has been to a considerable degree replaced by learning from records. In this regard, it is interesting to note the role played by men such as René López and Andy González—who have large record collections and who are also effective social and political historians, educators, impresarios, record producers, and even performers themselves—in educating other Latino musicians as to what their "traditional cultural symbols" are, their history, and the importance of their authenticity if they are to serve to "define their own identity."[24]

New York City has long been a magnet for immigration from the Caribbean, and its Latin populations make up small cities within the supercity. Emigration from Puerto Rico (ceded to the United States after the Spanish-American War in 1898, and given commonwealth status in 1952) has been significant ever since United States citizenship was granted to Puerto Ricans in 1917, and it reached a peak in the 1940s and early 1950s. Emigration from Cuba has been less extensive, but an important ingredient in *la salsa* in New York City has been the presence of Cubans of the poorer classes, especially black Cubans who came to the United States before the 1959 revolution. Thus for two generations New York has echoed with the strongly flavored music of the Caribbean: the Spanish-derived forms of the *danza*, the *seis*, and the *aguinaldo*, and the African-influenced *plena* and **bomba** of Puerto Rico, the Cuban **son** and **guajira**, the Afro-Cuban *rumba,* and the music of the Yoruban **lucumí** ritual (in Spanish *santería*).[25] (In listening to the batá drumming of the lucumí, we become aware that the most African-sounding music in the United States can be heard in the playing of Afro-Cuban groups in New York.) This mixture of the African with the Hispanic has been furthered by the fact that many early Puerto Rican immigrants settled in Harlem, in close proximity with African Americans.

The Rhythms of Caribbean Music

A basic ingredient of Afro-Caribbean rhythm is the *clave*, a rhythmic pattern whose constant repetitions unify the piece. At its simplest it is two measures in length, and consists in its skeletal form of five strokes distributed over two measures, as either "2+3" (Ex. 4-4) or "3+2" (Ex. 4-5).

Example 4–4. 2 + 3 clave

Example 4–5. 3 + 2 clave

The clave, as played on the *claves*, is a familiar sound in Latin music, but the clave is by no means invariably performed on that instrument, nor is it always overtly stated in its simplest form. What *is* invariably characteristic is the presence of a rhythmic ground (*tumbao*) built around the clave, and repeated (with subtle variations) throughout the piece. This ground (called by musicologist Roberta L. Singer the "pitch-timbre-rhythm complex") is traditionally executed, according to Singer, on two drums (the deeper *tumba* and the higher *segundo*), with the possible addition of maracas or claves along with a third drum, which is played in an improvisational way. In larger and more jazz-oriented ensembles, both the piano and the bass may take part in executing the tumbao.

Iberian-Afro-Indian music from Latin America has influenced what may be regarded as "mainstream" American music in ways far less superficial than the successive waves of popular Latin dance fashions. The "Latin tinge," therefore, is an important, if largely unacknowledged, hue in much of our music.

FURTHER READING

Studies that include music

Gerard, Charley, with Marty Sheller. *Salsa: The Rhythm of Latin Music*. Crown Point, IN: White Cliffs Media Company, 1989.

> Deals much more specifically with the music itself than does Vernon Boggs's *Salsiology*, with many musical examples (including the full score of an arrangement), an index, a discography, and a glossary.

Loza, Steven. *Barrio Rhythm: Mexican American Music in Los Angeles*. Urbana: University of Illinois Press, 1993.

> A well-done treatment of the subject, from 1769 to the present, with emphasis on developments in popular music over the past 50 years. Some transcriptions and complete texts of recent works. Includes index, bibliography, and discography.

Paredes, Americo. *A Texas-Mexican Cancionero: Folksongs of the Lower Border*. Urbana: University of Illinois Press, 1976.

> The 66 songs are interesting in themselves, but the extensive and informal prefaces to each section, and to each song, make this a valuable introduction to this whole regional music. The photographs are an extra bonus.

Rael, Juan B. *The New Mexican Alabado*. Palo Alto, CA: Stanford University Press, 1951. Reprint. New York: AMS Press, 1967.

> A study of the spiritual songs sung by New Mexican villagers and *penitentes*, especially during Holy Week; includes tune transcriptions.

Robb, John Donald. *Hispanic Folk Music of New Mexico and the Southwest: A Self-Portrait of a People*. Norman: University of Oklahoma Press, 1980.

> More extensive than his 1954 *Hispanic Folk Songs of New Mexico*, this is the major summary in published form of many years of collecting. The anthology (891 pages) includes many types of music, sacred, secular, and instrumental, with informative notes on each type. The songs include texts and English translations.

Stark, Richard B. *Music of the Spanish Folk Plays in New Mexico*. Santa Fe: Museum of New Mexico Press, 1969.

> Songs and texts of various versions of *Los Pastores* transcribed from recordings made between 1940 and 1968. Includes some songs from *Las Posadas* and from another folk play, *El Niño Perdido*.

Studies

Flores, Richard R. *Los Pastores: History and Performance in the Mexican Shepherds Play of South Texas.* Washington DC: Smithsonian Institute Press, 1995.

Herrera-Sobek, Maria. *Northward Bound: The Mexican Emigrant Experience in Ballad and Song.* Bloomington: Indiana University Press, 1993.

Paredes, Americo. *"With his pistol in his hand."* Austin: University of Texas Press, 1958.

> An extensive documentation of a ballad ("El Corrido de Gregorio Cortez") and its hero, which supplies valuable background information on the Texas-Mexico border country.

Peña, Manuel. *The Texas-Mexican Conjunto: History of a Working-Class Music.* Austin: University of Texas Press, 1985.

Roberts, John Storm. *The Latin Tinge: The Impact of Latin American Music in the United States.* New York: Oxford University Press, 1979.

> Deals with influences from all of Latin America; useful, even though the emphasis is on popular music.

Tinker, Edward Larocque. *Corridos and Calaveras.* Austin: University of Texas Press, 1961.

> Although this deals specifically with the corrido and related forms as found in Mexico, it is excellent background reading for the corrido as a genre. Especially fascinating are the reproductions of the old broadsides themselves, with their drawings by the famous artist José Guadalupe Posada, a forerunner of Rivera and Orozco. A delightful book, in a very artistic format.

Weigle, Marta. *Brothers of Light, Brothers of Blood: The Penitentes of the South-west.* Albuquerque: University of New Mexico Press, 1976.

> A well-documented, thorough, and sympathetic treatment of this brotherhood, counteracting the often exaggerated and sensational accounts that had appeared earlier.

Articles

From Latin American Music Review

Limon, José. "Texas-Mexican Popular Music and Dancing: Some Notes on History and Symbolic Process," 4, no. 2 (Fall–Winter 1983).

Peña, Manuel. "Ritual Structure in a Chicano Dance," 1, no. 1 (Spring–Summer 1980).

Singer, Roberta L. "Tradition and Innovation in Contemporary Latin Popular Music in New York City," 4, no. 2 (Fall–Winter 1983).

From Aztlán: A Journal of Chicano Studies *(UCLA Chicano Studies Research Center)*

Gutiérrez, Ramon. "Unraveling America's Hispanic Past: Internal Stratification and Class Boundaries," 17, no. 1 (Spring 1986): 79–102.

Hurtado, Aída, and Carlos H. Arce "Mexicanos, Chicanos, Mexican-Americans, or Pochos . . . Qué somos?: The Impact of Nativity on Ethnic Labelling," 17, no. 1 (Spring 1986): 103–30.

From Ars Musica Denver, *Lamont School of Music of the University of Denver*

Koegel, John. "Spanish and Mexican Dance Music in Early California," 7, no. 1 (Fall 1994): 31–55.

Summers, William John. "Recently Recovered Manuscript Source of Sacred Polyphonic Music from Spanish California," 7, no. 1 (Fall 1994): 13–30.

From Inter-American Music Review

Koegel, John. "Mexican and Mexican-American Musical Life in Southern California, 1850–1900" and "Calendar of Southern California Amusements 1852–1897; Designed for Spanish-Speaking Public," 13, no. 2 (Spring–Summer 1993): 111–43.

Projects

1. If you live in an area where there is a significant Mexican-American population that attends a Hispanic Catholic church, investigate the music performed in the church and assess its relationship to one or more of the types of Mexican-American musics treated in this chapter.

2. Attend a concert by a professional mariachi show band and write a review. Comment, among other things, on the makeup of the audience, the things to which the audience reacts most strongly, and the relationship of the music played to traditional Mexican music.

3. If you are fluent in Spanish, transcribe and translate one or more corridos that are in current circulation on recordings. (Among other sources, they are available from Norteña Records, San Antonio, Texas; and Arhoolie Records, 10341 San Pablo Ave., El Cerrito, California 94530.)

4. Investigate and describe in as much detail as you can the origin and characteristics of any specified number of the following Mexican musical/dance forms: huapango, jarabe, jota, malagueña, pasodoble, son (Mexican), son jarocho, zapateado.

5. Write a paper on the state of Chicano music today, including a discography, and a list of poet-musicians active in Chicano circles. Two periodicals listed in the Further Reading section might be helpful.

6. Investigate and describe in as much detail as you can the origin and characteristics of any specified number of the following Caribbean or South American-derived musical/dance forms: aguinaldo, bolero, bomba, bossa nova, bugalú, chachachá, danza, danzón, guaguancó, guajira, guaracha, habanera, mambo, mapayé, mixixe, merengue, pachanga, plena, rumba, samba, seis, son (Cuban), tango.

Notes

1. Joaquin Fernández, in a note to the author. Robert L. Vialpando, of Alcalde, New Mexico, is a collector and researcher of alabados.

2. "Dividido el Corazón" is on New World-80292. Side 1 is devoted to alabados sung by elderly members of the Penitentes who had belonged to the Brotherhood since the late nineteenth and early twentieth centuries. The pito is also heard. Robb's extensive *Hispanic Folk Music of New Mexico and the Southwest* includes many transcriptions of alabados, and one pito melody. The Penitente Manual, including the texts of the alabados, is painstakingly copied by hand by members of the Brotherhood; a sample page of such a copy is reproduced in Robb, op. cit., 619, and also in Bill Tate, *The Penitentes of the Sangre de Cristo* (Truchas, NM: Tate Gallery, 1968), 33.

3. See *Music of the Spanish Folk Plays in New Mexico* by Richard B. Stark (Santa Fe: Museum of New Mexico Press, 1969), and *Hispanic Folk Songs of New Mexico* by John Donald Robb. The Song from *"Los Pastores"* was recorded in a small town in south Texas in 1934.

4. The author is indebted to William John Summers, an eminent authority on the music of the Californian missions, for much of the information and insight on this topic. He has a forthcoming book on the subject. Meanwhile, readers are referred to his most comprehensive treatment of the subject, "Spanish Music in California, 1769–1840, A Reassessment," in *Report of the Twelfth Congress of the International Musicological Society, Berkeley, 1977* (Bärenreiter, 1981), 360–80. See also the articles in the reading list for this chapter.

5. Robert Louis Stevenson, "The Old Pacific Capital," in *Across the Plains*.

6. It has been estimated that in the seventeenth century, for example, there were more Africans than Spaniards in Mexico. See Robert Stevenson, *Music in Aztec and Inca Territory: Contact and Acculturation Periods* (Berkeley: University of California Press, 1977), 231, to which Claes af Geijerstam makes reference in his *Popular Music in Mexico* (Albuquerque: University of New Mexico Press, 1976), 11.

7. See John Koegel "Spanish and Mexican Dance Music in Early California" in *Ars Musica* (Lamont School of Music, University of Denver) (Fall 1994).

8. "Huapango" and "el valse" are on New World-80292, *Dark and Light in Spanish New Mexico*, with notes by Richard Stark. A polka and a waltz may also be heard on *Spanish and Mexican Folk Music of New Mexico*, Folkways 04426, with notes by John Donald Robb. Both waltz and the quadrille (las cuadrillas) owe their presence in Mexico to French influence in the nineteenth century, especially during the French occupation of 1862–67.

9. It must not be assumed that these cultural mixings occurred only north of the Rio Grande. As Geijerstam has pointed out, the waltz, the polka, the mazurka, and the schottische were imported into Mexico itself in the nineteenth century, reaching Mexico City mostly from Paris. See *Popular Music in Mexico*, 16.

10. The term *charro* refers to the highly skilled rope artists who performed in rodeos, or *chareadas*, and who wore the distinctive costumes from which the costumes of the mariachi musicians have been adapted.

11. *Mexican-American Border Music*, vol. 1, Arhoolie Folklyric CD 7001, includes "Que me gano con llorar," and is a good introduction to the early phases of this music.

12. Steven Loza, *Barrio Rhythm*, 47.

13. See *Crossing: A Comparative Analysis of the Mexicano, Mexican-American and Chicano* (San Pedro, CA: International Universities Press, 1983) by Maximiliano Contreras. Much information was also derived from a paper, "Mexicans and Mexican Americans in the United States—Past and Present," presented by Lawrence Cardoso at the Symposium "Ethnicity in American Culture" at the University of Wyoming in June 1985, and from a conversation with the musician-poet-painter José Montoya of Sacramento. See also "Unraveling America's Hispanic Past: Internal Stratification and Class Boundaries" by Ramón Gutiérrez, and "Mexicanos, Chicanos, Mexican-Americans, or Pochos . . . Qué somos? The impact of Nativity on Ethnic Labeling" by Aída Hurtada and Carlos H. Arce, both *Aztlán* 17, no. 1 (Spring 1986): 79–130.

14. This variant of "**Gregorio Cortez**" is transcribed from the earliest version to appear on phonographic records, about 1929. It may be heard on *Texas-Mexican Border Music*, vol. 2 (Folklyric 9004). The complete histories of the case and of the ballad are found in "With His Pistol in His Hand" by Americo Paredes (Austin: University of Texas Press, 1958).

15. See Dan William Dickey, *The Kennedy Corridos: A Study of the Ballads of a Mexican American Hero* (Austin: University of Texas Press, 1978).

16. John Donald Robb, *Hispanic Folk Songs of New Mexico*, 201–313. All four of the canciones mentioned here ("Cielito Lindo," "La Golondrina," "La Cucaracha," and "La Adelita") have great meaning for Mexicans and Mexican-Americans alike; their interesting histories are unfortunately too long to be recounted here.

17. "Mal Hombre" is on *Lydia Mendoza: Mal Hombre* Arhoolie Folklyric CD 7002.

18. See Chris Strachwitz and James Nicolopulos (compilers), *Lydia Mendoza: A Family Autobiography* (Houston: Arte Público, 1993), and Strachwitz's notes to recordings in the Arhoolie Folklyric series.

19. There is much detailed information, from which this brief summary has been drawn, in "Mexican and Mexican-American Musical Life in Southern California, 1850–1900" and "Calendar of Southern California Amusements 1852–1897; Designed for Spanish-Speaking Public" in the *Inter-American Music Review* 13, no. 2 (Spring–Summer 1993), by John Koegel.

20. Steven Loza *Barrio Rhythm: Mexican American Music in Los Angeles*, 233.

21. For more information on *nueva canción* see the article in *World Music: The Rough Guide* (London: Rough Guides, 1994), 569–76.

22. John Storm Roberts, *The Latin Tinge*, 57.

23. John Bennett, in *The New Ethnicity: Perspectives from Ethnology* (Proceedings of the American Ethnological Society) as quoted in Roberta Singer, "Tradition and Innovation in Contemporary Latin Popular Music in New York City," *Latin American Review* 4, no. 2 (Fall–Winter 1983): 183.

24. René López has said: "We consciously impart this whole sense of history to the people we come in contact with," See Singer, "Tradition and Innovation," cited above, from which this quote was taken. Roberta Singer is also coauthor of the notes for New World 80244, which was produced by René López.

25. Examples of bomba of Puerto Rico, the Cuban son and guajira, and the music of the Yoruban lucumí ritual (in Spanish *santería*) are included in *Caliente=Hot: Puerto Rican and Cuban Musical Expression in New York*, New World 80244–2.

Part Two

Three Prodigious Offspring
of the Rural South

Photo courtesy of the Southern Historical Society, University of North Carolina

The rural American South, in its former isolation and conservatism, fathered two musical offspring, reared in private within its confines and long unknown outside: the country music of white people and the blues of black people. Though unlike in significant ways, they share a patrimony and a native soil. Both have grown to become in our time mighty musical nations with three quarters of a century of commercial success behind them. Long segregated, they have both played their part in producing a third prodigious, electrified, urbanized offspring: rock.

How did the South come to father these prodigies? What were their antecedants, musically and culturally? What are their enduring characteristics? These questions we shall explore, and then trace the first two as they emerged from the isolation of folklore into the bright public arena of popular culture, from which emerged the third.

The South has constituted the largest and richest single reservoir of folklore we have. In the latter half of the twentieth century great changes have come to this region, so that it is no longer what it once was. But if we are seeking the origins of its folklore, we have to look at the South not as it is now, but as it existed for three centuries before our own time. The two key words are isolation and conservatism. The isolation was not only geographic (of the lowlands as well as the highlands) but also demographic—an isolation of the southern people, largely, from the greater mass of the American people. For once the frontier had passed through and moved on west, there was emigration *from* the South but until our time little significant immigration *to* the South. The conservatism owed a good deal to this isolation, but also to the almost exclusively agrarian economy; to the hierarchical (if not actually aristocratic) social and political structure; to the defensive attitude assumed almost monolithically by southern whites toward the institution of slavery and its equally problematic sequel, white supremacy; and, last but by no means least, to the prevailing orthodox religious modes of thought. Out of this soil, then, sprang the two most pervasive forms of rural music America has ever produced, and, as a second generation, a citified but visceral amalgamation that has revolutionized popular music throughout the world.

Chapter 5

Country Music

The latent popularity of "hillbilly" music,* fully revealed only after it had spread beyond its original geographical limits in the 1930s and 1940s, was one of the surprises of the century, at least to city-bred entrepreneurs and savants of popular culture. Its base of popularity was found not only in the rural South and, as might be expected, among its people who had emigrated to the cities and to other parts of the country, but also among rural white people elsewhere who had no cultural ties with the South at all. We are dealing, then, with the closest thing to a universal "people's music" that rural white Americans have had.[1]

Enduring Characteristics of the Music

Despite evolution and change, certain enduring musical characteristics have been identified with country music. The choice of instruments, the style of singing, the melody, and the harmony are all distinctive.

The Instruments

Country music is basically music for string band, originally played on those stringed instruments that were easily portable. The dominant instrument in traditional country music is the *fiddle*, which takes the lead not only in dance music, but often in the instrumental breaks in songs. The *mountain dulcimer* and the *autoharp* belong more to the folk origins of this music, and with a few exceptions did not survive long into country music itself (considered as a form of popular music that emerged in the 1920s). The *banjo* (possibly acquired in the lowlands, through contact with African Americans and blackface minstrelsy) became an early mainstay of country music. In the second quarter of this century it was

---

* The term "hillbilly" (like so many labels in art that have stuck) was originally derogatory. The first recorded use of the term appeared in a New York periodical in 1900 as follows: "A Hill-Billie is a free and untrammelled white citizen of Alabama, who lives in the hills, has no means to speak of, dresses as he can, talks as he pleases, drinks whiskey when he gets it, and fires off his revolver as the fancy takes him" (quoted by Archie Green in "Hillbilly Music: Source and Symbol," *Journal of American Folklore* [July–September 1965]): 204–28.

almost supplanted by the *guitar*, a more resonant instrument with a greater range. The *mandolin* entered country music in the 1930s, being at first associated with Bill Monroe and subsequently with the whole style known as "bluegrass," which also revived interest in the banjo. With its thin but penetrating tone, the mandolin competes with the banjo for the lead parts. Less easily portable is the *string bass* (always plucked rather than bowed), but it became established in country music as early as the 1930s, and has been essential in the bluegrass band since the 1940s.

An exotic addition to the hillbilly band came from as far west as Hawaii, probably by way of the Hawaiian bands popular in the early decades of this century. The Hawaiian *steel guitar*, with its sliding, wailing sound, was appropriated by country musicians as far back as the 1920s and 1930s. (These guitars are designed to be held flat and include a steel bar for slide playing. Similar sliding effects were obtained by many early African-American blues guitarists, stopping the strings with broken bottlenecks, or knife blades.) A guitar with a built-in resonator, which served to amplify the sound mechanically before the advent of the electric guitar, was known as the *dobro*.[2]

The piano, drums, saxophones, and trumpets, essentially alien to country music, were introduced in the country/jazz hybrid "western swing" in the 1930s. With "rural electrification" came the electric guitar in the 1940s (primarily associated with the need for a louder sound in honky-tonk music), and eventually, in the late 1960s, electric keyboards. Acoustic stringed instruments, however, remain the basis for any country music committed to its tradition.

The Style of Singing

A definitive manner of singing characterizes traditional country music. A direct carryover from the folksinging of the rural South, it is typified (as heard in bluegrass music) by a high, nasal, and somewhat strained tone. The "lonesome," impassive manner of delivery is suited to the impersonality of the ballad tradition. The clear, vibratoless tone so akin to that of the country fiddle also lends itself to the kind of vocal ornamentation familiar in this music: short slides and anticipatory flourishes heard in advance of the principal notes, especially in slow tunes such as "Wayfaring Stranger," as sung by traditional singer Roscoe Holcomb. This high, tense, rigid vocal quality was later modified under southwestern influence.

Essential to any consideration of vocal style is that utter sincerity of delivery without which country music is not genuine. Hank Williams Sr. expressed it vividly when asked about the success of country music:

It can be explained in just one word: sincerity. When a hillbilly sings a crazy song, he feels crazy. When he sings "I Laid My Mother Away," he sees her a-laying right there in the coffin. He sings more sincere than most entertainers because the hillbilly was raised rougher than most entertainers. You got to know a lot about hard work. You got to have smelt a lot of mule manure before you can sing like a hillbilly.[3]

Melody and Harmony

The folk music of the English and Scottish ballad tradition, as we saw in chapter 1, tended to preserve the old modal scales, with their attendant archaic-sounding melodic patterns and harmonies. A vestige of the old modality, in the form of the flatted seventh degree of the scale, can be heard in "**The Old Man at the Mill**" (Ex. 5–1).

Example 5–1. "The Old Man at the Mill"

As country music sought to expand its public the old modal tunes began to lose favor. Singers brought up in the older tradition still sang them privately but were reluctant to record them, or sing them for "outsiders."[4] New tunes came into use—tunes with harmonies of the utmost simplicity, which made them well adapted to guitar accompaniment. The melodies of two of the best-known country songs illustrate the harmonic vocabulary of most country music. Both imply the same three basic chords only; further, both tunes follow the outlines of their clearly implied harmonies. The first is "Wildwood Flower" (Ex. 5-2).

The tune of the second song, "**Wabash Cannon Ball**" (Ex. 5-3), follows its chord outlines even more faithfully; only seven tones in the entire tune do not belong to the prevailing chords.

Though "Wildwood Flower" has been unmistakably a country song ever since the Carter Family recorded it in the 1920s, the melody can be traced to

Example 5–2. "Wildwood Flower"

Example 5–3. "Wabash Cannon Ball"

sources outside the rural South—in this case, as in many others, to a parlor song
of the previous century. As the scholar D. K. Wilgus has said, "A good percentage of the lyric songs of the early hillbilly tradition seem to derive from the nineteenth century sentimental parlor song—and are often considerably improved in
the process."[5] Parlor songs (see chapter 12) were extremely popular with amateur
singers. Many of them were published, and therefore no doubt sung, with guitar
accompaniment as an alternative to the piano; this early adaptation to the guitar

must have made even easier their later passage into the repertoire of country musicians.[6] "**Lorena**," perhaps the most popular love song of the Civil War, was published in 1857 in versions for both guitar and piano accompaniment, and became in the 1950s a country music standard.

In country music, as in folk music, tunes are freely borrowed and adapted to make new songs. The tune of "Wildwood Flower" became the basis for Woody Guthrie's "The Sinking of the *Reuben James*."

Enduring Characteristics of the Words

Words are of paramount importance in country music. They exhibit certain pervasive traits that have consistently characterized this genre through its half-century of change.

Fundamental Attitudes

Country music is steeped in a paradoxical blend of realism and sentimentality. The realism reveals itself in a readiness to treat any human situation in song, and to deal unflinchingly with any aspect of life that genuinely touches the emotions. It shows up in extreme cases, for example, in the depicting of such grim scenes as the following:

> *He went upstairs to make her hope*
> *And found her hanging on a rope.*[7]

A later song, "Wreck on the Highway," updates this penchant for furnishing grisly details.[8] Such unsparing realism (a characteristic of the ballad tradition) contrasts strikingly with the conventionalized subject matter and treatment of most urban commercial song before 1950, and identifies country music as one progenitor of the subsequent "revolution" in American popular music.

Paradoxically, the obverse of this realism is a nearly universal tendency toward sentimentality—a sentimentality that may often strike one outside the tradition as excessive and tainted with self-pity.[9]

> *Walking down this lonesome road,*
> *I'll travel while I cry*
> *If there's no letter in the mail,*
> *I'll bid this world goodbye.*[10]

The sentimentalizing of objects is common, especially in the "weepers" of the later, more commercial phase of country music, such as "Send Me the Pillow You Dream On." The pathetic fallacy is frequently encountered: objects in nature, or even inanimate artifacts, may be endowed with the capacity for human feelings and even the ability to manifest them visibly. The lyrics of Hank Williams's "I'm So Lonesome I Could Cry" are typical in this regard.

Perennial Themes

The subjects of country songs and ballads, while diverse, group themselves around certain perennial themes. One is love:

> *Tell me that you love me, Katy Cline.*
> *Tell me that your love's as true as mine.*[11]

Another is death:

> *There's a little black train a-coming*
> *Fix all your business right;*
> *There's a little black train a-coming*
> *And it may be here tonight.*[12]

Still another is religion:

> *I am bound for that beautiful city*
> *My Lord has prepared for his own,*
> *Where all the redeemed of all ages*
> *Sing, "Glory!" around the white throne.*[13]

And a fourth is nostalgia:

> *There's a peaceful cottage there,*
> *A happy home so dear.*
> *My heart is longing for them day by day.*[14]

Trains figure prominently in country music, as they do in blues:

> *I'm riding on that New River train*
> *I'm riding on that New River train*
> *The same old train that brought me here*
> *Is going to carry me away.*[15]

The railroad train and the life of the rambler were both romanticized in rural thought. In recent times the truck and even the jet airplane have figured in country songs, but they have not seized the imagination with anything like the vivid intensity that the train has been able to evoke.

Songs about events were once an important part of country music, and any country singer could make up his own songs on important happenings of the day.

> *Come all you fathers and mothers,*
> *And brothers, sisters too,*
> *I'll relate to you the history*
> *Of the Rowan County Crew.*[16]

This trait shows country music's relation to the earlier ballad tradition. Many songs and ballads collected by Cecil Sharp in the southern highlands in 1916–18 appear in country music recordings of the 1920s and 1930s.[17] The ballad "John Hardy" was presumably based on an actual episode in 1894 that culminated in the execution of one John Hardy for murder in West Virginia. It was collected by Sharp in 1916, and was recorded commercially by the influential Carter Family in 1930.[18]

The ballad tradition was kept alive as event songs continued to be written. With the coming of commercialism, it became vital to hit the market as soon after the event as possible. A song based on General Douglas MacArthur's speech before Congress in 1951, after President Harry Truman removed him from command in Korea, was written and recorded by Gene Autry within hours of the event, while a song on the assassination of Senator Huey Long of Louisiana in 1935 was written two years *before* his death—and was even sung to him by its author.[19]

Dialect and Other Regionalisms

The early country singers naturally retained not only their regional accent in their songs but their dialect as well, with such usages as "a-going," "a-coming," "rise you up," and "yonders." With the first wave of commercial success and the broadening of country music's public, there was a tendency (on the part of singers like Jimmie Rodgers, for example) to drop the dialect and substitute standard English. In more recent country music a few vernacular survivals, such as the well-nigh universal "ain't," and the dropping of the final *g*'s of the *-ing* suffix ("ramblin'," "cheatin'"), have become clichés. The loss of an authentic vernacular, together with the introduction of such devices as more sophisticated rhymes ("infatuation," "sensation," "imagination"), has introduced an artificial conventionality to latter-day country music, which has already lost many of its distinctive regional characteristics in the general process of homogenization.

Commercial Beginnings:
Early Recordings, Radio, and the First Stars

We first encounter country music proper as it emerged from the folk tradition into the realm of popular music in the 1920s. Although commercial phonograph recording was established before the turn of the century, the widespread recording of jazz, blues, and hillbilly music did not come for another two decades, principally because recording executives either were only dimly aware that those genres existed or were unsure as to whether there was a market for such recordings, which is ironic in view of later developments! When recording companies did move into the area of hillbilly music (marketing it at first under such names as "old-time music" or "old familiar tunes"), they did so at least partly in response to growing competition from that other powerful new medium of the day, radio. Thus the roles of radio and phonograph recording in the dissemination and popularization of country music were elaborately intertwined from the start—and still are.

In 1923 Georgia moonshiner, circus barker, and political campaign performer Fiddlin' John Carson (who had recently become a locally popular radio performer) recorded "The Little Old Log Cabin in the Lane" and "The Old Hen Cackled and the Rooster's Going to Crow." This recording proved to be phenomenally and prophetically successful, and the move to record hillbilly music was on. Recording companies made excursions into the South, set up temporary studios, and began recording country musicians by the score, either singly or in groups. In other cases the newfound artists were brought to New York to record. A few who were recorded in the twenties became the stars of the ensuing period. These included Uncle Dave Macon (from Tennessee), the Carter Family (from Virginia), and Jimmie Rodgers (from Mississippi).

Radio broadcasting, until then an amateur's plaything, suddenly came of age in the 1920s. As receiving sets came within the economic reach of more and more Americans, broadcasting stations appeared and multiplied, and with them grew the demand for performers to cater to the new audience. Some stations in the South began almost immediately to broadcast country music by local musicians. In 1925 WSM in Nashville began a show, with two unpaid performers and without a commercial sponsor, that was to evolve into the *Grand Ole Opry*, the best-known and most influential country-music program. The early radio programs, like the early recordings, presented a highly traditional country music, still close to its folk origins.[20] But its very popularity generated winds of change.

Of the three stars of early country music mentioned above, the first two are representative of performers who never essentially changed their style or material

The Carter Family: Maybelle Addington Carter (guitar), Sarah Carter (autoharp), and Alvin Pleasant Carter. *Courtesy Frank Driggs Collection.*

in order consciously to appeal to a larger audience. David Harrison ("Uncle Dave") Macon (1870–1952) got his professional start playing banjo and singing in local fairs and tent shows, and the basis of his style and repertory was his background in nineteenth-century minstrel, circus, and vaudeville songs and routines. "Johnny Gray (Blow You Winds of Morning)," a quasi-ballad of unknown origin with an old refrain, shows his lively banjo style. He was a favorite performer on the *Grand Ole Opry* from 1925 to 1952.

The Carter Family (Alvin Pleasant, 1891–1960; his wife, Sara, 1898–1979; and his sister-in-law, Maybelle, 1909–78) came from a Virginia mountain background. Their varied repertory (which included not only nineteenth-century parlor songs but also early Tin Pan Alley songs and gospel hymns, as well as ballads and other folk material) made them very influential, as did their distinctive sound and style, with Sara Carter playing autoharp, and Maybelle Carter playing the melody on the bass strings of the guitar and the harmony and rhythm on the upper strings. "Wildwood Flower" is one of their best-known songs.

Jimmie Rodgers (1897–1933) based his career on traditional country music, but he contributed enormously to the popularization of that music, and in the process wore a number of different country hats. He recorded many types of songs: sentimental love songs, melancholy nostalgic songs, cowboy and railroad songs, and white blues. He was able to put across a great variety of material by the force of his sincerity and personality. His eclecticism was bound to lead him away somewhat from traditional country songs and style. He introduced the

Jimmie Rodgers circa 1928, dressed as a railroad brakeman. *Courtesy Frank Driggs Collection.*

famous "blue yodel" (of which his **"Mule Skinner Blues"** is representative) into country music, and was really one of the first popular "crooners." With the advent of Jimmie Rodgers, the attention and emphasis in country music shifted to the solo singer. The "Singing Brakeman" of Meridian, Mississippi (one of Rodgers's many stage names), had an extremely short career as a performing and recording artist. But in a mere six years (from his first trial recording in 1927 to his death in 1933) he recorded 111 songs, sold twenty million records, became internationally famous, and led country music into greener pastures than it had ever dreamed existed.

The interaction between the commercial country music of the thirties and what was held to be "folk music" shows how complex the relationship between the two had become after the advent of radio and recordings. Folklorists traveling through the South in the 1930s, in the first wave of collecting on behalf of the Library of Congress and others, "discovered" and collected songs that their singers had learned from the commercial recordings of Jimmie Rodgers!

Hillbilly music's native soil was the upland South, and it is the music from this hill country—played with banjo, acoustic guitar, mandolin, fiddle, string bass, dobro, and harmonica, and sung with a straight, unembellished vocal tone and unaffected regional accent—that has come to be unmistakably identified with the country music of the Southeast. But meanwhile the West was being heard from.

The West: The Cowboy Image

America has long pursued a love affair with its own romantic conception of the West and the cowboy. The western branch of country music has played its part in the propagation of this romanticism. For just as the Southwest is in large degree a cultural extension of the South, so is "western" music an extension and adaptation of hillbilly music.

The link is Texas. Here the southern influence, especially in east Texas, is notably strong. The country was settled primarily by Southern planters, and slavery and the raising of cotton flourished, along with Southern religion, culture, and folklore. But Texas is also, as the song goes, "where the West begins." The dry and spacious topography, the open range and the raising and transporting of cattle to the new railroads, and ultimately the industrialization following the oil boom produced a distinctive Texan economy. Culturally the influence of Mexican, Louisiana Cajun, and midwestern American culture distinguished Texas from the old South.

Authentic Cowboy Music

There is a rich store of authentic cowboy and frontier songs that were actually sung in the old West. "**The Buffalo Skinners**," already introduced as a native ballad in chapter 1, is an example. These were among the first folk songs, after African-American spirituals, to be collected and published in the United States.[21] Early singers like Jules Verne Allen and Harry "Haywire Mac" McClintock, who really had been cowboys, and Carl T. Sprague and Powder River Jack Lee, who learned songs at first hand from cowboys, made recordings of these songs in the 1920s.[22] But the cowboy image did not loom large in American popular culture until the advent of western movies and the "singing cowboy."

The Cowboy Image on Records and Film

The "western" part of the trade designation "country-and-western" was added as cowboy life began to be romanticized. Ken Maynard was perhaps the first singing cowboy; he sang two traditional songs in the film *The Wagon Master* as early as 1929. The genre—and the image—was well launched in the 1930s. Jimmie Rodgers, already a star as the "Singing Brakeman" from Mississippi, adopted the ten-gallon hat, Texas as his home state, and the role of singing cowboy. Native

Texans such as Gene Autry, Ernest Tubb, and Woodward Maurice "Tex" Ritter soon capitalized further on this image.* The Sons of the Pioneers, which included Leonard Slye (later Roy Rogers), was among the earliest singing groups. Rubye Blevins moved from her native Arkansas to California and became, as Patsy Montana, the first singing cowgirl. Her own song "**I Want to Be a Cowboy's Sweetheart**" became very popular, and marked a significant entry of women into the ranks of country singers.

Few actual cowboy songs went into country-and-western repertoire. The country music entertainer adopted cowboy dress (often in fancy and exaggerated form) and continued to sing country songs. Cowboy films made in Hollywood spurred the writing of popular songs based on western *themes*. Songs like "Tumbling Tumbleweeds" and "Cool Water," written by Bob Nolan (a Canadian by birth), and "The Last Roundup," by Billy Hill (who was born and grew up in Boston), became prototypes of the "western" song.

The West: Realism and Eclecticism
Honky-Tonk Music

The occupation of cowboy has not gone out of existence. The chronicling, in song, poem, and story, of the lives and traditions of real-life cowboys, as they have changed and adapted over the years, continues.[23] But the open range, with its freely roaming cows and cowboys, was largely fenced and gone by 1900, and the great cattle drives ended more than a century ago. A more realistic ambience of the West, particularly in Texas, has been for half a century that of small farm and oil-boom towns, of truck stops and taverns; its more realistic heroes and heroines the oil "boomers," the truck drivers, and their women. A new kind of "western" music evolved to fit this environment—the environment of the honky-tonk. The honky-tonk, which Bill Malone has described as a "social institution," was a generic term for the neon-light-emblazoned bars, taverns, saloons, dance halls, ballrooms, and nightclubs that grew up, generally on the outskirts of towns. The music evolved for this environment had to emphasize the louder and more incisive instruments; the electric guitar began to be used in the 1940s, as did that distinctly urban instrument the piano. Malone has pointed out that country musicians "found receptive audiences in the oil communities," but in the absence of live performers the music reached its consumers via the ubiquitous jukebox.

The music was no longer concerned with nostalgia for rural life, home, or family, or with traditional religion or mores; it dealt with harsh realities, preeminently loneliness and infidelity ("slippin' around"). "I'll Get Along Somehow," as recorded by Ernest Tubb, with a faintly ragtime beat and harmonies and the

---

*Their background was the farm, rather than the range, but farm life has never been successfully romanticized in America.

addition of a honky-tonk piano, typifies the genre. Texans have been the main purveyors of honky-tonk. In the 1970s and 1980s the Austin, Texas, "outlaw" wing of country-and-western music reincarnated the honky-tonk sound, style, subject matter, and spirit.

Hybridization with Jazz: Western Swing

Texas, at the crossroads of a variety of influences, was hospitable to bands that were more innovative and eclectic in their instrumentation and repertory than those of the more traditional Southeast. It is not surprising, then, that Texas was the locale where hybridization took place between country music and big-band jazz. The introduction of such hitherto alien instruments as saxophones, drums, and later trumpets into the string band of fiddles, mandolins, and guitars began as early as the 1930s. Bob Wills, most closely associated with this development, started his famous Texas Playboys in 1934. By the early 1940s the popularity of this eclectic blending of styles and repertory allowed Wills to move the band's base of operations from Texas to California, from whence he toured and recorded extensively. The mix became known as "western swing," and other bandleaders such as Milton Brown, Spade Cooley, Tex Williams, and Hank Penny cultivated it as well. California, more than Texas, nurtured this hybrid genre; Bakersfield-born Merle Haggard, among others, has been responsible for its recent revival.

Postwar Dissemination and Full-Scale Commercialization

The migrations and upheavals that attended both the Depression of the 1930s and the World War of the 1940s had the effect of spreading country music far beyond the provincial soil that had given it birth, dispersing its devotées to the cities and their suburbs, and to all parts of the country. This regional music thus acquired nationwide popularity, and became altered—deregionalized—in the process. This set the stage for its full-scale commercialization in the decades that followed.

Mainstream Stars of the 1950s and 1960s

The use of the suspect term "mainstream" here is prompted by the fact that the country music stars mentioned below clearly came out of, and continued to cultivate, the dominant characteristic traditions of country music.

Of these, Alabama-born Hank Williams (1923–1953) probably shone the brightest and cast the longest shadow—all the more remarkably since his career, like that of Jimmie Rodgers twenty years earlier, was brief (essentially 1947–52). His band, the Drifting Cowboys,* had a traditional instrumentation of fiddle,

---

*The pervasiveness of the western image is seen in the name Williams gave his band, and the stylized cowboy costume he sometimes wore, despite the fact that he had virtually no cowboy songs in his repertory.

guitars, steel guitar, bass, and occasional mandolin. His vocal style could be relaxed and rhythmic or highly intense, depending on his material, and his technique included such traditional effects as a modified yodel (as in "Lovesick Blues"), and an almost-sobbing break on emotion-laden songs (as in "I'm So Lonesome I Could Cry"). Many of his songs reflect both his own very troubled life, and country music's tendency toward sentimentality and self-pity. In spite of this, his range was broad. It is characteristic of country singers (as of blues and rock singers) that, unlike most of those in the fields of pop, jazz, or classical music, they write many of their own songs. Williams excelled in this regard; his memorable songs include "Your Cheatin' Heart," "Move It on Over," "Kawliga," "Honky-Tonkin'," and "Hey, Good Lookin'," as well as "I'm So Lonesome I Could Cry." Also placing him in the mainstream of country musicians is the fact that he wrote and recorded religious songs, including his well-known "I Saw the Light," based on an earlier gospel song.

Other stars who worked in an essentially traditional vein during country music's postwar surge of popularity were Hank Snow (Canadian-born, and known best for "I'm Moving On"), Johnny Cash (from Arkansas, basically traditional despite his early association with rockabilly), and Tennessee Ernie Ford (actually from Tennessee, and known for his performance of Merle Travis's "Sixteen Tons," and for his subsequent turn to gospel music). Of more recent popularity are Loretta Lynn (from Kentucky, known for her autobiographical song "Coal Miner's Daughter") and Merle Haggard, who came to prominence after his release from San Quentin prison in 1960.

Rockabilly and a New Generation of Performers and Fans

The influence of African-American musical styles has never been absent from country music; blues have been in the repertory from the beginning, and the debt of Dock Boggs, the Delmore Brothers, Jimmie Davis, Jimmie Rodgers, Bob Wills, and many others to blues and jazz is clear. In the 1950s a few white performers then in their twenties (principally Carl Perkins, Elvis Presley, and Jerry Lee Lewis, and to a lesser extent Buddy Holly and Johnny Cash) began copying the material and style of black blues and rhythm-and-blues singers such as Arthur Crudup, Little Richard, and Otis Blackwell. The nascent rock 'n' roll had a heavy impact on country music itself, splitting its constituency (many fans and performers alike left traditional country for rock, some to return later), and leaving its mark on Nashville and commercial country music, in the form of the rock beat, the electrification of the instruments, and the studio-produced sound.

The immediate progeny of this cross-fertilization was *rockabilly*—according to Gary Giddins, "an amalgamation of honky-tonk, country, blues, gospel, and boogie-woogie jack-hammered by white performers . . . [and] largely the creation of Sun Records, operated by Sam Phillips."[24] The mixture of ingredients in this music, which had such overwhelming appeal for youthful fans, is complex, as Giddins's summary indicates.* The persistent influence of rock on subsequent commercial country music is attributable in large part to the historic background and tastes of many country fans who grew up in the rockabilly era of the 1950s and 1960s. On the other hand, a somewhat different, and largely urban, genera-tion of youth brought up on the folk rock of Bob Dylan was introduced to coun-try music when Dylan visited it briefly in the late 1960s in the albums *John Wesley Harding* (1968) and *Nashville Skyline* (1969, including a duet with Johnny Cash).

Nashville and the Lure of Pop

The major changes in the move toward pop music had to do with the sound of the instrumental accompaniment—changes that were primarily associated, for a variety of reasons, with Nashville, Tennessee. Nashville had an early lead in establishing itself as a center for the commercial production and dissemination of country music, thanks to the presence there since 1925 of radio station WSM and its *Grand Ole Opry*. Recording began as a sideline in conjunction with the station in the 1940s. The availability of talent in the area, together with the increasing market for country music, caused major record companies to begin recording there instead of in New York or Chicago, and ultimately to establish their own studios in Nashville. Independent record companies also sprang up, and as more records were produced there the city acted like a magnet for performers from all over the South. The cycle of growth went on, and the combination of superbly equipped studios and an abundance of skilled engineers and versatile musicians available as session players led to the expansion of the Nashville recording indus-try to include all types of popular music. The city is also the home of a number of television studios, publishing houses, and booking agencies.

The characteristics of the "Nashville sound," which began to be evident in the 1950s, include the regular use of drums (which, except in the jazz-hybrid "western swing," had been foreign to country music), electric bass (sometimes pounding out a fairly heavy beat reminiscent of rock or boogie), a background of strings (definitely violins and not country fiddles!), and the use of female singers (often tightly disciplined groups) to provide an impersonal, anonymous kind of vocal backup. Studio techniques such as echo effects and overdubbing (adding material in later recording sessions) became standard. A common device for sus-taining interest in popular arrangements—raising the pitch a half step when

---

*In connection with the gospel ingredient in rockabilly, it is interesting to note that both Presley and Lewis came out of Pentecostal (specifically Assembly of God) backgrounds.

material is repeated—was adopted in Nashville productions; easy for today's facile session players, it sounds oddly out of place in country music, which has its roots in traditional tonality and ways of playing the instruments. (Loretta Lynn's "Coal Miner's Daughter," a Nashville production number as recorded in 1969, features this technique.)

The occasional whine of the steel guitar, the very occasional faint sound of a fiddle or banjo (often overdubbed), simple diatonic harmonies and melodies, and above all lyrics that still exude an inbred and ineradicable sentimentality are virtually all that remain to distinguish thoroughly "Nashvillized" country music from any other kind of "easy listening" fare.

Austin, Texas: "Outlaws" and Honky-Tonk

An alternative to the Nashville sound and concept is the neo-honky-tonk ("cosmic cowboy") music emanating from Texas, where honky-tonk began. Austin has a rather unique ambience that combines ranchers and cowboys with college students at the University of Texas. As a result, in Bill Malone's words, "a musical culture emerged which enveloped them all, and one which reflected a curious combining of images and symbols: hippie, Texan, and, above all, cowboy. . . ."[25] The best-known country musician to be associated with the Austin musical scene is Willie Nelson (b. 1933). After his move to Austin in 1972, his symbolic abandoning of the Stetson for a headband, earrings, and long hair while he went on purveying a brand of uncomplicated, pre-Nashville honky-tonk music, ensured his appeal to the three constituencies to which Malone referred: the hippie, the Texan, and the cowboy. (Nelson's 1975 recording of "**Blue Eyes Crying in the Rain**," a song recorded thirty years earlier by Roy Acuff, is an example of what Malone has called the "clean, uncluttered country music" that was a characteristic of Austin in this period.)

Country Music's Identity Crisis: Crossovers and Superstars

The identity of country music is precisely what was imperiled in the 1970s and 1980s. In the wake of its tremendous commercial success, the country music industry has, in Malone's words, "discovered that its best interests lie in the distribution of a package with clouded identity, possessing no regional traits . . . a music that is all things to all people . . . ."[26] This is a capsule description of country pop, which reflects the music's "ambivalence about its rural past" and the determination of its producers that it "not reek too strongly of rural or working-class life."[27] As the music itself has become more bland and less regional, many of its performers tended to move out and away from both the context and the material of country music. Tammy Wynette, Barbara Mandrell, and Dolly Parton have achieved superstar status in crossing over into pop styles and into the media of television and movies. In the other direction, pop singers like Kenny Rogers have successfully crossed over and achieved a measure of identification as country singers—though exactly what that designation now means, and to whom, is no longer as clear as it once was, as the identity of the audience for country music has also undergone a considerable shift.

From the perspective of the mid-1990s it appears there are some successful singers and composers who are appearing to re-adopt, in a highly commercial way, country music's basic identity and stance. Perhaps this is due in part to the swing toward social and political conservatism of the past decade or so. The image is by this time thoroughly Western, rather than Southern. Gone are photos of fiddlers in denim overalls, and of old wooden rockers on dilapidated porches. George Strait, for example, appears on album covers in immaculate Western garb—not just *clean*, but obviously *brand new*, and from the most expensive shops. The sound is studio-clean as well, though it does show an increasing use of acoustic instruments. (George Strait's "Blue Clear Sky" may be taken as representative of this phase of country music in the 1990s.) Of the many women singers and composers now marketed in the country music category (among them Tanya Tucker, Michelle Wright, Shania Twain, and Trisha Yearwood), Pam Tillis stands out as being the most conscious of country music's roots and sound. In "Deep Down" we hear recognizable mandolin and fiddle sounds, and her voice, instead of exhibiting the sexy pseudo-intimacy of many country-pop singers, is more reminiscent of the timbre of the earlier traditional country singers and the singers of ballads.

The Persistence and Revival of Traditional Styles
Bluegrass

The single strongest bastion of the musical tradition of the rural southeastern United States is bluegrass music. Yet bluegrass music as we know it today is scarcely fifty years old. Its origins, well documented, are within the living memory of many, and some of its originators are still playing and singing. It is less a literal *revival* of an older style than it is a new, highly demanding, highly professional virtuoso style *based* on and evolved from the music of the old string bands. The term "bluegrass" stands for an acoustic string band sound (fiddle, mandolin, banjo, guitar, and bass), and a singing style that stresses a high-pitched, straight tone. What has been repeatedly described as the "high, lonesome sound" is further enhanced by the choice of the "open-sounding" intervals of perfect fourths and fifths in the harmony parts in the choruses. There is also a pronounced blues influence, palpable not only in the presence of blues numbers in the repertory (including Bill Monroe's famous rendering of Jimmie Rodgers's **"Muleskinner Blues,"** and even more in his "Rocky Road Blues"), but also in the frequent blues inflections in fiddle and banjo passages. Example 5-4, an approximation of an Earl Scruggs chorus for 5-string banjo in **"Earl's Breakdown,"** shows these inflections, as well as the blues chord in the third and eleventh bars, and the speeded-up ragtime rhythms.

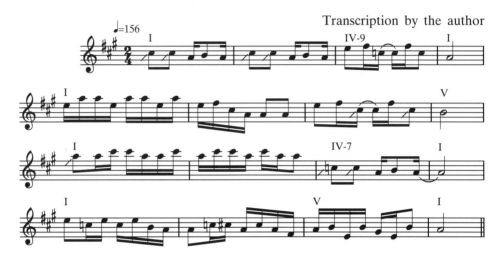

Example 5–4. "Earl's Breakdown" (excerpt)

There are slow, mournful bluegrass songs, but its most characteristic tempo is fast—often breathtakingly so. Bluegrass shares with bebop jazz (a revitalization of jazz by virtuosos that actually evolved about the same time) the distinction of being the fastest vernacular music we have—pushed to its limits by phenomenal players.

There is one man who, more than any other, was responsible for the evolution of bluegrass, and whose group, the Blue Grass Boys, gave it its name—Bill Monroe (1911–96). Monroe was a gifted mandolin player, guitarist, and singer who began his professional career performing with his two brothers, and proceeded, with persistence and integrity, to develop a style that was true to the old-time music. Monroe was not from the bluegrass country, but from farther west in Kentucky. Nor did the style evolve there; it came into being slowly, by degrees, in Atlanta (where the Blue Grass Boys were first assembled) and in Nashville (where they became part of the *Grand Ole Opry*).

Monroe's high, clear singing style and his mandolin playing were important hallmarks of the genre as was the reinstatement of the fiddle. But the most characteristic trademark of bluegrass in the popular mind is the incisive tone of the 5-string banjo, played with virtuoso technique. The banjo had all but disappeared in country music by the 1940s, but it had a dramatic revival in a picking style native to western North Carolina, as exemplified in the phenomenal playing of Earl Scruggs (b. 1924). Scruggs joined the Blue Grass Boys in 1945. His tenure with them was fairly brief; it is in the nature of professional careerdom that rising potential stars do not stay long with their mentors, but leave to form their own groups. But it was in the three short years when Scruggs and Monroe were playing together (along with three other outstanding performers, Lester Flatt, guitarist and singer, Chubby Wise, fiddler, and Howard Watts, bassist) that the "bluegrass sound" was essentially established. Flatt and Scruggs left in 1948 to form the Foggy Mountain Boys; they, the Stanley Brothers, the Lilly Brothers, Jim and Jesse McReynolds, Mac Wiseman, and Jimmy Martin, among others, continued the cultivation and evolution of bluegrass music.

Bluegrass has for some time, possibly because of its strict loyalty to acoustic instruments, had an existence independent of the more mass-audience-oriented and ambivalent country music. But the style has also by this time spawned substyles, branching off in several directions. The group Seldom Scene has purveyed a smooth honky-tonk bluegrass (as in "Bottom of the Glass" of 1974), and the Osborne Brothers were already producing in the 1960s a kind of neo-bluegrass (as in "Rocky Top" of 1967), adding piano and drums, sophisticated harmonic progressions, and lyrics that, with their corny references to such stereotypical images as moonshine, were pseudo-hillbilly. But traditional bluegrass flourishes as well, especially in the many summer festivals that have been taking place since the early 1960s and that encompass all the many styles the genre has produced. Lately, fiddler/vocalist Alison Krauss and her group, Union Station, have achieved country hits playing in traditional bluegrass style.

Other Aspects of Traditionalism
Mike Seeger, John Cohen, and the New Lost City Ramblers took a different course in relation to traditional music—that of establishing a repertory ensemble that, among other things, would keep alive older styles and older songs, such as those that had hitherto survived only on recordings from the 1920s and 1930s. Their recordings for Folkways and their *New Lost City Ramblers Song Book* embodied this approach.[28] And groups such as Horse Sense (led by Justin Bishop) and Riders in the Sky (led by Douglass Green) have specialized in researching and keeping alive traditional cowboy music.

In the year 1974 two interesting signposts appeared, pointing in opposite directions. *Grand Ole Opry* in Nashville moved from the historic Ryman Auditorium to its opulent new state-of-the-art home in Opryland. And Garrison Keillor, who had written a piece on *Grand Ole Opry* for the *New Yorker*, started his own radio show in St. Paul, *A Prairie Home Companion*. This return to the format and feeling of old-time radio, with its audience becoming involved as part of the show, was partly satirical and partly serious. The program has included jazz, ragtime, blues, gospel, ethnic music, and high school bands and choirs, as well as old-time country music and bluegrass, and the featured performers have been consistently either older traditional musicians such as Ralph Stanley, mid-generation established stars such as Emmylou Harris, or younger performers such as Peter Ostrushko, who played and sang out of a genuine understanding of and love for the music they were re-creating. In spite of Keillor's gifts as a storyteller, the enormous popularity of the program could not have been due to him alone; it was an indication that an increasing number of people were growing tired of the slick, homogenized productions, the hype, and the packaging of the pop music industry (including country-pop), and responded to the freshness and the down-to-earth lack of pretension of a kind of music that had not been stripped of the flavor or the eccentricities of either the region or the culture from which it had come. It is significant that this recognition and response could come even from those whose own background was very different from that of a Ricky Skaggs, or whose chronological age was far removed from that of a Ralph Stanley or a Bill Monroe. It is in the nature of youth to seek innovation and change, but it has also been the young in great numbers, both performers and audience, who in our time have recognized the value of the traditional aspects of our culture, and have been enthusiastic in cultivating them and keeping them fresh.

FURTHER READING

Reference works

Editors, *Country Music Magazine. The Comprehensive Country Music Encyclopedia.* New York: Times Books, 1994. 447 pp.

Collections of music

Dunson, Josh, and Ethel Raim, eds. *Anthology of American Folk Music.* New York: Oak, 1973.

> Transcriptions from the Folkways 3-cassette recorded anthology with the same title. Commentary and photographs are especially good. Includes blues and gospel music. This and the next entry constitute the basic anthologies in notation of old-time music, much of which has never been transcribed in this form.

Seeger, Mike, and John Cohen, eds. *The Old-Time String Band Songbook.* New York: Oak, 1976; now in Music Sales Corp. catalog.

> An important collection of transcriptions from recordings of songs popular in the 1920s and 1930s. Documentation, commentary, and photographs make this especially valuable.

> In addition, many of the folk music collections listed in chapter 1 contain material that is relevant to early country music, especially the Appalachian collection of Cecil Sharp.

Studies

Cash, Wilbur J. *The Mind of the South.* New York: Knopf, 1941.

Linn, Karen. *That Half-Barbaric Twang: The Banjo in American Popular Culture.* Urbana and Chicago: University of Illinois Press, 1991.

Malone, Bill C. *Country Music, U.S.A*. Rev. ed. Austin: University of Texas Press, 1985.

      The best comprehensive work available on the subject; its revised edition has been updated, and is longer by 140 pages.

———. *Singing Cowboys and Musical Mountaineers: Southern Culture and the Roots of Country Music.* Athens, GA, and London: University of Georgia Press, 1993.

Reid, Jan. *The Improbable Rise of Redneck Rock*. Austin, TX: Heidelberg, 1974.

      A lively, personal, and informative account of the Austin scene.

Rosenberg, Neil V. *Bluegrass: A History*. Urbana: University of Illinois Press, 1987.

Tichi, Cecilia. *High Lonesome: The American Culture of Country Music*. Chapel Hill: The University of North Carolina Press, 1994.

Wolfe, Charles K. *Grand Ole Opry: The Early Years, 1925–1935*. London: Old-Time Music, 1975.

Articles

Green, Archie. "Austin's Cosmic Cowboys: Words in Collision." In *"And Other Neighborly Names": Social Process and Cultural Image in Texas Folklore*, ed. Richard Bauman and Roger D. Abrahams. Austin: University of Texas Press, 1981, 152–94.

Lornell, Kip. "Early Country Music and the Mass Media in Roanoke, Virginia." *American Music* 5, no. 4 (Winter 1987): 403–16.

      Regional study of the kind needed to supplement one's understanding of any kind of American music.

Rosenberg, Neil V. "Image and Stereotype: Bluegrass Sound Tracks." *American Music* 1, no. 3 (Fall 1983): 1–22.

Projects

1. Interview a number of people, from varied backgrounds, on the subject of country music, with a view to ascertaining the degree of correlation (if any) between a like or dislike of country music and a basically rural or urban background and orientation. It may be well to play some recorded examples as part of the interview. Include yourself as one respondent if you like.

2. Investigate the state of country music in your own area to determine whether there are live performances of it by local groups, professional or amateur, and what styles are favored. If there is a sizable public for this music, try to determine something about its makeup. If possible, interview some local performers.

3. Do a study contrasting rock lyrics with those of country music. In what ways are they similar (e.g., choice and range of subject matter, frankness in its treatment) and in what ways different (e.g., presence or absence of sentimentality, sophistication, use of consciously "poetic" imagery, etc.)?

4. Compare the treatment of the man-woman relationship in a typical honky-tonk song of the 1940s with that of a typical popular song (Tin Pan Alley–Hit Parade type) of the same period.

5. Make the same comparison suggested in 4. above, using a 1970s or 1980s neo-honky-tonk song ("outlaw" or "redneck," as exemplified by, say, Willie Nelson or Waylon Jennings) with a "mainstream pop" song of the last decade or so.

Notes

1. It would be interesting to speculate as to just what accounts for this popularity among those who feel strong ties to rural life and mores, wherever they happen to live, as well as for the scorn with which this music is regarded among those who belong culturally to the city and its milieu. It is perhaps not too great an oversimplification to state that the line between those who appreciate country music and those who hold it in contempt may be drawn with fair accuracy on the basis of whether their background, attitudes, and values are basically rural or urban/suburban. But times and tastes change, and this thesis may have to be modified in view of the recent increase in popularity of country music among urban listeners.

2. From the American practice, now familiar, of adopting a brand name (e.g., Kleenex, Xerox) as a generic name for a product in common use. As such the word is now usually not capitalized.

3. Quoted in Malone, *Country Music, U.S.A.*, 2d ed., 242. For an anecdote on the relation between experience and sincerity see Maurice Zolotow, "Hillbilly Boom," *Saturday Evening Post*, quoted in Linnell Gentry, ed., *A History and Encyclopedia of Country, Western, and Gospel Music*, 2d ed. (Nashville, TN: Clairmont, 1969), 60–61.

4. Clarence Ashley, an old-time musician, recorded almost as an afterthought during one session in 1930 his version of "The House Carpenter," a venerable English and Scottish ballad from the Child canon. It turned out to be one of his most memorable recordings. It can be heard in *Anthology of American Folk Music*, vol. 1 (Smithsonian/Folkways 2951).

5. D. K. Wilgus, "An Introduction to the Study of Hillbilly Music" in the *Journal of American Folklore*, reprinted in Gentry, *A History and Encyclopedia of Country, Western, and Gospel Music*, 2d ed., 229.

6. "Listen to the Mocking Bird," published in 1855, became a favorite with country fiddlers (see *Smithsonian Collection of Classic Country Music*).

7. "Snow Dove," also known as "The Butcher Boy," on *Mountain Music Bluegrass Style* (Smithsonian/Folkways 40038).

8. "Wreck on the Highway" may be heard on *Roy Acuff's Greatest Hits*, Columbia CS 1034.

9. For a provocative discussion of sentimentality as a characteristic attitude of the South, and some speculation as to its origins, see Wilbur J. Cash, *The Mind of the South* (New York: Knopf, 1941), especially 82–87, 126–30.

10. "No Letter in the Mail," as sung on *Mountain Music of Kentucky* (Smithsonian/Folkways 40077).

11. "Katy Cline," as sung on *Mountain Music Bluegrass Style* (Smithsonian/Folkways 40038).

12. "Little Black Train," as sung by Dock Boggs, in *Dock Boggs*, vol. 2 (Smithsonian/Folkways 2392).

13. From "No Disappointment in Heaven," as sung by Dock Boggs, Folkways 2392 (cited above).

14. "'Mid the Green Fields of Virginia," sung by the Carter Family, on the album of the same title (RCA ANL–1–1107[e]).

15. "New River Train," on *Mountain Music Bluegrass Style* (Smithsonian/Folkways 40038).

16. "Rowan County Crew," as sung by Dock Boggs on *Dock Boggs*, vol. 1 (Folkways FA–2351).

17. Among these are "The Wagoner's Lad" in Cecil Sharp, *English Folk-Songs from the Southern Appalachians*, vol. 2 (London: Oxford University Press, 1932), 123, recorded in 1928 by Buell Kazee, on *Anthology of American Folk Music*, vol. 1 (Smithsonian/Folkways 2951); and "Sally Ann" (Sharp, 351), recorded by Clarence Ashley, on *Old-Time Music at Clarence Ashley's* (Smithsonian/Folkways 40029).

18. Sharp, 35; recorded on Smithsonian/Folkways 2951 (cited above).

19. See Doron Antrim, "Whoop-and-Holler Opera," reprinted in Gentry, *A History and Encyclopedia* (cited above), 65–70.

20. For examples illustrative of this phase of "old-time" music, an excellent and representative selection of material from the early recordings by such artists as Clarence Ashley, Buell Kazee, Uncle Dave Macon, Dock Boggs, the Stoneman Family, and the Carter Family is available in *Anthology of American Folk Music* (Smithsonian/Folkways 2951–53).

21. *Songs of the Cowboys*, collected by Nathan Howard "Jack" Thorpe, was published in New Mexico in 1908, followed by *Cowboy Songs and Other Frontier Ballads*, collected by John Alan Lomax, in 1910.

22. Several of these are included in New World 314–15. One of the best known of these, "When the Work's All Done This Fall" (based on a poem by the cowboy poet D. J. O'Malley), is included, as recorded by Carl T. Sprague in 1925, both in New World 314–15 and in the *Smithsonian Collection of Classic Country Music*.

23. The vitality of cowboy poetry, always an important adjunct to cowboy song, is illustrated in the surprising growth of events such as the annual Cowboy Poetry Conference in Elko, Nevada, and its numerous progeny springing up elsewhere in the West.

24. Gary Giddins, in notes to New World 249, *Shake, Rattle & Roll: Rock 'n' Roll in the 1950's*.

25. Malone, *Country Music, U.S.A.*, 2d ed., 394. See also Reid, *The Improbable Rise of Redneck Rock* (Austin, TX: Heidelberg, 1974), for a personal, informative account of the Austin scene, and those who have had a part in it.

26. Malone, *Country Music, U.S.A.*, 2d ed., 369.

27. Ibid., 378.

28. See *New Lost City Ramblers* (Smithsonian-Folkways 40036) and *Out Standers in Their Field* (40040). The songbook has been reissued as *The Old-Time String Band Songbook* (New York: Oak, 1976).

Chapter 6

Blues and Soul: From Country to City

If country music has become a mighty (and a wealthy) nation, the blues has prospered and increased mightily also, and the range of its influence on our music has been even broader. In tracing the blues through its folk phase in chapter 2, we noted that its emergence came with the fundamental changes that accompanied the abolition of slavery. The blues was not a communal expression. It was (and is) the lament, the comment, often mocking or ironic, of the solitary individual, bereft of the support of a close-knit society, facing *alone*, on personal terms, a hostile or indifferent world. Yet long before our time the lament had become an entertainment, the solitary singer's comment had crystallized into a form that could be printed and sold, and the lone cry had become a commodity. The blues had become, in a word, popular music—even before the first recordings of it appeared.

But the legacy of its folk beginnings remained to characterize the blues indelibly: the way the voice is handled, the blues intonation, the range and treatment of its subjects, and above all the basic blues feeling that has its roots in a solitary experience and view of life. Those who were to become its first professionals had, like their white hillbilly counterparts, served their apprenticeship in traveling tent shows and minstrel and medicine shows, or in playing and singing for all-night parties and dances, or even (as many blind singers did) in performing for passersby in front of country stores or on city streets.

Early Published Blues

It was inevitable that a type of music being sung and played in cities and small towns in the lowland South from the Piedmont to Texas would eventually find its way into print. This happened first in 1912, when by coincidence within a period of two months blues were published in St. Louis ("Baby Seals Blues"), Oklahoma City ("Dallas Blues"), and Memphis ("Memphis Blues"). "Memphis Blues" had been widely played in that city for three years before its publication, by the enterprising composer-bandleader who, more than any other early professional, was to promote the blues as popular music and bring it to a wide public—William C. Handy (1873–1958). Handy's early experiences with the performance and publication of these compositions are interestingly set forth in his autobiography, *Father of the Blues*. In the beginning, "Memphis Blues" netted him $50, with the real profits for years going to others. But Handy was to learn quickly. If the nickname "father of the blues" is something of an exaggeration (Bruce Cook has said that a more accurate one would be "rich uncle"),[1] his place in blues history is still important, and his ties with its roots are perfectly genuine.

The Music of the Early Blues

By the time the blues were being composed and arranged for broad popular consumption, the musical form had been developed and extended. It came to include at least two and sometimes three strains, often in the relationship of verses-with-chorus. The three-phrase, 12-bar pattern with its usual harmonic plan (as outlined in chapter 2) was standard for at least one of the strains, but there were also strains cast in the standard European 16-bar form. These early published blues, as a matter of fact, showed a mixture of influences. The blues elements were often quite attenuated, and the music was sometimes pure ragtime, with its more elaborate European harmonies, as in the second strain of Handy's "Memphis Blues." At times still other influences were evident; the best-known strain of the most famous blues of all, the "St. Louis Blues," is actually, as Handy wrote it, a 16-bar tango! As he notes in his autobiography, the effect of this tango rhythm—the "Spanish tinge" as noted jazz pianist-composer Jelly Roll Morton described it—on black dancers for whom he played was not lost on the observant Mr. Handy, and he used it again in his "Beale Street Blues" and "Aunt Hagar's Children."

The Texts of the Early Blues

The blues as published for general public consumption were distinct from the earthy blues of the tent shows that were later to become so popular on recordings. Each had its own public and its own standards of what was admissible in terms of subject matter and language, but there was some commonality of musical and textual ideas. The recently invented telephone was an irresistible metaphor in blues, as it was in early gospel music. Handy made a practice of noting down folk phrases he heard here and there ("Goin' where the Southern cross' the Dog"; "Ma man's got a heart like a rock cast in de sea") and incorporating them into his songs. But in the published blues of Handy and others the rhymes are more exact, the lyrics more facile, employing clever plays on words, and the subjects (as in Handy's "Wall Street Blues") artificially remote from the soil in which the blues had germinated.

Classic City Blues

The blues as a more or less standardized form of popular music for a large public (mostly black, but with a growing white element) enjoyed what has been called its "classic" period from 1920, when the first recordings were made and sold, until the onset of the Depression in the early 1930s. Personal-appearance tours (mostly on vaudeville circuits) and nightclub appearances were a mainstay for the more popular blues singers, and there were some radio performances and even some films. But the principal medium for the propagation of the blues was the phonograph recording. In a development parallel to that of instrumental jazz and white country music, thousands of blues performances by hundreds of singers were recorded, and millions of copies sold.

The period of the classic city blues was dominated by the female blues singer. Various reasons have been advanced for this, but the most likely ones have to do with the nature of show business at the time and the success of the women singers in tent and vaudeville shows. Unlike the folk blues—which, as we have seen in chapter 2, encompassed a wide range of subjects—the classic blues were almost exclusively concerned with man-woman relations from the woman's point of view. The treatment of sexual themes ranged from the frank earthiness of much of Ma Rainey's material to the kind of smirking double entendre typical of the sleazier vaudeville shows—a type of lyric exploited in both city and country blues by record companies eager to bolster sales in the early years of the Depression, when the amazingly prosperous era of the classic blues was waning.

The recording of blues was regarded at the outset as a risky venture. The first singers recorded were not really blues singers, but professional entertainers with experience in cabaret and vaudeville singing. Real blues singers in the Southern tradition began to be recorded a few years later. Of these by far the best known and most influential were Ma Rainey (1886–1939) and Bessie Smith (1894–1937), both of whom began recording blues in 1923.

Ma Rainey's early career sheds light on the milieu in which the classic blues evolved. Both her parents were minstrel-show performers, and she herself was singing on the stage by the time she was fourteen. She acquired her familiar nickname, "Ma," when, at age eighteen, she married William "Pa" Rainey, a minstrel performer and they began touring with their song-and-dance routine. (She herself preferred to be called "Madame" Rainey.) Thus she had had more than twenty years of professional experience in touring circus, variety, and minstrel shows by the time she made her first blues recording. Of all the classic blues singers she remained closest to the vernacular blues tradition. She never sang professionally outside the South, except to make recordings in New York and Chicago during a four-year period that ended in 1928. By then, a recording

Gertrude "Ma" Rainey. *Courtesy New York Public Library.*

executive is said to have expressed the opinion that Ma's "down-home" material had gone out of fashion. During this brief period she recorded with some of the leading jazz musicians, but also with a traditional Southern jug, kazoo, washboard, and banjo band.

Ma Rainey's lyrics reflected the country blues range of subject matter, and went beyond the perennial man-woman themes to touch on poverty, alcoholism, prostitution, homosexuality, and topical references (as in "Titanic Man Blues"). She recorded in Chicago and New York with a pickup group that included many of the important blues and jazz performers of the time. In "**Countin' the Blues**" (see Ex. 6-1, p. 105), her "Georgia Jazz Band" includes trumpeter Louis Armstrong and pianist Fletcher Henderson. Contemporary accounts and pictures indicate that she was a stocky, imposing woman, imbued with what must have been a commanding stage presence and an uncanny degree of what can best be described by that much-abused term "charisma." In her surviving recordings what we hear, dimly transmitted through primitive recording techniques, is a voice and a kind of singing devoid of the slightest trace of artificiality.

Bessie Smith, eight years younger than Ma Rainey, began her career as the latter's protégée, though she declined to acknowledge this in later years. She and Ma Rainey began recording about the same time, but Bessie Smith eventually became far better known, and was undoubtedly a more versatile singer. She became identified wholly with the sophisticated city blues tradition, and her material was tailored largely for this market. Like Ma Rainey she worked with the leading jazz musicians, and recorded with piano (with Fletcher Henderson, for example), with piano and one instrument (quite often with Joe Smith or Louis Armstrong playing muted blues cornet), with a small jazz combo, and even with choral background in some early "production numbers." **Mama's Got the Blues,**" recorded with Fletcher Henderson as pianist, is a typical 12-bar slow blues, with lyrics traditional for the period. Her mastery of the idiom and the forcefulness and directness of her delivery are undisputed. But Bessie Smith, too, was out of fashion by the time she made her last recordings in 1933.

Other singers in the classic blues tradition included Ida Cox, Bertha "Chippie" Hill, Clara Smith, Sippie Wallace, and Victoria Spivey, all of whom performed with major jazz musicians of the 1920s and 1930s. It was the day of the woman blues singers, and while there have been eminent black female popular singers since (Ella Fitzgerald, Billie Holiday, Sarah Vaughan, and Aretha Franklin), none after the classic period has been so exclusively identified with the blues. The dominant role in blues singing has since passed largely to men.

Blues and Jazz

The blues had evolved structurally in such a way as to demand the complementing role of an answering voice (or instrument) at the end of each sung line. This manifestation of call-and-response is a distinguishing feature of the blues. The solitary blues singer filled in his own breaks on his guitar; in the city blues the piano, and later the collaborating instrumentalist, took up this function. An interesting example of distinctive jazz breaks provided by a small combo can be heard in Ma Rainey's **"Countin' the Blues,"** in which each break in the three-line blues form is taken in turn by cornet, clarinet, and trombone. These collaborations provide some of the finest moments in early jazz.

At this time "blues" and "jazz" were taken by some to be one and the same. While they are distinct traditions, their parallel development is a rather complex history of periodically strong influence and identification. At the same time that the rural blues was slowly taking shape, something like its urban counterpart was having a hand in the early formation of jazz. There were bands in New Orleans (and possibly in Memphis and other cities as well) playing music by 1900 that was called "blues." We will never know what the blues played by these early bands sounded like. But the identification of blues with jazz remained exceptionally close through the classic blues period. Then, in the 1930s, began a gradual divergence; the blues declined somewhat, and jazz evolved in other

Example 6–1. "Countin' the Blues"

directions. While the blues as a harmonic and formal design can be heard in all ages of jazz, the blues references, as we advance through the so-called modern period, become increasingly attenuated. Recently, under the impact of the reenergized urban blues and the synthesis called "soul" music, jazz has been forcibly pulled back to a closer relation with its blues roots.

Boogie-Woogie

Boogie-woogie is essentially a solo piano form, as is ragtime, but quite distinct from it in origin and style. Its progenitor is the blues. Its sound is unforgettable—a driving left hand with a hypnotically repeated pattern (the musical term for this, *ostinato*, is related to our word "obstinate"), the right hand often insisting equally obstinately on its own repeated figures; and, underlying all, blues form and harmony. It was spawned as piano entertainment in bars, nightclubs, and related establishments. Generically, boogie-woogie was probably an adaptation of what blues singer-guitarists had been doing, with their intricate, ostinato-like accompaniments. Early boogie-woogie soloists would often sing along, or talk to their audience, while they were playing.

Boogie-woogie, transferred out of the environment of its origins, went through a period of short but intense popularity in the late 1930s. This is apt to obscure the fact that it is a much older phenomenon. Jelly Roll Morton has said that many piano performers in his early days (shortly after the turn of the century) played in what must have been something like this style of piano blues with heavy ostinato-like left hand. W. C. Handy mentions adopting and orchestrating for his group a type of piano music played in the bordellos of the Mississippi delta region around the turn of the century; it was called "boogie-house music."

There is a relationship between boogie-woogie and the big bands of the 1930s, especially in Kansas City, where the "jump" style was in many ways a translation of boogie idioms to the jazz band, just as the idioms of ragtime had been transferred to traditional jazz a generation earlier. Although the craze for it subsided somewhat in the 1940s, boogie-woogie remained a potent musical style. With its driving ostinato and blues form, it was to emerge as a major influence on rock 'n' roll in the 1950s, as can be heard, for example, in the work of Jerry Lee Lewis.

Boogie-woogie's resources are limited. Nevertheless, within those limitations a considerable amount of variety is found—variety of tempos (not all boogie is fast), of left-hand patterns, and of general feeling. In "**Mr. Freddie Blues**," a boogie-woogie treatment by Meade "Lux" Lewis of an earlier blues by J. H. Shayne, the typical ostinato bass and the 12-bar blues form are exceptionally clear.

The Absorption of Country Blues into Popular Music

The fascinating evolution of the blues itself from African-American field cries, calls, and hollers has already been traced in the place where it really belongs— that is, as part of the unfolding story of African-American folk music. In this chapter, it only remains to trace the passage of rural blues into the realm of popular music.

Recordings of city blues by female singers in the early 1920s were very successful. As the business of selling records by mail grew it was realized that a large market existed among the rural Southern black people for recordings of their own singers. The ice was broken for male blues singers when Papa Charlie Jackson recorded his "Lawdy Lawdy Blues" in Chicago in 1924. (The piece was not really a blues, nor was Jackson a blues singer, but a minstrel and medicine-show performer from New Orleans, who accompanied himself on a 6-string banjo. The parallel with the first female singers to record blues commercially is interesting.) When this yielded an encouraging amount of commercial success the search for traditional country blues performers was on, and there soon followed recordings by singers from across the entire South, from Florida (Blind Blake) to Texas (Blind Lemon Jefferson).

"Race records" was the trade term used for several decades for recordings by black musicians intended for black consumers. For the earliest recordings, singers were brought to Chicago, where they worked in "studios" often primitive even by the standards of the time. But expeditions through the South with recording equipment were also undertaken. The engineering and production of the records were for the most part as cheap as the promotional material was crass, and usually little attempt was made to preserve the masters. The records themselves, especially those made in the 1920s, became very rare indeed. With few exceptions the singers themselves were exploited while being treated with disdain.

A few country blues singers, survivors in a harsh environment, did eventually became well known and frequently recorded, the beneficiaries of two developments in the cities: the urban folk-song movement of the 1930s and 1940s (see chapter 1), which brought Leadbelly (Huddie Ledbetter) into prominence, and in the 1960s the folk-song revival movement, with its attendant folk festivals, at which country blues performers such as Robert Pete Williams, Mississippi John Hurt, Lightnin' Hopkins, Son House, and the team of Sonny Terry & Brownie McGhee regularly performed. Terry & McGhee went on to successful careers in New York.

Urban Blues

There is no music that better epitomizes the harsher aspects of urban life, especially for African Americans, than the urban blues. The heartwood of the blues is rural, but at the layer where it is continuing to add living tissue it is wholly of the city. Thus the blues, like a great proportion of the black populace whose music it is, made the move from country to city.

The move toward modern urban blues was signaled by the introduction of that quintessentially urban instrument the piano into the ensemble. The combination of piano and guitar was used by the influential team of Leroy Carr and Francis "Scrapper" Blackwell in the 1930s (their **"Blue Night Blues"** is representative), and the piano almost invariably figured in Chicago blues recordings of the period. The style of piano playing, except for traces of ragtime, was, not surprisingly, essentially that of the blues-related boogie-woogie, with its heavy and incessant left-hand ostinatos clearly presaging the main features of rock 'n' roll. Also to be noted was the addition of drums to many of the Chicago groups. But this was a transitional period in the citification of the blues; some recordings still included such down-home instruments as the harmonica and even the washboard. The blues, just before World War II, had one foot in the city and one still in the country.[2]

After the war a number of blues singers born in the South, and with strong blues roots there, began recording in the 1950s and 1960s, mostly in Chicago, a brand of hard-driving blues with a strong beat, backed by electric guitar (which they often played themselves), bass, drums, and sometimes electric organ and/or piano. This blues was strongly influenced by the gospel tradition, a background from which many of the singers came. These include Howlin' Wolf (1910–76, born Chester Arthur Burnett), Muddy Waters (1915–83, born McKinley Morganfield), John Lee Hooker (born in 1917), all from Mississippi, and Willie Mae "Big Mama" Thornton (1926–84, born in Alabama). Muddy Waters's "Hoochie Coochie Man" is typical. These artists defined a type of urban blues that was very influential on later blues and rock musicians, especially in England, where many of them toured.

Meanwhile in the West, typically Kansas City, blues singers were often backed by jazz bands, with heavily pounding rhythm sections, and featuring prominently the wind instrument that became the blues singer's alter ego, the saxophone. The wailing, honking, screaming saxophone often took a complete chorus after the singer had sufficiently established the mood. This in turn affected vocal style. The modern blues singer has a microphone, of course, but the shouting style that Midwest blues singers like Joe Turner (whose "Shake, Rattle and Roll" became a musical icon of nascent rock 'n' roll) and Jimmy Rushing had to adopt to be heard, unamplified, over the big band sounds of Kansas City, has remained as a characteristic of much blues singing today. As Amiri Baraka has put it: "These Southwestern 'shouters' and big blues bands had a large influence on Negro music everywhere. The shouter gave impetus to a kind of blues that developed around the cities in the late thirties called 'rhythm and blues,' which was largely huge rhythm units smashing away behind screaming blues singers."[3]

The symbolic distortion forced upon that most sensitive of all musical instruments, the human voice, by the stridency and abrasiveness of a stark urban milieu is summed up by Baraka: "Blues had always been a vocal music . . . but now the human voice itself had to struggle, to scream, to be heard."[4]

The guitar, by now invariably electric, remained as an element of continuity in the blues band. If we add to this a small vocal ensemble, usually female, for the blues singer to "play" to, which gave the responses to his or her calls and echoed the key phrases, we have virtually complete the medium of the urban blues that, by the early 1950s, had been given the commercial designation "rhythm-and-blues." "A Fool in Love,"[5] with a vocal group taking over the role of the blues saxophone, is illustrative.*

This rhythm-and-blues, especially as conventionalized by such entertainers as Chuck Berry and Bo Diddley, was still performed by black musicians for an almost exclusively black audience, reached either in person or via recordings—a market rivaling that for the race recordings of city and country blues thirty years earlier. But it also unquestionably formed the basis for the music—rock 'n' roll—that won a vast young white audience from the mid-fifties on. So closely, in fact, did early rock 'n' roll performers imitate black models that the early recordings of the white singer Elvis Presley (who spent his adolescent years in the blues ambience of Memphis) sold primarily to black audiences.

The Soul Synthesis

A broader synthesis of black musical styles, and one embodying many elements of the blues, is embraced in the concept of "soul." Charles Keil writes: " 'Soul' may be partly defined as a mixture of ethnic essence, purity, sincerity, conviction, credibility, and just plain effort."[6] The ethnic orientation of "soul" is clear; it began to evolve, as Keil points out, after the Supreme Court's school desegregation decision of 1954, one of the landmarks in a decade that saw the aspirations of African Americans take a definite turn toward strengthening racial and cultural *identity*, rather than achieving integration per se.

As a concept, soul embraces a wide spectrum of life's aspects, from religion to sex to food; indeed, it emphasizes a kind of synthesis of everything, and the communication and sharing of experience and strong emotion. As Keil has said: "For many Negroes, life is one long sacrificial ritual. The blues artist, in telling his story, crystallizes and synthesizes not only his own experience but the experiences of his listeners."[7]

Musically, soul is a synthesis as well—of blues, jazz, and gospel. Its foremost artists among blues singers have been Ray Charles, B. B. King, Bobby Blue Bland, Junior Parker, Aretha Franklin, and Ike and Tina Turner. Of their performances, Keil has said: "The word 'ritual' seems more appropriate than 'performance' when the audience is committed rather than appreciative."[8] No better example of this can be cited than B. B. King's **"Sweet Little Angel,"** as recorded live at the Regal Theater, a famous blues venue in Chicago, in 1964. It consists of five choruses of 12-bar blues, the first and last featuring King's electric guitar. The audience reaction gives a feeling for the ritual of an authentic performance of soul.

---

* "A Fool in Love" is on *Roots: Rhythm and Blues*, Smithsonian/Folkways RBF 20. Both "Shake, Rattle and Roll" and "A Fool in Love" illustrate in their lyrics the blatant sexist stance, the first from the male and the second from the female point of view, which characterized much of rhythm-and-blues.

Blues in the 1990s

Many changes have affected blues in the 1990s. The recordings that are being produced are both fewer and technologically and stylistically slicker. As Mary Katherine Aldin has noted, "The good old days of producing on a shoestring and selling records at gigs have all but disappeared." Live concerts have become more expensive and more gargantuan. "The juke joints of the 1930s and even the folk clubs of the 1960s have been replaced," as Aldin has pointed out, "by blues festivals that draw tens of thousands. . . . The audience usually cannot get closer than binocular distance, and the sense of immediacy, urgency, and intimate communication so essential to the blues experience has all but disappeared."

She further calls attention to more fundamental changes as well when she asserts that

> . . . not a single young artist is carrying on the tradition of, say, John Lee Hooker or Son House . . . one reason is that the young people growing up today come from a different background. They don't learn field hollers, don't pick cotton, aren't sharecroppers. They work city jobs, even in the small towns, and the music of the auto mechanic or car-wash operator is, by its very nature, going to be a more urbanized sound, so that what David Evans called "the solo work song that for years provided blues with its basic vocal and melodic material" no longer exists.[9]

Gender and racial shifts are noteworthy as well. White male blues singers such as Johnny Winter and William Clarke have come into prominence, as has the interracial women's group Saffire: The Uppity Blues Women.

Among blues men and women prominent today (some of whom are already in their fifties or older) are Johnny Copeland, Robert Cray, Albert Collins (who, although each a full-fledged artist on his own, formed a very successful trio), Clarence "Gatemouth" Brown, James Cotton, KoKo Taylor, Taj Mahal, Joe Lewis Walker, Son Seals, and Kenny Neal.

Reflecting many of these changes, as well as ties to the past and its traditions, is "We're Outa Here," by Clarence "Gatemouth" Brown, recorded in 1991.* It consists of twenty 12-bar blues choruses in a fast tempo over a pronounced boogie bass pattern—one that was already old in the 1930s. The fairly large band includes winds that play jazz riffs. There are solo choruses for guitar and piano, but only three choruses with vocals! The whole exhibits a virtuosity that is a match for that of bebop jazz and bluegrass breakdowns.

*"We're Outa Here" is on *No Looking Back*, by Alligator Records.

Clarence "Gatemouth" Brown. *Photo by Robert Barclay.*

Whatever the present and future state of the blues, there can be no doubt of its importance up to this point. Blues authority Paul Oliver has called it "one of the richest and most rewarding of popular arts and perhaps the last great folk music that the western world may produce."[10]

FURTHER READING

Baraka, Amiri. *Blues People*. New York: Morrow, 1963.
> A survey by an eminent black writer, who uses music to illustrate and illuminate the history of his people in America.

Charters, Samuel. *The Bluesmen*. New York: Oak, 1967.
———. *Sweet as the Showers of Rain*. New York: Oak, 1977.
> These two titles constitute a two-volume expansion of the author's earlier *The Country Blues* (New York: Rinehart, 1959).

Cohn, Lawrence, ed. *Nothing But the Blues: The Music and the Musicians*. New York: Abbeville, 1993.
> A compilation of eleven chapters by various authors, at 432 pages in large format this is the most comprehensive up-to-date general work on the subject.

Cook, Bruce. *Listen to the Blues*. New York: Scribner's, 1973.

Ferris, William, Jr. *Blues from the Delta*. New York: Da Capo, 1984 (reprint of 1979 ed.).

Handy, W. C. *Father of the Blues*. New York: Macmillan, 1941.

> In spite of the obvious kind of exaggeration implicit in its title, Handy's autobiography contains a wealth of background information, written from the standpoint of firsthand professional experience, on America's popular music business during the first four decades of this century.

————, ed. *Blues: An Anthology*. New York, 1926. Reprint. New York: Macmillan, 1972.

> A famous collection of early published blues by Handy and others. A 1949 edition includes a rather extensive and valuable essay, "The Story of the Blues," by Abbe Niles. This is included in the most recent edition, which also incorporates additional blues, and guitar-chord symbols.

Harrison, Daphne Duval. *Black Pearls: Blues Queens of the 1920s*. New Brunswick, NJ: Rutgers University Press, 1988.

Keil, Charles. *Urban Blues*. Chicago: University of Chicago Press, 1966.

> Still an indispensable study, and one of the few to deal adequately and from a variety of angles with the modern urban component of the blues. His annotated outlines of blues styles (Appendix C) is valuable.

Oliver, Paul. *The Story of the Blues*. New York: Chilton, 1969.

> A comprehensive study, profusely illustrated with photographs, this is a basic source, though concentrating mainly on the rural and "classic" blues. There is a fine bibliography and discography.

Shaw, Arnold. *Black Popular Music in America*. New York: Schirmer Books, 1986.

Taft, Michael. *Blues Lyric Poetry: An Anthology*. New York: Garland, 1983.

> Lyrics of more than 2,000 blues songs, transcribed from reissue LPs. Published with a companion three-volume concordance.

Titon, Jeff Todd. *Early Downhome Blues: A Musical and Cultural Analysis*. Urbana: University of Illinois Press, 1977.

> In addition to cultural background, photographs, and reproductions of contemporary advertisements, this study includes transcriptions from forty-eight blues recordings of the 1920s, with musical analysis, thus making it one of the most musically thorough and useful studies in the field.

See also various works in the reading lists for chapter 2 (additional background on the folk phase) and chapter 15 (jazz, especially the early jazz so closely related to blues).

Projects

1. Based on W. C. Handy's autobiography (and any other sources you can find) describe in a brief essay what life was like for a black musician in the Deep South in the first quarter of the twentieth century.

2. Assemble a list of at least five male and five female blues singers (besides Ma Rainey and Bessie Smith) who recorded between 1920 and 1930, with a brief biographical sketch of each. Cite at least one recording for each, and listen to as many others as you can.

3. Compare three recordings of Mississippi delta blues performers with three recordings of Texas blues performers. Describe them, and determine to what extent they either support or contradict the stylistic generalizations made in the chapter.

4. Make a collection of urban blues lyrics since 1950 (including rhythm-and-blues and soul). Compare them, in scope and treatment, with those in Paul Oliver's study *The Meaning of the Blues*, which are predominantly rural and date from before 1950.

5. Make a study of urban gospel music, and its relation to the urban blues.

6. Make a study of a commercial style such as the "Detroit sound" or "Motown" (as represented, say, by the Supremes). How much does it owe to the blues? Analyze the similarities and differences between such a stylization and the more mainstream blues tradition—the "blues continuum."

Notes

1. Bruce Cook, *Listen to the Blues*, 122.

2. A good single collection documenting this phase is *Blues Roots/Chicago—the 1930's* (Smithsonian/Folkways RF016).

3. Amiri Baraka, *Blues People* (New York: Morrow, 1963), 168.

4. Ibid. 171–72.

5. Rhythm-and-blues, like the earlier race records, is a vast commercial category. Charlie Gillett has written: "As a market category . . . 'rhythm and blues' was simply a signal that the singer was black, and recording for a black audience." The album *Straighten Up and Fly Right: Rhythm and Blues from the Close of the Swing Era to the Dawn of Rock 'n' Roll* (New World 261) gives a broad sampling of styles from the 1940s and early 1950s, with excellent notes. Also valuable is *Roots: Rhythm and Blues*, Smithsonian/Folkways RF020, on which "A Fool in Love" can be found.

6. Keil, *Urban Blues*, especially chapter 7, "Soul and Solidarity." The quote above appears on p. 160.

7. Ibid. 161.

8. Ibid. 164.

9. Quotes by Mary Katherine Aldin are from *Nothing But the Blues*, 390, 392, and 398–99.

10. Paul Oliver, *The Story of the Blues*, 168.

Rock and Its Progeny

Rock has become, at the end of this century, virtually *the* worldwide popular musical culture. (Some would eliminate both "popular"and "musical" as modifiers.) As such, it deserves treatment that is reasoned, informed, and as thorough as the brevity that is necessarily imposed on a concise edition will allow. The volume of writings on rock has become staggering; to deserve a serious place among the flood of books and articles on the subject, this modestly proportioned chapter must pursue a judicious path through the mazes that inevitably confront anyone seriously attempting to negotiate the jagged and confusing topography of rock, avoiding both the sycophantic tone of its single-minded enthusiasts, and the polemics of its committed detractors, and concentrating most of all on the music itself.

Much of rock is "goodtime" music, eminently music to dance to; in its lyrics, much of it is concerned with the man-woman relation. These aspects (though certainly not its *sound*) rock shares with the popular music whose beginnings preceded it by more than a century. But it differs from previous forms of mass entertainment in being to a greater extent an expression of revolt. It is also fair to say that rock is essentially the product and expression of urban culture—some have said of "street culture."[1] Although the "street" has never been the home of rock performers or of most of their devotees, rock is nevertheless as distinctly an outgrowth and expression of urban life and values as country music is of rural life and values. Traceable ultimately to common origins in the rural South, these two have grown apart, musically and socially (and one might almost say politically), and have become the musical property of two distinctly different constituencies that are still identifiable, in a cultural if not literal sense, as *city* and *country*. Together they account for the major portion of our popular music.

Characteristics of the Music
The Basic Makeup of the Rock Band
Underlying the profuse variety of sounds in rock's forty-year history, there is a basic aggregation of three obligatory sound sources. Because rock, like its prog-

enitors, blues and country music, has as its basic vehicle the song, the *human voice*, invariably amplified (the microphone is one of the icons of rock), is indispensable. A second indispensable element is the amplified sound of plucked strings—invariably the *guitar* (or guitars), nearly always electric, usually backed up by its larger cousin, the electric bass. The third indispensable element is the *drum set*. These three constitute an irreducible core of sound; they are all that are needed for rock's sound signature, and often all that are present.* Of the optional additions, first in importance would be the keyboard instruments: at first, of course, the traditional piano, now more often than not, electronic keyboard(s). The next most frequently heard option is the saxophone, exemplifying rock's relation to rhythm-and-blues. To this core whatever else is added (banjos, sitars, flutes, violins, a brass section, a full symphony orchestra) is essentially frosting on the cake.

Style Traits

Rhythm

The most obligatory rhythmic element of rock is the *beat*, as maintained by the drummer and the bass player, sometimes with the assistance of the rhythm guitarist and the keyboard player. Forthright, loud, and insistent, this rhythmic ground often incorporates a simple melodic figure in the bass, called a *bass riff*, which is obsessively repeated, and which shows rock's strong relationship to blues-derived boogie-woogie. This is apt to be most noticeable in the music of those black artists whose work comes directly out of rhythm-and-blues, from Chuck Berry in the 1950s to "the artist formerly known as Prince" in the 1980s. Another rhythmic feature of rock that is close to its roots is the prominent "backbeat"—the strongly marked offbeat *reaction* to the basic pulse that is so typical a feature of black music-making, in which the drummer has simply picked up and imitated the hand-clapping, for example, of black audiences, sacred and secular. It can be heard in pieces as otherwise dissimilar as "Maybellene" (1955) by Chuck Berry, and "Born in the USA" (1985) by Bruce Springsteen. In certain substyles the rock beat can become more complex, showing its derivation from a combination of the boogie-woogie bass,[2] and the rhythms of the Latin band.[3]

Melody and Harmony

In terms of melody and harmony, rock owes much more to both the blues scale and the modes of Anglo-Celtic folk music than it does to the harmonies and the progressions of the European-derived popular music of Broadway and Tin Pan Alley, which it largely replaced. By the way of illustrating this, Example7-1

---

* The jazz ensemble, even the smallest, has likewise its own irreducible core of instruments: piano, bass, and drums—again, sometimes all that is present.

shows, in their simplest form, the harmonies of the most important strains of "Daisy Bell" (1892, by Henry Dacre) and "The Wind Cries Mary" (1967, by Jimi Hendrix). In each there are only five chords used; four of these are common to both songs. The difference is in their usage—a difference that becomes audibly apparent when Example 7-1 is played. It is most striking in the final phrase of each; the Tin Pan Alley song confirms its comfortable conventionality by stating the time-honored dominant-to-tonic cadential progression three times, while the rock song, which never uses that progression at all, ends on quite a different kind of cadence, preceding the final tonic with the subtonic chord, a chord prevalent in both folk music and the blues.

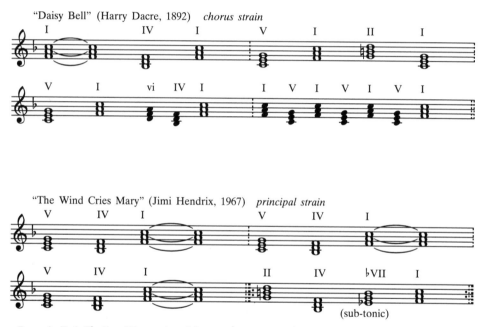

Example 7–1. Tin Pan Alley and rock harmonies compared

Vocal Styles

The heritage of the blues is apparent in the vocal styles used in rock; the shout, the cry, the groan (of either pain or ecstasy), use of falsetto, the mumbled slur deliberately "throwing away" portions of the lyrics—all these have their roots in blues and gospel singing. While these are basic resources of rock singing, it is also true that vocal styles in popular music tend to be highly individual; tone quality, inflection of the voice, manner of delivery, even accent, become identifying "trademarks" of a particular singer. The highly individualized styles of extremely popular singers become prototypes, imitated by those who follow.

Black blues singers such as Joe Turner, Muddy Waters, and John Lee Hooker were influential on early rock 'n' roll vocalists; there developed subsequently a Bob Dylan type of delivery, a Beatles style of singing and inflection, a David Byrne manner of monotone half-recitation, and so on.

The Sound Studio

Since the 1960s, rock musicians and producers have taken full advantage of a continually evolving technology in the production of the basic vehicle of rock, the sound recording. Synthesized sounds, complex echo and reverberation effects, and the multiplying of layers of sound through overdubbing have become commonplace ingredients of the music, and effects not easily duplicated in live performances are taken for granted on recordings. The sound studio has become itself a sound resource; as Evan Eisenberg has put it, "The real cooking is done in the studio."[4]

Characteristics of the Words

Words have an ambivalent role in rock. On the one hand, there are rock fans, and even some performers themselves, who say that they never pay attention to the lyrics. In a sense, the *sound* of rock is the emotive *message* of rock. At times the very sound may in fact overwhelm the lyrics, either rendering them inaudible or reducing them to elemental fragments or vocal ejaculations, building with the sound to an intense climax.

On the other hand, there is a sense in which rock, like country music, and like the folk music that was the source of them both, is fundamentally word oriented; its vehicle is the song, not, as in jazz, the instrumental number. This has given rise to a close scrutiny of rock lyrics.

Rock Lyrics and the Blues

Early rock 'n' roll, coming as it did directly out of rhythm-and-blues, naturally reflected this patrimony in its lyrics. From Roy Brown's "Good Rockin' Tonight," as recorded by Wynonie Harris in 1947, to Chuck Berry's "Rock 'n' Roll Music" a decade later, the family likeness is clear: a celebration of energy, of vitality, of movement, of sex, of the very act of making the music itself. Like rhythm-and-blues, it was music for dancing. The classical blues form itself (*aab*) did appear in rock 'n' roll, as it had in rhythm-and-blues; its repetition of a single line followed by a concluding line can be found as a kind of relic of classical blues in the choruses of such early rock 'n' roll songs as "I Can't Go On," "Good Golly, Miss Molly," and "Maybellene." But the broader range of blues lyrics was missing from early rock 'n' roll, which was little else than music to dance to. In general, the growing popularization of rock 'n' roll, and the subsequent evolution of rock, created a widening separation from blues lyrics in both form and content.

Rock Subject Matter
Love: Romantic, Real-life, and Altruistic

Many rock songs are about love-in-real-life, whether joyous, poignant, or painful. These songs express the same emotions in varying degrees of poetic sophistication, from the simple and straightforward "I Want to Hold Your Hand" (John Lennon and Paul McCartney, 1963)—

> *Oh please say to me, you'll let me be your man.*
> *And please say to me, I want to hold your hand . . .*
> *And when I touch you I feel happy inside*
> *It's such a feeling that my love I can't hide—*

to the more graphically metaphorical "I Feel the Earth Move Under My Feet" (Carole King, 1971)—

> *I feel the earth move under my feet,*
> *I feel the sky tumbling down,*
> *I feel my heart start tremblin' whenever you're around—*

to the more philosophical implication of "Kathy's Song" (Paul Simon, 1965):

> *And so you see I have come to doubt*
> *All that I once held as true;*
> *I stand alone without beliefs,*
> *The only truth I know is you.*

There is another class of lyrics that goes still further, and treats love as a more universal and at the same time more subjective feeling—love of fellow beings, love of the earth, love of life itself. Perhaps a manifestation of the same impulses that motivated the "flower children," and closely related to pro-environment, antiviolence, antidiscrimination, and antiwar sentiments, these songs have come from a wide range of composers and lyricists, from the Beatles ("Mother Nature's Son") to Bob Marley ("One Love," 1977).

> *One love, one life,*
> *Let's get together and be all right.*

The epic Woodstock gathering in 1969 drew from folk-rock singer/composer Joni Mitchell the advice to "get back to the garden" (of Eden) in "Woodstock."

A new altruism manifested itself in the 1980s and 1990s, addressing humanitarian issues in a positive manner. This has been associated with the production of large-scale benefit concerts and recordings, including the 1979 series of concerts presented by the Musicians United for Safe Energy (MUSE, against nuclear power), Band Aid, in 1984, to raise money for the underprivileged in Ethiopia, and the 1985 superstar album *We Are the World*, produced as a project to raise money for the relief of hunger in Africa, which included thirty-six stars in its roster of performers.

Sex in and of Itself

Folk blues, as we have seen in the previous chapter, treated sexual themes in a frank, matter-of-fact way; rhythm-and-blues tended to do the same. When this music began to reach a wider young public, it encountered heated opposition from the older generation in general, and from parents in particular. Those interested in producing it on a commercially profitable scale began to censor— by disguising or transmuting—references to sex, often in metaphors such as dancing or automobile driving—images common enough in the culture, to be sure. This is especially apparent in the "cover" versions of black rhythm-and-blues songs.[5]

The reappearance of overtly sexual lyrics in rock was due again to the influence of the blues. The young British groups that emerged in the 1960s were greatly influenced by American blues singers such as Howlin' Wolf, Muddy Waters, and Bo Diddley. The new groups, best typified in this regard by the Rolling Stones, introduced a more direct treatment of sex into rock; in particular, the aggressiveness and bravado illustrated, for example, by Muddy Waters's "Hoochie Coochie Man" as reflected in such Stones songs as "Satisfaction," "Parachute Woman," and "Play With Fire." The early (1964) "I'm a King Bee" was a reworking of an actual blues number.

Sexual themes have been addressed more explicitly since the mid-1970s, beginning with *disco*, and exemplified by Donna Summer's "Love to Love You Baby" (a "seventeen-minute orgasm"). Prince (Rogers Nelson) in albums of the early 1980s preempted the breaching of a broad range of taboos, from masturbation to group sex, oral sex, and incest. Beginning in the 1980s *heavy metal* groups such as Kiss, The Who, AC/DC, Judas Priest, and especially Mötley Crüe, have purveyed both sex and violence, often combined, and rendered still more explicit by visual promotional material and videos.

Dissent

Rock was born as an underground form. Its forebear, rhythm-and-blues, was to many a cultural outcast. When it was popularized and adopted by the mass of youth as "rock 'n' roll" in the 1950s, its threatening aspects diminished. But its identity as a vehicle of protest has been periodically reasserted since. Events of broad public concern have been reflected in rock songs. The Vietnam War was addressed by Country Joe and the Fish in "I-Feel-Like-I'm-Fixin'-to-Die" (Joe MacDonald, 1967)—

> *Come on all of you big strong men,*
> *Uncle Sam needs your help again.*
> *He's got himself in a terrible jam,*
> *Way down yonder in Vietnam.*
> *So put down your books and pick up a gun;*
> *We're gonna have a whole lotta fun.*

and by Jefferson Airplane in "Volunteers" (1969).

The rap of the 1980s and 1990s has brought out explicit warning protests about conditions of ghetto life, such as the "The Message" by Grandmaster Flash and the Furious Five (1981).

There has been a ratcheting up over the years of the degree of rancour expressed; at times it has approached a vicious level of alienation and hatred. On the subject of parents, for example, we need only compare the relatively goodnatured antiparental satire of "Yakety-Yak" of the 1950s (in which youth objects to having to do household chores in order to receive an allowance) with the more sober challenge posed by Bob Dylan's "The Times They Are A-Changin'" of 1963 (in which parents are asked if they wouldn't please get out of the new road if they didn't find themselves able to help), and then with the threatening vitriol of Ozzy Osbourne's "Rock 'n' Roll Rebel" (1983), who threatens his parents that if they try to make him conform, he will make them regret that they had been born.[6] Another kind of dissent (as in "grunge" or "punk") is that which is extremely introverted, expressing resignation, self-doubt, self-deprecation, and a kind of desperate and nihilistic malaise.[7]

The Psychedelic and the Surreal

When rock left the realm of simple good-time music in the 1950s and confronted the troubled 1960s with increased sophistication, the imagery of some of its lyrics became less direct, less rooted in the obvious realities of a tangible, everyday world, and more given to the exploration of the visionary and the surreal, as experienced in a subjective mental state denoted by the term "psyche-delic." For a comparatively brief period (the late 1960s), rock lyrics found their way into paths explored by poetry and painting three-quarters of a century earlier, creating and juxtaposing fantastic images with obscure or subliminal significance—a carefree life beneath the waves in a yellow submarine; a dream-world of ambulatory chessmen and a smoking caterpillar, which we enter by falling down a rabbit hole (one mapped out for us a century ago by Lewis Carroll); a courtroom scene in which an electric guitar, victim of a highway accident is brought before a jury.[8] Though the rock ambience of the 1960s began to include (and indeed to imply) the widespread use of drugs everywhere, it was the street and drug culture of San Francisco that most explicitly expressed and came to typify it. But the "acid-rock" phase was relatively short-lived, and it cannot be maintained that *all* psychedelic images or mental states in rock lyrics refer to the use of drugs.

Rock Lyrics as Poetry; Rock as Art

The claims of rock lyrics to the status of poetry are based on their creating an *esthetic distance* from the subject, sacrificing the directness of approach to a subject that is the very attribute by which we recognize folk art. It is the difference between the unabashed, unreflective, sensual exuberance of Roy Brown's "Good Rockin' Tonight"[9] and the obscure, ambiguous introversion of David Byrne's "Memories Can't Wait," in which the party is in the mind.[10] Rock, in its more sophisticated forms, has replaced folkness with artfulness. Since rock has its very roots in folkness, this artfulness presents an interesting paradox. Simon Frith has noted: "The irony was that it was on the basis of its folk conventions that rock developed its claims as a 'high art' form."[11]

Some Conclusions Concerning Rock's Style Traits

"Body Language": The Kinesics of Rock

We cannot consider our treatment of rock's style traits to be complete without taking into account what Larry Worster has called attention to as "the movement of the body in the rock experience."[12] To see a rock performance, either live or on film or video, is to recognize that rock is music not only for the ear, the mind, and the emotions, but for the body as well. This is apparent in the total *involvement* of the audience, but it applies to the performers themselves in the very act of performance. The very gestures of playing the guitar (the electric guitar is, along with the microphone, the other indispensable icon of rock) can be exaggerated into a sensational mime show in itself, with the strings intimately caressed, savagely attacked, or even (apparently) played with the teeth.

The bodily response to the beat can be magnified and endowed with a degree of energy that can erupt into an onstage choreography of volcanic proportions.

The *Apollonian* and the *Dionysian* in Rock

Mention of "body language" leads to a consideration of the dichotomy that began to appear in the 1960s between the *Apollonian* and the *Dionysian* aspects of rock. The two principal British "invaders" of the 1960s typified this dichotomy. The Beatles can be thought of as representing the Apollonian temperament—calm, poised, and disciplined—while the Rolling Stones represent the Dionysian—undisciplined, frenzied, orgiastic. Of course, as in the human experience itself, this dichotomy is more constructively viewed not as an immutable division, but as a continuum. In the center is a kind of balance of Apollonian and Dionysian tendencies—tendencies present in the work of every artist. But if the distinction is to have any meaning, it will have to be related to specific traits. Consider for a moment the following points of contrast: the Apollonian is represented by (1) minimal (though by no means absent) gesturing in performing, (2) no extremes of visible *effort* in performing, (3) a sound volume *relatively* moderate, (4) an absence of an overt "working" of the audience, (5) stage dress not significantly different from that of the audience (e.g., The Grateful Dead, Bruce Springsteen, current rap artists). By contrast the Dionysian is represented by (1) exaggerated gestures in performing the music (especially in the case of guitarists), and an often violent stage choreography (e.g., Elvis Presley—with whom, possibly, it all began, Jerry Lee Lewis, Jimi Hendrix, The Rolling Stones, The Who), (2) extreme visible effort expended in performing—sweating and the like (e.g., Bruce Springsteen), (3) extremely loud sound volume, (4) an obvious "working" of the audience (as one performer put it, "Work them up almost to the point of orgasm, and then keep working until you drop"), (5) exaggerated costuming. (Costuming is of course integral to most performing, with the exception of folk music, country blues, and rap; it became a trademark of country music as soon as that music became commercial. But what is meant here is, for example, the exaggeration of "glitter" rock and some "New Wave"—of David Bowie, Elton John, Alice Cooper, Kiss, etc.)

A Brief History of Rock's Times and Styles
Roots in Black Music

Recordings of rhythm-and-blues, the taproot of rock 'n' roll, had a somewhat narrow market in the early 1950s, largely racially defined.* Had this music

---

* But there was already evident in the parent rhythm-and-blues the influence of popularization, even of Tin Pan Alley—as indicated, for instance, in the adaptation of old "standards" from popular music, such as "Blueberry Hill" or "Blue Moon," without regard for the incongruity inherent in juxtaposing cliché "pop" lyrics with the earthier musical style of the blues.

remained, as it began, nearly the exclusive province of a young black audience, the history of American popular music would have been different. As it happened, black rhythm-and-blues, played on black radio stations in the large cities, and recorded and sold through outlets primarily intended for the black public, began to become popular with an increasingly large group of white youth. This coincided with a period of low inventiveness and pallid offerings from the established white popular music industry, and of increased independence and dissatisfaction with conventionality on the part of many young whites.

It was a disc jockey on a Cleveland radio station, Alan Freed, who first realized the potential inherent in the popularity of black rhythm-and-blues among white adolescents. In 1951 he began programming the music extensively. (It is probably true that he invented the name "rock 'n' roll"; his early radio program was called "Moondog's Rock and Roll Party.") He also arranged live stage shows of black rhythm-and-blues performers for predominantly white audiences. In 1954 he moved to New York as disc jockey for WINS, which quickly became the city's leading popular music station.

By 1954 white groups were "covering" (recording their own versions of) popular black rhythm-and-blues recordings; Bill Haley's "Shake, Rattle, and Roll" of that year, a version of an earlier recording by the blues singer Joe Turner, was among the first of the very popular "covers." But rock 'n' roll, as a new form of white popular music *based on* black rhythm-and-blues, began to evolve as a distinct music, and the black artists who were among the most popular with the growing constituency of whites were those whose styles were closest to the new idiom—Chuck Berry (b. 1926; his "Maybellene" has been cited above), Bo Diddley (Elias McDaniel, b. 1928), Fats Domino (b. 1928), and Little Richard (Richard Penniman, b. 1935). Conversely, rock 'n' roll as a primarily white phenomenon began with those white performers who most closely patterned their work on black models—men such as Bill Haley (1925–81), whose "Rock Around the Clock" (1955) has been recognized as the first white rock 'n' roll hit, and Elvis Presley (1935–77), who was strongly imprinted with the blues ambience of Memphis. It was Presley (whose coming was presaged by his early producer's search for a "white boy who could sing colored") who most forcefully exemplified the combination of black and white influences that constituted early rock. His famous "Heartbreak Hotel" (1956) accomplished the symbolic feat of achieving popularity in both black (rhythm-and-blues) and white (country-and-western) markets. A comparison of the rhythm-and-blues hit "Hound Dog" as sung by Willie Mae "Big Mama" Thornton in 1952 with the cover by Elvis Presley in 1956 shows both the similarities and the differences, as rhythm-and-blues gave rise to rock 'n' roll.

White Country Music and Early Rock

If black rhythm-and-blues was the taproot of rock, white country music was also an important root. Country music evolved out of folk roots as a conservative regional music. By the 1950s, however, its public was no longer so narrowly limited. The electric guitar had long been used in country music, and the singing guitarist, as basic to white country music as to black country blues, became the mainstay of the early rock ensemble, as typified by performers like Bill Haley, Elvis Presley, Carl Perkins (b. 1932), and Buddy Holly (1936–59), all of whom were identified with *rockabilly*.*

Rock and the Recording Industry

Given the new technology that allowed recordings to be produced nearly anywhere in the country, early rock belonged to the "indies"—small independent record companies that had been mainly responsible for supplying the hitherto limited black rhythm-and-blues market and now expanded and multiplied to meet the new demand for rock 'n' roll. This market was extremely volatile. Hits would zoom into prominence overnight, and disappear almost as fast. As in the early publishing days of Tin Pan Alley, a single hit would be enough to establish a company. The major companies, representing the conservative and declining Tin Pan Alley tradition, found themselves left out of this market. This fact had more than economic significance. As Larry Worster has pointed out: "Independence from the major corporations meant independence from the control of 'normal' mores, values, or ideological alliances. Hence Elvis and the other 'sexy' stars of the 50s were able to rise to stardom despite their controversial images; they were not controlled by the corporations."

The "Clean Teen" Market, and the Reentry of the Majors

By the early sixties a vast teenage market had emerged to be catered to. It was in catering to this market that the major record companies regained their dominance. This younger market had its own concerns to be addressed. The preoccupation with cars, for example, was reflected in any number of "hot rod" songs, such as "Little Deuce Coupe," which, in a manner curiously typical of folk art, combines vernacular expressions with oddly technical descriptions of the car's mechanical features. From California came surfing songs (best represented, probably, by the highly successful and polished recordings of the Beach Boys,

*See chapter 5, p. 90.

The Beach Boys. *Courtesy New York Public Library.*

whose "Surfing USA" became a classic). The surfing cult spread rapidly across the country, having little to do, ultimately, with the actual practice of the sport; as Belz remarks, "The surf itself had been obviated as an essential ingredient."[13]

New Infusions and Developments of the 1960s

The British Influence

The pervasive and continuous influence of English artists and groups on American rock since the 1960s fits a pattern of the long historical interdependence of British and American popular music. In one direction, English ballad opera was a staple here in Colonial times; the English music hall provided songs and a song style for our musical comedy in the nineteenth century; and Gilbert and Sullivan has been almost as popular here as in England. British folk music, a subtly pervasive presence in nearly all English music, was a source of one of the most important strains of American folk music. In the other direction, our blackface comedy, ragtime, blues, and jazz were each, in their heyday, exports that were much in demand. A broad segment of the younger British public has always followed avidly developments in American popular music—especially the fruits of our black popular culture. There have been times when the devotion to some particular phase was stronger in England than in America generally. The sixties was such a time. The earthier manifestations of the blues, which no longer enjoyed very wide popularity here, were being assiduously cultivated by a segment of British youth. Muddy Waters, Big Bill Broonzy, Howlin' Wolf, Sonny Terry, and Brownie McGhee were known in England not only from their recordings but from personal tours. As adherents of a later style, such men as Chuck Berry and Bo Diddley were well known and influential in England after they had been largely supplanted here.[14] What the English groups gave back to America turned out to be America's own black rhythm-and-blues, filtered through the temperament and experience of British youth, and giving off echoes, when the beat was a little less relentless, of the music hall and, further in the background, of English folk music.

The Rolling Stones, representing the Dionysian temperament, explored and extended the somewhat limited range staked out by the shouting, "bragging" blues, producing aggressive statements (and becoming effective personal symbols) of revolt, nihilism, and sexual bravado. The other group, representing the Apollonian aspects of rock, transcended the limiting range of the hard-edged blues. The Beatles (John Lennon, 1940–80, Paul McCartney, b. 1942, George Harrison, b. 1943, and Ringo Starr [Richard Starkey], b. 1940) began their meteoric journey across the mid-century skies of popular culture by a reintroduction of innocence—an infectious pleasure in music-making akin to what was felt in the folklike singing and playing of early black rock 'n' roll artists like Chuck Berry, and of white rockabilly singers such as the Everly Brothers. (Indeed, such questions as the probable influence of the vocal style and close harmonies of the Everly Brothers' songs of the early 1960s on the Beatles cannot be ignored; the British "invasion" brought with it much that was already our own.)

This innocence is nowhere more apparent than in their famous "I Want to Hold Your Hand" of 1964. It proved to be the quality that opened the way to a much broader range of expression for the Beatles, which their collective talent enabled them to explore. In the process came inevitably sophistication, but also musical and poetic development. Their work, from folk beginnings, gradually came to acquire that aesthetic distancing from its subject that gave it the genuine stance of art. The *Sgt. Pepper's Lonely Hearts Club Band* album (1967), in its entirety, probably best signaled that development, of which even segments of the world of fine-art music had to take notice. Writing from the vantage point of this world, musicologists such as Wilfred Mellers and composers such as Ned Rorem could regard the Beatles' work as almost pointing the way toward a kind of salvation for fine-art music, or at least one avenue of escape from the paralyzing dilemma of noncommunication in which it found itself in the 1960s.

The eclecticism that the Beatles' work came to embody (running the gamut from synthesized sound to Renaissance music and Indian ragas) was widely imitated, and has become endemic. From the mid-sixties on, so interwoven are the stories of British and American rock that it is impossible to trace native rock music without nearly constant references to what British groups are doing.

Folk Rock, Protest Rock, and Psychedelic Rock

Here in the United States the protest movements of the 1960s, as expressed in the folk and neo-folk music treated in chapter 1, created their resonances in rock. This was evidenced in the *folk rock* of the Byrds (whose "Turn, Turn, Turn" was a version of Pete Seeger's adaptation from the book of Ecclesiastes), and in much of the work of the Grateful Dead and other San Francisco groups. Folkness, protest, and the use of drugs were combined aspects of the mammoth outdoor festival at Woodstock, New York, in August 1969, which created, however briefly, a sense of community (a "Woodstock Nation"), not only among the half million young people who attended, but among the like-minded young throughout the world. Unfortunately, the negative potential of such mass gatherings was tragically revealed by the violence at the Altamont, California, concert by the Rolling Stones in December of that same year, which dealt a severe blow to the aspirations, and the acceptance by the broader public, of the "Woodstock Nation."

Black Rock: Soul and Motown

African-American rhythm-and-blues, the dominant parent of rock, continued to evolve among black musicians in the "soul synthesis" treated in the preceding chapter. Arnold Shaw has written that in the 1960s, "black music became blacker than it had ever been, more Gospel-oriented than it had ever been. The development came with an intensification of the struggle for equality, the rise of black nationalism, the growth of black pride—'Black is Beautiful'—and the emergence of a black-power movement."[15] The blues shouting, screaming, and grunting over a rock band backup of a bass riff and a strong backbeat of James Brown's "Cold Sweat" of 1967 are representative of this aspect of the *soul* of the 1960s. In contrast to this, the *Motown* sound (derived from "Motor Town," a nickname for Detroit) was represented by the Supremes, who were, to use Brock Helander's words, "prime purveyors of the sophisticated, highly commercial, and sometimes bland vocal group sound that found acceptance with white audiences as well as with black." "You Can't Hurry Love" by Diana Ross and the Supremes (1966) is representative.

The Complexities and Diversities of Rock from the 1970s to the Present
Hard Rock and Heavy Metal

The loud, aggressive, superheated, Dionysian aspects of rock were continued and exaggerated in *hard rock* and *heavy metal*.* The beginnings of hard rock can be detected in the sound, actions, and stance of Elvis Presley himself, in his cover of "Hound Dog," and in Jerry Lee Lewis and Little Richard. Hard rock emerged more overtly in those British bands that were following in the footsteps of the American hard-edged blues performers such as Howlin' Wolf and Muddy Waters—principally the Rolling Stones, but also Cream, with Eric Clapton. As hard rock became more the "mainstream" in the early 1970s, with performers like Bob Seger, the aggressive fringes adopted the features associated with heavy metal. As Joe Stuessy describes the distinction:

> If hard rock was loud, heavy metal was louder; if hard rock was simple and repetitive, heavy metal was simpler and more repetitive; if hard rock singers shouted, heavy metal singers screamed; if hard rockers experimented with distortion and feedback, heavy metalers distorted everything; if hard rock favored long instrumental improvisations, heavy metal offered longer, louder, and more dazzling instrumental solos; if hard rock was *countercultural*, heavy metal would come to specialize in the *anticultural*.[16]

The British seemed to lead in this development, with groups such as Led Zepplen (whose "Whole Lotta Love" of 1970, with its heavy bass riff and obsessive repetition in the main sections, its electronic manipulation and sound effects in a middle section, and the explicit sexuality of its lyrics, is representative). Presently, Led Zepplen and other British groups, principally Black Sabbath and Judas Priest, took heavy metal a further step out of the mainstream by introducing and capitalizing on occult themes of black magic, witchcraft, and devil worship, as well as the darker aspects of Celtic and Greek mythology, and of medieval lore, all of which were more familiar to British youth who grew up surrounded by castles, and whose cultural heritage included dark myths and legends, than to Americans, for whom the scariest themes were those from horror movies. These themes were exaggerated, of course, in the cover art and promotional posters and advertising. American heavy metal groups of the 1970s included Iron Butterfly, Blue Cheer, Van Halen, MC5, and Blue Öyster Cult.

---

*The aptly descriptive designation "heavy metal" is said to have come from the lyrics to a 1968 song performed by the group Steppenwolf that included the phrase "heavy metal thunder."

The rock group Kiss. *Courtesy New York Public Library.*

A further step away from mainstream rock were the visual and theatrical aspects of some heavy metal. Black leather and elaborate hardware, including chains, had become familiar in costuming. Makeup contributed to the creation of fantastic and abnormal stage personae. Alice Cooper (the name of the band, which was also the stage name of the lead singer, Vincent Furnier, was derived from the name of a woman allegedly burned at the stake for witchcraft in the 1500s) featured black eye makeup. Kiss, another group, used full character makeup, personifying what one observer has identified as "the bloody, ghoul-like image of a cat, a lover, a spaceman, and a devil."[17] The fascination engendered in a jaded public by the sensational packaging of androgynous stage personae, such as Ziggy Stardust (a character portrayed by David Bowie) and Boy George, must account in part for their success. Stage action pursued a demonic path from the routine destruction of musical instruments (by The Who and others) to the killing of live animals onstage (by Alice Cooper and Ozzy Osbourne).

While heavy metal, to qualify as such, incorporates much of the time the loudness, the pounding beat, and the distortion which is its trademark, this frequently masks musical sophistication and virtuosity, especially on the electric guitar. In Blue Öyster Cult's "(Don't Fear) The Reaper" (the Grim Reaper being death itself) of 1976, there can be heard, over and between the statements of the obsessive four-note bass riff, guitar solos of considerable complexity. Classically trained Edward Van Halen brought a new level of performance to the electric guitar; any of the Van Halen albums illustrate this, but the famous "Eruption" of 1978 is an astounding display of virtuosity, which includes a transformed quote from a famous Kreutzer study known to every student of the violin.

Punk, Hardcore, and New Wave

In a popular art form fed from the underground, there is always a *new* underground ready to emerge when the current underground becomes generally accepted. In the 1960s, '70s, and '80s there were a succession of these. The British group the Sex Pistols has been described as the "archetypal punk rock band," noted "for their adamantly incompetent playing, cynically vituperative and anticommercial lyrics, and deliberate onstage vulgarity."[18] At the grassroots level, *punk* was the music of teenage "garage bands"—bands with little musical skill, but with energy and an attitude, overwhelmingly negative. Nowhere is this "nihilistic punk metabolism"[19] more evident than in the names of the groups, which call up images normally considered aberrant, repulsive, or destructive— the Mutants, the Ghouls, the Weirdos, Circle Jerks, Flesheaters, Twisted Sister, Crime, Damage, Slash, Search and Destroy, and Black Flag (a symbol for anarchy, but also a well-known brand of insecticide).

The 1980s brought changes to the underground scene. *Hardcore*, while still expressing dissent in a rough-edged and purposely unimaginative musical style, presents songs that focus on specific issues, rather than anger for its own sake. Lyrics* could be found that dealt, for example, with the use of live animals in scientific experiments ("Mad Scientists' Ball" by Dead Silence), with the environment ("Progress" by Clown Alley), and with tyranny and oppression ("Dr. Harley" by Rhythm Pigs). Heavy satire, in the manner of Jonathan Swift, was heard in "Kill the Poor" (1980) by The Dead Kennedys, a San Francisco group. The lyrics "satirically praise the U. S. government for developing the neutron bomb that can kill people and leave property undamaged and suggest that, in order to save money otherwise wasted on welfare, the bomb be used to kill poor people." [20]**

Also out of punk there came a movement more sophisticated in both music and lyrics, known as *new wave*. It was best represented in the work of David Byrne, leader of Talking Heads ("talking head" is a TV term for a head-and-shoulders shot of a person talking—turn off the sound on a TV discussion program, and this is all you are aware of). As a measure of the musical and textural sophistication, the backup vocal group has its own material, sometimes creating a kind of counterpoint in which solo singer and vocal group or groups sing contrasting

* Lyrics are typically so difficult to understand in performance that they are published on lyric sheets, which accompany the records, or in fan magazines known as "fanzines."

** As a similar instance of vitriolic satire, Katherine Charlton cites Irish satirist Jonathan Swift's *A Modest Proposal*, from the eighteenth century, in which he suggested that the English solve the problem of starvation in Ireland by eating Irish children.

Bob Marley. *Courtesy New York Public Library.*

material, either sequentially or simultaneously. "Once in a Lifetime" (1980) from *Remain in Light* is illustrative. The satire, instead of attacking a political target, was turned to more quasi-philosophical questions and couched in the obscure language and metaphors of some contemporary poetry. This intellectual stance drew the attention both of a public not previously known for its devotion to rock and of the mass media. David Byrne widened his range from that of singer-guitarist-composer for a band with quasi-punk beginnings to become a film director, actor, designer, photographer, and writer.

Reggae

American rhythm-and-blues, reaching the Caribbean island of Jamaica via radio and records, became very popular around mid-century with the predominantly black population. The Jamaican music that evolved from this influence, *reggae* (an outgrowth of the earlier *ska*), spread to the United States, and indeed worldwide, in the 1970s and early 1980s. The rhythm of reggae, like that of Calypso music from another part of the West Indies (Trinidad), is strongly Caribbean in its syncopation. The heavy relentless beat of hard rock is replaced by a more melodious ostinato, and the offbeats are ornamented with a complex overlaying of cross-rhythms, performed with a variety of Latin percussion sounds, either acoustic or synthesized. The lyrics of many of the songs express concern for the poor and downtrodden, but usually without the angry and threatening tone of heavy metal, and often in the storytelling form of the ballad (as in "Buffalo Soldier," about the conscripting of black men into the Union Army to kill Indians). The most popular group was Bob Marley and the Wailers, whose "Get Up Stand Up" (1973) is representative of the style, and the positive nature of their "message" songs.

Rock's Peripheral Offspring

Rock, potent and fecund, has in the last quarter century not only evolved into a family of different styles in itself, but in its contact with other forms of popular music has fathered many "natural children" on its periphery. Space allows us merely to note the existence of disco, soft rock, country rock, and the fusion of rock with jazz, and with the classical musics of both West and East.

The Rock Video

Until the 1980s the visual presentation of rock songs—apart from live performances, which had become spectacularly elaborate in the case of superstars—had been confined to films. Rock remained primarily an aural form, with radio and records its prime media. But with the combined advance of videotape technology and cable TV with its multiple channels, this changed. In August 1981 MTV, the first all-rock channel on cable television, began broadcasting. Record album promoters, who had long been in the habit of sending free albums to radio stations for airplay, now hastened to produce and send free video versions of new songs to MTV, and to the other TV stations, which soon began to broadcast rock videos. The video became a powerful new weapon in the endless battle to promote artists and records. Rock videos are not intended primarily for sale themselves, but are designed to sell the records they are "about." As such, they provide consumers with an elaborately crafted visual *iconography* of the performer, with his or her image built up to larger-than-life proportions. Sometimes they are merely visually edited presentations of live performances (similar in effect to TV coverage of a baseball game), with close-ups of the performers, and shots of the frenzied audience, including girls rushing the stage to kiss the male star, and others "stage diving"—jumping on stage and then diving into the audience waiting to catch them.

"Conceptual" videos, on the other hand, use intercutting to outside scenes, sometimes featuring the star in some imaginary story situation (which may illustrate the song's "plot" or meaning, or be unrelated to it). In the more elaborately "staged" videos, such as those of Michael Jackson, there is a rapidly paced collage of fantasy images, placing the star in a series of exotic surroundings. At times this results in segments with a sustained mood; at other times there is a break-neck pace, the eye bombarded with the kaleidoscope of fast-changing images using all of the manipulative techniques available—slowed-down or speeded-up motion, superimposed images, rapid zooming, distortion, "morphing" (where one image changes into another), and cartooning. These are devices familiar from the TV commercial, with which the rock video, which is also a sales pitch, has much in common.

There are some rock videos, such as Pearl Jam's "Jeremy," that deal in social commentary, with comment or interpretation, beyond what is in the song itself, added visually. But for the most part rock videos, like the records they are designed to sell, deal in entertainment, not real life. It has been pointed out, with justification, that the more sexually oriented videos (produced and directed by men) present a male "dream world" in which women (numerous, attractive, and afflicted with nymphomania) are presented as devoid of individuality, unique-ness, humanity, or any capacity for genuine feelings.

Rap and Hip Hop

In concluding our survey of rock, we come full circle to confront once again, as we did in the 1950s with rhythm-and-blues, the potency of African-American musical styles in American popular music—this time, in the 1980s and '90s, with the emergence of *rap*. Rap does not transcend, but rather celebrates (in the minds of some black writers) the separateness of black culture, and black popular music. It has been hailed as bringing together "a tangle of some of the most com-plex social, cultural, and political issues in contemporary American society."

Rap music has been defined by Tricia Rose as "a form of rhymed storytelling accompanied by highly rhythmic, electronically based music."[21] Shaw has called it "rhymed street slang delivered at breakneck speed."[22] It emerged from the street culture of the South Bronx in New York City in the mid-1970s. Its antecedents can be found in African chanted recitation, in spoken blues and the spoken inter-polations of soul singers, and in the "toasting" of Jamaican disc jockeys (the recitation of doggerel over prerecorded segments of rhythm).[23] It was recorded by small independent record companies, and the release of "Rapper's Delight" by Sugarhill Gang in 1979 brought it into broader notice. An early and by now classic hit was "The Message" (1981) by Grandmaster Flash and the Furious Five. The piece had a specific political and social message about conditions in the black ghetto, and eventually appeared in a video version. As is typical of pure rap, it has spoken (not sung) patter, against a backup reduced to the essentials of rhythm, overlaid with occasional electronic effects. As rap has evolved it has brought in other ingredients of rock—the rock guitar and the bass riff, for example.

Yet rap remains distanced from rock. Perhaps it is more related to the talking blues; perhaps its narrative aspect marks it as some kind of extension of the ballad. Wherever placed, rap certainly is, as Rose has said, "a black cultural expression," and as such cannot be well understood apart from this culture. The term "hip hop" evidently has multiple meanings. Hyphenated as *hip-hop*, it has been defined as a primarily electronic subgenre of rap, of which "The Message" is cited as an example. But *hip hop*, unhyphenated, is also used (by Rose) to denote the culture itself, of which the major components are graffiti, breakdancing, and rap.

FURTHER READING

Unfortunately for the serious reader, many of the books available about rock have little to offer but what Gammond has called "the nauseous claptrap of the pop publicist." Well-executed historical writing is rare; serious critical writing still rarer. Reference works date rapidly but are useful. This list begins with three of the best of these, then proceeds to historical and critical writing.

Reference works

Helander, Brock. *The Rock Who's Who*. 2d ed. New York: Schirmer Books, 1996.
> 849 tightly packed yet readable pages, with extensive discography, and a comprehensive index listing individuals, groups, and songs, and an extensive bibliography by individuals.

Larkin, Colin, ed. *The Guiness Encyclopedia of Popular Music*. 6 vols. New York: Stockton , 1995.
> Entries A–Z by individuals, groups, and shows. Bibliography by artist and subject.

Stambler, Irwin, ed. *Encyclopedia of Pop, Rock, and Soul*. Rev. ed. New York: St. Martin's, 1989.

Historical and critical writing

Belz, Carl. *The Story of Rock*. 2d ed. New York: Oxford University Press, 1972.
> Valuable, in spite of its age.

Charlton, Katherine. *Rock Musical Styles: A History*. Dubuque, IA: Wm. C. Brown, 1989.

Frith, Simon. *Sound Effects: Youth, Leisure, and the Politics of Rock 'n' Roll*. New York: Pantheon, 1981.

Gillett, Charlie. *The Sound of the City*. Rev. ed. New York: Pantheon, 1984.

Gore, Tipper. *Raising PG Kids in an X-rated Society*. Nashville: Abingdon, 1987.
> If this subject interests you, read both this and chapter 5 in Walser, below, and make up your own mind.

Marcus, Greil. *Mystery Train: Images of America in Rock 'n' Roll Music*. New York: Dutton, 1982.

Pattison, Robert. *The Triumph of Vulgarity: Rock Music in the Mirror of Romanticism*. New York: Oxford University Press, 1987.

Rose, Tricia. *Black Noise: Rap Music and Black Culture in Contemporary America*. Hanover & London: Wesleyan University Press, 1994.

Stuessy, Joe. *Rock and Roll: Its History and Stylistic Development*. Englewood Cliffs, NJ: Prentice-Hall, 1990.

Walser, Robert. *Running with the Devil: Power, Gender, and Madness in Heavy Metal Music*. Hanover & London: Wesleyan University Press, 1993.
> If the subject of violence, sex, etc., in heavy metal interests you, read Walser's chapter 5 and the Gore book, cited above, and make up your own mind.

Periodicals

Rolling Stone. Biweekly (New York).
> This has become a general-interest periodical, with a special emphasis on popular music but with articles on American culture, politics, and art.

Popular Music and Society. Quarterly, Bowling Green State University Popular Press, Bowling Green, OH.
Popular Music. Monthly, Cambridge University Press, England.

These last two periodicals publish scholarly and increasingly specialized articles on rock

Projects

1. Find and listen to two early "covers" (recordings by white musicians derived from earlier recordings by black musicians) from the 1950s, and their original versions. Write a descriptive comparison, trying to account for the differences.

2. Do a taped essay on the role of the disc jockey in modern popular music, beginning with Alan Freed. Include taped excerpts of several current disc jockeys, with a brief commentary on their delivery, content, and style.

3. Interview a local disc jockey, and produce a paper profiling the job (both positive and negative aspects) and recording his or her opinions or current trends in popular music, the influence and responsibilities of the disc jockey, etc.

4. Interview the manager, or a knowledgeable employee, of a local record store, and produce a paper on a topic such as (1) the buying habits of the local publics (e.g., percentages for rock, for country, for classical, for folk, for soul, for "underground," etc.); (2) any recognizable characteristics (e.g., apparent age, occupation, dress, behavior, etc.) of the various publics; (3) the store's handling of "underground" recordings; (4) the effect of rock videos on the sales of specific albums; (5) their experiences in the handling of hit albums (the predictability of hits, the buying rush—how strong and how *long*, etc.); or make up your own approach.

5. Make a study of the complex array of popularity charts in *Billboard* magazine, the trade journal of American popular music.

6. If you have some background or interest in English literature, assemble a small collection of rock lyrics from the 1990s and try to confront the question of rock "poetry"—the quality and consistency of the imagery, the extent to which it can stand on its own as poetry, and so forth.

7. Describe and analyze the theatrical aspects of a live rock concert you have attended.

8. Write a paper entitled "The Rock Video as Synthesized Theater."

9. Tipper Gore's *Raising PG Kids in an X-rated Society* and Robert Walser's *Running with the Devil: Power, Gender, and Madness in Heavy Metal Music*, chapter 5, present opposing views on a topic of importance to parents. Read both, make up your own mind, and then present your own views in a paper.

Notes

1. The titles of two fairly early books on rock, both dating from the early 1970s, express these aspects of revolt and urban ("street") ambience. George Melly's *Revolt into Style* (Garden City, NY: Anchor/Doubleday, 1971) deals primarily with the British scene, but takes its title from a comment that Elvis Presley had turned "revolt into a style." Charlie Gillett's *The Sound of the City*, 1st ed. (New York: Dell, 1970) begins with an introduction subtitled "Dancing in the Street," wherein he writes that "rock and roll was perhaps the first form of popular culture to celebrate without reservation characteristics of city life that had been among the most criticized. In rock and roll, the strident, repetitive sounds of city life were, in effect, reproduced as melody and rhythm" (1). Simon Frith, however, writes: "Rock 'n' Roll . . . has celebrated street culture both for its participants and for its suburban observers, and by the mid-1960s such a celebration meant more to the latter group" (in *Popular Music 1: Folk or Popular? Distinctions, Influences, Continuities*, ed. Richard Middleton and David Horn [Cambridge: Cambridge University Press, 1987], 168).

2. The link with boogie-woogie (see chapter 6) is shown clearly in such numbers as Lloyd Price's "Mailman Blues" (New World-249), but it is also in Little Richard's "Every Hour" on the same album. Both are in the classical 12-bar blues form.

3. The Latin beat is clearly illustrated in Leiber and Stoller's "What About Us?" written for the Coasters. Dating from 1959, this was perhaps rock 'n' roll's first protest song (New World-249). An interesting mixture of Latin and African rhythms can be heard in "New Orleans" on the same album.

4. Evan Eisenberg, *The Recording Angel: Explorations in Phonography.*

5. The much-cited example of successive versions of Hank Ballard's "Work with Me, Annie" makes this point. The original, from 1954, had a blues form with a strong backbeat. Its code phrase, "work with me," was thereafter laundered to "roll with me" (as sung by Etta James), and then to "dance with me" (as sung by Georgia Gibbs).

6. The author is indebted to Joe Stuessy for the last two examples, found in his book *Rock and Roll: Its History and Development.*

7. For one example see "Blank Generation" by Richard Hell. The lyrics are quoted in *Best of New Wave Rock* (New York: Warner Bros., ca. 1978), 51.

8. See "Yellow Submarine," by Lennon and McCartney for the Beatles (Capitol SW 153); "White Rabbit," by Grace Slick for Jefferson Airplane (RCA LSP 3766); and "Electric Guitar," by David Byrne for the Talking Heads (SIRE SRK 6076).

9. Roy Brown, "Good Rockin' Tonight" (copyright 1948): Wynonie "Blues" Harris's 1947 recording of the rhythm-and-blues classic is on NW–261, which reprints the lyrics.

10. David Byrne "Memories Can't Wait" is on *Fear of Music* (Sire SRK 6076), with complete text.

11. Simon Frith, *Sound Effects: Youth, Leisure, and the Politics of Rock 'n' Roll* (New York: Pantheon, 1981), 30.

12. Larry Worster, in correspondence with the author.

13. Belz, *The Story of Rock*, 97.

14. As Muddy Waters said to an American college audience, "I had to come to you behind the Rolling Stones and the Beatles. I had to go to England to get here!" Quoted in Arnold Shaw, *Honkers and Shouters* (New York: Macmillan, 1978), 526.

15. Arnold Shaw, *Dictionary of American Pop/Rock*, 364.

16. Joe Stuessy, *Rock and Roll: Its History and Stylistic Development*, 306.

17. Katherine Charlton, *Rock Musical Styles: A History*, 164.

18. Brock Helander, *The Rock Who's Who*, 2d ed., 615.

19. Peter Belsito and Bob Davis, *Hardcore California: A History of Punk and New Wave* (Berkeley, CA: The Last Gasp of San Francisco, ca. 1983).

20. Katherine Charlton, *Rock Musical Styles: A History*, 207–08. "Kill the Poor" is on Cherry Red Records Cherry 16.

21. The quotes from Tricia Rose in this and the preceding paragraph are found in *Black Noise: Rap Music and Black Culture in Contemporary America*, 2.

22. Shaw, *Dictionary of American Pop/Rock*, 301.

23. See John Rockwell's article on rap in the *New Grove Dictionary of American Music.*

Part Three

Popular Sacred Music

Photo by Dorothea Lange

America is too young to have been able to nurture such highly cultivated worship music as is represented, for example, by the rich flowerings of Gregorian chant, elaborate settings of the Roman Catholic Mass, or the Lutheran cantata. Nor, the question of time aside, have the conditions been present that could have produced such flowerings. The reasons are many—our broad spectrum of religious denominations, our inbred distrust of the ecclesiastical organization and wealth that are indispensable for building a tradition of highly refined religious art, and our increased secularization. The intensity of focus has been lacking here that in Europe, from the Middle Ages up to the time of the social and industrial revolutions, could put large resources of talent at the service of the Church, and produce, at the apex, a *Notre Dame Mass* or a *St. Matthew Passion*. Thus our output of what might be called cultivated religious music has been meager, and up to now mostly derivative.

At the relatively unconscious and unlearned level of folk, or near-folk, art, on the other hand, we have produced religious music that, in accord with its homely character, has become deeply embedded in the culture of a broad segment of our people. Thus the most significant of our religious music is that which has remained closest to folk sources. Like popular music (and it is popular music in the sense of the large market it has had for a century and a half, and the commercial establishment that has grown up to serve this market), it draws its significance not primarily from its aesthetic value but from its meaning in the lives of those who sing it, and from the response it evokes. Indeed, immediacy and depth of response, without the distancing of any art-consciousness, are part and parcel of the phenomena of both folk and popular art. Charles Ives, one of our greatest composers but also a perceptive thinker, pointed up in the epilogue to his *Essays Before a Sonata* the importance of this near-folk music to those whose music it is. He is speaking to the American composer, but his words have substance for anyone who would understand American music:

> The man "born down to Babbitt's Corners" may find a deep appeal in the simple but acute Gospel hymns of the New England "camp meetin'" of a generation or so ago. He finds in them—some of them—a vigor, a depth of feeling, a natural-soil rhythm, a sincerity—emphatic but inartistic—which, in spite of a vociferous sentimentality, carries him nearer the "Christ of the people" than does the *Te Deum* of the greatest cathedral. . . . [If] the Yankee can reflect the fervency with which "his gospels" were sung—the fervency of "Aunt Sarah," who scrubbed her life away for her brother's ten orphans, the fervency with which this woman, after a fourteen-hour work-day on the farm, would hitch up and drive five miles through the mud and rain to "prayer meetin'," her one articulate outlet for the fulness of her unselfish soul—if he can reflect the fervency of such a spirit, he may find there a local color that will do all the world good. If his music can but catch that spirit by being a part with itself, it will come somewhere near his ideal—and it will be American, too.

Chapter 8

From Psalm Tune to Rural Revivalism

Psalmody in America

Probably the first musical sounds from the Old World that the indigenous inhabitants heard what is now the United States were the psalm tunes sung by Protestant settlers and sailors. French Huguenots were singing psalms from their psalter in Florida half a century before the landing of the English Separatists at Plymouth. At the other edge of the continent, the California Indians were fascinated by the psalm singing of Sir Francis Drake's men in 1579. When the first permanent settlements in Massachusetts were established, psalters were an important part of the few precious possessions brought over. Psalm tunes were the most important body of religious music in constant use throughout those colonies founded by the English and Dutch, almost until the time of the Revolution. They were subsequently largely replaced by the music of hymns, anthems, and fuging tunes, but many of the old psalm tunes have survived, and tune names such as "Toulon," "Windsor," "York," "Bristol," "Old 104th," "Old 112th," "Old 120th," and the famous "Old 100th" bespeak their presence in every major modern hymnal.

Calvinism and the Psalms

A glance at a map of Europe, together with some understanding of the situation there at the time of the Reformation, will make clear why it was the psalm tune, rather than the Lutheran chorale or the venerable and cultivated music of the Roman Catholic Church, that dominated our early religious music on the eastern seaboard, and, with its related progeny, left its mark on our sacred music for three hundred years. We cannot here fill in the background; suffice it to say that most of our earliest permanent settlers there brought with them not only their psalters and their psalm tunes, but their pronounced aversion to state religion and temporal ecclesiastical hierarchy and power—all of which, to them, was summed up in one word: "popery." This was to have a profound effect on the development of American consciousness and culture.

Calvinism dominated the religious practices of a large portion of our early east coast settlers. Music in the Calvinist churches was rather severely limited to the unaccompanied unison singing of metrical versions of the psalms. This was but one manifestation of the ancient and ever-present dichotomy between the musician and the theologian on the question of music in worship. The musician wishes to use the utmost skill and craft, and give the music free rein; the theologian wishes to keep music simple and ensure its subordination to the worship itself. The controversy is nearly as old as the Christian Church itself, and the history of church music is the history of the swinging of the pendulum back and forth between the two positions. The Church recognized, as the Greeks had long before, the power of music over the human emotions. As two recent writers have aptly summarized the situation: "The Christian church has carried on a long, often fruitful relationship with music, governed, however, by the kind of uneasy truce man had struck with fire."[1] It so happened that in the sixteenth century the pendulum swung decisively to the side of strict control of music, in both the Roman Catholic Church and the new Reformed Church, but much more drastically and completely in the latter. In the Reformed Church, the new broom had no weight of musical tradition to encumber it. Psalm singing, then, was the product of a musical simplicity enforced on theological grounds.

Psalm Tunes and Psalters

With John Calvin's exhortation to psalm singing came the need for metered and rhymed versions of the psalms, and tunes to which they could be sung by entire congregations, and not by trained choirs. This need was met by a series of psalters, the first published in Strasbourg in 1539. The sixteenth century thus saw the establishment of two great bodies of sacred tunes, the Lutheran chorales and the psalmody of the Reformed Church. They share similar characteristics (as well as some of the same tunes): they are easily singable melodies of fairly simple construction, with vestiges of the old modal scales already encountered in our study of folk music.

The most significant psalter, for us, was the first book printed in what is now the United States, *The Whole Booke of Psalmes Faithfully Translated into English Metre*, published in Boston in 1640 and nicknamed the *Bay Psalm Book*. It was no mean achievement for a community of fewer than twenty thousand people that had established itself on the edge of the American wilderness scarcely more than a decade before. The motive of these scholars is revealed in characteristic words at the close of the preface (see Fig. 8-1).

> If therefore the verſes are not alwayes
> ſo ſmooth and elegant as ſome may deſire
> or expect; let them conſider that Gods
> Altar needs not our polliſhings: Ex. 20. for
> wee have reſpected rather a plaine tranſla-
> tion, then to ſmooth our verſes with the
> ſweetnes of any paraphraſe, and ſoe have
> attended Conſcience rather then Elegance,
> fidelity rather then poetry, in tranſlating
> the hebrew words into engliſh language,
> and Davids poetry into engliſh meetre;
>
> that ſoe wee may ſing in Sion the Lords
> ſongs of prayſe according to his owne
> will; untill hee take us from hence,
> and wipe away all our teares, &
> bid us enter into our maſters
> ioye to ſing eternall
> Halleluiahs.

Figure 8–1. From the preface to the *Bay Psalm Book* (facsimile reprint, University of Chicago Press, 1956).

Two Divergent "Ways"

By the 1720s a hundred years of psalm singing in America had produced two discernible traditions, simultaneous but widely divergent. They amounted to a written and an oral practice. In the written practice, the tunes would be sung as they were notated in the psalmbooks of the time. But psalmbooks were few, and few in the congregations, especially in rural areas, could read music. This led to the practice of "lining out," in which the deacon, or precentor, sang or recited each line before it was sung by the congregation. This oral practice, called the *Usual Way*, led to a severe shrinking in the number of tunes in common use, and a marked slowing of the tempo. (One observer noted, "I myself have twice in one Note paused to take Breath.") This folk practice in singing the psalms has persisted to this day in the parts of the Old World from which it came, as can be heard in the Gaelic psalmody as sung in the Free Church of Scotland on the Isle of Lewis, in the Outer Hebrides.*

For an example of the survival of the Usual Way in this country, we could listen to the singing in some rural churches in the South, especially in the

*This unusual sound can be heard on *Gaelic Psalmody*, issued in 3 cassettes by Lewis Recordings, 42 Newvalley, Stornoway, Isle of Lewis PA86ODH, Scotland.

Appalachians. In "**Amazing Grace**," as sung in a Baptist church in Kentucky, for example, we can hear the "lining out," and the slow, individualized singing. (See Ex. 8-4, p.150)

Reform and Instruction

Opposition to the Usual Way on the part of a more musically literate portion of the populace grew more outspoken as time went on, and came to a head in the 1720s. What the reformers, or proponents of what was called *Regular Singing*, wanted to make happen could be accomplished only by teaching people to read music. This is exactly what they set out to do. Instruction books such as *An Introduction to the Singing of Psalm Tunes in a Plain and Easy Method* (Rev. John Tufts) appeared in the 1720s, and went through many editions. As intimated in their titles, these books represented only the first of a long series of assaults by American ingenuity on the perennial problem of how to make music easier for the uninitiated. From *An Introduction . . . in a Plain and Easy Method* through *Ragtime in Ten Easy Lessons* this elusive goal has been pursued—often with some success.

But no one has ever learned to perform music just by reading a book. The need for instruction by a "master," and for practicing together under his tutelage, produced one of the most important and pervasive musical and social institutions in our early history—the singing-school.

The Singing-School Tradition

That uniquely American institution, the singing-school, may have had its beginnings in New England, but ultimately it spread far and wide. In the cities its descendants are represented by the numerous choral societies, great and small. In rural areas it retained its original characteristics longest; here, as a social as well as musical gathering, it brightened the routine of lives that were otherwise all too often harsh and dreary. The firm place and meaning of the singing-school in rural American life before this century can hardly be better attested to than by the following excerpt from the reminiscences, in folk verse form, of a pioneer woman writing of her life in Sangamon County, Illinois, in the mid-nineteenth century.

> *We had so few things to give us pleasure*
> *The memories of such times I love to treasure.*
> *Our singing school, where we looked forward to meet*
> *Our beloved teacher, and his pupils to greet.*
> *Our singing books, few here now, ever saw*

The old patent notes, fa, sol, la, sol, fa, me, la.
There were some good voices to lead the rest,
All long since gone to the home of the blest.
I seem to hear their voices now singing, loud and clear
And almost feel their presence hovering near.

How the Singing-Schools Worked

From the 1720s on, the singing-school movement gradually picked up momentum, and the period 1760 to 1800, encompassing the Revolution and the founding of the new nation, saw its greatest activity, especially in New England. The singing-school was a private venture, taught by an itinerant master. The school would be advertised in advance in the community, and subscriptions taken. The singing-school itself was not a denominational institution, and in fact the instruction did not always take place in the church; a room in a schoolhouse or local tavern was sometimes used. Two or three meetings a week for three months seems to have been a common schedule. If the singing-master had published a tunebook the pupils would be expected to buy and use it, thus somewhat augmenting his income, which was seldom large.[2]

The solmization syllables (fa, sol, la, mi) were invariably taught as a basis for learning to sing the correct pitches, and the words of the pieces were not allowed to be sung until the syllables had been mastered. As an ingenious device for getting the tempo exact, homemade pendulums (of a length carefully specified) were recommended, and Billings gives the following directions for making them in the preface to his *Continental Harmony*: "Make a pendulum of common thread well waxed, and instead of a bullet take a piece of heavy wood turned perfectly round, about the bigness of a pullet's egg, and rub them over, either with chalk, paint or white-wash, so that they may be seen plainly by candle-light." (It was usually stipulated that the students bring their own candles.) At the close of the term, there was almost always a public concert, or "exhibition." The pupils thus got a chance to show off what they had learned; the singing-master then moved on to another community.

Contemporary accounts show that the pupils were mostly young people. It seems, from the directions for the conduct of a singing-school that have survived, that the teacher's ability to keep order was at least as important as his ability to teach music—an observation that has a familiar ring. Yet there is little doubt that the singing-schools generally accomplished their objectives very well. After the term was over, one or more of the ablest pupils might start teaching themselves, or even try their hand at composing psalm settings, anthems, or fuging tunes. Thus the singing-schools, in addition to raising the general level of musical literacy and expanding the repertory of music available, played a vital part in encouraging the development of native composers.

Billings of Boston and His Contemporaries

Not every singing-master became a composer, of course, but the number that did is substantial. In fact the singing-school movement gave us our first school of indigenous American composers, who worked under the most fruitful conditions a composer can experience: writing music for which there is a clear demand and appreciation on the part of a well-defined public. This fruitful period for our first native composers did not last long—near-ideal conditions for art never do—but the productivity was intense (one scholar has termed it a "golden age"), for one authority has estimated that by 1800 there were over a thousand different compositions in print in American tunebooks, most of them by native composers.[3]

The singing-masters and composers were for the most part humble craftsmen, artisans, or small businessmen, who composed and taught in addition to plying their trades. The names and trades of these native pioneers read like a litany of eighteenth-century New England names and occupations, and perhaps help to give the flavor of the singing-school movement in a way nothing else can: Supply Belcher, tavernkeeper; David Belknap, farmer and mechanic; William Billings, tanner; Amos Bull, storekeeper; Oliver Holden, carpenter; Jeremiah Ingalls, cooper; Jacob Kimball, lawyer; Abraham Maxim, farmer and schoolteacher; Justin Morgan, horse breeder; Timothy Swan, hatter.

William Billings (1746–1800), the best known among these, was also the most prolific, inventive, and enthusiastically dedicated. In 1770, at the age of twenty-four, he published the first tunebook in America consisting entirely of music by a single composer; his *New-England Psalm-Singer* contained more than 120 compositions. In the next quarter century he brought out five more books, whose titles give something of their flavor and usage: *The Singing Master's Assistant* (1778), *Music in Miniature* (1779), *The Psalm-Singer's Amusement* (1781), *The Suffolk Harmony* (1786), and *The Continental Harmony* (1794).

He became quite well known in his time. Yet he was never able to give up his tanning trade permanently, and in fact records show him to have held down several civil posts in order to help make ends meet for himself and his family—even keeping hogs off the streets, and keeping the streets clean in Boston's Eleventh Ward. He died in severe poverty.

Billings, a friend of Samuel Adams and Paul Revere, was an ardent patriot, and his patriotic song **"Chester"** (Ex. 8-1) was one of the most popular songs of the Revolution. With its first stanza, it appeared in 1770 in *The New-England Psalm-Singer*; during the Revolution further stanzas were added, with the names of five British generals, and the boast that "Their Vet'rans flee before our Youth,/ And Gen'rals yield to beardless Boys"—and it was in this form that it appeared in *The Singing Master's Assistant* of 1778.[4]

Example 8–1. "Chester"

Billings was a colorful and energetic writer of prose as well, as his salty, conversational, and sometimes lengthy prefaces to his tunebooks attest. His philosophical approach to music, as well as to politics, was one of independence and self-reliance. Oft-quoted statements of his—such as "Nature is the best Dictator"; "I don't think myself confin'd to any Rules for Composition laid down by any that went before me"; and "I think it best for every Composer to be his own Carver"—may, taken out of their own context and the context of his work, suggest a degree of rebellious iconoclasm far beyond Billings's actual intent, or what his works show. Nevertheless, he was among the first to sound here a note of independence that was more fully orchestrated half a century later by Emerson, and again a full century later by Charles Ives.

Perhaps the best summation of Billings as man and composer is contained in an entry in the diary of the Rev. William Bentley of Salem, made a few days after Billings's death. Bentley, one of America's best-educated men of his time, moved in circles unfamiliar and even inaccessible to Billings. Nevertheless, his insight into Billings's work and importance moved him to write: "Many who have imitated have excelled him, but none of them had better original power. . . . He was a singular man, of moderate size, short of one leg, with one eye, without any address, & with an uncommon negligence of person. Still he spake & sung & thought as a man above the common abilities."*

Yankee Tunebooks by the Hundreds

Billings was but one among many. An examination of the singing-school period during its golden age gives an impression of tremendous activity and vitality. By 1810 about three hundred of the distinctive tunebooks, homely in appearance and typography, had been published. Their oblong shape gave rise to the terms "long boys" and "end-openers." The titles of these old books tell us much. Some show the classical education or aspirations of their compilers: *Urania; Harmonia Americana*. Some of the titles show clearly the books' use and purpose: *The Musical Primer; The Easy Instructor; The Psalmodist's Assistant; The Psalmodist's Companion; The Chorister's Companion*. Many bespeak their own locale: *The Massachusetts Compiler; The Vermont Harmony; The Harmony of Maine; The Worcester Collection of Sacred Harmony; The Essex Harmony*. The word "harmony" was widely used: *The American Harmony, The Northern Harmony; The Union Harmony; The Federal Harmony; The New England Harmony; The Christian Harmony*; and, as a final distillation, *The Harmony of Harmony*. To close the list, there appeared (with singular appropriateness to their environment) *The Rural Harmony* and *The Village Harmony*.[5]

The Music of the Tunebooks

The venerable psalm tunes are well represented in some of the earlier collections (*Urania*, for example), but along with these appear the tunes for the short non-scriptural *hymns* to original texts, and the larger and more ambitious *anthems*— more elaborate settings of scriptural texts, adapted Scriptural texts, or original texts. It is evident that by this time hymnody had fairly well succeeded in replacing psalmody.

The *canon* (or *round*) does not appear frequently, although Billings has given us a beautiful example in his first publication, the justly famous **"Jesus Wept"** (Ex. 8-2).

Of particular interest are the famous *fuging tunes* (the term, though derived from *fugue*, was very possibly pronounced "fudging" in contemporary usage). Alan Buechner describes it simply as a piece that "begins like a hymn and ends like a round." It was the second section, or *fuge*, that was distinctive, with its rather informally constructed homespun imitative entrances of the voices. The fuging tune was very popular in its day: the effect of hearing the successive

*The phrase "without any address" should not, despite his poverty, be taken as meaning that Billings was among the homeless. This usage of the word "address" is now uncommon, and describes Billings as one who lacked either the capacity for "skillful management," or a tactful and cultivated manner of speaking, or possibly both.

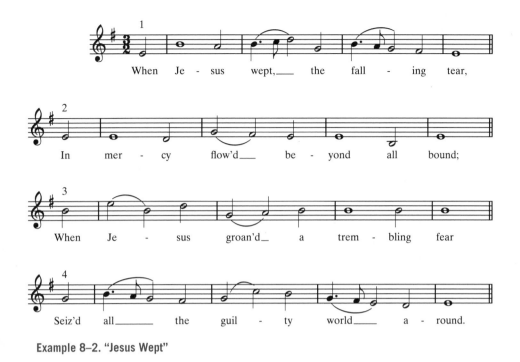

When Je - sus wept,___ the fall - ing tear,

In mer - cy flow'd___ be - yond all bound;

When Je - sus groan'd___ a trem - bling fear

Seiz'd all___ the guil - ty world___ a - round.

Example 8–2. "Jesus Wept"

entrances coming from different parts of the U-shaped meetinghouse gallery must have thrilled both singers and congregation alike. Billings describes these pieces as being "twenty times as powerful as the old slow tunes." Although he composed many himself, there were other composers of the time who favored them even more, and it has been found that over a thousand were published by 1810. The fuging tune later fell into disfavor among reformers of church music, who urged that it was both too crude and too lively as music for worship. But its appeal among the rural folk persisted, and fuging tunes in considerable numbers appear in the shape-note songbooks of the nineteenth century. **"Amity"** by Daniel Read, a Revolutionary War soldier who became a storekeeper and maker of combs, is an excellent example of this popular form.

A number of the larger anthems and set pieces were written for specific occasions or observances—for Thanksgiving, for a Fast Day, for Ordination, for Christmas,* for Easter, for thanksgiving "after a victory," to commemorate the landing of the Pilgrims, and so on. Some were of a still more topical nature, as illustrated by Billings's famous "Lamentation Over Boston," a spirited paraphrase of Psalm 137 commemorating the British occupation of the city during the war.

---

* It is not clear in what circumstances and by whom Billings's Christmas pieces were sung, as the Puritans had suppressed traditional Christmas customs as "Prophane and Superstitious" in the seventeenth century, and this proscription was in effect until the mid-nineteenth century, at which time Christmas was still a regular working day in Boston. See McKay and Crawford, *William Billings of Boston*, 144–45.

The End of an Era, and the Suppression
of the Indigenous Tradition in the Urban East

America's expansion, which began in earnest with the opening of the nineteenth century, manifested itself in two directions at once: in the growth of our cities in size, complexity, and sophistication; and in the continuous rolling westward of our frontier. Both had profound effects on American thought, life, and art—including our indigenous religious music. By 1810 an "anti-American" reform movement had successfully established a trend away from the native, unschooled, innocent art of the pioneer tradition, and toward the closer imitation of European models. The fuging tune especially was castigated. In 1807 the preface of a new compilation characterized the fuging tunes as "those wild fugues, and rapid and confused movements, which have so long been the disgrace of congregational psalmody." The reformers prevailed, to the extent that one observer wrote in 1848, "The good old days of New England music have passed away, and the singing-masters who compose and teach it, are known only in history as an extinct race."[6]

The Frontier and Rural America in the Nineteenth Century

That the music of the New Englanders was in fact far from extinct is now clear to us. As is often the case, in the rural areas the "old ways"—and the old music—were clung to tenaciously long after they had been replaced in the cities. And the frontier, southwestward into the long valleys of the Appalachians and beyond into the broad river valleys of the Ohio and the Tennessee, was an extension of rural America. We can follow the movement of the singing-school tradition along these paths just by tracing the continued appearance of its odd oblong books of tunes. Moving out of Boston and Philadelphia, we find compilations being made in Harrisburg, Pennsylvania; in the Shenandoah Valley of Virginia; in Hamilton, Georgia; in Spartanburg, South Carolina; in Lexington, Kentucky; in Nashville, in Cincinnati, in St. Louis. The titles tell a story of both continuity and movement. As lineal descendants of *The New England Harmony* and *The Harmony of Maine*, we find *The Virginia Harmony, The Kentucky Harmony, The Knoxville Harmony, The Missouri Harmony, The Western Lyre, The Southern Harmony*, and, finally, the famous *Sacred Harp*. These books clearly revealed their ancestry—in their shape and appearance; in their prefatory introductions to the "Rudiments of Music"; in their continued use of the four solmization syllables (fa, sol, la, mi); in their hymns in three and four parts, with the melody buried in the middle of the texture in the tenor voice; and in their sprinkling of more ambitious anthems and fuging tunes. Pieces by Billings himself were almost invariably included; far from being "extinct," William Billings and some of his contemporaries have turned out to be the most continuously performed composers in American history. Indeed, their music has already entered its third century. The singing-schools continued to flourish in the nineteenth century, fulfilling their dual musical and social function much as they had done in New England in Colonial times. Later came the institution of annual gatherings, or "singings," some lasting two or three days, with "dinner on the grounds" a fixed feature.

Thus we see that the "old ways" did not die. Two important additions were made, however, as the native tradition moved out of the East into the South and West. One was the development of the famous shape notes, and the other was the infusion of the folk element into the music.

The Shape Notes

John Tufts's *An Introduction . . . in a Plain and Easy Method* in the early eighteenth century was only the first of many attempts to simplify and speed up the process of teaching people to read music. There appeared in 1801 a book by William Little and William Smith called, appropriately, *The Easy Instructor*, which introduced a simple but ingenious device: the use of differently shaped notes for each of the four syllables then in use to indicate degrees of the scale. In the key of F major, for example, the scale with its syllables would look like Example 8-3.

| Fa | Sol | La | Fa | Sol | La | Mi | Fa |

Example 8–3. The shaped notes

Example 8-5, on page 151, shows the entire folk hymn **"Wondrous Love"** in shape-note notation. The device appears to have caught on rather quickly and well. *The Easy Instructor* was reissued in various editions for thirty years; by the time it ceased publication there were at least eighteen other songbooks in print using the same device. *The Easy Instructor* was first published in the urban East (Philadelphia). The shape-note method was so readily adopted by the compilers of the traditional rural songbooks, however, that its vast literature—for so long all but unknown to outsiders—has taken on the name "southern shape-note hymnody."[7]

Infusion of the Folk Element

Another important development as this rural hymnody moved southwest at the beginning of the nineteenth century was a fresh infusion of the folk element into the tune collections. Folk or folkish tunes of Anglo-Celtic cast, given sacred words and spare, austere harmonic settings, were found in the new books, along-side the established hymn tunes, anthems, and fuging tunes. This had already begun in New England. The "borrowing" of folk tunes to supply the needs of sacred music—"plundering the carnal lover"—is a venerable practice. The great body of Lutheran chorale tunes, for example, contains its share of melodies that began life as folk or popular tunes, in some cases love songs.

A folklike melody of unknown origin variously known as "Harmony Grove," "New Britain," "Redemption," "Symphony," or "Solon" appeared in shape-note hymnody at least as early as 1831 in *The Virginia Harmony*, with a text beginning

There is a land of pure delight
Where saints immortal reign.

It became far better known with the text that was later associated with it, which has given it the title by which we know it —**"Amazing Grace."**

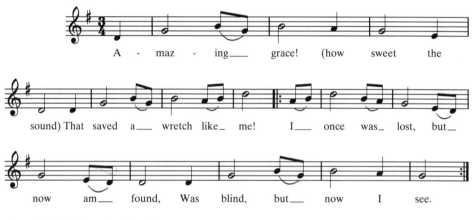

Example 8–4. "Amazing Grace"

The harmony of these hymns abounds in austere open consonances (octaves, fifths, fourths). The spare openness of the harmonic texture contributes as much as the modality of the tunes, to the distinctiveness of this music, which must be actually *heard* (preferably live) to be appreciated. This style is nowhere better illustrated than in the three-voice setting of the famous folk hymn **"Wondrous Love,"** as found in *The Southern Harmony*. The folk tune is in the middle, or tenor, voice.

It is interesting to note that some American composers in the 1930s and 1940s, such as Aaron Copland and Virgil Thomson, writing at a time when American classical music had begun to find its own voice, would tend to adopt similarly lean textures and sounds.

Example 8–5. "Wondrous Love"

Revivalism and the Camp Meeting

Successive waves of religious revivalism have swept America since 1800. Their impact on our indigenous religious music was most pronounced in the period of the expanding frontier before the Civil War, for it was on the frontier that revivalism nurtured its most striking manifestation: the camp meeting. The camp meeting in turn nurtured, for its own needs, one of our most distinctive forms of religious music: the revival spiritual. In order to understand the origin, nature, and function of the revival spiritual, let us turn our attention briefly to the camp meeting itself.

The Colonial South was far from being a devout society. The fundamentalist faith that later became so ingrained there was established as a result of two factors. One was the hardship of what amounted to a frontier existence throughout the antebellum South for the "plain folk" who made up the bulk of the population—mostly white subsistence farmers, who were continually forced to move and take up less arable land as the large slave-worked plantations spread into the fertile lowlands. This kind of existence bred a need for the reassurance and consolation that could be supplied by an evangelical religion—a religion that held out the promise in the hereafter of all the good that was so elusive and pitifully transient in the here-and-now. The other factor was the unremitting effort of the three most popular denominations after the Revolution: the Presbyterians, the Baptists, and the Methodists (the latter most especially, with their organized hierarchy and their corps of indefatigable circuit-riding preachers). These two factors set the stage for the Great Revival of the early nineteenth century.

At its beginning it was called the Kentucky Revival, for that state was its fertile seedbed. Of all the newly opened territories west of the Appalachians, Kentucky was the first to attract settlers, and it acted as a kind of staging area for those who were eventually to move on. By 1800 it was a "boom" state, having a greater population (over 200,000) than all the other states and territories outside the original thirteen colonies combined. It was about this time that revivalism in its most sensational form came to this raw frontier state.

The early camp meetings of the Kentucky revival were huge, chaotic, turbulent affairs. Many people traveled for days to get there. The famous camp meeting of August 1801 at Cane Ridge, in the gently rolling country of Bourbon County, northeast of Lexington, lasted six days, and estimates of the number in attendance ran between ten and twenty-five thousand. The preaching, praying, shouting, and singing went on day and night.

According to one of the many eyewitness accounts,

> The noise was like the roar of Niagara. The vast sea of human beings seemed to be agitated as if by a storm. I counted seven ministers, all preaching at one time, some on stumps, others in wagons, and one . . . was standing on a tree which had, in falling, lodged against . . . another. Some of the people were singing, others praying, some crying for mercy in the most piteous accents, while others were shouting most vociferously. . . . A strange supernatural power seemed to pervade the entire mass of mind there collected. . . . Soon after I left and went into the woods, and there I strove to rally and man up my courage.
>
> After some time I returned to the scene of excitement, the waves of which, if possible, had risen still higher. The same awfulness of feeling came over me. I stepped up on to a log, where I could have a better view of the surging sea of humanity. The scene that presented itself to my mind was indescribable. At one time I saw at least five hundred swept down in a moment as if a battery of a thousand guns had been opened upon them, and then immediately followed shrieks and shouts that rent the heavens.[8]

But in spite of the undenied excesses of the early camp meetings, their emphasis on emotionalism, and the dubious significance of many of the "conversions," most careful observers now conclude that the positive influence of the camp meetings outweighed the negative. As Charles Johnson has summed it up, "Among all of the weapons forged by the West in its struggle against lawlessness and immorality, few were more successful than the frontier camp meeting. This socioreligious institution helped tame backwoods America."[9]

The Revival Spiritual

Singing was a vital part of revivalism from the beginning. Another account of Cane Ridge tells of the powerful impulse of song: "The volume of song burst all bounds of guidance and control, and broke again and again from the throats of the people." Still another eyewitness reported that at the camp meetings the "falling down of multitudes, and their crying out . . . happened under the singing of Watts's Psalms and Hymns, more frequently than under the preaching of the word."[10] All agree that the singing was loud. "The immediate din was tremendous; at a hundred yards it was beautiful; at a distance of a half a mile it was magnificent."[11]

What was sung at the camp meetings? Since it was for so long a matter of purely oral tradition, evidence must be pieced together. The reference above to "Watts's Psalms and Hymns" refers to the words; certain hymns, and bits and pieces of hymns, of eighteenth-century English divines such as Isaac Watts were much used. Though pocket-sized "songsters" with just the words began to appear about 1805, the tunes were not written down and published until the 1840s. From these later collections we can form some notion of the camp-meeting repertory, since we know what the hallmarks of the true revival spiritual were. The tunes had to be lively and easily learned. There was an almost unvarying reliance on the verse-chorus form; everyone could at least join in on the choruses, even if they didn't know the verses, or if the leader introduced unfamiliar ones or even made them up on the spot. A further development along the line of what has been called "text simplification," for the sake of mass participation, was the single-line refrain, interpolated after a couplet of original text or even after every line. With the crowds joining in on the refrains, this turned the singing into the familiar call-and-response pattern. Indoor church hymns could be transformed into revival spirituals by this process.

It is interesting to observe this at work in the case of one of the most popular hymn texts of the time. The original hymn "Canaan" by the English clergyman Samuel Stennett (1727–95) describes in Blakean imagery the beauties of heaven. The first of many verses runs:

> *On Jordan's stormy banks I stand,*
> *And cast a wishful eye,*
> *To Canaan's fair and happy land,*
> *Where my possessions lie.*
> *O, the transporting rapturous scene,*
> *That rises to my sight!*
> *Sweet fields array'd in living green,*
> *And rivers of delight.*

In the revival-song version shown in Example 8-6, only one couplet at a time is used, with a typical chorus added, spelling out in more homely language of action and urgency the conviction that the believer is actually *going* to the promised land so poetically described. The result is a spirited and popular revival spiritual that was first printed in William Walker's *Southern Harmony* in 1835.

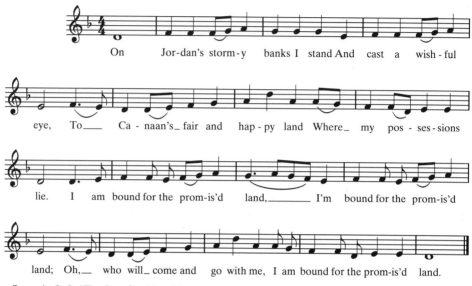

On Jor-dan's storm-y banks I stand And cast a wish-ful eye, To__ Ca-naan's_ fair and hap-py land Where_ my pos-ses-sions lie. I am bound for the prom-is'd land,_____ I'm bound for the prom-is'd land; Oh,_ who will_ come and go with me, I am bound for the prom-is'd land.

Example 8–6. "The Promised Land"

A further stage in the "revivalizing" of this hymn is illustrated in Example 8-7, in which a one-line refrain is interpolated after every line of the text. Both the words and music of the refrain then become the basis for an added chorus. The whole appears in *The Revivalist* of 1868, set to a folkish tune that has a decidedly Irish lilt.

Repetition was carried even further through the use of a form in which a single word is changed to make each new stanza, as can be seen in Example 8-8, from *The Social Harp* of 1855. According to George Pullen Jackson, this spiritual was probably sung with "fathers" only in the first verse, then "mothers" in a second. Further multiplication of verses was easy, using "brothers," "sisters," "friends," "neighbors," and so on. This pattern was to persist in vernacular religious song, especially among African Americans; it proved useful in the "freedom songs" of the Civil Rights movement of the 1960s—songs that were most often adaptations of old spirituals and hymns.

The revival spirituals were also distinguished by the import of their texts. These emphasized the basic themes of the prevailing theology—especially salvation, its attendant joys, and the glories of a heaven that was far removed from the present life. The examples already cited have been replete with expressions that

Example 8–7. "On the Other Side of Jordan"

Example 8–8. "Way Over in the Promised Land"

pervade the spirituals: "promised land," "Canaan," "the other side of Jordan."
Along with the descriptions of heaven and its joys is a dissatisfaction with this
present life that amounts at times to a rejection of the world and, if not actually
a wish for death, at least a poignant anticipation of the joys and release from pain
it would bring to the righteous saints who had been converted:

> *Our bondage it shall end, by and by, by and by.*

> *I am a stranger here below.*

> *This world is not my home.*

How blest the righteous when he dies!
How gently heaves the expiring breast
How mildly beams the closing eyes
When sinks a weary soul to rest.

Sweet home! Oh, when shall I get there?

Parallel Traditions: White and Black Spirituals

The African-American spiritual has been treated extensively in chapter 2. Parallel traditions of these "spiritual songs" existed among blacks and whites, as has been documented, for example, by George Pullen Jackson, who included in his *White and Negro Spirituals* a comparative list of 116 tunes from both. Thus white rural hymnody—folk hymns and, especially, revival spirituals—may have furnished a great deal of raw material, at least, for black spirituals. John Lovell, Jr., the African-American author of *Black Song: The Forge and the Flame*, has written: "There is hardly any doubt that the Afro-American songmaker borrowed from the hymns he heard, and from the Biblical stories he picked up."

The main opportunities for this transmission occurred not in the large slave-holding areas of the South, and not through the master-slave relationship, but precisely in those regions and under those conditions that nurtured the folk hymn and the revival spiritual among whites—in the uplands and on the frontier, among the plain folk and at the camp meeting. The camp meeting, a frontier institution, was probably the site of as uninhibited a meeting of the races as could be encountered in that time. Many of the early camp-meeting preachers, such as Lorenzo Dow and Peter Cartwright, preached against slavery, and were in fact among our earliest abolitionists.

Music Among Our Smaller Independent Sects

Conditions in America have been such as to nurture from the beginning, despite glaring episodes of intolerance and persecution, a lively tradition of religious independence and nonconformity. Many sects either have been transplanted to this country or have sprung up here, where, especially in the eighteenth and nineteenth centuries, they found the space necessary to provide the measure of isolation and self-sufficiency they so deeply desired. Prominent among these sects were the Moravians and the Shakers. It is fitting to close to this chapter on early American religious music with one of its great masterpieces, the Shaker spiritual "'Tis the Gift to be Simple" (Ex. 8-9). This song gives expression to the basic Shaker themes of simplicity and humility, and stands as a consummate achievement of innocent religious art. It is included in the hope that it will be *sung* as well as listened to.

'Tis the gift to be sim-ple, 'tis the gift to be free, 'Tis the gift to come down where we ought to be, And when we find our-selves in the place just right, 'Twill be in the val-ley of love and de-light. When true sim- -pli-ci-ty is gained, To bow and to bend we shan't be a-sham'd, To turn, turn will be our de-light, 'till by turn-ing, turn-ing we come round right.

Example 8–9. "'Tis the Gift to be Simple"

FURTHER READING

Facsimile editions

Modern facsimile reprints of old books are interesting in themselves, as well as giving us firsthand acquaintance with this music. A selection, arranged in chronological order, follows:

The Bay Psalm Book. Boston, 1640. Reprint. Chicago: University of Chicago Press, 1956.

Tufts, John. *An Introduction to the Singing of Psalm Tunes*. 5th ed. Boston, 1726. Reprint. Philadelphia: Musical Americana, 1954.

Billings, William. *The Psalm-Singer's Amusement*. Boston, 1781. Reprint. New York: Da Capo, 1974.

———. *The Continental Harmony*. Boston, 1794. Reprint. Cambridge, MA: Harvard University Press, 1961, with an introduction by Hans Nathan.

Wyeth, John. *Wyeth's Repository of Sacred Music, Part Second*. 2d ed. Harrisburg, PA, 1820. Reprint. New York: Da Capo, 1964.

   The first-shape-note publication to include folk hymns. This reprint edition has an excellent introduction by Irving Lowens.

Mason, Lowell. *The Boston Handel and Haydn Society Collection of Church Music*. Boston, 1822. Reprint. New York: Da Capo, 1973.

   A landmark of the "better music" movement, this interesting book retains the form and appearance of the older books, but contains very little American music, and was the harbinger of a flood of later popular urban collections.

Walker, William. *The Southern Harmony*. Philadelphia, 1854. Reprint. Los Angeles: Promusicamericana, 1966.

   The revised edition of this important shape-note publication, which appeared first in 1853.

White, B. F., and E. J. King. *The Sacred Harp*. 3d ed. Philadelphia, 1860. Reprint. Nashville: Broadman, 1968.

> This reprint of another very important shape-note publication includes George Pullen Jackson's essay "The Story of the Sacred Harp 1844–1944."

Modern editions of music, including scholarly editions and anthologies

The Music of Henry Ainsworth's Psalter (Amsterdam, 1612). Ed. Lorraine Inserra and H. Wiley Hitchcock. I.S.A.M. Maonograph no. 15. Institute for Studies in American Music, 1975.

> Contains both facsimiles and transcriptions of all the thiry-nine tunes, with extensive commentary, and a table of the tune sources.

The Music of the Bay Psalm Book, 9th edition (1968). Ed. Richard G. Appel. I.S.A.M. Monograph no. 5. Brooklyn: Institute for Studies in American Music, 1975.

> This contains both facsimiles and transcriptions in modern notation of the 11-page supplement to the 9th edition (the first to include music) of the Bay Psalm Book, preceded by a short commentary.

Billings, William. *The Complete Works of William Billings*. Boston: American Musicological Society and Colonial Society of Massachusetts, 1981.

> A scholarly edition in four volumes with extensive notes by the editor, Karl Kroeger.

Jackson, George Pullen. *Spiritual Folk-Songs of Early America*. New York, 1937. Paperback reprint. New York: Dover.

> This important collection has 250 complete tunes and texts, with sources and notes, and an extensive introduction. It is the basic annotated compendium of tunes and texts in the shape-note tradition.

Many publishers with substantial sacred choral music catalogs now include editions of music from the New England singing-school tradition. An example is Concordia, of St. Louis, which has a rather extensive series, *Sacred Choral Music from Colonial America by William Billings*, with useful notes.

Studies, some with incidental musical examples

Buechner, Alan C. Notes to the record album *The New England Harmony*. Folkways 32377 (1964).

> This excellent 32-page booklet has much valuable information on the singing school tradition. The booklet is available separately from Folkways, although the record album is nearly indispensable as well.

Cobb, Buell E., Jr. *The Sacred Harp: The Tradition and its Music*. Athens: Brown Thrasher Books, University of Georgia Press, 1989

Jackson, George Pullen. *White Spirituals in the Southern Uplands*. Chapel Hill: University of North Carolina Press, 1933. Paperback reprint. New York: Dover, 1965.

> The basic history of the shape-note movement and its background. It includes the seven-shape branch. It also includes a listing, with initial-phrase quotations, of the eighty most popular tunes in the tradition.

Lorenz, Ellen Jane. *Glory, Hallelujah! The Story of the Campmeeting Spiritual*. Nashville, TN: Abingdon, 1978.

> Includes music and words for forty-eight "northern campmeeting spirituals."

Lowens, Irving. *Music and Musicians in Early America*. New York: Norton, 1964. Chapters 2, 3, 8, 14, 18.

> A collection of valuable articles by one of the most eminent scholars in American music.

MacDougall, Hamilton C. *Early New England Psalmody*. Brattleboro, VT, 1940. Reprint. New York: Da Capo, 1969.

McKay, David P., and Richard Crawford. *William Billings of Boston: Eighteenth-Century Composer*. Princeton, NJ: Princeton University Press, 1975.

> It includes much valuable background information, including a complete survey of sacred music in New England to the time of Billings. It is now a basic work on Billings himself and his time.

Scholes, Percy A. *The Puritans and Music in England and New England.* Oxford, England: Clarendon Press, 1934. Reprint. New York: Russell & Russell, 1962.

> A valuable and copiously documented treatise correcting the stereotype of the Puritans as being universally and implacably opposed to music, the fine arts in general, and the appreciation of beauty.

Stevenson, Robert. *Protestant Church Music in America.* New York: Norton, 1966. Paperback, 1970. Chapters 1, 2, 3, 7.

> A brief but invaluable survey, written with a broad perspective of the subject by a noted scholar. Begins with the all-but-forgotten Huguenot settlements in Florida more than half a century before the landing of the Pilgrims. Excellent bibliography.

Titon, Jeff Todd. *Powerhouse for God: Speech, Chant, and Song in an Appalachian Baptist Church.* Austin: University of Texas Press, 1988.

Projects

1. If you like to sing folk songs, learn a psalm tune (from *The Music of Henry Ainsworth's Psalter, The Music of the Bay Psalm Book, 9th edition* (1698), Marrocco and Gleason, *Music in America,* or any other authentic source—see the reading list for this chapter); fit a psalm text of the same poetic meter to it from the Bay Psalm Book (or any other early translation); and add it to your repertoire. You may sacrifice historical authenticity to the extent of contriving a tasteful accompaniment to it on the guitar if you wish.

2. Find three psalm tunes (*besides* "Old 100th"!) that are still in use and appear in modern hymn collections in this country. Find out as much as you can about the origins of the tunes, and in which early psalters they appeared. Find and consult early versions of the tunes if possible. (Most hymnals have a good index of composers and sources, which can help, as can the index of tune names. The *Hymnal of the Protestant Episcopal Church in the U.S.A.*, for example, is rather rich in tunes from the old psalters of the sixteenth and seventeenth centuries.)

3. Read William Billings's prefaces to his *Continental Harmony*—both "To the several Teachers of MUSIC, in this and the adjacent States" and "A Commentary on the preceding Rules: by way of Dialogue, between Master and Scholar." Comment on what these treatises seem to say about Billings himself: his sense of humor, his ability and ingenuity as a teacher, and his views on music, especially vocal music.

4. Investigate music among a small independent sect such as the Moravians, the Shakers, the Seventh-Day Baptists of the Ephrata Cloister, the Mennonites, or the followers of Johannes Kelpius (the "Hermit of the Wissahickon").

5. Find three folk hymns from the shape-note tradition that are included in present-day hymnals. As in project 2 above, find out what you can about the tunes and put together a brief commentary.

6. Find three revival spirituals in present-day hymnals. As in projects 2 and 5 above, find out what you can about the tunes and put together a brief commentary. The Lorenz book in the reading list may be helpful.

7. Write a brief paper comparing the camp meetings of the Kentucky Revival with large outdoor rock festivals from Woodstock to Lollapalooza.

Notes

1. David McKay and Richard Crawford, *William Billings of Boston* (Princeton, NJ: Princeton University Press, 1975), 8.

2. There is evidence that singing-masters sometimes took their pay in produce—Indian corn, for example. For this and many other interesting details of the New England singing-school tradition, see Alan Buechner, "Yankee Singing Schools and the Golden Age of Choral Music in New England: 1760–1800" (Ph.D. dissertation, Harvard University, 1960), and, based on this, his copious annotations to the recording *The New England Harmony* (Folkways FA–2377).

3. McKay and Crawford, *William Billings of Boston*, 23.

4. "Chester" can be heard on *The New England Harmony* (Smithsonian/Folkways 2377) in a performance with a small "gallery orchestra" of woodwinds and cello.

5. Fortunately, several of these books are now available in facsimile reprint form, including Lyon's *Urania*, Belcher's *Harmony of Maine*, and Billings's *Continental Harmony* and *Psalm-Singer's Amusement*.

6. See Robert Stevenson, *Protestant Church Music in America*.

7. Not long after the invention of the four-shape system, a system of seven shapes was devised, in 1832—one shape for each tone of the diatonic scale, and for each of the syllables used in continental European practice (do, re, mi, etc.) The seven-shape, seven-syllable system did become established in portions of the South. But although the seven-syllable system ultimately triumphed everywhere else in the English-speaking world, it did not succeed in dislodging the four-syllable (fa, sol, la, mi) practice from its stronghold in *Sacred Harp* circles—nor has it to this day.

8. From the autobiography of James B. Finley, quoted in Charles A. Johnson, *The Frontier Camp Meeting* (Dallas: SMU Press, 1955), 64–65.

9. Ibid., vii.

10. From a letter written in Kentucky in 1803, printed in the *Methodist Magazine*, London, that year. Quoted in Johnson, *The Frontier Camp Meeting*, 57.

11. Samuel E. Asbury, quoted in Gilbert Chase, *America's Music, From the Pilgrims to the Present*, 3d ed. (Urbana: University of Illinois Press,1987), 204.

Chapter 9

Urban Revivalism and Gospel Music

The opening decades of the nineteenth century witnessed the beginnings of a growing cultural cleavage between the city and the country. The products of our native school of church composers were progressively cast aside by those dedicated to what they saw as the improvement of church music, who turned to Europe not only for "rules" as to what was correct, but also for actual tunes. *The Boston Handel and Haydn Society Collection of Church Music*, compiled by Lowell Mason and published in 1822, was a landmark. Gone were the fuging tunes; there was not a single piece by Billings, Ingalls, or Swan. Instead, there were European hymn tunes, as well as adapted tunes by Handel, Mozart, Haydn, and Beethoven.[1] The inexorable divergence between "highbrow" and "lowbrow" in American tastes after 1800 applied to religious music as well. For the worship services of the urban churches that had a pronounced liturgical bent, coupled with a substantial tradition and an intellectual, even aesthetic, dimension to their appeal (Episcopal, Lutheran, Presbyterian to some degree, as well as Roman Catholic), a hymnody continued to develop along the lines Lowell Mason helped to establish—cultivated and eclectic, selecting and adapting from a wide range of traditions. Any recent hymnbook of these denominations (such as *The Hymnal of the Protestant Episcopal Church in the United States of America* [1982]) will illustrate this. Here medieval plainchant, Lutheran chorales, Calvinist psalm tunes, and melodies by classical and modern composers rub shoulders with American folk hymns such as "Kedron."

On the other hand, after 1800 the broadly popular evangelical denominations and sects continued to demand a popular type of song, particularly for special occasions such as revival meetings, which incorporated many features of the old camp-meeting spiritual.

Urban Revivalism After the Civil War:
The Moody–Sankey Era of Gospel Hymns

Hymn tunes have been called by Robert Stevenson "pre-eminently the food of the common man," and nineteenth-century America had a seemingly insatiable hunger for this food. In the period following the American Revolution, the demand for popular hymnody was met by drawing upon the wealth of folk music in the possession of the rural people, thereby creating the folk hymn. After the Civil War, folk music, no longer a very vital part of the lives of a now much larger and increasingly citified populace, could not be drawn upon to satisfy this demand. Instead, it was met by a large number of hymn writers and composers, most of whom had only a modest amount of formal training but had an instinctive feel for what would best appeal to the great numbers of Christian believers, many of them new converts. These hymn writers and composers maintained a prodigious output of what have come to be known as *gospel songs* or *gospel hymns*. The production of these became especially copious after the revivalism of Dwight Moody and Ira Sankey swept the country beginning in 1875. In that year Sankey published, with P. P. Bliss, a volume called *Gospel Hymns*. This was followed by five sequels, culminating in *Gospel Hymns Nos. 1 to 6 Complete* in 1895, a compendium of more than seven hundred hymns and songs that typify the genre. As comprehensive as such a collection might seem, it represents only a fraction of the simple, homely songs and hymns produced.*

The models for these gospel songs did not come from the European-influenced collections of Mason and others; rather, their lineage was from the earlier camp-meeting song via the Sunday school songs for children that began to be published in mid-century. Their optimistic stance is revealed in the titles of collections such as *Happy Voices*, *The Sunny Side*, and *Golden Chain*. A new feature of revivalism was that singing the gospel became as important as preaching the gospel; therefore, to reach the masses the gospel hymn had to be of the utmost simplicity, governed by a conventionality that virtually amounted to a formula. With extremely rare exceptions, all the tunes were in the major mode, in contrast to the dour minor and modal tunes of the old rural folk hymns. The major mode was thought to be more cheerful and optimistic, and reinforced better the millennial spirit of the revivalist preaching of the day—preaching that replaced the grim pessimism and preoccupation with death and eternal judgment that had characterized pre–Civil War preaching and the songs that went with it. The tunes were harmonized with the three most basic chords, embellished occasionally with some chromaticism in the style that has since become known as "barbershop harmony." The form is nearly always that of verse and chorus. The chorus is a feature that not only shows a direct descent from the earlier revival spiritual,

*Fanny Jane Crosby (1820–1915), using hundreds of pen names in addition to her real name, worked for years under a contract that called for the production of three songs a week. How far she exceeded even this is indicated in her own statement: "I have often composed as many as six or seven hymns in one day." It is no wonder that her total output has been estimated at more than eight thousand hymns.

but also relates the music to the commercial secular songs of Tin Pan Alley. This chorus often embodies a sort of polyphony even more rudimentary than that of the old fuging tunes; the lower, or men's, parts simply repeat short phrases that have just been sung by the upper, or women's, parts, thus illustrating the perennial delight that the most naive manifestations of counterpoint have for the musically innocent. The chorus of "**Sweet By-and-By**" (Ex. 9-1), one of the best-known hymns of the 1895 collection *Gospel Hymns Nos. 1 to 6 Complete*, illustrates this feature.

As this example shows, the music was written on two staves in four-part harmony. The tune was now on top, in the soprano: this made it more prominent for congregational singing. The four-part harmonizations were also eminently convenient for the mixed solo quartet of soprano, alto, tenor, and bass (often paid professionals) that was a popular feature in churches from the Civil War on.

The words, as might be expected, show the same preoccupation with the central theme of salvation as did those of the revival spiritual, though there is less gloomy dwelling upon death and, with the increased cheerfulness that pervaded popular theology, a great deal more sentimentality.*

Despite the ephemeral nature of most of this gospel music, a few survivals, of enormous popularity and some distinction, have found their way into modern hymn collections. They have become woven into America's musical consciousness, as Charles Ives shows when he quotes them so liberally in his works, and as other more recent composers like Virgil Thomson have demonstrated in their treatment and transformation of them. An English writer has characterized as "at best . . . honestly flamboyant and redolent of the buoyancy of the civilization that created New York and Pittsburgh and Chicago."[2] Representative examples of these hymns with their evocative titles and the names of their composers are "Hold the Fort" ("for I am coming") and "Let the Lower Lights Be Burning" by P. P. Bliss; "Sweet Hour of Prayer," "He Leadeth Me," and "Just as I Am" by William B. Bradbury; "Beautiful River" ("Shall we gather at the river?"), "Where Is My Boy Tonight?" and "I Need Thee Every Hour" by Robert Lowry; "What a Friend We Have in Jesus" by Charles C. Converse; "Bringing in the Sheaves" by George A. Minor; "Jesus, Lover of My Soul" by Simeon P. March; and "Beulah Land" by J. R. Sweney.

The Billy Sunday–Homer Rodeheaver Era: Further Popularization

The turn of the century saw further popularization and even secularization of evangelical song. There was a greater emphasis on informality and entertainment

---

*The intimate relation of many of these gospel songs to country music is explored in chapter 5.

Example 9–1. "Sweet By-and-By"

Homer Rodeheaver. *Courtesy New York Public Library.*

in revival meetings; the piano replaced the old reed organ, and Homer Rodeheaver (associated from 1909 to 1929 with the evangelist Billy Sunday) added trombone solos to his singing and piano playing to liven up the proceedings. In mid-career Rodeheaver made full use of the new media of radio and recordings; he also published extensively, through the Rodeheaver Company of Winona Lake, Indiana. His *Christian Service Songs* (for which practical orchestrations were available) went through many editions. It included older traditional material (standard tunes by Handel, Mendelssohn, and the like, and by the Americans Mason and Root) but is best known for the popular sacred and semisacred songs that characterized the era, among them "Brighten the Corner Where You Are" (Charles Gabriel, 1913), "In the Garden" (C. Austin Miles, 1912), and "The Old Rugged Cross" (George Bernard, 1913).

After a decline during the Depression era, urban revivalism again began attracting attention with the activities of Billy Graham. The music accompanying his meetings was conservative, with a return to the repertoire represented in the Moody–Sankey *Gospel Hymns*.[3] With the advent of television evangelism, the emphasis, as in the Sunday–Rodeheaver era, is again on entertainment, eclecticism, and commercialism.

Gospel Music After the Advent of Radio and Recordings

Following the course of jazz, blues, and country music, what Charles Wolfe has called "the fourth great genre of grass roots music"—gospel music—entered the commercial arena of the radio and the phonograph in the mid-1920s, and was profoundly influenced by both media. In the seventy years since, two parallel traditions, black and white, have developed, both drawing to a significant degree on the same reservoir of nineteenth-century gospel hymnody, but each reacting in its own way to popular secular currents of the times—white gospel music to those of white country music, and black gospel music to those of blues and jazz.

Southern White Gospel Music

Twentieth-century white gospel music in the South had its musical roots in the rural shape-note tradition described in the preceding chapter, and, instrumentally, in the folk music of that region. Its religious roots were in evangelical revivalism, and in the Holiness and Pentecostal[4] movements that around the turn of the century began to sweep across the whole country, taking root especially in the South, the Midwest, and California, where they made converts among the poor, both black and white. At first the musical fare in the white churches was that of the rather staid gospel hymns of the Moody–Sankey era, which began to reach rural southerners in shape notes as early as 1890.* But by the 1920s a new kind of gospel song was becoming more popular—a type more indigenous to the region, which reflected the influences of both secular country ("hillbilly") music and, to a certain extent, Tin Pan Alley. The texts emphasized more down-to-earth, homely, and even topical metaphors. As in secular country music and the blues, the train motive appeared in songs like "Life's Railway to Heaven" and "The Glory Train"—the latter with Jesus as "our great conductor," who "has been this way before." The faithful are admonished: "Get your ticket and be ready, / For this train may come today . . . Have your baggage checked for glory, / So you'll meet with no delay."

In "The Royal Telephone" of 1919 we find the chorus:

> *Telephone to glory, O what joy divine!*
> *I can feel the current moving on the line;*
> *Built by God the Father for his loved and own,*
> *We may talk to Jesus thru this royal telephone.*[5]

---

*By that time the four-shape system, as preserved in *Southern Harmony* and *The Sacred Harp*, had largely given way to a seven-shape system, which had been introduced in the mid-nineteenth century and which persists in publications to this day.

The texts tended to anticipate the joys of heaven, as in "Where We'll Never Grow Old" (1914), "When the Roll Is Called Up Yonder (I'll be there)" (1921), and "**Can the Circle Be Unbroken**" (ca. 1907). There was emphasis on the semisacred "message" song, which simply advocated cheerful optimism, as in the popular "Give the World a Smile," or indulged in sentimentality, as in "If I Could Hear My Mother Pray Again."

Musically, the melodic and harmonic vocabulary of twentieth-century white gospel music has been basically the same as that which had proved so workable and popular in the nineteenth century. The verse-chorus form is nearly always used, with the chorus containing the kind of antiphonal "answering" effects already illustrated in "**Sweet By-and-By.**" The principal musical differences between the urban gospel hymns of the nineteenth century and the Southern white gospel songs of the twentieth have been in the manner of their performance. In early recordings before much commercial influence was evident (and in more recent revivals of earlier styles), we hear the staid hymns of the Moody–Sankey era "ruralized" and "southernized" by being given an instrumental accompaniment of guitar, banjo, and mandolin (more rarely fiddle), with characteristic introductions and instrumental choruses. The singing style, in the early period was that familiar from recordings of Southern folk music. "**Sweet By-and-By**" as sung and played by traditional musicians Harry and Jeanie West is an example of a nineteenth-century gospel hymn "ruralized" in this way.

Charlie D. Tillman, composer of "Old Time Religion" (a song associated more than any other in the popular mind with white gospel music) and "Life's Railway to Heaven," was among the first to broadcast this music, in 1922 in Atlanta. Record companies, discovering the sales potential of secular hillbilly music and blues, were also looking for artists to record gospel music. Performers who already had a reputation for doing mostly secular songs and ballads also recorded some gospel songs—among them Bascomb Lamar Lunsford, Uncle Dave Macon, the Stoneman Family, the Carter Family, and the Stanley Brothers. Since then virtually all country singers have included in their repertory some gospel songs.

In the face of a persistent trend toward the commercialization of white gospel music since the 1930s, a few groups continued to perform it with the traditional sound and spirit. One of these was a mixed quartet (originally a father, son, and two daughters) from Texas that had the somewhat misleading name of the Chuck Wagon Gang thrust upon them. From the late 1930s to the early 1970s, they achieved considerable and enduring popularity, on radio and recordings, singing mostly old songs such as "**The Church in the Wildwood**," familiar from the seven-shape-note books, in a conservative manner to a simple guitar accompaniment; only in the late 1950s was an electric guitar sometimes substituted. By the 1960s, with the rewards of commercial success becoming ever larger, as the careers of successful country and rock groups showed, two distinct motivations for performing gospel music had emerged. As Malone puts it, "The sense of religious mission no doubt still burned brightly in the lives of many gospel singers, but an increasing number viewed the music as just another facet of popular music, or as an avenue for entrance into different kinds of performing careers."[6]

In the 1980s popular commercial gospel groups such as the Florida Boys, a male quintet, most typically purveyed a slick, studio-produced product, with a large pop/soft-rock backup group with drums and a mixture of electric and acoustic instruments, strangely at odds with the very conservative old-line evangelical message of the words. Their repertory, while mostly new, includes an occasional older song such as Tillman's "Life's Railway to Heaven," done in a very stylized evocation of the "old-time" way.

Outside the gospel movement itself, some folk revivalists have taken a renewed interest in songs from the old seven-shape-note repertory, and it is not unusual to hear, in the old singing style, songs like "The Lonesome Road," "Can the Circle Be Unbroken" (in its more recent variant, "Will the Circle Be Unbroken"), and of course the perennial "Amazing Grace."

Black Gospel Music: The Roots

African-American gospel music had its religious roots in the turn-of-the-century Holiness movement. The Holiness sects are based on a highly personal, vivid, and emotional religious experience—an experience that involves, ultimately, possession by the Holy Spirit. This possession shows itself in emotionally charged expression and movement—moaning, singing, speaking in tongues, and dancing (the term "shout" can refer to a dance as well as a song). This seemingly unbridled expression—the one and only outlet for pent-up emotions in the lives of the poor of both races, who made up the majority of adherents of the Holiness sects—elicited amusement and scorn from the world at large.[7] (The derogatory term "Holy Rollers" was frequently heard.) Since these believers were already among the outcasts of society, the contempt only strengthened the sense of community they felt in their worship. Though the Holiness and Pentecostal adherents were always in a minority numerically among church members, the freedom of expression that they encouraged, especially in music, had a special appeal and gave them, eventually, an influence disproportionate to their numbers. The singular fact is that it was just these scorned modes of worship, this rejected music of the disinherited, that ultimately came to influence not only a large segment of

American religious music, white and black, but indirectly a great spectrum of our popular music as well.

We cannot go very far in understanding the conditions under which black gospel music developed unless we understand something of the role of the black preacher. W. E. B. Du Bois has said: "The Preacher is the most unique personality developed by the Negro on American soil. A leader, a politician, an orator, a 'boss,' an intriguer, an idealist—all these he is, and ever, too, the center of a group of men, now twenty, now a thousand in number."[8] In the Holiness church, all that was required to be a preacher was that one have the combination of qualities enumerated by Du Bois, and that one feel the "call" to preach. An indispensable gift was the ability to elicit a response from the congregation. As, in the course of his exhortation, the responses became more frequent and more intense, the sounds of preacher and congregation together gradually merged into song. Early entrepreneurs recorded many of these sermons-into-songs, in conditions not unlike those of the storefront churches where the actual services took place. It is estimated that over seven hundred "sermons" were recorded in the 1920s and early 1930s. Recordings in archival collections, such as "Jesus Rose from the Dead," give at least some flavor of what the Sanctified services were like.[9]

The black Holiness churches welcomed the use of instruments. There were the characteristic percussion instruments (the tambourine, the triangle, and later the drums) as well as the guitar and its urban replacement, the piano. But the services could also include, especially on the recordings of the 1920s, the trumpet, trombone, and string bass, as can be heard in **"I'm on the Battlefield for my Lord."** The music, in fact, often has the sound and feel of early jazz. To conclude, however, that jazz influenced the music of the Sanctified churches is to get the picture as much backwards as forwards; they grew up together, and jazz may well owe as much to the music of the Holiness churches as it does to the streets and brothels of New Orleans. One small clue is the fact that the traditional jazz standard "When the Saints Go Marching In" is actually a Sanctified "shout." Early gospel singers such as guitar-playing Rosetta Tharpe, who came out of the Church of God in Christ, recorded "Daniel in the Lion's Den" with bass, drums, and boogie-woogie piano; and Sister Ernestine Washington recorded, among other pieces, "Does Jesus Care?" with Bunk Johnson's jazz band.*

Black gospel music, unlike its white counterpart, was a music of the cities. Its roots can be found not only in what preachers and their congregations were doing in many humble storefront Holiness churches, but also in the music of many blind street evangelists. Blind Willie Johnson (1902–50) was a street

*"Daniel in the Lion's Den" is on *Brighten the Corner Where You Are*, New World 224, and "Does Jesus Care" is on *The Asch Recordings* 1939–1947, A/A1.

singer in Dallas. His "God Moves on the Water," one of many songs based on the sinking of the *Titanic* in 1912,[10] shows him to have been the religious counterpart, in terms of style and guitar technique, to blues singers such as Blind Lemon Jefferson.[11] Memphis, world headquarters of the Church of God in Christ, the largest black Sanctified denomination, was a center for Sanctified music in the 1920s. For further evidence of the influence of Sanctified singing on jazz, listen to the singing of Sister Bessie Johnson, who together with Sister Melinda Taylor recorded "**He Got Better Things for You**" as the Memphis Sanctified Singers (1929). The growling, rasping vocal quality is exactly what jazz musicians were imitating on trumpet and trombone.[12]

The Methodist minister and composer Charles Albert Tindley (1851/59–1933) has been called the "progenitor of black-American gospel music." In the first decade of the twentieth century he was writing songs in what became the prototypical form and style of gospel music—simple melodies and harmonies, in verse and chorus form. Among these were "I'll Overcome Some Day" of 1901 (the chorus of which entered, by a circuitous route, the Civil Rights struggle a half-century later as "We Shall Overcome"); "What Are They Doing in Heaven" of the same year (one of several songs to cross over into the white gospel tradition); "We'll Understand Better By and By" (1905); and "Stand by Me" (also 1905). The center of Tindley's work was Philadelphia, where he wrote songs for "new arrivals in the North who poured in daily, most of them poor and illiterate, and who valued highly the simple, direct, and emotional life style of which Tindley spoke."[13]

By the 1920s the gospel music indigenous to the Holiness churches was beginning to be introduced to other African-American denominations as well. But the phenomenal growth of modern gospel music as it is known today did not begin until the 1930s.

Modern Black Gospel Music's First Phase: The 1930s, 1940s, and 1950s

The one person most responsible for the initial propagation of modern gospel music was Thomas A. Dorsey (b. 1899). After an early career as a blues singer, composer, and pianist—as "Georgia Tom" he had played and recorded blues with Ma Rainey and Tampa Red—he was first drawn to gospel music in 1921. For a while he continued to play and record blues, but from 1932 on he devoted himself wholly to the blues' sacred counterpart. It was in that year, a year of personal tragedy, that he wrote his most famous song, "Precious Lord." Dorsey proved to be an indefatigable promoter, organizer, and manager, as well as composer, of gospel music. He published his own compositions, and went from

Clara Ward. *Courtesy Frank Driggs Collection.*

church to church in Chicago, and later from city to city, with singers such as Sallie Martin and later Mahalia Jackson, performing and promoting gospel music. Dorsey published his songs not in book collections, as had been the case with popular sacred music up to this time, but rather (in the manner of Tin Pan Alley) as sheet music. In his capacity as organizer and promoter, he started with Sallie Martin the National Convention of Gospel Choirs and Choruses. "**I'll Tell It Wherever I Go**," which Sallie Martin recorded with Dorsey at the piano, illustrates the seminal style of "gospel blues" in its early stages.

Thanks in part to Dorsey's promotional activity, the solo gospel singer began to assume more importance. During this first phase of modern gospel music it was women singers who dominated, just as in the 1920s female singers had dominated the classic urban blues. In fact, the two greatest influences on the first two generations of women gospel soloists were the music of the Holiness churches*

*Of women singers prominent in the first three decades of gospel music Mahalia Jackson, Rosetta Tharpe, Marion Williams, and Ruth Davis either came out of Holiness backgrounds or were strongly affected by the music, and Willie Mae Ford Smith joined a Holiness church in 1939, at the age of thirty-three.

and the singing of blues singers like Ma Rainey and Bessie Smith. The first generation of singers included Roberta Martin (1907–69), who began as the pianist for Dorsey's chorus; Mahalia Jackson (1911–72), with whom Dorsey toured as pianist from the mid-1930s until around 1950; Willie Mae Ford Smith (b. 1906); and Sister Rosetta Tharpe (1915–73). The second generation included such singers as Clara Ward (1924–73), Marion Williams (b. 1927), Ruth Davis (1928–70), and Albertina Walker (b. 1930). These women developed distinctive styles that were individual blends of certain enduring characteristics of gospel singing: the bending of notes, the sliding into or between pitches, the bending of rhythms (in common with jazz singers), the repetition of syllables or words, the interpolation of extra words or exclamations, and a range of vocal effects that included shouting, falsetto, and a hoarse, rasping, or growling vocal quality. Roberta Martin's "Ride On, King Jesus" and Mahalia Jackson's "**Didn't It Rain**" are illustrative of their distinctive styles.

In the beginning the basic accompanying instrument was the piano, played in a "gospel" style, which, quite unlike the accompaniments played for congregational hymn singing, owed a great deal to ragtime, stride piano, and other popular styles. Soon it was common to add bass and drums to the piano; in the 1950s the electric organ became an indispensable part of the ensemble. A small vocal group (mostly female, but occasionally including men) was frequently added, but the soloist tended to dominate; the vocal backup group merely added support, and reiterated key phrases of the soloist for emphasis. When gospel music began to enter the commercial arena with recordings, radio appearances, and tours, many soloists formed their own groups, such as the Roberta Martin Singers, the Davis Sisters, the Clara Ward Singers, and later the Caravans.

The above capsule description helps to define the traditional gospel group led by the female "diva," but the other type of group important in gospel music's first phase was the male ensemble—usually a quartet that sang unaccompanied, dressed in business suits. The unaccompanied male gospel quartet predated modern gospel music; early quartets in what Boyer has termed the "folk" phase, up until 1930, were built on the nineteenth-century tradition of the Fisk Jubilee Singers and others. In the period 1930–45, termed by Boyer the "gospel" or "jubilee" period, groups adopted mannerisms from the more rhapsodic aspects of Holiness singing and from the rhythmic aspects of jazz; a characteristic number would start slowly, with florid improvisation, and then work up to a highly rhythmic ending. This period merged imperceptibly into Boyer's next phase, that of "sweet" gospel, in which a lead singer emerged as dominant, with the rest of the group forming a close harmony background and responding to the lead.[14] Well known in this period were the Blue Jay Singers, the Golden Gate Quartet, the Soul Stirrers, and the Dixie Hummingbirds. "**When the Gates Swing Open**," by the latter group, is representative.

Styles in Black Gospel Music Since Mid-Century

Since mid-century, and especially beginning in the 1970s, gospel music has evolved along two fairly distinct lines: "contemporary" and "traditional." Underneath the difference in style and sound, the basic distinction between the two types lies in the way each regards its public. For "contemporary" gospel the public is an audience to be entertained, and perhaps soothed and comforted; for "traditional" gospel, it is a congregation to be charged with religious ecstasy.

Traditional gospel music, even on recordings, always conveys the ambience of an actual service. Even though the location may be Carnegie Hall (and it is much more apt to be an actual church) the congregation is palpably there, and participating. The "sermonette" before the song (an innovation evolved out of the old recorded preachers' sermons by Willie Mae Ford Smith, Dorothy Norwood, Inez Andrews, and other old-line gospel singers) or the pastor's exhortation is delivered over an instrumental background that merges into the next song. The instrumentation of piano, electric organ, electric guitar, electric bass, and drums is in the direct line of the tradition evolved since the 1930s. The choir, singing in an altogether homophonic texture, is an important element. Numbers now appear for chorus alone, representing a resurgence of actual choral singing in gospel music. More frequently the chorus is used for backing up the soloist, singing a verse or chorus of the song, or sometimes repeating short phrases, in the background, under the soloist's improvisation. The soloists tend to sing in a "hard gospel" style, highly charged emotionally. The fast numbers, driven by the accompaniment (all the instruments except the organ can be considered a rhythm section), are highly rhythmic and syncopated, and often incorporate hand-clapping.

"**I Feel the Spirit**," by Clarence Eggleton, illustrates features of traditional gospel music today. It is essentially a choral piece, with improvised solo interjections toward the end, as the intensity builds.[15] The text is simple; the principal ingredient being:

> *I feel the Spirit moving in this place;*
> *He's all over me, I can't hold my peace.*

with subsidiary lines used intermittently:

I feel like Jeremiah in his heart as a burning fire;
Shut up in my bones; Spirit won't leave me alone.

Approximately half way through the piece, there is a *vamp*, in which typically, as a means of increasing the intensity, the text becomes more condensed, with more repetition:

I feel the Spirit moving . . .	[4 times]
moving . . .	[6 times]
I feel like Jeremiah, etc.	[2 times]
I feel the Spirit moving . . .	[8 times]
moving . . .	[6 times]
in this place.	

At this point there is an *apparent* end, with applause, but the instruments keep the momentum going, and there is a reprise with even more repetition:

I feel the Spirit moving . . .	[10 times]
moving . . .	[6 times]
in this place.	

The intensity and momentum built up by this means has to be heard (preferably live) to be appreciated. During the vamp the leader may go down and circulate among the congregation, and the congregation may respond to the highly charged emotional momentum established by the music and go into a "shout," dancing or moving rhythmically. In a live situation this may go on for as long as half an hour before leader and ensemble bring it to a close; recordings obviously must edit these vamps.

Although there is a considerable overlap between "traditional" and "contemporary" gospel music, the latter tends to sound as if it is more at home in the concert hall than in church, and often more in the recording studio than either. The singing style and vocal quality of both soloists and choir tend to be smoother, more polished, and more pop-oriented, with less of the emotion-driven "edge" that characterizes traditional gospel singing. Solo cuts may have a soft-rock or soft-rhythm-and-blues background, with velvet-voiced studio backup singers replacing the incisive and committed voices of the historic gospel choir. Instrumentally there is a heavy reliance on a battery of electronic keyboards, and on studio electronic manipulation. Brass instruments and even a full orchestra augment or replace the basic piano-organ-drums sound of traditional gospel. Heilbut has summed it up in these words: "The eclecticism of 'contemporary gospel' derives from several sources: the academic training of many young choir directors; the example of the highly complex recording techniques of a Stevie Wonder or Michael Jackson; and the simple financial lure."[16]

In live performances and on live recordings, "audience" has replaced "congregation." Perhaps the trend toward multiracial concert audiences accounts in part for Boyer's observation that congregational response during many contemporary gospel concerts consists of smiling, soft weeping, and clapping, most often on a primary, rather than a secondary beat, that is, shunning the "backbeat" so traditional in black music. Where a section of a song would have previously elicited a moan, shout, or vocal utterance, the audience response is only applause at concerts of contemporary gospel.[17] Boyer goes on to note the loss of "participation"—a passive role has replaced the formerly active one.

Andraé Crouch, one of the leaders of contemporary gospel, goes so far in the lyrics of one of his songs as to disown gospel's roots in the worship of the Holiness churches:

> *You don't have to jump no pews,*
> *Run down no aisles,*
> *No chills run down your spine;*
> *But you know that you've been born again.*
> *Don't you know my hands didn't shake,*
> *The earth didn't quake,*
> *No sparks fell from the sky;*
> *But I know that I've been born again.*[18]

Secularization and Commercialization
in African-American Gospel Music

The evolution of "contemporary" gospel style so briefly described above is only one manifestation of what has been happening to African-American gospel music since mid-century. In 1961 two significant events occurred: Mahalia Jackson sang at one of John F. Kennedy's inauguration parties, and Clara Ward and the Ward Singers started singing in nightclubs. Mahalia Jackson's appearance symbolized the widespread acceptance of gospel music, Clara Ward's its secularization. Recent developments include black gospel's move from shabby storefront churches to concert extravaganzas; the appearance of black gospel stars and groups at jazz festivals and in night clubs; a secularizing of the material, whereby "message" songs, expressing optimistic or altruistic sentiments but avoiding the words "God" or "Jesus," could be sung to a broader audience, and thus earn both popularity and money;* and a"song exchange" between gospel and secular pop music, wherein pop songs could be "gospelized," and their popularity appropriated.

Gospel music today presents a pluralistic picture. In its commercial aspect, as represented by contemporary gospel, it now accounts for a significant segment of the American popular music industry. At the grassroots level of church and community choirs, on the other hand, traditional gospel music is flourishing; ensembles such as the New Jerusalem Baptist Church Choir in Flint, Michigan, or the Sacramento Community Choir in California are giving live performances and producing "live" recordings that have a resounding authenticity. Gospel has become multiracial, and other Christian denominations, including such liturgically conservative ones as the Roman Catholic Church, have instituted gospel choirs, as have many colleges and universities. A network of teachers, workshops, and conventions (especially the large Gospel Music Workshop of America) is active in propagating and offering instruction in gospel music, not only in the United States but in other countries as well. Gospel music, following jazz and rock 'n' roll, now belongs to the long succession of exports of American popular music—all of which have stemmed from African-American roots.

FURTHER READING

Studies on twentieth-century gospel music, black and white
Boyer, Horace Clarence. "A Comparative Analysis of Traditional and Contemporary Gospel Music." In *More Than Dancing*, ed. Irene V. Jackson. Westport, CT: Greenwood, 1985.
———. "Contemporary Gospel Music." *Black Perspectives in Music* 7 (Spring 1979): 5–58.
Harris, Michael W. *The Rise of the Gospel Blues: The Music of Thomas Andrew Dorsey in the Urban Church*. New York and Oxford: Oxford University Press, 1992.
      A serious and well-documented study of a seminal figure, including transcriptions illustrating musical style. The work's thoroughness sheds light on many aspects of black gospel music.
Heilbut, Tony. "The Secularization of Black Gospel Music." In *Folk Music and Modern Sound*, ed. William Ferris and Mary L. Hart. Jackson: University Press of Mississippi, 1982.
Malone, Bill C. *Southern Music—American Music*. Lexington: University Press of Kentucky, 1979.
      This has more material specifically on gospel music than does his *Country Music, U.S.A.*
Oliver, Paul. *Songsters and Saints: Vocal Traditions on Race Records*. Cambridge: Cambridge University Press, 1984.
      Well-documented and well-written study of blues and gospel recordings made in the late 1920s.
Reagon, Bernice Johnson, ed. *We'll Understand It Better By and By*. Washington, DC, and London: Smithsonian Institution Press, 1992.
      Ten scholars, musicians, and educators contribute substantial articles on six major figures, plus an overview. There are many musical examples.
Wolfe, Charles K. "Gospel Goes Uptown: White Gospel Music, 1945–1955." In *Folk Music and Modern*

*It should be noted, however, that some gospel songs have social or political "messages" having nothing to do with entertainment; "Move on Up a Little Higher," "Surely God Is Able (to carry you through)," "I'm Climbing Higher and Higher (and I won't come down)," all by the Rev. W. Herbert Brewster, and "How I Got Over" by Clara Ward, as sung during the Civil Rights struggle of the 1950s, carried more than religious implications, just as spirituals had before Emancipation.

Sound, ed. William Ferris and Mary L. Hart. Jackson: University Press of Mississippi, 1982, 80–100.

Historical and religious background

Anderson, Robert Mapes. *Vision of the Disinherited: The Making of American Pentecostalism*. New York: Oxford University Press, 1979.

Goodspeed, Rev. E. J. *A Full History of the Wonderful Career of Moody and Sankey in Great Britain and America*. New York, 1876. Reprint. New York: AMS, 1973.

Sizer, Sandra S. *Gospel Hymns and Social Religion: The Rhetoric of Nineteenth-Century Revivalism*. Philadelphia: Temple University Press, 1978.

Projects

1. Make a survey of religious music in the repertory of currently popular country music stars, including types of songs and, if possible, their origin. To what extent has the "message" song superseded the overtly religious or gospel song? How does the situation now compare with that in the generation of Hank Williams Sr.? Of the Carter Family?

2. Make a survey of "Christian music" in the urban churches today, with emphasis on your own area if you live in a city. For each church you survey, characterize the basic repertory as being, for example, "revivalist," "traditional, with strong European influence," "folk," "pop," "ethnic," "consciously multi-ethnic," or whatever. Determine whether there is more than one *constituency* for music in the same church, and hence more than one distinct repertory, with perhaps even separate services for each.

3. Using W. E. B. Du Bois's description of the African-American preacher in *Souls of Black Folk* as a point of departure, carry this into our own time by writing a paper on the social and political roles of the black preacher since mid-century. Has the relationship of preacher to congregation carried over into the relationship of speaker to audience? In what ways?

4. Make a study of the music in the black churches in your area. How does it relate to the gospel music described in this chapter? What part do older hymns or spirituals play in the repertory? Are there differences in musical preferences between one denomination and another?

5. Listen to some examples of both "traditional" and "contemporary" gospel music. In an essay, make your own comparisons between them, evaluate what you see as the function of each, and conclude with a well-reasoned expression of your own preference.

Notes

1. The hymn tunes in Lowell Mason's *The Boston Handel and Haydn Society Collection of Church Music* (1822), which were made out of "beautiful extracts from the works of Haydn, Mozart, Beethoven and other eminent modern composers," were in most cases highly adapted from the original melodies. Many were taken from an English publication of 1812 by William Gardiner called *Sacred Melodies from Haydn, Mozart and Beethoven*. Gardiner's (and Mason's) borrowings can still be found in twentieth-century hymn collections. Some of the tunes still in use are "Sardis" and "Germany (Fulda)" by Beethoven, and "Austria" (the Austrian national hymn) by Haydn, though most have different names in the Mason collection.

2. Erik Routley, *The Music of Christian Hymnody*, quoted in Stevenson, *Protestant Church Music in America* (cited above), 112.

3. Appropriately, Ira Sankey's reed organ is now in the possession of the Billy Graham Evangelistic Association. George Beverly Shea, the musician for years most closely associated with Graham, can be heard singing one of Sankey's best-known songs, "The Ninety and Nine," accompanied by this organ, on New World 224.

4. The terms "Holiness," "Sanctified," and "Pentecostal" are sometimes used interchangeably to describe this general movement, which was actually made up of several distinct movements and many sects, as manifested in many practically independent denominations and churches. The term "Pentecostal" is not universally applicable to the movement as a whole, since it connotes a particular emphasis

on the phenomenon of glossolalia, or "speaking in tongues," which not all Holiness churches or adherents practice. The terms "Apostolic" and "Church of God" (or "Church of God in Christ") are frequently encountered as names of the Holiness churches. The Holiness and Pentecostal denominations were frequently racially integrated early in this century but have since become largely segregated. See Robert Mapes Anderson, *Vision of the Disinherited: The Making of American Pentecostalism* (New York: Oxford University Press, 1979).

5. A close variant of "The Royal Telephone," called "Telephone to Glory," was recorded several times by black gospel singers in the 1920s: see Paul Oliver, *Songsters and Saints* (New York: Cambridge University Press, 1984), 205. The metaphor lives on: the Mighty Clouds of Joy, a present-day black gospel quartet, recorded a distant variant with the title "Call Him Up."

6. Malone, *Southern Music—American Music*, 113.

7. One black Baptist lady, describing Holiness worship, said to Tony Heilbut, "To me, it's just like going to a movie; they *amazing*." In Heilbut, *The Gospel Sound* (Third Limelight Edition, 1989), 173.

8. William E. B. Du Bois, *The Souls of Black Folk: Essays and Sketches* (Chicago: McClurg, 1903), chapter 10, as quoted in Oliver, *Songsters and Saints*, 140. On the capacity for showmanship, and even for "clowning," that was involved, see Heilbut, "The Secularization of Black Gospel Music" in William Ferris and Mary L. Hart, eds., *Folk Music and Modern Sound* (Jackson: University Press of Mississippi, 1982), 103.

9. "Jesus Rose from the Dead" is on *An Introduction to Gospel Song*, Folkways/Smithsonian RF–5, which includes three more sermons. The *Anthology of American Folk Music*, vol. 2 (2952), includes two sermons by the Rev. Gates and one each by the Rev. McGee, the Rev. Moses Mason, and the Rev. D. C. Rice. All were recorded between 1927 and 1931.

10. Paul Oliver points up an interesting contrast between the races in their responses to the Titanic disaster: for whites it could be accounted for by "human error or folly," while blacks attached far more metaphorical significance to it as "indicating the inevitability of God's judgment on the arrogance of those who believed themselves invincible." See his *Songsters and Saints*, 223.

11. Some blues singers did record gospel songs, usually under different names. Blind Lemon Jefferson's recording of "I Want to Be like Jesus in My Heart" was released under the name of Deacon L. J. Bates, and Charley Patton recorded gospel songs as Elder J. J. Hadley. There were token releases by other blues singers as well. See Oliver, *Songsters and Saints*, 202–4.

12. See Oliver, *Songsters and Saints*, 195–96.

13. Horace Clarence Boyer, "C. A. Tindley: Progenitor of Black-American Gospel Music," *Black Perspectives in Music* 11, no. 2 (Fall 1983): 113.

14. Horace Clarence Boyer's chronology of male gospel ensembles can be found in his article in *The New Grove Dictionary of American Music*, vol. 2, 254–59. This can be compared with Heilbut's chronology in chapter 3 of *The Gospel Sound*.

15. "I Feel the Spirit" can be heard on *Take Me to the Water: The Gospel Music of Clarence Eggleton*. CD, Epiphany Enterprises, 916-478-9325.

16. Heilbut, "The Secularization of Black Gospel Music," 113. Examples of contemporary gospel music may be heard in virtually any album by Andraé Crouch, the Winans, Al Green, or the Hawkins Family. "Contemporary" gospel is a product in which there is indeed a fine line, often subtly crossed, between the sacred and the secular. The secularization of which Heilbut speaks sometimes involves not only adopting the "highly complex recording techniques of a . . . Michael Jackson," but imitating, in a muted way, the latter's sex appeal as well, as album photos of Al Green or Edwin Hawkins, with open shirt and necklace, show.

17. Horace Clarence Boyer, "A Comparative Analysis of Traditional and Contemporary Gospel Music" in *More Than Dancing*, ed. Irene Jackson (Westport, CT: Greenwood, 1985), 143.

18. "You Don't Have to Jump No Pews (I've been born again)" on the album *Autograph*, produced by Lexicon Music, Inc., SPCN–7U57–10740.

Popular Secular Music

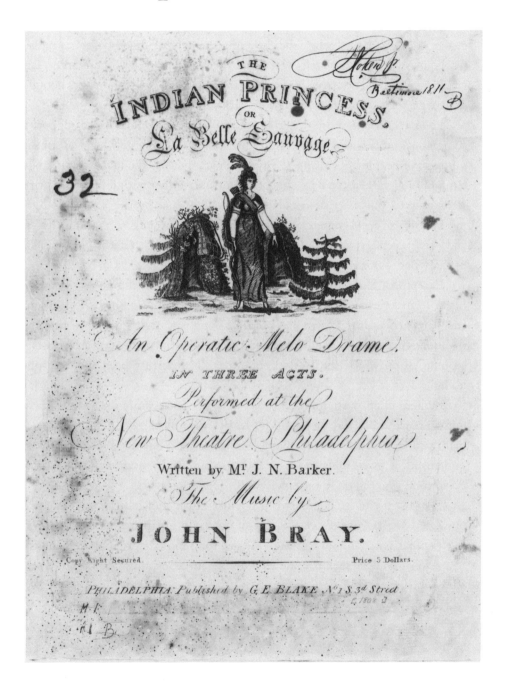

A by-product of the growth of cities, and the consequent specialization of human endeavor, is the evolution of a popular culture (produced for the mass of the populace by specialists) as distinct from a folk culture (made for people in smaller groups, or cultural "villages," by people who are themselves members of the village). If we illustrate this by an analogy with the production of another commodity we consume in great quantities—our daily bread—a first stage in this evolution is reached when the home-baked is replaced by the store-bought. A second stage is reached when that baked in the neighborhood bakery is replaced by the mass-produced plastic-wrapped article for sale in the supermarket; large, efficient baking plants serve huge areas, and the bread looks and tastes about the same whether we buy it in Arizona or Vermont.

Popular music requires a certain critical mass of population to support the commercial process devoted to its production. It will emerge whenever sufficient numbers of people are willing to pay for an art that has the look or sound of the familiar (it always has some points of resemblance either with folk art or with the well-accepted fine art that people know), that is made easily affordable by the mechanisms of its commercial distribution, and that adds something desirable and even necessary to their lives without being too difficult to understand. Its primary purpose is to entertain.

Except for the products of the Yankee singing-school composers, we did not begin to make our own distinctive kind of popular music until the Jacksonian era—an era of cultural as well as political populism. It was not until the end of the nineteenth century that the making of popular music became an industry—an industry in which the United States has for a century been the undisputed leader.

Because of the vast market, those who can successfully create this kind of music are naturally very well paid for it. But the gift of creating something that many people will regard as memorable, and that will be immediately and widely in demand, is mysterious and rare, and there are never very many around at any given time who can do it extremely well.

The distinctions made between popular music and folk, ethnic, or fine-art music are distinctions of *function*, not of quality or ultimate value. The superlative popular song, the "evergreen," the one song in perhaps a hundred thousand that resonates in the memory and feelings of generation after generation, is surely one of the glories of American music.

Chapter 10

Secular Music in the Cities from Colonial Times to the Jacksonian Era

Musical life in the largest American cities (Philadelphia, New York, Boston, Charleston, and Baltimore) during the Colonial and Federal periods was by no means primitive or dull. Music historians, together with performers specializing in the re-creation of early music, have illuminated the existence of a lively and varied musical culture in our growing urban centers. To re-create a sense of what this musical life was like is the purpose of this chapter.

Concerts and Dances

The giving of public concerts for which people pay admission presupposes a certain critical mass of population that will include enough people with the means, the leisure, and the inclination to support such endeavors. For the first hundred years of eastern seaboard settlement this was not the case. But by the middle of the eighteenth century, public concerts were being given fairly regularly in Philadelphia, New York, Boston, and Charleston.*

What were these concerts like? Many of the early ones would hardly fit our notion of a formal concert of classical music; the music itself was varied and popular, but in addition the program could include dramatic recitations, card tricks, balancing acts ("a dance upon wire"), and other "Manly Feats of Activity." Another pleasurable aspect of concert life was the outdoor concert in the summer months, modeled after English practice. Two attractions existed then that have been familiar to patrons of outdoor summer concerts ever since—fireworks and ice cream!

Dancing in the Eighteenth and Early Nineteenth Centuries

That the range of pleasures offered by these events was agreeably broad is demonstrated by the fact that the concert proper was nearly always followed by "proper music . . . to wait upon such ladies and gentlemen, as may choose to dance."

---

*Oscar Sonneck determined that the first "concert of music on sundry instruments" was given in Boston in 1731.

"The concert will terminate by a ball" was the pleasant and in fact nearly obligatory promise put forth in most advertisements. The kind of dancing that would have gone on at these balls varied with time and place. In Colonial times, especially among the landed gentry of the southern colonies, it is likely that the elegant *minuet*, and possibly also the more intricate *gavotte*, would be danced. After the Revolution, these dances, with their suggestions of monarchy and aristocracy, fell out of favor. The *country dances*, on the other hand, enjoyed the widest popularity throughout the period. Of English origin, they were done in all the colonies and states, by all classes of society, in urban as well as rural settings. A French importation, the *cotillion*, became the *quadrille* (which in time gave rise to the more typically rural *square dance*). Both the country dance, with its typical lining up of dancers in opposing rows (as in the later *Virginia reel*), and the quadrille, with its square set of eight dancers, were social dances, as contrasted with later couples dances such as the *waltz* and the *galop*. The music for country dances came from a variety of sources. Fortunately, some of it has been preserved in manuscript books, mainly for the use of the fifers and fiddlers who played for dancing. Many tunes used for eighteenth-century dancing are still familiar to us today, including "The Rakes of Mallow," "The Irish Washerwoman," "Soldier's Joy" (which in its countless variants became a staple in the fiddler's repertory), and "The College Hornpipe" (better known to us today as "The Sailor's Hornpipe").

Example 10–1. "The College Hornpipe"

The Performers

Who were the musicians that furnished the music for the first hundred years of our urban musical life? Contemporary advertisements show those who plied the trade of "music master" to have been of a hardy, resourceful, and versatile breed. In addition to being music masters, many were also dancing masters and fencing masters; they were thus equipped to minister to more than one need of the polished aristocrat of the day, especially in the southern colonies. Many also offered a variety of musical instruments for sale—as well as tobacco and other sundries. It is known that a great many African Americans were accomplished musicians, and played for dances in the northern as well as the southern colonies and states.*[1]

The child prodigy was evidently a great attraction at concerts, promoted by parents who were professional performers, and who seized the opportunity to capitalize on an unsophisticated public's curiosity and eagerness to be amazed. The ages of such children were naturally featured in their announcements. A certain "P. Lewis, Professor of Music" presented an entire program in Boston in 1819 in which his children—aged eight, seven, and four—were the sole performers; the concert was exceptional only because the children were so young and so numerous.

The century 1730–1830 was a period of gradual transition from the amateur to the professional. Though the word "amateur" does not appear at first, his identity was made plain by the use of the word "gentleman," as distinguished from the professional, who was designated as "professor." By this the "gentleman amateur" not only maintained his distinction of class, but insulated himself from judgment by professional standards. An advertisement of a concert in Charleston in 1772 makes both these points plainly: "The vocal part by a gentleman, who does it merely to oblige on this occasion." After the privations of the Revolution had passed, the flow of professional immigrants increased, mostly on account of the increased appetite for musical theater in the cities. This resulted in the gradual reduction of the amateur, "gentleman" or not, to a distinctly subordinate role in the growing musical life of the cities.[2]

The Composers

Who were the composers of this music? Late in the eighteenth century it began to be common to print programs, especially in the newspapers. We find, as might be expected, that the composers were mostly European; Haydn, Pleyel, Handel, Stamitz, and Corelli appear frequently. After the Revolution, with the coming into prominence of the professional musician, we find the names of those, either immigrants or native-born, who must be recognized as our first American composers, including among the native-born Francis Hopkinson, Samuel Holyoke, and Oliver Shaw, and among the immigrants Alexander Reinagle, James Hewitt, and Rayner Taylor.

*Some of the scant information we have on this subject comes from contemporary newspapers, in advertisements about slaves—either "for sale" or "runaway." These indicate that the most common instrument played was the fiddle, but the fife, drum, flute, banjo, and French horn also appear in the lists.

Concert Music

The programs played at these concerts were much more varied than we are accustomed to. As the frequent appearance of the phrase "Concert [earlier spelled "Consort"] of Vocal and Instrumental Musick" indicates, songs were nearly always included. The instrumental pieces were overtures, symphonies (not usually performed in their entirety, as later audiences would come to expect), sonatas, and concertos or solos for various instruments. Popular solo instruments were the violin, the guitar, the "German flute" (the transverse flute, in contrast to the recorder), the French horn, and the harp.

Programmatic pieces intended to depict momentous events (usually battles, but sometimes travels by sea or land, which in those days were also momentous and could be equally hazardous) began to appear toward the end of the eighteenth century. *The Battle of Prague*, by the Bohemian-born Frantisek Koczwara (Franz Kotzwara), showed up on numerous programs for half a century, and was a kind of prototype. American contributions to the genre were represented by *The Battle of Trenton*, a pastiche arranged from various sources by James Hewitt, and after the French Revolution, *The Demolition of the Bastille*, by John Berkenhead. These programmatic pieces persisted well into the nineteenth century.[3]

The Audiences

What were the audiences for these concerts like? For one thing, they could be noisy—though not as noisy as theater audiences. Nevertheless, the admonition by the performer who "finds himself obliged to request that silence may be observed during his performance" was not unusual. They could even be rowdy; one concert manager advertised that "every possible precaution will be used to prevent disorder and irregularity," while another promised that a "number of constables will attend to preserve order."

On another point, it is clear that audiences did not represent the broad spectrum of the populace at large—an advertisement in Charleston in 1799 makes it clear that "persons of color" will not be admitted, for example. And from the same city in 1782 we find an announcement to the effect that "gentlemen of the navy, army [referring to officers during the British occupation of the city] and the most respectable part of town" would be admitted. It is clear that concerts, at least in the early part of the period, were primarily for "gentlemen." "Ladies" typically were admitted on the "gentleman's" ticket, sometimes two for each.

Bands and Military Music

The functions of military music throughout history have been manifold: to dignify ceremonial functions, to lift morale, to enable soldiers to march in step together, and, of supreme practical importance, to convey signals and commands. The last two needs, essential but utilitarian, were met by the simplest means— that which has long been known as *field music*. For eighteenth-century foot soldiers this meant drums and fifes, which were incorporated into each company unit. The fifers often were young boys. Collections of music for the fife existed in print and manuscript in the eighteenth century, and the tunes were often those of songs or dances of the period. "**Lady Hope's Reel**" was one such tune. It is shown in the first two lines of Example 10-2 as it was written down by a fifer in the Revolutionary War, Giles Gibbs Jr., who was seventeen years old when he copied out these tunes in the summer of 1777. He was captured and killed by a British raiding party in 1780. Example 10-3 presents the tune as edited, with reference to other sources, for a modern edition of *Giles Gibbs, Jr.: His Book for the Fife*.

Example 10–2. "Lady Hope's Reel" I

Example 10–3. "Lady Hope's Reel" II

To fulfill more elaborate functions, larger ensembles, known as *bands of music*, were formed. The basic makeup was a pair of oboes, a pair of French horns, and one or two bassoons, often with a pair of clarinets either replacing or supplementing the oboes. **"Washington's March"** (one of many to bear this title) illustrates the sound. This was a kind of ensemble well known in Europe, and masters such as Haydn and Mozart wrote a considerable amount of what was basically outdoor music for this ensemble, or augmented versions of it. "Bands of music" were usually employed by the regimental officers themselves, and were used on social as well as military occasions. Made up of fairly skilled musicians, who often played stringed instruments as well, they came to play a rather prominent role in the musical life of the times, especially during the time of the Revolution. These bands played for military ceremonies and parades, at which the public were often spectators. They also played for dances for the officers and their ladies, and even gave public concerts, and on occasion played in the theaters.

Musical Theater

The musical theater, in its many varied forms, was the institution on which most of the musical life in the cities centered in this period, especially after the Revolution. It was usually the theater that employed those professional musicians who were active here, and that attracted performers, composers, and impresarios from Europe (mostly from England).

In the eighteenth century, music was a nearly universal accompaniment to theatrical performances of all kinds. Even what we would regard today as straight drama (the plays of Shakespeare, for example) was usually presented with interpolated songs, dances, and incidental music. What is generally regarded as the first theater in the colonies was built in Williamsburg, Virginia, in 1716, and there is evidence that musicians were employed in this enterprise from the very beginning.[4] Furthermore, it has been shown that the majority of stage works produced here were actually "musicals"—belonging to one of the many various, confusing, and overlapping types that will be alluded to presently.

But if music was nearly always present in the theater, and its presence taken for granted, it was the most ephemeral ingredient of any production, and its providers were subordinate and often anonymous. The music for operas, or related musical genres, was often appropriated from other sources to begin with; it was also frequently changed from production to production, and from city to city, as the show traveled. The music was not usually published, and it was subsequently often lost altogether. From the truly impressive number of musical stage works presented here in the century between 1730 and 1830 a disappointingly small amount of the actual music has survived.

Theatrical Genres

There existed in this period a vast array of entertainments in which music was a major ingredient. Until about 1800, the forms we would most recognize today as "musicals" were the famous ballad opera and its often less precisely defined successors, the pastiche opera and the comic opera. What they had in common was spoken dialogue, which was interspersed with songs, and sometimes with dances and choruses. The music was in a style familiar to its public. For the most part the characters and situations were drawn from everyday life.

The original ballad opera was the famous *The Beggar's Opera*, first performed in London in 1728. With its already-popular tunes, its memorable low-life characters, and its satirization of the conventions of the imported upper-class Italian opera of its day (which it nearly put out of business for a time), it was an instant success, and was soon widely imitated. Though the initial intensity of its popularity, and the heyday of ballad opera in general, was over in London in a decade or so, a certain few operas of this genre proved to be amazingly long-lived, especially in America. *The Beggar's Opera* itself was performed in Providence, Rhode Island, by a "Sett of Inhabitants" (amateurs) at least as early as 1746, and by a professional company in New York by 1750.[5] Julian Mates has written that "it was *The Beggar's Opera*, in most places, which introduced the musical to America."[6] It was a staple of the repertory through the remainder of the eighteenth century, and has been revived, in various forms, ever since.

By 1800 ballad operas and pastiches were no longer being written, and a new genre, the *melodrama*, appeared, which coexisted with comic opera for the rest of the period with which this chapter deals. The melodrama introduced wordless instrumental music as an accompaniment to stage action. An American "Operatic Melo-Drame" that has survived is **The Indian Princess, or La Belle Sauvage**, first performed in Philadelphia in 1808. It is based on an American subject—the story of Captain John Smith and Pocahontas. In each of the three acts there is music to accompany stage action, as for example "Smith brought in prisoner," "Smith is led to the block," "The Princess leads Smith to the throne," "She supplicates the King for his pardon," and "Smith is pardoned—general joy diffused." Also of interest is the inclusion of the Irishman, Larry, and his lament—an early appearance of the ethnic characters that were such a feature of the popular musical theater in the late nineteenth century.

Political independence of the colonies from England was declared in 1776, but cultural independence evolved much more slowly. For three-quarters of a century more, the legacy of English comic opera, with its comic characters, its homely but pungent satire, and its popular, folklike songs, was entertaining Americans, if not continuously in the large cities of the eastern seaboard, then in crude, sparsely documented, but keenly enjoyed performances in frontier towns and cities. The tenacity of the pieces themselves was amazing. An example is *The Poor Soldier* (a favorite of George Washington), written by an Irish playright, John O'Keeffe, and first performed in London in 1783. It reached the United States in 1785, and after a successful New York run of nineteen performances by the famous Old American Company, it was taken on the road by that company. Thereafter, until the end of the eighteenth century, hardly a year went by without a performance of *The Poor Soldier* somewhere, by some company. In 1801 it was done in Cincinnati—the first play performed in the Northwest Territory—and continued to be played throughout the Ohio Valley for twenty years. *The Poor Soldier* was part of the American theatrical scene in one form or another almost until the Civil War; the same was true of *Love in a Village*, both thriving alongside the circus and the minstrel show (see chapter 11).

In addition to the comic operas, there was a bewildering variety of theatrical entertainments, all of which employed music in some form. Theatrical presentations hardly ever consisted of just a single play, and could go on for four or five hours! There were shorter "afterpieces" that followed the main play or opera, sometimes known as *farces*. *Interludes* were even slighter pieces that went between the acts of longer works. In addition, there were forms such as the *pantomime*, in which stage action and speech were accompanied by wordless music. A species of pantomime popular in America featured the old stock-comic figures of the *commedia dell'arte*, especially that of Harlequin. Like a character in a "sit-com," Harlequin appears in many settings, in pieces with titles such as "Harlequin Doctor," "Harlequin Barber," "Harlequin Balloonist," "Harlequin Pastry-cook."

Theaters and Audiences

The first theatrical performances in the colonies were given in buildings made for other purposes—often in taverns or warehouses (though not in churches). The first musical in America, in 1735, was given in the Courtroom in Charleston, South Carolina. By mid-century, theaters had been built in most cities. The space for the audience, according to a plan that remained basically unaltered to the twentieth century, was divided into three distinct parts: at the bottom level was the "pit" (now called the "orchestra"); above this, in a horseshoe shape around the walls, were one or more tiers of boxes; and above the boxes was the gallery. The distribution of the audience was rigidly defined: "ladies and gentlemen in the boxes, the pit occupied almost entirely by unattached gentlemen, and the gallery 'reserved for the rabble.'"[7] An announcement of 1759 quotes the following prices: "Box, 8 shillings. Pit, 5 shillings. Gallery, 2 shillings."[8]

The behavior of audiences was, by our standards, notoriously bad. There was loud talking and often card playing in the boxes, and coming and going, with the slamming of doors. Prostitutes, who used the theater (in Sonneck's words) "as a kind of stock exchange,"[9] were by custom assigned the upper boxes. Liquor was served to the "unattached gentlemen" in the pit. It was not until the end of the century that the custom of allowing some of the audience to sit on the stage during the performance was abolished. But the greatest disturbances came from the gallery. It was customary for people in the gallery to interrupt the orchestra's performance by shouting down requests for popular tunes—requests that, if not complied with to their satisfaction, would result in loud demonstrations. A letter to a New York newspaper as late as 1802 describes the behavior of the gallery "gods": "The mode by which they issue their mandates is stamping, hissing, roaring, whistling; and, when the musicians are refractory, groaning in cadence." The habit of the gallery's throwing objects at the orchestra, and into the pit, was notorious. "As soon as the curtain was down, the *gods* in the galleries would throw apples, nuts, bottles and glasses onto the stage and into the orchestra." Mates quotes a report of a performance in 1794 "when half the instruments in the orchestra were broken by missiles from the upper reaches of the theater."[10] Thieves and pickpockets in the theaters were common. Feelings in the audience (often motivated by the volatile political issues of the day) ran high, especially in the Federal era and after the French Revolution; certain tunes were associated with certain factions (pro- or anti-Federalist, pro- or anti-French, and so on), so that managers and orchestra leaders had to be extremely judicious in the choice of music, in order not to provoke the riots that were all too common in the theaters of the day.

Popular Song

Popular song—enjoyed by the general populace and not associated with the stage or the concert hall—is at once the most widespread kind of music-making and the most difficult to chronicle. Secular songs were not published complete with lyrics and music together until the last decade of the eighteenth century. Before that time, popular songs were disseminated in print for the most part by the publication of the words alone, either as single-sheet *broadsides*, or in collections called *songsters* (see chapter 1). By the time of the Revolution, newspapers, of which there were a great many in the colonies, had become another medium for the publication of lyrics, especially topical verses dealing with the patriotic and political matters that were of so much concern at the time.[11] It is not possible to determine now whether all of these versifications (often crude by literary standards) were in fact meant to be sung, but the strength of the ballad tradition, the number of tunes known to be in wide circulation, and the fact that in many cases the names of the tunes were given justify our including this vast output in our consideration of popular song. Many patriotic songs, including "Yankee Doodle" and the many sets of words associated with it, were first disseminated in this manner.

One very popular song that was parodied in broadsides of the time was "The Dusky Night" or "A-Hunting We Will Go." The tune is given in Figure 10-1 as it appeared in a copybook of 1797.

Figure 10–1. "The Dusky Night" or "A-Hunting We Will Go" as written out in 1797. Note the differences between this tune and the version that is familiar today.

The first version of the song, as used in a revival of *The Beggar's Opera* in England, is:

> *The Dusky Night rides down the Sky,*
> *When wakes the Rosey Morn,*
> *The Hounds all join the Jovial cry,* (2x)
> *The Huntsman winds his Horn.* (2x)
>
> *(Chorus)*
>
> *Then a Hunting let us go.* (4x)

The broadside parody, attacking the British desire to raise more revenue from the colonies, appeared in journals of the day in New York and Philadelphia. Known as the **Junto Song**, it substitutes "A-taxing we will go" for the original words of the chorus.

There was no very clear dividing line between sacred and secular in this period, and religion was often invoked in political and military struggles. William Billings's "**Chester**," especially with the updated topical verses added for its second version of 1778, is said to have been the most popular song of the Revolutionary War.*

The turn of the century saw the beginnings of change, gradual but significant, in our urban secular music. In terms of the medium of dissemination, the publishing of songs individually, rather than in sets, marked the beginning

---

*Both the music and the words of "Chester" are quoted in chapter 8, Example 8-1.

of *sheet music*, which became, during the nineteenth century, the basis for the entire popular music industry, known later as Tin Pan Alley. In the first quarter of the nineteenth century the growth in sheer volume of music published was in marked contrast to the last quarter of the eighteenth; in the period 1801–25 nearly ten thousand titles appeared of secular music alone.[12] The range, in terms of songs, was broad—from topical songs on political or patriotic themes, crude but timely, to settings of the poetry of Shakespeare, Sir Walter Scott, or Thomas Moore. This very breadth was symptomatic of a divergence of taste that was to lead, as the century progressed, to the fragmentation of our musical culture.

FURTHER READING

Books

Camus, Raoul F. *Military Music of the American Revolution*. Chapel Hill: University of North Carolina Press, 1976.

> Basic work by a leading authority.

Hamm, Charles. *Yesterdays: Popular Song in America*. New York: Norton, 1979.

> The first five chapters deal with this period.

Lambert, Barbara, ed. *Music in Colonial Massachusetts. 1630–1820*. 2 vols. I: *Music in Public Places*. II. *Music in Homes and in Churches*. Charlottesville: University Press of Virginia, 1980, 1985.

Lowens, Irving. *Music and Musicians in Early America*. New York: Norton, 1964.

> Articles on various topics, from the seventeenth century to the mid-nineteenth.

Mates, Julian. *The American Musical Stage Before 1800*. New Brunswick, NJ: Rutgers University Press, 1962.

> Popularly written, readable, with copious documentation.

Porter, Susan L. *With an Air Debonair: Musical Theatre in America 1785–1815*. Washington, DC: Smithsonian Institution Press, 1991.

> Unquestionably the most thorough and comprehensive work on the subject. Includes a painstaking clarification of the various confusing genres. Appendix A consists of a checklist of musical entertainments performed in the United States during the period, giving librettist, composer, genre, and the date and place of the first performance in America. Appendix B gives a list of theater performances in five American cities, 1801–15.

Sonneck, Oscar George. *Early Concert-Life in America (1731–1800)*. New York: Musurgia, 1949. Reprint of 1906 ed.

> An indispensable work by a pioneering scholar in American music; all of the quotes in the chapter from contemporary newspaper accounts are from this book or *Early Opera in America*. Sonneck's painstaking study of contemporary newspapers up to 1800 is being expanded in a project carried out by the Sonneck Society that bears his name.

———. *Early Opera in America*. New York: Benjamin Blom, 1963. Reprint of 1915 ed.

Modern collections or anthologies

Anderson, Gillian, comp. and ed. *Freedom's Voice in Poetry and Song*. Wilmington, DE: Scholarly Resources, 1977.

> This compendious "inventory of political and patriotic lyrics in colonial American newspapers" concludes with a songbook with 92 songs and 8 poems.

Keller, Kate Van Winkle, and Ralph Sweet, eds. *A Choice Selection of American Country Dances of the Revolutionary Era, 1775–1795*. New York: Country Dance and Song Society of America, 1976.

Twenty-nine dance tunes on single staff, with directions for performing the dances.

Rabson, Carolyn, comp. and ed. *Songbook of the American Revolution*. Peaks Island, ME: NEO Press, 1974.
Single-staff tunes, with suggested chords; annotations and sources.

Articles in American Music *by subject*

Theater

Borroff, Edith. "Origin of Species: Conflicting Views of American Musical Theater History," 2, no. 4 (Winter 1984): 101–12.

Brooks, William. "*Pocahontas*: Her Life and Times," 2, no. 4 (Winter 1984): 19–48.

Hoover, Cynthia Adams. "Music in Eighteenth-Century American Theater," 2, no. 4 (Winter 1984): 6–18.

Mates, Julian. "The First Hundred Years of American Lyric Theater," 1, no. 2 (Summer 1983): 22–38.

Shapiro, Anne Dhu. "Action Music in American Pantomime and Melodrama, 1730–1913," 2, no. 4 (Winter 1984): 49–72.

Song

Tawa, Nicholas E. "Songs of the Early Nineteenth Century. Part 1: Early Song Lyrics and Coping with Life," 13, no. 1 (Spring 1995): 1–26.

———. "Serious Songs of the Early Nineteenth Century. Part 2: The Meaning of the Early Song Melodies," 13, no. 3 (Fall 1995): 263–94.

Projects

1. If you are a country dance enthusiast, write a paper on the eighteenth-century forebears of either the "square dances" or the "line dances" that are popular today.

2. As revealed in this chapter, audiences in the eighteenth century were often inconsiderate and ill-behaved. From personal observation, write a paper on the behavior of present-day audiences for a variety of events in a variety of locations: a classical concert, a jazz concert, a rock concert, a concert of folk music, and so on. To what would you attribute the differences, both between the eighteenth and the twentieth centuries, and between various kinds of contemporary events?

3. As a group project, work up the presentation of a scene from an eighteenth-century ballad opera. Include some of the songs if possible, although the spoken dialogue of the printed texts alone will make a comprehensible scene. A copious source, available in larger libraries, is W. Rubsamen, ed., *The Ballad Opera: A Collection of 191 Original Texts of Musical Plays Printed in Photo-Facsimile* (New York: Garland, 1974).

4. Sketch a plot and scenario for a modern-day "ballad opera," dealing in a comical and even satirical way with some current issue or event. Read the texts of several ballad operas in preparation for this (see project 3 above for a source); the scenes should be short and the characters few, and allowance should be made for the inclusion of "airs," which can be parodies of existing popular songs.

5. Write a paper on the history of *The Beggar's Opera*, including such twentieth-century reincarnations as the Brecht/Weill *Threepenny Opera*.

6. Study the modern edition of *Disappointment: or, The Force of Credulity* (Madison, WI: A-R Editions, 1976), an eighteenth-century ballad opera that was not performed until 1937. Read the two articles on the subject by Carolyn Rabson in *American Music* (1, no. 1 [Spring 1983]: 12ff, and 2, no. 1 [Spring 1984]: 1ff). Write an article, in a lively journalistic style, describing the piece and its history.

Notes

1. See Southern, *The Music of Black Americans*, 2d ed., chapters 2 and 3.

2. The circumstances attending, and contributing to, replacement of the amateur by the professional musician are treated with sympathy and perception by Richard Crawford in his notes to New World–80299, *Music of the Federal Era*.

3. The best single sampling of concert music of the period is to be found on New World–80299 *Music of the Federal Era*, which treats both vocal and instrumental music, including an excerpt from the ubiquitous *The Battle of Prague*. It does not accurately reflect the *proportion* of American music on concert programs of the Colonial period, which were dominated by European music.

4. See Mates, *The American Musical Stage Before 1800*, 40.

5. See David McKay, "Opera in Colonial Boston." (*American Music*, 3, no. 2 [Summer 1985]: 140), and O. G. Sonneck, *Early Opera in America* (New York: Benjamin Blom, 1963), 15.

6. Mates, *The American Musical Stage Before 1800*, 142.

7. Ibid., 64.

8. Quoted in Sonneck, *Early Opera in America*, 26.

9. Ibid., 121.

10. Mates, 73.

11. Gillian Anderson, examining issues of 126 newspapers, found nearly 1,500 such lyrics printed during the ten-year period 1783–93. See her *Freedom's Voice in Poetry and Song*.

12. See Richard J. Wolfe, *Secular Music in America, 1801–1825: A Bibliography* (New York: New York Public Library, 1964).

Chapter 11

Popular Musical Theater from the Jacksonian Era
to the Present

The age of Jackson, characterized by westward expansion and a new degree of political populism, marked the beginning of a new era of *cultural* populism as well. One useful yardstick of this new populism was the music publishing industry, which was expanding rapidly and catering to a much broader segment of the people. New methods of lithography made possible the use of black-and-white illustrations in sheet music in the late 1820s, and colored illustrations in the 1840s[1]—developments that were clearly linked to a growing popular market, as can be seen in the popular nature and appeal of illustrated sheet music published in the 1820s and 1830s. Thus the period from 1820 to 1840, which saw the admission of three new western states into the union (Missouri, Arkansas, and Michigan), the opening of the Erie Canal, and the construction of the Baltimore and Ohio Railroad to carry paying passengers as far west as Harpers Ferry, also saw the mass publication of sentimental popular favorites such as "Woodman! Spare That Tree!"—and also, for less genteel tastes, "Massee Georgee Washington and General Lafayette," "My Long-Tail Blue," "Jim Crow," and "Zip Coon,"—all illustrated with blackface figures with exaggerated features, dress, and poses.[2]

As the country was expanding westward, so were its cities growing rapidly, both on the more settled eastern seaboard and in the Ohio and Mississippi valleys. And as the cities grew, so did the number and size of the theaters, and the audience for the vast array of theatrical entertainments that we noted in the last chapter—comic operas, musical romances, melodramas, farces, and pantomimes. Two forms in particular—the *olio*, a kind of variety show that predated vaudeville, and the *circus*, which had incorporated comic song-and-dance acts into its original format—prepared the way for the first of a succession of truly indigenous forms of popular musical entertainment.

Minstrelsy and Musical Entertainment Before the Civil War

The first of these indigenous forms, and one that swept the country by mid-century, was the blackface minstrel show. It was based on what had become by then a common source of entertainment among the broader masses, both in America and in England: the parodied portrayal of any people who would be seen as exotic to the majority of urban theatregoers. This included rural people, Irish people, German people, Jewish people and, as early as the eighteenth century, people of African descent in this country.

The faculty of black people for spontaneous song and dance, and for unbridled comedy, was well known to observers such as Lewis Paine.* Spending some time in Georgia in the 1840s, he described the festivities after a corn shucking:

> The fiddler walks out, and strikes up a tune; and at it they go in a regular tear-down dance; for here they are at home. . . . I never saw a slave in my life but would stop as if he were shot at the sound of a fiddle; and if he has a load of two hundred pounds on his head, he will begin to dance. One would think they had steam engines inside of them, to jerk them about with so much power; for they go through more motions in a minute, than you could shake two sticks at in a month; and of all comic actions, ludicrous sights, and laughable jokes, and truly comic songs, there is no match for them.[3]

It is clear from this that there was abundant material here for imitation by white entertainers, once they saw its potential. The original black minstrelsy was an informal, spontaneous, and exuberant affair of the plantation. But its reputation spread. Thus it came about that the native songs, dances, and comedy of the slaves first reached the general American public in the form of parodies by white entertainers.

The Beginnings of Minstrelsy

Impersonations on the stage of the black man by the white were already taking place in the eighteenth century, both here and in England. Two American entertainers, George Washington Dixon (1808–61) and Thomas Dartmouth "Daddy" Rice (1808–60), did blackface song-and-dance routines in the 1820s and 1830s. Dixon introduced the songs "Long Tail Blue" (referring to the blue swallowtail coat associated with the black urban dandy) and "Coal Black Rose." Rice was famous for his song-and-dance routine "Jim Crow," which he introduced in 1832 and which, according to a well-known story, he adapted from the singing and movements of a black man he encountered in Cincinnati.[4]

Familiar and very popular as single acts in olios and circuses, the impersonation of blacks had, by the 1830s, evolved into two stage types. One, typified by

*Paine, a white man from Rhode Island, went to the South for an extended stay on business and was sentenced to prison there for helping a slave to escape.

Gumbo Chaff or Jim Crow, portrayed the ragged plantation or riverboat hand, joyous, reckless, uncouth. The other, typified by Zip Coon or Dandy Jim, was a citified northern dandy, with exaggeratedly elegant clothes and manners. The extent to which some songs of the minstrel period have entered into the great body of perennial American tunes is illustrated by the fact that the tune of "Old Zip Coon" has been perpetuated since the Civil War as "Turkey in the Straw."

The minstrel show itself was put together in the early 1840s. It consisted of songs (both solo and "full chorus"), dances, jokes, conundrums, satirical speeches, and skits. The performers, only four in number at first, seated themselves in a rough semicircle on the stage. In the middle were the banjo player and the fiddle player. The two "end men" played the tambourine and the bones, and these, along with the inevitable foot-tapping of the banjo player, provided a kind of rhythm section. It was the end men who indulged in the most outrageous horse-play. The bones, which were in the beginning actually just that, were held one pair in each hand and rattled together. The fiddle played the tune more or less straight, while the banjo, instead of merely strumming chords as it would in the later jazz band, played an ornamented version of the tune. Since the banjo music was eventually written down and published, we know not only that it presupposes a good deal of agility, but also that the lively and syncopated rhythms were similar to those that would appear later in ragtime.

What did the early minstrel band actually sound like? Hans Nathan, in his *Dan Emmett and the Rise of Early Negro Minstrelsy*, has this to say:

> The volume of the minstrel band was quite lean, yet anything but delicate. The tones of the banjo died away quickly and therefore could not serve as a solid foundation in the ensemble. On top was the squeaky, carelessly tuned fiddle. Add the dry, "ra, raka, taka, tak" of the bones and the tambourine's dull thumps and ceaseless jingling to the twang of the banjo and the flat tone of the fiddle, and the sound of the band is approximated: it was scratchy, tinkling, cackling, and humorously incongruous.[5]

The coming to town of the touring minstrel show was as eagerly anticipated as the coming of the circus, with which it had a good deal in common. The troupe's arrival was signaled by the inevitable parade through town, winding up at the theater where the evening performance was to be given. At this performance the public's expectations of an evening of vivid and diverting entertainment were seldom disappointed; they laughed hard at the comic songs, repartee, conundrums, and grotesque antics of the end men, and the skits and parodies that made up the second half of the show. But there also may have been some

Mt. Vernon, Ohio. Home of Daniel Decatur Emmett, Author of "Dixie."

Daniel Decatur Emmett. *Courtesy New York Public Library.*

moist eyes in the crowd at the close of the sentimental songs, ranging from "Old Black Joe," "My Old Kentucky Home," and "Old Uncle Ned" to such later (and less slave-oriented) songs as "She May Have Seen Better Days" or "Just Tell Them That You Saw Me."

Dan Emmett

Daniel Decatur Emmett (1815–1904) was a pioneer performer in minstrelsy, and one of the most important composers and authors of its early folkish and rough-hewn material. Born in a small Ohio town just emerging from the backwoods, Emmett grew up in a frontier society similar to that in which Lincoln was raised, with all its virtues and vices—its examples of courage and fierce independence, its violence and prejudices, and above all, its rough-and-ready humor. At eighteen, he enlisted in the army, where he mastered the drum and fife. In the late 1830s he began appearing in circuses, singing and playing the drums, and later the banjo and the fiddle.

Blackface singing and dancing with banjo accompaniment were by this time common in the circus; of the four performers who formed the original Virginia Minstrels in New York City in 1843 (Dan Emmett, Frank Brower, William Whitlock, and Richard Pelham), at least three had had experience in touring circuses. The Virginia Minstrels, the first group to use the classic instrumentation described above (fiddle, banjo, tambourine, and bones) and the first to put together a whole evening of minstrel music, dancing, and skits, caught on with both public and press in New York and Boston. The popularity of this entertainment in the United States was so great that many imitators and competitors soon appeared—E. P. Christy and his troupe among them. Emmett himself was active for over twenty-five years as an "Ethiopian" performer, and as composer-author of songs and skits, especially for the shows' finales, the "walk-arounds." His song **"De Boatman's Dance"** (Ex. 11-1) became so well known as to achieve the status of a folk song. A lively pentatonic tune, with its emphatic repetition of short motives, it is typical of the exuberant songs of early minstrelsy.

Example 11–1. "De Boatman's Dance"

It was for Bryant's Minstrels that Dan Emmett wrote "Dixie" (full title, "I Wish I Was in Dixie's Land") in 1859. Perhaps the most phenomenally popular song of the nineteenth century, it was minstrelsy's greatest single legacy to American music. It soon acquired a significance entirely unintended and even resented by its composer, when it was adopted by the Confederacy at the outbreak of the Civil War.

Stephen Foster and Minstrelsy

Stephen Collins Foster (1826–64) was minstrelsy's best-known composer. He was not, as Emmett was, a minstrel performer himself, but in 1845 he began writing "Ethiopian songs," at first for the enjoyment of a group of friends. In Cincinnati he met a member of a professional minstrel troupe (the Sable Harmonists), who introduced his "Old Uncle Ned" in one of their programs. In 1848 he wrote "Oh! Susanna," selling it outright to a Pittsburgh publisher for $100. It became enormously popular. The next year he signed a contract with the leading New York publisher, Firth, Pond & Co., and committed himself to a songwriting career. In 1852 he made a brief steamboat trip down the Ohio and Mississippi to New Orleans—his only visit to the South. Stephen Foster will be considered more fully in the next chapter, in connection with American popular song.

Zenith and Decline

The minstrel show reached its zenith in the years just prior to the Civil War. After the war, minstrelsy lost much of its original flavor and character, becoming, as Nathan has said, "an efficient large-scale variety show which favored less and less the dry, tough humor of Emmett's texts and tunes and the primitive style of his performances."[6] The *revue* indeed did replace the minstrel show almost completely in New York in the 1860s. But the latter continued strong in smaller centers of population and in rural America. After the Civil War, African-American musicians themselves began to participate, and all-black minstrel companies, such as the Georgia Minstrels, the Original Black Diamonds (of Boston), Haverly's Genuine Colored Minstrels, and W. S. Cleveland's Colossal Colored Carnival Minstrels, toured for another half-century or so. Minstrelsy thus became both a training ground and a source of employment for many black musicians who later branched out in the direction of blues or jazz. W. C. Handy was one, as was "Ma" Rainey, who toured widely in the South with various minstrel shows and circuses in the first two decades of this century. Other jazz figures who played for a time in minstrel bands include Bunk Johnson, Lester Young, and Jelly Roll Morton.[7]

Despite the (nominally) free status of blacks, and the drastically changed social and economic conditions in the South after the Civil War, the basic characterization of black people in postwar minstrel songs remained virtually the same as during slavery, with continued nostalgic references to idyllic plantation life. These were performed, and often also composed, by blacks themselves. The songs of James Bland (1854–1911), the best-known black songwriter for the minstrel stage, are typical in this regard. "Oh, Dem Golden Slippers," "In the Evening by the Moonlight," and "Carry Me Back to Old Virginny" were all composed about 1880; in terms of their characterization of black people and depiction of conditions in the South, they could have been written thirty years earlier. But the nostalgically clothed stereotype was what audiences continued to want to hear.

Less than a generation later, there were the beginnings of change. Around the turn of the century, performers such as the team of Bert Williams (1874–1922) and George Walker (ca. 1872–1911), black singers-comedians who also wore blackface makeup, helped to bring new standards of integrity to the stage portrayal of the black man. As George Walker said in 1906:

> The one hope of the colored performer must be in making a radical departure from the old "darkie" style of singing and dancing. . . . There is an artistic side to the black race, and if it could be properly developed on the stage, I believe the theatergoing public would profit much by it. . . . My idea was always to impersonate my race just as they are. The colored man has never successfully taken off his own humorous characteristics, and the white impersonator often overdoes the matter.[8]

Playing eventually in shows such as *In Dahomey* (1902) and *In Bandana Land* (1907), Williams and Walker were part of the first wave of black shows with black performers at the turn of the century—as we shall see.

From the Civil War Through the Turn of the Century

Immediately after the searing and costly War between the States, the popular musical stage entered a period of exuberant growth, characterized by foreign importation and native experimentation. With the great leaps in industry and transportation, and the heterogeneous, enriching inflow of immigrants, a new and energetic era was beginning. Above all, the cities grew, and with them the wealth and expectations of all but the poorest of their inhabitants. In an era of affluence and expansion the public was in the market for—and got—new theatrical diversions.

The New York Stage in the 1860s

New York City's dominance as America's entertainment capital was well established by the mid-nineteenth century. It was the first stop for touring artists and companies from Europe, and already the magnet toward which all native talent was drawn. Beginning in the 1860s, it became the fantasy-land of that dream of every producer, the "Broadway hit." Let us, very briefly, pay our respects to the first of these, *The Black Crook*. Produced in 1866 in Niblo's Garden, the best-appointed theater in New York, with its stage completely rebuilt for the occasion, the original production lasted five and a half hours and was a spectacle lavish beyond anything that had been seen previously. Its thin, derivative melodramatic plot was overwhelmed by huge ensemble numbers, costumes, extremely elaborate scenic effects and changes, and, as a significant ingredient, the dancing of no fewer than two hundred French ballet dancers in "immodest dress." *The Black Crook* actually looked more to the past than to the future. None of its ingredients was new; what *was* new was the prodigally lavish scale of the production (said to have cost more than $35,000, an astounding outlay for the time), and the fact that it ran for 474 performances and grossed more than a million dollars.

Vaudeville

After the impetus of *The Black Crook*, the New York stage became the arena for continued experiment on a new scale. One form emerged that was to become a prominent and typically American entertainment for half a century—*vaudeville*. Its antecedents were to be found in the minstrel theater, the English music hall, and, more immediately, the lowbrow entertainments offered in beer halls and saloons to which the name "burlesque" had come to be applied. But in the 1880s Tony Pastor, called the "father" of vaudeville, successfully turned it into clean, family entertainment. Vaudeville typically was a succession of individual acts, including dancers, acrobats, jugglers, magicians, and animal acts, usually headlined by a well-known comedian or singer.

Importations from London, Paris, and Vienna

The American popular stage languished musically until the importation of comic opera of exceptionally high quality from London, Paris, and Vienna beginning in the last quarter of the century. W. S. Gilbert and Arthur Sullivan in London, Jacques Offenbach in Paris, Johann Strauss Jr. in Vienna—each of these represented a peak of achievement in English, French, and German comic opera, all coming at about the same time. It was an unprecedented era of concentrated brilliance, which cast beams on this side of the Atlantic as well.

The London "invasion" came first; *H.M.S. Pinafore* was heard (in a stolen version) in Boston in 1878, and became prodigiously popular at once. After *Pinafore*, there followed in short order *The Pirates of Penzance* (premiered in New York by the author's own company, to protect its rights), and then *Iolanthe, The Sorcerer,* and *Princess Ida*, climaxed by the phenomenal success of *The Mikado* in 1885.

The new popularity of English comic opera created a popular audience for other European light operas as well, and both French *opéra bouffe* and Viennese operetta (which had been given here earlier in their original languages) were presented in English translations. After a lull in the nineties, Viennese operetta again enjoyed a great period of popularity here with the advent of *The Merry Widow* by Franz Lehár in 1907 and *The Chocolate Soldier* by Oskar Straus in 1909. A host of operettas more or less on the Viennese model were subsequently produced by our immigrant composers.

The Americanization of the Musical

While these foreign importations were enjoying their popularity, there was gradually emerging a more indigenous kind of musical show. The Harrigan and Hart comedies of the period represented an important early step toward the Americanization of the musical. Portraying with humor the Irish, the Germans, and the African Americans in believable comic situations growing out of the everyday lives of everyday people, they were an immediate success. The first was *The Mulligan Guard Ball* (1879), and this was followed by many Mulligan Guard sequels with the same characters, much in the manner of a television situation-comedy series. The songs, all by David Braham (1834–1905), a London-born musician who came here at the age of fifteen, became popular at the time in their own right and were sometimes borrowed for other shows. Songs such as "**The Babies on Our Block**" from *The Mulligan Guard Ball* illustrate the Irish flavor that was brought to the musical stage by these shows.*

The movement toward the Americanization of the musical comedy of this period culminated in the shows and songs of George M. Cohan (1878–1942), an energetic and ambitious showman who came up from vaudeville to become an author, composer, stage director, and performer who dominated the musical stage in the first two decades of this century. In describing Cohan, the one word inevitably used by writers is "brash." The directness of his style, his informality, and above all his fast pace (Heywood Broun described him as "a disciple of perpetual motion") brought new vitality to the theater. Cohan was right for his time, and fittingly marked the last stage in the adolescence of our popular

---

*Irish characterization had been introduced to the American popular musical stage at least seven decades earlier in the melodrama *The Indian Princess*, as we saw in the preceding chapter.

musical theater, sounding a decisive note of independence from Europe. His three most important and characteristic shows came early in the century: *Little Johnny Jones* in 1904 (which included "The Yankee Doodle Boy"), and *Forty-five Minutes from Broadway* and *George Washington, Jr.*, in 1906. (*The Little Millionaire*, the last of this genre, came in 1911.) Of the first three, each has its American hero (a jockey, a reformed gambler, a young super-patriot), and the three shows together contain the best of Cohan's show tunes.

The First Half of the Twentieth Century
Black Musicians on Broadway: The Emergence from Minstrelsy

Late in the nineteenth century it began to be apparent that the contributions of black musicians to America's popular musical stage need not—in fact *could not*—be forever limited to the caricatured renditions of the minstrel stage. Change, however, was painfully slow.

Two important landmarks came in 1898. Robert Cole produced the first full-length all-black musical show, *A Trip to Coontown*. But more successful and memorable was an all-black musical comedy sketch, *Clorindy, the Origin of the Cakewalk*, with music by the talented and classically trained musician Will Marion Cook (1869–1944). **"Darktown Is Out Tonight"** gives the flavor of the music. With its characteristic music, dancing, and choral singing, *Clorindy* created a sensation and opened the doors for black music and musicians on the Broadway stage, performing for predominantly white audiences. The first wave of black musicals followed. Will Marion Cook himself wrote a succession of shows. The next three were unsuccessful, but three hits followed: *In Dahomey* (1902), satirizing the scheme to colonize American blacks in Africa; *In Abyssinia* (1906), an extravaganza laid in Africa; and *In Bandana Land* (1908), set in the American South. The team of Cole and the Johnson brothers wrote two musicals, *The Shoo-Fly Regiment* (1906) and *The Red Moon* (1908), and J. Rosamund Johnson wrote the music for *Mr. Lode of Koal* (or *Kole*), of 1909. Thus the first period of activity of the black musical lasted for a decade.

After a lull during the second decade of this century, a second era of black musical shows was inaugurated in 1921 by the famous *Shuffle Along*, with lyrics by Noble Sissle and music by Eubie Blake. It was essentially a revue. Some of its fast numbers (of which "I'm Just Wild About Harry" was the most famous) are imbued with the ebullient but easygoing momentum of ragtime and early jazz; some (such as "Bandana Days") are almost pure George M. Cohan. Of its slow songs, some are in the style of the standard sentimental show tune ("Love Will Find a Way"), which the authors feared, needlessly, might not be accepted by a white audience from black singing actors; other slow tunes are close to the blues ("Daddy, Won't You Please Come Home").

Shuffle Along is credited with helping to initiate the Harlem Renaissance of the 1920s—a period of unprecedented cultural activity and rising intellectual and artistic self-esteem among American urban blacks. From that time until the Depression many all-black shows played Broadway. Blake and Sissle wrote three more, and among others of note were *Keep Shuffling* (1928) and *Hot Chocolates* (1929), with music by Thomas "Fats" Waller (1904–43). A more recent black idiom, rhythm-and-blues, was brought to Broadway in a lavishly staged black adaptation of a classic story and film musical (*The Wizard of Oz*) called *The Wiz* (1975).

Operetta, and Three Immigrant Composers

Building on the basic style, form, and approach of operetta, three immigrant composers brought a consistently high level of competence to the popular musical stage. During the forty years from Victor Herbert's first success, *The Wizard of the Nile* (1895), to Sigmund Romberg's last Viennese piece, *May Wine* (1935), there was hardly a time when there was not an American operetta on the Broadway stage. Its three great American exponents were Victor Herbert, Rudolf Friml, and Sigmund Romberg. All three were European-born, and all received there a thorough musical training (though Romberg's was more practical than formal, gained by hanging around the very epicenter of German-language operetta, the Theater-an-der-Wien in Vienna). All came to America, thus fully trained and equipped, in their twenties.

Victor Herbert (1859–1924), born in Dublin and trained in Germany, had the broadest musical experience and competence of the three. He entered the field of the popular musical show at the relatively late age of thirty-five, but once in, he knew that the theater was his métier. He was extraordinarily facile, composing over forty operettas. His major contributions were made in the two decades between *The Wizard of the Nile* (1895) and *Eileen* (1917), and included *The Fortune Teller* (1898), *Babes in Toyland* (1903), *Mlle. Modiste* (1905), *The Red Mill* (1906), *Naughty Marietta* (1910), and *Sweethearts* (1913). In addition to his gift for producing a memorable melody, Herbert's virtuosity as a composer enabled him to handle ensemble and choral scenes (e.g., the opening scene of *Naughty Marietta*, with its street cries) with a skill and inventiveness heretofore associated only with opera.

Rudolf Friml (1879–1972), born in Prague, was another thoroughly schooled musician, who was in his early years a concert pianist. His range was somewhat narrower, but between 1912 (*The Firefly*) and 1928 (*The Three*

Musketeers) he produced some enduring operettas, including *Rose Marie* (1924) and *The Vagabond King* (1925).

Sigmund Romberg (1887–1951) was more versatile than Friml. He identified himself completely with the popular musical theater, writing music for numerous revues for the Shuberts and others, including annual "editions" of *The Passing Show* between 1914 and 1924. But his forte was operetta, with a pronounced Viennese flavor, and his main contributions were *Maytime* (1917), *The Student Prince* (1924), *The Desert Song* (1926), *The New Moon* (1928), and *May Wine* (1935).

From the works of these three composers, we can arrive at a working definition of that form so popular in America from the Gay Nineties to the Depression—the operetta, or "light opera." Its setting was exotic, belonging to another place and time—Vienna, Heidelberg, Hungary, Paris, even eighteenth-century New Orleans. The characters often included royalty or nobility, frequently incognito, but gypsies, brigands, and opera singers were also favorites. The plot usually involved either concealed identity or concealed fortune, and the hoary theatrical device of look-alikes was employed. The music was tuneful, often memorably so, and like its Viennese counterpart, it placed its greatest faith in its waltzes, which really epitomized the genre.

The Revue

Thriving during the same period as the operetta was an even lighter form of entertainment, usually associated with the late spring or summer portion of the season. The trade names were many: "passing show," "follies," "scandals," "vanities." It was a succession of single acts, usually lacking even a pretense of dramatic thread or interest. Into it went the ancient elements of song-and-dance, burlesque, spectacle, and the display of feminine beauty.

The Musical in Its Maturity: *Show Boat* to *West Side Story*

The musical show had its period of greatest achievement in the thirty years that began with *Show Boat* (1927) and ended with *West Side Story* (1957). During this time the musical set itself new musical-dramatic problems (the term "musical *comedy*" was no longer appropriate), and solved them, without ceasing to captivate and entertain its audience. It was a period of sustained creation by major writers devoting their talents principally to the live musical stage, and it was, moreover, a period when the popular stage still had its audience. Broadway was in a clear position of leadership, and supplied America (and much of the world) with its best popular music.

A glance at the thirty years under consideration reveals the domination of five superbly equipped and successful composers: Jerome Kern (1885–1945),

A scene from the 1994 revival of *Show Boat*. *Photo by Michael Cooper.*

Irving Berlin (1888–1989), George Gershwin (1898–1937), Richard Rodgers (1902–79), and Cole Porter (1891–1964), each of whom wrote music for a least a dozen shows. Four others also made important contributions: Kurt Weill (1900–50), and near the end of the period, Frederick Loewe (1901–88), Frank Loesser (1910–69), and Leonard Bernstein (1918–90). During these thirty years, only one year passed without the appearance of a new show by at least one of these nine composers; in most years there were two or three. Their shows and the best known of their hundreds of songs are so familiar that a mere listing would be pointless. It will be more profitable here to consider certain aspects of the musical itself—areas in which innovation and evolution occurred during its era of greatest achievement.

The Evolution of Dramatic Values

During this period there was a great widening and deepening of the dramatic dimensions of the musical—a gain in both range and verisimilitude, without compromising the musical's essential nature as entertainment. Subject matter, plot, characterization, and range of emotion were all broadened. A brief look at six shows of the era should substantiate this.

Show Boat (1927: music by Jerome Kern, book and lyrics by Oscar Hammerstein II) was adapted from Edna Ferber's novel. It put real characters in believable situations—Magnolia, the sheltered daughter of the Mississippi show boat's owner, who survives a broken marriage with a riverboat gambler to make her way to the top as a musical comedy star; the half-caste Julie, singing two love songs that shattered the conventional sentimental mold, "Can't Help Lovin' Dat Man" and "Bill" ("an ordinary boy"). Also worthy of note was the realistic and sympathetic portrayal of African Americans on the stage.

Pal Joey (1940: music by Richard Rodgers, lyrics by Lorenz Hart, book by John O'Hara) was based on O'Hara's stories, which the author himself had suggested as a framework for a musical. It is strongest in characterization: the hero is a crass, selfish opportunist, finally abandoned by the two women who have, each in her own way, been used by him. The shoddy nightclub milieu of Chicago marked a new venture into the seamier aspects of realism. Vera's unsentimental love song to a heel, "Bewitched, Bothered, and Bewildered," gained musical force through Rodger's characteristic device of the almost obsessive development of a small melodic motive. So novel for 1940 were the elements thus introduced into a Broadway musical that *Pal Joey* did not succeed with the public until its revival twelve years later.

Lady in the Dark (1941: music by Kurt Weill, lyrics by Ira Gershwin, book by Moss Hart) plunges us into the realm of psychosis and the dream fantasy. The theme was not new to the musical; Rodgers and Hart had explored it in 1926 in *Peggy-Ann*, as did Romberg in *May Wine* (1935). But *Lady in the Dark* presents an almost clinical treatment of the subject, as the heroine, Liza, undergoes psychoanalysis. The dream sequences, more than mere surrealistic burlesque, have a genuine bearing on the heroine's problems, and the three men among whom she must choose are real, three-dimensional characters. The dramatic resolution is neatly paralleled by a musical one; the mysterious tune Liza remembers from childhood, which has haunted the play as a fragmentary motive, appears at the end, completed and harmonized, as "My Ship."

Carousel (1945: music by Richard Rodgers, lyrics and book by Oscar Hammerstein II, based on the play *Liliom* by the Hungarian playwright Ferenc Molnar) has elements of tragedy and symbolic fantasy, with a finale built on the age-old theme of redemption—heavy fare for a musical show. The hero is an outcast who must conceal his tenderness beneath a bullying, swaggering exterior. Thus he cannot, in life, communicate his love to Julie, nor can she to him—"If I Loved You" is as much as they can ever say to one another. His suicide brings an opportunity for redemption; stealing a star that he gives to the daughter he has never seen in life, he conquers the alienation that was threatening to warp her existence as it had his. Music has an ample role; the entire prelude is pantomimed to a carousel waltz, and there is a ballet-pantomime sequence in the second act.

Two more Rodgers and Hammerstein collaborations brought innovations in theme and setting. *South Pacific* (1949), one of the best-crafted musicals of the period, dealt ironically in song with the issue of interracial marriage, in "You've Got to Be Taught" ("to hate and fear"). These virtuosos of the form were able next to execute the remarkable feat of bringing an exotic Oriental setting to the stage (*The King and I*, 1951) and treating it tastefully, without resorting either to crude spectacle or to caricature, and without subjecting the audience to imitations of Oriental music. They also showed the extent to which sentimental convention could be discarded depicting a relationship between two principals in which the love interest is present only by muted implication.*

Satire and "Social Significance"

In the troubled political and economic climate of the 1930s, the theater did what it has always done in such times—it assumed the role of commentator, satirist, and gadfly. Political satire had never been completely absent from musical comedy, here or abroad, as a close look at Gilbert and Sullivan reveals. What was new was the fact that the musical show, hitherto the realm of entertainment, fantasy, and escape, began to get itself involved to an extent previously unknown. The treatment given this theme represented a rather wide spectrum of approaches.

Three shows by the team of George Gershwin (music), Ira Gershwin (lyrics), and George S. Kaufman and Morrie Ryskind (book) were brilliantly acidic and made use of outrageous fantasy. The shows were *Strike Up the Band* (1930), *Of Thee I Sing* (1931), and *Let 'Em Eat Cake* (1933). *Of Thee I Sing*, with its right combination of the fantastic (a beauty contest to determine who is to be the new First Lady, "Miss White House"), good show songs, and genuinely humorous satire (the vice-president is such an anonymous figure that he cannot get a library card because he cannot produce two references)—was the most successful of the three, and the first musical to win the Pulitzer Prize.

Two shows of this period had an even more conscious emphasis on "social significance." *Pins and Needles* (1937) was a very successful revue produced by the

*Five years later the authors of *My Fair Lady*, an otherwise nearly perfect piece, felt obliged to make a concession to conventional sentimentality by bringing Eliza back to Henry Higgins in a dénouement that is weak and unconvincing dramatically, and that George Bernard Shaw had specifically ruled out in the postscript to his *Pygmalion*, on which *My Fair Lady* was based.

garment workers' union, and ran (with updating) for three years. *The Cradle Will Rock* (1938: music, lyrics, and book by Marc Blitzstein) was a hard-hitting propaganda piece.

At the other end of the spectrum were shows that treated their themes with a lighter touch—musicals making use of satire, rather than satire taking the form of musicals. The veteran Irving Berlin wrote the music and lyrics for *Face the Music* (1932) and *As Thousands Cheer* (1933), both with books by Moss Hart, and *Louisiana Purchase* (1940), with book by Morrie Ryskind. Rodgers and Hart's one venture into this field was *I'd Rather Be Right* (1937). Cole Porter successfully satirized not only American politics but the Soviet Union in *Leave It to Me* (1938). The hit of the show was the very nonpolitical "My Heart Belongs to Daddy," which brilliantly etched one of Cole Porter's favorite hard-bitten female types. Porter returned to political satire, again of the Soviet Union, in *Silk Stockings* (1955).

Increased Sophistication of Musical Resources

During the period under consideration, the Broadway show utilized more fully and freely the musical means that had long been at the disposal of classical composers. One of these was counterpoint—the sounding together of two or more melodies. It is by nature an undramatic device, in a form where words are important, and where the attention, for greatest dramatic effect, should be focused on only one thing at a time. But carefully introduced, it can be effective, if only as a foil for the otherwise constant monody. This is the basis for the ensemble number, which may involve, for example, two characters ("Marry the Man Today" from *Guys and Dolls* is a superb and witty illustration, incorporating a quasi-canonic echoing effect between the voices); or the superbly crafted ensemble near the end of the first act of *West Side Story*, when five characters present three different interpretations of what "tonight" means to them. Occasionally even imitative counterpoint has its place: Kern included a fugue in *The Cat and the Fiddle* as early as 1931, and the "Fugue for Tinhorns" (actually a three-part canon) in *Guys and Dolls* is one of the most effective opening numbers in any musical. To accompany the dance sequence "Cool," Bernstein used a fugue effectively in *West Side Story*.

Beyond an increased broadening and sophistication of technique, the musical during this period came gradually to assign a far greater role to music itself; there was more of it, and it was given more work to do. Instead of being called upon only when it was time for a song or dance, it underscored dialogue, accomplished transitions, or arranged itself in a sequence of movements that became the equivalent of the operatic scene. Furthermore, in the best musicals the entire score had a unity to it. Jerome Kern took a large step in this direction in the score of *Show Boat* when he employed a few key motives, associated with certain characters, at appropriate moments in the background. This was a technique long known to opera, but new to the musical.

Increased Importance of the Dance

Another evolutionary development was the increased attention lavished on the dance. Song and dance had always gone together on the entertainment stage. But a new era began when George Balanchine, the noted Russian-born choreographer and ballet master, who had come to the United States in 1933, was called upon to create a special jazz ballet for the Rodgers and Hart show *On Your Toes* (1936). The result was the famous "Slaughter on Tenth Avenue," an extended "story" ballet sequence within the musical. From that time forward, choreography and dance, in whatever style is appropriate, have become integrated ingredients in the best musicals, especially telling in drama and fantasy sequences, as in *Carousel* and *Allegro*. For *Oklahoma!* (1943) a new orientation for the dance was required, and Agnes De Mille created what were essentially folk-ballet sequences. The musical *On the Town* (1944), with score by Leonard Bernstein, had actually originated as a ballet, *Fancy Free*, by the same composer, with choreography by Jerome Robbins. Robbins also contrived the dance and movement for *West Side Story*, in which they played an important role in the unfolding of the action—indeed this was one of the few musicals conceived and directed by a choreographer. The score itself is nearly a succession of dances, with dance rhythms underlying even the love song. The two contrasting types (jazz-rock and Latin) in juxtaposition express the essential conflict that is the basis of the modern urban plot derived from Shakespeare's *Romeo and Juliet*.

The Musical Since the Advent of Rock

Another forty years have passed since *West Side Story*, and these decades have wrought profound changes in the American popular musical stage. Late in the 1950s, Broadway began to lose the ear of its hitherto large public—an ear it had been able to take for granted in the three decades we have just been considering, when the best of America's popular tunes were from Broadway shows. Partly to blame was the decline of the big bands, which were no longer there to function as a medium for the dissemination of these tunes. The "hit parade" was over. Partly it was the fact that Broadway itself was in something of a slump—a dry transitional period, when the great composers were gone or were past their most productive period, and the new talent had not yet matured. (When a new generation did arrive, it would strike out in dramatically new directions.) But for the most part, it was the fact that receptiveness to show tunes, and to the whole ambience of the musical, was narrowing, especially among younger people, as the new and affluent youth market turned to rock 'n' roll, no longer interested in the wares of Broadway. Radio first, and eventually the record industry, followed the market; a gulf began to open up between the musical and the broad public. At least partly in response to this situation, several things happened to the musical show, as its new generation of practitioners took over.

The Broadening of Sources and Subjects of the Musical

In the second half of this century, the musical continued to mine the familar sources of ore for subjects: books, plays, and even operas (*La Bohème* for *Rent*, 1996). But it also searched farther and farther afield for its stories and ideas, from the Bible to the comic strip and the fairy tale. In a reversal of the usual process of producing a film version of a musical, older films became the basis for new musicals. Two spectacle musicals, *Grand Hotel* (1989) and *Sunset Boulevard* (1993), are only among the latest, both based on classic American films decades old. Show business itself has been a favorite subject—often in portrayals of the more selfish, ruthless, insensitive, and pathetic side of what goes on behind the scenes. Beginning in the 1960s there has been a special reliance on the show built around a striking female personality (whether real or fictional), and often designed as a vehicle for one star. As lighter entertainment, the revue, which virtually died out during the heyday of the story musical, has again been culti-vated, often as a retrospective of the work of a single composer, lyricist, or choreographer.

As a final gesture in what amounted to a progressive elimination of a plot as an ingredient in the musical, a show can simply be based on a *concept*. The con-cept could be the tangled relationships of sex, love, and marriage (*Company*, 1970); it could be the trauma of dancers desperately trying to be hired for shows (*A Chorus Line*, 1975); it could be the painter and his painting, and hence the relationship of art to life (*Sunday in the Park with George*, 1984). Or it could sim-ply be the elaborately costumed setting of a series of descriptive verses by a well-known poet about a well-known domestic animal (*Cats*, 1981).

Not only has there been a steadily widening range of sources, settings, and concepts, but, following trends in literature and on the legitimate stage, *themes* new to the popular musical stage have been introduced in the past decade. There could be mentioned in passing the onstage horror and bloodthirstiness of *Sweeney Todd*. Of deeper contemporary significance is the theme of homosexual love, which appeared in *La Cage aux Folles* (1983), and was central to *Falsettos* (1992, by William Finn, based on two earlier works by the same author, *March of the Falsettos* and *Falsettoland*, with the same sets of characters). These works of the early 1990s deal with AIDS, as does the 1996 rock musical *Rent*.

The Diminished Role of Music in the Musical Show

The music of the musicals has acquired, in most shows, increased sophistication: a more supple handling of form, a more ingenious use of ensembles, more effective scoring, a capacity for integrating into the whole a greater variety of musical styles, and so on. But with all this polish, it is paradoxical that, in the musical after mid-century, the music itself has mattered less in the whole scheme of things. It is no longer the single most significant ingredient, especially in terms of what had formerly been the most memorable part of the earlier musicals—the singable, hummable song. There might actually be more music (it is practically continuous in *Sweeney Todd* and *Dreamgirls*), but it is subservient to other aspects. On the decline of the overall role of music, and hence of the composer, observers are generally in agreement. Gerald Bordman has written: "Emphasis on composers in earlier shows has now passed to librettists, directors, and choreographers."[9]

What has taken the place of music as a prime ingredient in the musical? For one thing, *words*. Lyrics have acquired new brilliance, wit, and sophistication. Penetrating and urbane, at times earthy, the best are replete with clever rhymes, especially internal ones. In our time, the worthiest successor to Ira Gershwin as a lyricist is Stephen Sondheim (b. 1930). An example of exceptional intricacy of both meter and rhyme scheme is found in his "**Beautiful Girls**," the opening number of *Follies*. The rhyme scheme is one of elegant complexity, with no less than four different rhyming "distances" used simulataneously. As Example 11-2 shows, the widest distance is one of 16 measures of music. Most striking are the internal rhymes—those at a distance of less than the standard 4-measure phrase. Of these there are three kinds: five at 2 measures, two at 1 measure, and two ear-catching rhymes at a half-measure. The entire song is worth a close look, as a vivid illustration of the way in which the sophisticated musical can sound catchy and familiar, and yet embody the most subtle intricacies in musical form, prosody, and rhyme.

Elaborate scenic and stage effects have become an integral (and expensive) ingredient in the musical. Shows such as *The Wiz* (taking us from Kansas to the fantasy land of Oz), *Sweeney Todd* (with its overwhelming portrayal of London at its seamiest), and *Barnum* (putting us *in* the circus) were notable for their stunning visual elements. By the time we get to *Sunday in the Park with George* (where an artist's painting is assembled in its brilliant color before our eyes), so far had staging preempted song that one critic mused that the audience might well leave the theater "humming the scenery."[10] Yet in 1984, this was only the beginning. Since then the series of spectacle shows—shows in which stage effects are possibly the most memorable ingredient—have followed one upon another, each striving to outdo the last in overwhelming the audience: *Les Misérables*, *Phantom of the Opera*, *Grand Hotel*, *Sunset Boulevard*, *Miss Saigon*, and *Titanic*.

Hats off, here they come, those Beautiful girls. ⟶
That's what you've been waiting for. ⟶
Nature never fashioned a flower so fair. ⟶ 2
No rose can compare, ⟶
    Nothing respectable ⟶ 1 16
    Half so delectable. ⟶

                   16

Cheer them in their glory, diamonds and pearls, ⟶
Dazzling jewels by the score. ⟶
This is what beauty can be, ⟶
    Beauty celestial, ⟶ ½ 2
    The best, you'll ⟶
        agree: ⟶
All for you, these beautiful girls!

Example 11–2. "Beautiful Girls"

Among the new musicals today there is a cleavage between the sophisticated shows (with far-out subjects, treatments, and messages, high critical acclaim, and small audiences) and the more popular shows—mostly the spectacles such as *Les Misérables* and *Phantom of the Opera*. These two types of shows are epitomized by the two most powerful figures in the business today. As John Lahr has put it, the musical today is "caught between the boulevard nihilism of Stephen Sondheim, which doesn't send in the crowds, and the boulevard bravado of Lloyd Webber, which does."

The audience has a third choice—the revivals. A scanning of the periodicals during the last five years or so reveals that of the shows that are reviewed, mostly in New York, approximately one fourth are revivals—going back as far as seventy years, to *Show Boat*. And of course the percentage of revivals is much higher in other cities throughout the country, and on the stages of college and community theaters—perhaps, after all, more accurate indicators of American taste in any period than what occupies the more fashionable and trendier stages of Manhattan.

In Conclusion, a New Live Musical

In the current confused, fragmented, and generally moribund state of the American musical—what critic John Lahr has described as "once a glorious fun machine, now yet another fabulous theatrical invalid"[11]—a new production is, as of this writing, creating a good deal of excitement. The media have labeled it a "rock opera," but there is far more to *Rent*, by Jonathan Larson (1960–96), than just another trendy low-life musical. Drugs, homosexuality, AIDS, poverty, the homeless, and four-letter words (as well as support groups, phone machines, and cellular telephones) place it unequivocally in our time. But they are part of the *setting*; it is the realistic portrayal of believable characters on the stage, and their experiences and feelings, that ultimately engages our attention. Like many successful musical shows, *Rent* is based on a story that has already been staged—in this case the opera *La Bohème* by Puccini, to which it pays homage not only in its basic plot, but in specific crucial scenes as well, most notably the meeting of Mimi and Roger (Puccini's Rudolfo), and in the final scene, that of Mimi's death. (Larson actually quotes Puccini here, but it is Musetta's waltz that we hear.) The music is well crafted, and combines the timbres, textures, and vocal styles of contemporary popular music (not exclusively rock) with well-established compositional techniques, as exemplified by a canon in "Will I?," and a ground bass (actually as basic to rock as to seventeenth- and eighteenth-century music) in "Seasons of Love." "Santa Fe" is a song of visionary escape from the dreary life of New York City. A real tour de force is the finale, in which three previously heard tunes and lyrics are combined, two at a time, in a moving climax. This finale reiterates the essential message of the show. Benny, a former fellow-bohemian turned entrepreneur, has declared in the first act that "this is Calcutta, Bohemia is dead." The rest of the extended bohemian family have been determined to prove him wrong, and the last words are those of one of the three songs recapitulated in the finale: "There's only now, there's only here; give in to love or live in fear. No other path, no other way, no day but today." Having neither the "boulevard nihilism" of a show by Sondheim nor the surface glitter, the spectacular sets, and the "boulevard bravado" of a show by Webber, *Rent* may, with its directness, its sympathetic portrayal of believable characters, and its craftsmanship, open up new possibilities and give new hope to the currently chaotic and ailing stage musical.

FURTHER READING

Reference works
Bloom, Ken, ed. *American Song: The Complete Musical Theatre Companion.* 2d ed. New York: Schirmer Books, 1996.
> Extensive two-volume work including entries, by show, on over 4,800 productions and indexes by songs, people, and year of production.

Minstrelsy
Nathan, Hans. *Dan Emmett and the Rise of Early Negro Minstrelsy.* Norman: University of Oklahoma Press, 1962.
> An important study of the early minstrel show, as well as of Emmett himself. Nearly half the work consists of a valuable anthology of all types of minstrel material by Emmett and others, including, for example, the complete text of a skit or "extravaganza."
Toll, Robert C. *Blacking Up: The Minstrel Show in Nineteenth Century America.* New York: Oxford University Press, 1974.

The Civil War to World War I
Riis, Thomas L. *Just Before Jazz: Black Musical Theater in New York, 1890 to 1915.* Washington, DC, and London: Smithsonian Institution Press, 1989.
> Thorough piece of work, with lists of songs by shows, many photos, and 69 pages of sheet music facsimiles.

Mainly twentieth century
Bordman, Gerald. *American Musical Theatre: A Chronicle.* 2d ed. New York: Oxford University Press, 1992.
———. *American Operetta: From* H.M.S. Pinafore *to* Sweeney Todd. New York: Oxford University Press, 1981.
———. *American Musical Comedy: From* Adonis *to* Dreamgirls. New York: Oxford University Press, 1982.
———. *American Musical Revue: From* The Passing Show *to* Sugar Babies. New York: Oxford University Press, 1985.
Mates, Julian. *America's Musical Stage: Two Hundred Years of Musical Theatre.* Westport, CT: Greenwood, 1985.
> Main emphasis on the earlier period.
Mordden, Ethan. *Better Foot Forward: The History of the American Musical Theater.* New York: Grossman (Viking Press), 1976.

Music
Piano-vocal scores are not included, as they are available for practically all of the important musicals of the twentieth century, beginning with Victor Herbert. Three useful collections of mostly earlier material are:

Appelbaum, Stanley, ed. *Show Songs from "The Black Crook" to "The Red Mill."* New York: Dover, 1974.
> Includes sixty songs from fifty shows, with commentary by the editor, and illustrations.
Fremont, Robert A., ed. *Favorite Songs of the Nineties.* New York: Dover, 1973.
> Includes some show songs.
Jackson, Richard, ed. *Stephen Foster Song Book.* New York: Dover, 1974.
> Forty of Foster's songs in their original published versions, with original sheet music covers and notes on the songs by the editor. All the important minstrel songs are included.
Great Songs of Broadway. New York: Quadrangle/New York Times, 1973.
> Seventy-four songs from sixty-three shows, from 1901 to 1971. General introductions by Alan Jay Lerner and Jule Styne, but no introductions to individual songs or shows.

Projects

1. Make a study of the early circus in America, and its relation to other forms of popular musical theater.

2. Make a study of the old-time minstrel skit with music known as "The Arkansas Traveler." For a start, consult the versions in Seeger and Cohen's *The Old-Time String Band Song Book* (see the reading list for chapter 5), and in Carl Sandburg's *Folk-Say.*

3. Compare the text of an original play with the "book," or libretto, of a musical show based on that play. Note technical changes and changes of plot, emphasis, and characterization. What do you think were the reasons for the changes? (Examples would be *Oklahoma!* vis-à-vis *Green Grow the Lilacs*; *Carousel* vis-à-vis *Liliom*; *The Most Happy Fella* vis-à-vis *They Knew What They Wanted*; and *My Fair Lady* vis-à-vis *Pygmalion.*)

4. Make a brief study of the use of the popular musical theater as an instrument of propaganda in any given age.

5. Attend a performance, and do a careful review, of a musical show written since 1970. Assess such things as dramatic verisimilitude, depth of characterization (do the characters seem "real," believable,

three-dimensional?), appropriateness of the songs to the situations in which they are sung, and distinctiveness and quality of the songs. Include a brief account of the breadth of your own acquaintance with musical comedy.

6. Select two show songs of the 1920s or 1930s and two show songs of the 1980s or 1990s, and do a comparative study of their lyrics; include a comparison of their language and subject, as well as of their form, prosody, and rhyme scheme.

Notes

1. See D. W. Krummel's article "Publishing and Printing of Music" in *The New Grove Dictionary of American Music*, vol. 3, 652.

2. See Hans Nathan, *Dan Emmett and the Rise of Early Negro Minstrelsy* (Norman: University of Oklahoma Press, 1962), 35–58.

3. Lewis W. Paine, in *Six Years in a Georgia Prison* (New York, 1851), quoted in Eileen Southern, ed., *Readings in Black American Music*, 2d ed. (New York: Norton, 1983), 91.

4. See Nathan, *Dan Emmett*, 50–52. For the full story, as told in the *Atlantic Monthly*, see Charles Hamm, *Yesterdays: Popular Song in America* (New York: Norton, 1979), 118–21.

5. Nathan, *Dan Emmett*, 128. The sound is recreated on New World 338, *The Early Minstrel Show*.

6. Nathan, *Dan Emmett*, 276.

7. See Marshall Stearns, *The Story of Jazz* (New York: Oxford University Press, 1956), chapter 11.

8. Gilbert, *American Vaudeville*, 284.

9. Gerald Bordman, *American Musical Comedy from* Adonis to Dreamgirls (New York: Oxford University Press, 1982), 189.

10. Douglas Watt, *New York Daily News*, May 3, 1984.

11. John Lahr in *The New Yorker*, July 26, 1993.

Chapter 12

Popular Song, Dance, and March Music from the Jacksonian Era to the Advent of Rock

A half century ago, when little serious attention was given to the study of popular culture, a writer began his history of popular music with the assertion that it "is an index to the life and history of a nation."[1] The songs that are enjoyed and sung by a broad segment of the populace do indeed afford a vivid picture not only of the life and history, but also of the attitudes, feelings, motivations, prejudices, mores—in fact, the dominant worldview—of an era. Popular songs fulfill this role even better than does the popular musical stage. Musical theater, for all of its popularity, could not possibly reach and be enjoyed by the masses to the extent that popular song can. An age that numbered its theatergoers in the tens of thousands would number in the millions those who sang its songs.

Popular Song from the 1830s Through the Civil War

At the beginning of the preceding chapter we noted the changes that were then under way in American social, political, and cultural life, and the developments in music printing that went hand in hand with the growth of a mass market for sheet music. The growth of this market, however, and with it the birth of distinctively American song, was related to far more than technology. Nicholas Tawa begins his book *A Music for the Millions* by observing:

> A turbulent era in American history opened with Andrew Jackson's election to the presidency and his passionate attack on privilege. It closed with Lincoln's election and the onset of the Civil War. From 1828 to 1861, new democratic beliefs and practices interspersed themselves aggressively among older aristocratic ways of thinking. . . . Inevitably, music reflected the social, economic, and political upheaval of these years. The once-dominant European-derived composition mirroring a narrow, leisured constituency was soon overwhelmed by a different type of musical work, one imbued with ideas favored by the common citizenry and exposed in the simplest verbal and melodic terms—the American popular song.[2]

The Parlor Song

The most flourishing genre of the period was what has become known as the parlor song. These songs were purchased by, and sung in the living rooms of, the rapidly expanding numbers of middle-class families in cities and towns—to the accompaniment (kept purposely simple) of the piano, the harmonium (reed organ), or the guitar. Indeed, simplicity and directness of expression were values that were prized in these songs, even when they were performed by professionals.

Melodies from Italian operas, principally those of Rossini (1792–1868), Donizetti (1797–1848), and Bellini (1801–35), were in circulation here with English words, and were more popular in America in the antebellum period than is generally supposed.[3] But the basic models for the new popular song are to be found much closer to oral tradition. Irish folk melodies, especially as adapted and given new words by the Irish poet Thomas Moore (1779–1852), were popular here throughout the nineteenth century, beginning with the first printing of Moore's famous collection *Irish Melodies* in 1808. The unadorned attractiveness and accessibility of the melodies (some of which are clearly related to dance tunes) helped win them wide acceptance. Then, too, Moore's new words often struck a note of melancholy and nostalgia that somehow, paradoxically for a new country with ever-widening possibilities, seemed in accord with nineteenth-century sentiments. Much of Moore's large collection is unfamiliar today, but a few of the songs have entered permanently into the body of American song, including "Believe Me, If All Those Endearing Young Charms," "The Minstrel Boy," "The Last Rose of Summer," and "The Harp that Once Through Tara's Halls." Other imports from the British Isles were popular here, and helped set the American parlor song on its course. The most popular of these were "Home, Sweet Home" (1823), "Long, Long Ago" (1833), and a pathetic song of parting, "Kathleen Mavourneen" (1841).

Surveying our native-born American songs, we find many that were sentimental or nostalgic in tone—often having to do with separation, usually by death. "Flow Gently, Sweet Afton" (1838), with music by the American J. E. Spilman on a poem by Robert Burns, was one.[4] "The Ocean Burial" (1850), a "favorite and touching ballad" with music by George N. Allen to words by Rev. Edwin H. Chapin, was another.* George Frederick Root wrote such sentimental songs on the subject of death as "The Hazel Dell" (1853) and "Rosalie. the Prairie Flower" (1855). The best known of the sentimental songs of love, separation, and death by Stephen Foster began to appear in the 1850s, including "The Village Maiden" (1855), "Gentle Annie" (1856), and, perhaps his most famous

---

*The words to "The Ocean Burial," which begin "O! bury me not in the deep, deep sea," were later brought ashore and transformed into the text for one of the most popular of all cowboy songs, "Oh, Bury Me Not on the Lone Prairie."

Henry Russell. *Courtesy New York Public Library.*

song in this vein, "Jeanie with the Light Brown Hair" (1854). The misery and hopelessness of poverty were not often dealt with in the parlor song, but one example, suffused with a degree of genuine sympathy, stands out: Stephen Foster's "**Hard Times Come Again No More**" (1855).

Touring Professionals: Henry Russell and the Hutchinson Family

Parlor songs were not confined to the parlor; in the period before the Civil War professional singers were on the road giving concerts. These performers played an important role in shaping public taste, in acquainting the public with new songs, and in promoting them. That even songs for the "parlor" could profit by such promotion is shown by the sheet music covers, which frequently advertised songs as having been "sung by," or even "sung with distinguished applause by," some popular singer.

One of the most successful and influential of these was the Englishman Henry Russell (1812–1900 or 1901), who visited the United States twice between 1836 and 1844. A most effective singer who also played his own piano accompaniments, he pioneered as a "one-man show" at a time when few other performers could hold the interest of an audience for an entire evening by themselves. His style and his material (he performed mostly his own songs) were designed to be spellbinding. His diction was such that every word was understood. Thus he was eminently fitted for popularity at a time when the main purpose of both singer and song was to arouse the emotions.

His songs tell us much about what was popular with antebellum audiences. Of his sentimental songs the best known are "The Old Arm Chair" (1840) and "**Woodman! Spare That Tree!**" (1837). Both have as their basis a special kind of sentimentality prevalent in the nineteenth century—sentimental attachment to a particular object.* More overtly dramatic were such extended scenic monologues as "The Ship on Fire" and "The Maniac." Real spellbinders that depended for their effect on acting ability as well as singing, these were almost like one-man operatic scenes.

Many of Russell's songs espoused social causes; the emotions so effectively aroused in his hearers were meant to be directed toward the alleviation of some current evil. This accorded with a prevalent view of the time as to the *moral* function of art, and especially of song. "The Maniac" was not merely a melodramatic scene; it called attention to the wretched conditions in the mental asylums of his day. "The Dream of the Reveller" (1843) dealt with the evils of alcohol abuse, and after his return to England Russell wrote many antislavery songs. Thus, what Russell's compatriot Charles Dickens was aiming to do by literary means Russell apparently aimed to do with song.**

Among the foremost American performer-composers to follow Henry Russell's example were the Hutchinson Family Singers. From a rural New England background of strong convictions, they composed and sang songs supporting many of the causes in which they so firmly believed. The cause that most absorbed them during the 1840s, their period of greatest activity, was the abolition of slavery. They sang frequently at antislavery meetings and rallies, appearing with the most radical abolitionists of the time, Wendell Phillips and William Lloyd Garrison. They participated in street marches, and on their tours

*This kind of sentimentality has survived in American popular culture and is frequently found in country music, as shown in songs such as "Picture on the Wall" and "Send Me the Pillow that You Dream On."
**It is revealing to note that Henry Russell's sincerity may have been simply part of his act. George Frederick Root was disillusioned to find that Russell, in the privacy of his dressing room, was "much amused at the grief of his weeping constituents." See Root *The Story of a Musical Life*, p. 18, as pointed out in Richard Crawford *The American Musical Landscape*, p. 153.

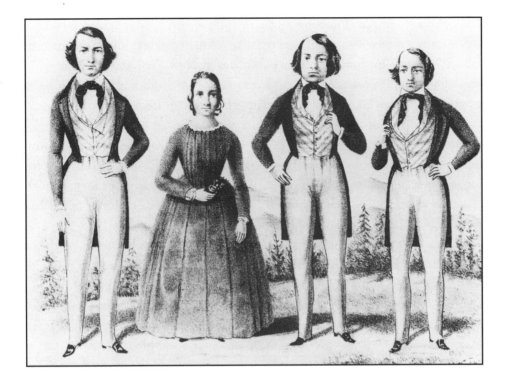

The Hutchinson Family. *Courtesy New York Public Library.*

they refused to sing in halls that would not admit blacks. They were well acquainted with Frederick Douglass, the escaped slave who settled in Lynn, Massachusetts, and they traveled with him to England. Abolition was by no means a universally popular cause, even in the North, and the Hutchinsons were hissed on occasion when they sang songs deemed "political." Their most famous abolitionist song, "**Get Off the Track**," was often sung to mixed reactions; it inspired wild enthusiasm among abolitionist sympathizers, and abuse, vocal and sometimes physical, from others.

Stephen Foster

Without doubt the best-known composer of the entire century was Stephen Collins Foster (1826–64). Although the popular Foster image is based on a good deal of misinformation and misinterpretation, the facts, insofar as modern objective scholarship can determine them, are more interesting than the fiction, and his accomplishments, his legacy, and his influence are undeniably impressive.

Foster was born as the ninth child into a fairly prosperous family in Pittsburgh. It was not to be expected, either of his family or of the mercantile environment of Pittsburgh in the 1830s, that his aptitude for music would be especially encouraged. Pursuing music in spite of this, Foster achieved enough success with some of his songs in the late 1840s (notably "Oh! Susanna") to induce him to sign contracts with publishers in New York and Baltimore. He actually became a professional songwriter in the 1850s and was able, for a time, to support himself in this way. His contracts provided for the payment of continuing royalties on sales—potentially a very favorable arrangement. But by the mid-1850s, serious problems began to surface, as manifested in his being persistently in debt (mostly to his brothers); in periodic, and ultimately prolonged, separations from his family; in a failure to manage prudently such resources as he had; and finally, in the alcoholism that defeated him in his last years in New York.

Foster's output of songs can be divided roughly into two categories: parlor songs and songs for the minstrel stage. The songs he wrote for the minstrel stage (described variously on their covers—"plantation melody," "plantation song," "Ethiopian melody") are with few exceptions his most enduring. The comic songs, with their inherent rhythmic vitality and their simple but catchy melodic lines, show, of all his output, the closest relationship to the rough-hewn folk songs of the antebellum frontier. These exuberant, high-spirited songs for the minstrel stage include "Oh! Susanna" (1848), "Camptown Races" (1850), "Nelly Bly" (1850), "Way Down in Ca-i-ro" (1850, with its original piano part marked "a la banjo"), "Ring de Banjo" (1851), and "The Glendy Burk" (1860). The dialect so typical of minstrel material was used in Foster's early songs (such as "My Brudder Gum," and "Ring de Banjo"), but he dropped this mannerism in his later songs, rightly thinking that it would restrict the universality of their appeal.

The sentimental minstrel songs (Foster himself used the word "pathetic"), unlike the comic songs, portray blacks with a profound sympathy, as human beings capable of feeling the pain of separation, and the unending weariness of a life of servitude—a weariness to be relieved only by an often welcome death. The grief of separation—whether from loved ones or from an irrevocable past—is uppermost in the four best-known "pathetic plantation" songs: "Old Folks at Home," "My Old Kentucky Home," "Old Black Joe," and "Old Uncle Ned."

A consideration of Foster's "pathetic plantation songs" would be incomplete without taking account of the appearance in 1852 of Harriet Beecher Stowe's novel *Uncle Tom's Cabin*, the central theme of which is slavery. The novel achieved instant popularity, and was almost immediately adapted for the stage; William Austin writes that nine versions of it were produced in New York before the end of 1852. Foster originally conceived "My Old Kentucky Home" with the play in mind, though he changed his final version, deleting the name Uncle Tom. At one time or another, however, at least four of his plantation songs—"Old Folks at Home," "My Old Kentucky Home," "Massa's in de Cold, Cold Ground" (sung by chorus), and "Old Black Joe"—were sung in stage versions of *Uncle Tom's Cabin.**

Songs of the Civil War

Uncle Tom's Cabin was only one of many portents of the tragedy of epic proportions that America was to live through in the next decade. Our greatest national trauma (more lives were lost in the Civil War than in all of America's other wars combined) left an indelible mark on all aspects of our culture. Popular song was quick to mirror the war's events, its ideals, its motivations, its slogans, and, of course, its anguish. By the time of the Civil War, the popular music publishing industry was in place and functioning. It was able to get songs to the public with an immediacy that rivaled that of the newspapers. Within a few days of the Confederate bombardment of Fort Sumter, which began the war, George F. Root's "The First Gun Is Fired!" was in print. More than in any other period in our history, popular song was the journalism of the emotions.

To fill the immediate need for songs, both sides rushed to fit new words to existing tunes. New verses to "The Star-Spangled Banner" were attempted by both sides. "The Yellow Rose of Texas"[5] became "The Song of the Texas Rangers," and Henry Russell's famous "**Woodman! Spare that Tree!** (touch not a single bough)" became "Traitor! Spare that Flag! (touch not a single star)." The ambivalence of Maryland as a border state was illustrated by the fact that both sides converted the German song "O Tannenbaum" into "Maryland, My Maryland," but with two sets of words urging diametrically opposed loyalties. At a time when secessionist feelings were running high, "Dixie" was used in a show in New Orleans (with no credit given to Dan Emmett as the composer); from there it spread rapidly throughout the South, becoming virtually the musical symbol of the Confederacy. It was not exclusively the property of the South, however; it could be found, with appropriate words, in virtually every state.

The other song most often associated with the Civil War is "The Battle Hymn of the Republic." It was originally a camp-meeting song with the words "Say, brothers, will you meet us on Canaan's happy shore?" then became a marching song used by Union regiments with the somewhat crude words "John Brown's body lies a-mouldering in the grave" (referring to the abolitionist Brown's raid on the arsenal at Harper's Ferry in 1859), then finally the loftier hymn, with words by Julia Ward Howe, that we know today.[6] As rallying songs, the South had "The Bonnie Blue Flag" (1861), a "southern patriotic song" with

---

*William Austin has thoroughly explored Foster's relation to the Stowe novel, and the plays that were made from it, in his *"Susanna," "Jeanie," and "The Old Folks at Home": The Songs of Stephen Foster from His Time to Ours.*

an Irish lilt, by Harry Macarthy, and the North had George F. Root's "**The Battle Cry of Freedom**" (1862), an immensely popular song.*

As the war dragged on and hopes for an early end were cruelly disappointed, the tenor of the new songs that appeared began to change. Among sober songs put into the mouths of soldiers in the field were "Just Before the Battle, Mother," by Northern composer George F. Root, and another by one of the best of the composers who cast in their lot with the South, John Hill Hewitt. Setting a poem by a Northern woman, Ethel Lynn Beers, of Goshen, New York, Hewitt produced in "All Quiet Along the Potomac Tonight" a song that transcended sectionalism and treated with a combination of sympathy and irony the death of a lone soldier on guard duty.

A subject only recently explored is the attitude toward African Americans portrayed in popular songs of the time. One researcher, Caroline Moseley, has found it mostly negative, even in the Unionist and abolitionist songs of the North.[7] Other songs written by white songwriters portrayed attitudes of black people themselves toward the war and ultimate emancipation. The very popular "Kingdom Coming" (1862), a dialect song by Henry Clay Work, couched in jubilant terms the anticipation of freedom. The chorus goes:

> *De massa run? ha, ha!*
> *De darkey stay? ho, ho!*
> *It mus' be now de kingdom comin'*
> *An' de year ob Jubilo!*

The song was indeed written by a white man (one whose father had been jailed in Illinois for his activities in helping runaway slaves to escape), but it is also known to have enjoyed wide currency among blacks; entering oral tradition, it achieved something of the status of a folk song, along with "Steal Away" and other songs that had specific reference to freedom in this present life.

Popular Song from the Civil War Through the Ragtime Era

The half-century between the Civil War and World War I witnessed changes that mark it as the beginning of the modern age. As such it presents contradictory images. Westward expansion, epitomized by the completion of the transcontinental railroad in 1869, a scant four years after Lee's surrender at Appomattox, was perceived as progress, yet it was accomplished at the shameful cost of killing off many of the original inhabitants who had lived on the land for centuries, and

---

*On the printed sheet music of another of Root's songs there appears this note: "In the Army of the Cumberland, the Soldiers sing the Battle-Cry when going into action, by order of the Commanding general."

destroying the survivors' way of life. Industry and invention flourished, manufacturing and selling goods undreamed of in any previous time, and raising the material standard of living (for most) far above what it had been; this was perceived as progress, and was celebrated in the many fairs and expositions that were held. Yet it was achieved only with a frightful waste of natural resources, and in many cases workers who produced the goods were exploited beyond the point of endurance, and strife between management ("the bosses") and the newly formed and struggling labor unions reached shockingly bloody proportions. Cities grew and prospered, as did the nation overall, yet corruption among those who governed was all too common. Immigrants poured into the country from both Europe and Asia; their hopes and prospects for a better life were on the whole justified, yet discrimination, and worse, degraded many and worked against their entering the mainstream of American life.

The Gilded Age (to use Mark Twain's famous term) has been given many interpretations. For all its excesses—its "crass materialism" and flagrant examples of corruption and waste—the age of "rowdy adolescence" was also a time of solid accomplishments as well; schools, colleges, and libraries were built as well as bridges and railroads, and there was Chautauqua as well as burlesque.

Popular Song Before Tin Pan Alley

Popular song, which had itself become an industry by the end of the century, did not mirror the full range of the contradictory images described above. The most popular topical songs were those that presented the positive aspects of events; Henry Clay Work's enthusiastic tribute to progress "Crossing the Great Sierra" (published in 1869 after the completion of the railroad) was more successful than his sympathetic and prophetic lament "The Song of the Red Man" (1868), which has the following lines:

> *Driven westward we came, but the paleface was here,*
> *With his sharp axe and death-flashing gun;*
> *And his great Iron Horse now is rumbling in the rear*
> *O my brave men! your journey is done.*[8]

A few well-established songwriters wrote songs about social issues. Work, the composer of "The Song of the Red Man," also wrote one of the most popular temperance songs, "Come Home, Father" (1864). George Frederick Root wrote "The Hand That Holds the Bread" in 1874, in support of the Grange movement rallying farmers against middlemen and monopolists. Septimus Winner wrote "Out of Work" in 1877, reflecting one of the frequent depressions of the period.

But except for a few of the temperance songs, songs of social comment were not big items in the general marketplace. Songs such as "No Irish Need Apply," "Drill, Ye Tarriers, Drill," "**The Farmer Is the Man Who Feeds Them All,**" and "The Dodger," all from this period, have survived doggedly only in the quasi-oral tradition of their constituencies.

The Civil War left a legacy of bitterness, war-weariness, sorrow, and a general depletion of spirit. Songs of gentle sentiment were popular. "Whispering Hope (Oh how welcome thy voice)" (1868, by Septimus Winner) speaks of comfort after sorrow—a mellifluous duet in waltz time. There was a preoccupation with growing old; three typical songs of love and remembrance in old age are all still well known: "When You and I Were Young, Maggie" (1866), "Sweet Genevieve" (1869), and "Silver Threads Among the Gold" (1873). Even the waltzing exuberance of "The Flying Trapeze" (1868), with its gracefully arching melody expressive of the swings of the aerialist, and its ruefully comic final verses, is tinged with the sadness and hopelessness of lost love:

> *Once I was happy, but now I'm forlorn,*
> *Like an old coat that is tattered and torn.*

In many ways the popular song of the period was linked more to the past than to the future. There was (relatively) an innocence, a sincerity, and, above all, an artistic and business climate in which the individual, regardless of location or commercial connections, could still succeed. Charles Hamm reports that Thomas Westendorf, who wrote "I'll Take You Home Again, Kathleen" in Plainfield, Indiana, was later sent a check for $50 each month for many years "in gratitude" by the publisher—who, having bought the song outright, was under no contractual obligation to do so. (The publisher, John Church & Co., was based not in New York, but in Cincinnati.) The whole story (beginning with a "hit" coming out of Plainfield, Indiana!) would have been, if not unthinkable, at least highly unlikely two decades later.

Tin Pan Alley: Popular Music Publishing Becomes an Industry

As American cities became larger, wealthier, and more sophisticated in the last two decades of the nineteenth century, two things happened that affected popular music. One was the increased vitality, and ultimately the Americanization, of the popular musical stage, as we saw in the last chapter. The other was the gradual emergence of a centralized industry for the publication and promotion of American popular songs. Both phenomena were centered on New York City.

Broadway and Tin Pan Alley were interrelated in complex ways, but were never one and the same. They cohabited the same area in the beginning—what was then the theater district of East 14th Street in Manhattan, where Tony Pastor's famous Opera House, the home of vaudeville, was located. But their close relationship grew looser over time, and as the musical theater developed, under the powerful influence of the great show composers of the new century, the *stratification* of American popular song took place. In terms of craftsmanship and sophistication, Broadway show songs, from Victor Herbert to Jerome Kern and George Gershwin, were at the top. As Nat Shapiro has written, "The Broadway musical is traditionally the primary source of superior popular music in this country."[9] Beginning in the 1890s, theater songs dominate the great canon of American popular song, which includes most of the "evergreens" such as "Smoke Gets in Your Eyes."

Slightly below the theater songs is a class of songs that began to appear in the 1930s, the movie songs. This category also includes a number of evergreens: "The Way You Look Tonight," "You'd Be So Nice to Come Home to," "Over the Rainbow," and "Laura" are among them.

Beyond theater songs and movie songs was that vast category of songs purveyed by the music publishing companies known collectively as Tin Pan Alley. These songs issued forth in prodigious quantities, only the tiniest fraction of which attained "hit" status. Most of them were short-lived, manufactured to conform to the passing fashions of the year, the season, the month. Yet here, too, as we shall see, were some "evergreens."*

New York's dominance in popular song publishing was not achieved at the hands of the old-line publishers—certainly not at the hands of publishers who would send monthly checks to songwriters out of sheer gratitude. As Sanjek has put it,

> Much as would the post–World War II music houses when faced with the annoying presence of hillbilly and race music, the established arts- and parlor-music publishers failed to perceive the future. It was in the hands of music publishers specializing in new popular American music—first formed around 1885, whose founders . . . were, as one of them, Isidore Witmark, remembered, "youngsters who had caught on and had a fair notion of the direction in which they were headed. What they knew least about was music and words, what they

---

*While it was not too uncommon to find composers contributing to two of the three strata here defined, Irving Berlin was virtually the only songwriter to contribute to all three—composing extensively and successfully for Broadway, Hollywood, and Tin Pan Alley.

cared about least might be answered in the same phrase. They discovered that there was money in popular song."[10]

The basic vehicle for the dissemination of the popular song, and therefore the basic commodity of the industry, continued until the 1920s to be sheet music. The money in popular song, it was realized by these new entrepreneurs, was in songs that sold not in thousands of copies, but in millions. In the 1880s sales began to climb toward this goal, and in 1892 the song that perhaps more than any other symbolizes the era—"After the Ball," by Charles K. Harris—sold over two million copies in its first few years, with sales eventually reaching over ten million.

For a song to reach anything even approaching this volume of sales (few did, and most barely paid for their printing costs), of course it had to be publicized, and this became a profession in itself, in which ingenuity and brashness paid off. The exploits of song "pluggers" included, but were not limited to, bribing performers across a wide spectrum, from professionals (who could be credited as coauthors of a song, with their picture on the cover), to hopefuls who sang on the popular amateur nights, to the Italian *padrone* who leased street organs to immigrant organ-grinders.*

As to the form of the songs themselves, the earlier four-part chorus, typical of the Stephen Foster era, was replaced by the solo "chorus" (the older name stuck, though it was no longer literally accurate). In the conventional Tin Pan Alley song, it was the "chorus" that had the identifiable "tune"; the "verse," with its lead-in narration, was the part hardly anyone remembered, and it was frequently omitted, especially when the tunes were later used as jazz "standards." The squarer 4/4 meter of the typical antebellum song had given way to 3/4; the waltz-song dominated the field—songs such as "After the Ball" (1892); "Daisy Bell," better known as "A Bicycle Built for Two" (1892, by Harry Dacre); "The Band Played On" (1895, by Charles Ward); and "Meet Me in St. Louis" (1904, a promotional song for the world's fair of that year by Kerry Mills).

There was a broad range of songs that played quite deliberately on the sentiments, written out of sincere feelings (here we think of Paul Dresser) or out of shrewd calculation as to what would sell (and here we think of Charles K. Harris), or, as is more likely in most cases, a combination of the two. Perhaps, as has been suggested, these songs offered an opportunity for emotional release, even if vicarious, at a time when the outward display of emotion was not acceptable in

* The novelist Theodore Dreiser left a valuable account of how the whole process worked in an article for *Metropolitan Magazine* in 1898, which is quoted at some length in Isaac Goldberg, *Tin Pan Alley: A Chronicle of American Popular Music.*

Protestant middle-class society. Prominent in this genre were the songs about women either bought or betrayed—women not as objects of romance, but as objects of pity. So much have these songs been associated with the period that their very titles have entered the language as phrases symbolic of the late Victorian age: "She May Have Seen Better Days" (1894), "Mother Was a Lady" (1896), "Take Back Your Gold" (1897), "She Is More to Be Pitied Than Censured" (1898), "Only a Bird in a Gilded Cage" (1900). Songs about separation by death were numerous; familiar are "**My Gal Sal**" (Paul Dresser's most famous song, of 1905) and "Dear Old Girl" (1903). Many a song that is actually about death reveals the fact only in the verse; the better-known chorus has more general sentiments. Examples are "'When You Were Sweet Sixteen" (1898), "You Tell Me Your Dream, I'll Tell You Mine" (1899), and "In the Shade of the Old Apple Tree" (1905). More blatantly pathetic "tearjerkers" are represented by "In the Baggage Coach Ahead" (where "baby's cries can't waken" the dead mother being transported by train), published in 1896 and composed by Gussie Davis, who was (according to Eileen Southern) the first black songwriter to succeed in Tin Pan Alley.*

The Ragtime Song

The nature and origins of ragtime, whose brief but intense flowering began in the 1890s and was over before 1920, will be considered in the next chapter. Ragtime, in its revival, has come to be regarded as essentially music for solo piano. In its day, however, ragtime had a far broader meaning. The ragtime song or *coon song* we tend now to see as a vulgarized offshoot of pure ragtime, with its essential characteristics diluted. Both in the crudity of its words and in the grotesque caricatures of its sheet music covers, the coon song appears today as grossly insulting to black people. In its day, however, the ragtime song was a popular manifestation of the "'ragtime craze," and these songs were written and sung by black as well as white performers. With all its vulgarity, it brought a new dimension to American popular song. As Arnold Shaw has said, "Coon songs were an infusion into the pop music scene of high spirits, revelry, and rhythmic drive, much as Rhythm and Blues was later in the 1950s," and he also makes the point that, as in the case of rhythm-and-blues half a century later, the coon song was as much a style of singing as it was a type of song.[11] The lineage of the female "coon shouter" starts perhaps with Mama Lou, in Babe Connors's St. Louis brothel, who may have been the writer of "Ta-Ra-Ra Boom-De-Ay" and "The Bully," songs

*The cover of this famous example gives a picture and byline to Imogene Comer, "Queen of Descriptive Vocalists," while at the same time taking opportunistic advantage of the scenario to advertise "The Empire State Express of the New York Central . . . Fastest Train in the World."

that were later popularized on the New York stage by the white singer May Irwin (1862–1938).

The white composer Frederick Allen ("Kerry") Mills produced a memorable little "ragtime cakewalk" called "At a Georgia Camp Meeting," published in 1897 as a piano piece and in 1899 as a song. The tune, with its ragtime syncopations, became very popular, and was much associated with a dance craze called the cakewalk that swept America and even invaded Europe. (The cakewalk, originally a plantation slave dance, had appeared in exaggerated form as the minstrel show "walk-around" for years.)

So persistent, and evidently popular, was the "darky" image in song that it was present even in songs whose well-known *choruses* gave little hint of it. "Ida! Sweet as Apple Cider" (1903) and "Coax Me" (1904) have faint traces of dialect, and references to a "dusky maid" and "dusky lovers" in their verses. Even the well-known "Mighty Lak' a Rose" (1901, by Ethelbert Nevin—a song that did not come out of Tin Pan Alley) shows a clear relationship to the long tradition of black dialect songs reaching back to the 1840s and before.

We have briefly sketched the rich mix that was popular song in the two decades surrounding the turn of the century—years when the "marvelous hit-machine" was being built. Before we follow popular song further into the twentieth century, let us look at another important ingredient in our popular musical culture: the American band.

The Band in America After the Jacksonian Era
Bands and Band Music to the Time of Sousa

As was noted in chapter 10, the wind band was an important part of the American musical scene in the Colonial and Federal periods. Subsequent European experimentation and invention resulted in improvements in brass instruments, making them more flexible and capable of producing the full range of chromatic tones. These improvements, as well as the greater durability and carrying power of brass instruments (important for outdoor functions), led to the gradual elimination of clarinets, oboes, and bassoons and the rise of the *brass band*, which dominated the scene until well after the Civil War. A sampling of the music played by these bands includes quicksteps, polkas, schottisches, and waltzes—a fair reflection of the dances that were popular at the time. (The **Blondinette Polka**," the music of which was found in a collection dated 1862, is representative.)

With the coming of the Civil War came the need for brass bands in ever-greater numbers. The standard Civil War band was small by present-day standards, consisting of a dozen brass players and five drummers. But even before hostilities ceased, there was a portent of things to come. When Patrick Gilmore, then in New Orleans, was asked by General Banks to provide music for the inauguration of the new governor there, he assembled a band of five hundred and a chorus of six thousand (including schoolchildren) and put on the first of his many mammoth concerts, climaxed by the firing of fifty cannon (electrically controlled from the podium) and the ringing of all the church bells in the city.

After the war, Gilmore expanded on the concept of the concert event of huge proportions. The ultimate came in 1872 as a World Peace Jubilee, for which he assembled two thousand instrumentalists and choruses of twenty thousand in a specially built coliseum that seated a hundred thousand. This Jubilee lasted eighteen days, and to augment the entertainment, Gilmore invited bands from England, France, and Germany, as well as Johann Strauss and his orchestra from Vienna. Patrick Gilmore never again assembled anything on this scale (in its day the equivalent, in complexity and the sheer numbers involved, to the modern Olympic Games), but the "jubilee" concept—under the more modern designation "festival"—is still a related cultural phenomenon worldwide, and the assembling of large instrumental forces survives in the "massed bands" heard today wherever school bands and bandsmen gather.

Less spectacular but ultimately more significant was the work that Gilmore did beginning in 1873 in developing his 22nd Regimental Band in New York into a combination concert and touring band. He was to establish a pattern for bands that lasted half a century. He played summer concerts at Manhattan Beach, and winter concerts in Gilmore's Garden.* In the spring and fall, Gilmore's band toured.

A typical band program of the late nineteenth century would show a judicious mixing of classical favorites, numbers by featured "headline" soloists, and popular songs and hymns. The classical ingredient consisted of transcriptions from the orchestral repertoire, mostly operatic overtures. Classical selections were always balanced by popular numbers; the soprano soloists who appeared with the bands might sing operatic excerpts, but would be sure to include songs such as "Silver Threads Among the Gold," and even popular hymns such as "Nearer My God to Thee." Touring concert bands like Gilmore's, and later Sousa's, played much the same role in the dissemination of popular songs as did the big dance bands of the 1930s and 1940s. Featured instrumental soloists were big attractions; these included accomplished performers on the saxophone, baritone horn, and trombone. But by far the most popular "stars" with the bands were the cornet soloists. The cornet had developed into an extremely facile virtuoso instrument, which was to the band what the violin as a solo instrument was to the orchestra.

*This establishment, originally P. T. Barnum's Hippodrome, ultimately became Madison Square Garden, and under that name moved later to a succession of new locations.

Gilmore tempered the sound of the brass band with the gradual reintroduction of woodwind instruments, which in time became numerically dominant, until by the end of the century the concert band consisted, in rough proportion, of one-third clarinets (the equivalent of the orchestra's violins), one-third other woodwinds, and one-third brass; the percussion section was somewhat smaller in proportion than in the brass band days. Under Gilmore and Sousa, who were both very discriminating and demanding musicians, the professional concert touring band developed into an ensemble that in terms of dynamic range, tone quality, blend, phrasing, and precision was comparable to the best orchestras of its day.

John Philip Sousa and the Band from the 1890s to the 1930s

The most important single figure in the development of the American band and its music, John Philip Sousa (1854–1932), began his independent professional career as an orchestral violinist (he played under the popular French composer and conductor Jacques Offenbach in Philadelphia in 1876) and a conductor with traveling musical shows. In 1880 he was invited to direct the U.S. Marine Band. By this time he had heard, and been impressed by, Gilmore's band, and he perceived the potential of the wind band. He reorganized the Marine Band and its repertoire thoroughly and raised it to a position of excellence and renown, even securing permission to take it on tour. In 1892 he formed his own independent band, which he conducted, except for an interval of training bands for the Navy during World War I, until his death in 1932.

Paying and treating his musicians well, Sousa at the same time made of his band a profitable business, with stockholders. It was essentially a touring ensemble, and except for a very few regular engagements (such as those at Manhattan Beach, New York, and Willow Grove, Pennsylvania) the band was on the road a great deal. He followed Gilmore's example in balancing his programs between popular and classical selections; furthermore, he kept up with the times in terms of popular music. His solo trombonist, Arthur Pryor, was from Missouri, the cradle of ragtime, and he arranged and taught the band to play this new music. (Pryor's composition *Lassus Trombone*, in this vein, was long a popular band number, especially with trombonists.) Sousa's band took ragtime to Europe in 1900, and his turn-of-the-century programs, with their "plantation songs and dances" and "coon songs," show that contemporary popular derivatives of black American music had a place on his programs. He later incorporated some form of jazz into his programs.

Considering his active public life, Sousa's creative output was phenomenal. He completed twelve operettas, eleven suites, seventy songs, nearly a hundred other instrumental pieces of various kinds, and over two hundred arrangements and transcriptions, as well as three novels and an autobiography. But he is best known for his marches. Between 1877 and 1931 he composed 136 of them, an imposing proportion of which (one could cite "The Washington Post,"* "Semper Fidelis," "The Thunderer," "The Liberty Bell," "King Cotton," "El Capitan," and "The Stars and Stripes Forever") have, along with some of the songs of Stephen Foster, entered the domain of our permanent national music. Nor is their popularity limited to America; like the Foster songs and the waltzes of Johann Strauss Jr., they have become part of a world music.

Sousa had a flourishing grassroots tradition on which to build. The 1890s, when his own band was touring and establishing its reputation, was the great era of American bands, especially in the towns and small cities in the Midwest. Town bands furnished music both functional and entertaining, and they were a strong focus of community pride. Before the advent of movies and later of radio, it was town bands, along with singing and theatrical groups, that accounted for most of what local entertainment and culture existed; these attractions were augmented by such traveling entertainments as circuses, minstrel shows, lecturers and performers on the Chautauqua circuit, and occasional visits by the bands of Alessandro Liberati, Frederick Innes, Thomas Brooke, Patrick Gilmore, and even Sousa himself.[12]

The Band from the 1930s to the Present

The decline of the professional concert/touring band began at about the time of Sousa's death in 1932. Subsequently there were two significant developments. The first was the passing of leadership to the *academic* band movement; college and university bands developed in size, in excellence, and in general esteem, especially in the Midwest. The second development, the creation of new works specifically for wind band, was related to this but was also the outgrowth of the work of Edwin Franko Goldman (1878–1956), whose professional band countered the general trend of decline. The Goldman Band performed continuously from 1918 to 1979, under the leadership of Edwin and later his son, Richard Franko Goldman (1910–80). In the 1950s Richard Franko Goldman began to commission new works. Thus it was that works for the newly developed "symphonic band" or "symphonic wind ensemble" began to come from established composers. This flow of new works for band reached its peak in the 1950s and 1960s; there was hardly a major American composer of the time who did not

---

* "The Washington Post March," composed in 1889 for a ceremony honoring the student winners of an essay contest sponsored by that newspaper, attained instant and widespread popularity, and became indelibly associated with a new dance, the two-step.

contribute at least one work for band, including Virgil Thomson, William Schuman, Walter Piston, Peter Mennin, Vincent Persichetti, Howard Hanson, Paul Creston, and Ross Lee Finney.

Popular Song from Ragtime to Rock

We now return to popular song where we last left it, at the close of the ragtime era, in order to describe the three decades between 1920 and 1950—decades that have generally been regarded as the "golden years" of Tin Pan Alley.

The Major Media Shift and the Role of the Big Bands

These "golden years" began with three developments that drastically changed the *media* by which popular song reached the public, and thus brought fundamental changes to the entire industry. The phonograph recording became a significant factor after the turn of the century, radio in 1922, and the sound movie in 1929. After 1920, the consuming public shifted gradually from an active to a passive role, as the phonograph and the radio replaced the parlor piano as a source of music in the home. Even that intermediate stage represented by the player piano ("canned" music produced by a "live" instrument) was edged out, sales of player pianos having reached their peak in 1923.

As the Depression arrived in the early 1930s, radio and the new talking pictures became the dominant media, dealing a severe blow to the phonograph—which did not really recover its position until the end of the decade, with recordings of the popular swing bands. Radio thus became a prime means for the dissemination and plugging of songs, as it has remained to this day (in changed form, and with a more specialized audience and material). Many of the prominent bands performed on weekly broadcasts in the 1930s, either from a permanent base or by remote hookup while on tour. Singers with the bands became increasingly important as purveyors of new popular songs. Some bandleaders were themselves composers, and a few of the best songs in this period came from the bands.

Stability and Pluralism in Popular Music Between the Wars

While the big technological media shifts had profound effects on the popular music industry, the nature and style of popular song itself changed little in this period. But if popular song was essentially static during this period, it was also pluralistic. The stratification referred to earlier in relation to the beginnings of Tin Pan Alley was a fact of our cultural life throughout this period. Sanjek points up this cleavage in taste—this pluralism—in describing the policies of Tin Pan Alley publishers in the 1930s:

Well-written songs possessing any poetic qualities were rejected immediately, because it was the general Tin Pan Alley feeling that true sheet-music buyers had little or no interest in them and therefore they were "not commercial." Those "great" songs of the 1930s, beloved by cultural elitists and social historians, were well known only to a minority of Americans—those who were better educated and more affluent than the average radio "fan" and who had access to the Broadway stage and other sophisticated entertainment.[13]

This view does seem to be borne out by a few statistics. Hamm has compiled a list of the "top forty" songs between 1900 and 1950, in terms of those most often recorded. Of these, only twelve (30%) are from plotted Broadway shows, another six (15%) are from revues (a form descended from vaudeville), and the other twenty-two (55%) are nonshow Tin Pan Alley songs.[14]

The mainstay of Tin Pan Alley in this period was the ballad, a type of love song providing most of the "standards"—those few songs that in quality and appeal transcended the quantities of ephemera produced. As a sample of the best the Alley had to offer in these three decades (again excluding show and movie tunes), here is a select list of half a dozen independent songs: "I'll See You in My Dreams" (1924, Isham Jones, one of many songs by bandleader/composers); "Blue Skies" (1927, Irving Berlin); "Star Dust" (1929, Hoagy Carmichael; this perennial, one of the most frequently recorded of all popular songs, began as a quasi-ragtime piano piece, which was later slowed down and given lyrics by Mitchell Parish); **"Stormy Weather"** (1933, Harold Arlen; written by this veteran Broadway composer for Harlem's Cotton Club, where it was introduced by Ethel Waters); "Blue Moon" (1934, Richard Rodgers, one of his few songs not introduced in a show or movie); and **"You Go to My Head"** (1938, J. Fred Coots).

Tin Pan Alley and Its Relation to Jazz and Black Vernacular Music

Many of the leaders of the dance orchestras and big bands of the period composed and introduced songs. Duke Ellington contributed many, most of which are decidedly instrumental in character. **"I'm Beginning to See the Light"** (1944), a collaborative effort of Duke Elllington, Johnny Hodges, and Harry James, is a typical song to come out of the stylistic milieu of the big band in that its melody is made up of *riffs*—short melodic fragments repeated over changes of harmony.

Aside from these songs by band leaders of the period, the typical popular song between the wars (whether from Broadway, Hollywood, or Tin Pan Alley) had little relationship to jazz or other black vernacular music. The one exceptional bridge was the blues. Harold Arlen was perhaps the closest to jazz and blues of any of the major songwriters of this period. As Alec Wilder has written,

"He, more than any of his contemporaries, plunged himself into the heartbeat of the popular music of his youth, the dance band." Wilder goes on to show how Arlen's "don't-worry-about-the-mud-on-your-shoes attitude," characteristic of blues and jazz, is illustrated in songs like "Sweet and Hot" (1930), "Between the Devil and the Deep Blue Sea" (1931), "I Gotta Right to Sing the Blues" (1932), "That Old Black Magic" (1942), and especially the memorable "Blues in the Night" (1941).[15]

Though they were distinct the one from the other, there was a symbiotic relationship between jazz and popular music in this period. Jazz was heavily indebted to Broadway, Hollywood, and Tin Pan Alley for its "standards"—songs whose melodies and chord progressions became the basis for jazz arrangements and improvisations, such as the hundreds of renditions of "Star Dust," Coleman Hawkins's "Body and Soul," Charlie Parker's "Embraceable You," and the score of bebop versions of "How High the Moon."

For its part, popular music was indebted to jazz for a continuously revitalized rhythmic basis, and for the jazz arrangements by popular hot bands that contributed their flavor to, and helped promote, the songs. Performances by such singers as Bing Crosby, Ethel Waters, Mildred Bailey, Jack Teagarden, Billie Holiday, Lena Horne, Sarah Vaughan, and Ella Fitzgerald, backed up by bands such as those of Benny Goodman, Teddy Wilson, Artie Shaw, Harry James, and Duke Ellington, impart, through interpretation, a jazz or blues flavor to songs that do not necessarily possess it inherently.

Finally, the relation of black vernacular dance to popular music in this period is crucial. Since the turn of the century, innumerable vernacular dances have entered the mainstream of popular dance. The Charleston, the shimmy, the black bottom, and various "animal dances," such as the turkey trot, the grizzly bear, and the bunny hug, began, despite opposition, to coexist with and gradually replace the older polkas, schottisches, and waltzes. (One animal dance—possibly made up by the popular and influential team of Vernon and Irene Castle before World War I—was the fox-trot, which became "respectable" and survived well into the period under consideration.) The toddle was danced to Dixieland jazz. But the dance that became indelibly associated with swing jazz came out of places like the Savoy Ballroom in Harlem in the late 1920s (the home ground of many of the hottest bands). First known as the lindy hop (after Charles Lindbergh's famous flight), it became more broadly familiar as the jitterbug. Although most of the young could and did do it, when performed by accomplished jitterbuggers in its more flamboyant and elaborate form it was a dance to watch as well. It was the dance symbol of hot jazz, and the interaction and mutual stimulus between a hard-driving swing band and a group of equally hard-dancing, frenzied jitterbuggers on the dance floor were undeniable.

The Decline of Tin Pan Alley and the
Dispersion of the Popular Music Industry

After mid-century, an upheaval in the popular music industry, leading to its dispersion and decentralization, began in the "provinces," far removed from the creaking but still functioning Broadway–Hollywood axis. Regional and ethnic musics began to account for significantly larger shares of the market. Coming out of teeming and troubled urban areas like Chicago, Detroit, and Philadelphia was black rhythm-and-blues; from the South and West came white hillbilly music, given the trade name country-and-western. As an offspring of both came rock 'n' roll.

There is an interesting parallel between this development and the beginnings, half a century earlier, of Tin Pan Alley. Although the birth of Tin Pan Alley was marked by the centralization of the industry, and the rock era by its decentralization, there is a sense in which the advent of rock marks the completion of another cycle in the periodic *democratization* of American popular music. It was with the beginning of another such cycle, in the Jacksonian era of a century and a half ago, that we began the story this chapter has attempted to tell.

FURTHER READING

Reference

Pollock, Bruce, Nat Shapiro, and Barbara Cohen-Stratyner, eds. *Popular Music: An Annotated Index of American Popular Songs*. Detroit: Gale, 1964–96.

> This 22-volume (to date) series includes *Popular Music, 1900–1919*; *Popular Music, 1920–1979* (8 volumes in 1); *Popular Music, 1980–1989* (6 volumes in 1), and individual volumes from 1990 on. Entries are alphabetical by year and title, and include composer, lyricist, publisher, and some information about performances, recordings, awards, and so on. Composers and lyricists are indexed separately, and there are introductory essays.

Books

Austin, William W. *"Susanna," "Jeannie," and "The Old Folks at Home": The Songs of Stephen Foster from His Time to Ours*. New York: Macmillan, 1975.

> A perceptive study of the complex array of meanings that Foster's songs have had in a variety of contexts.

Goldberg, Isaac. *Tin Pan Alley: A Chronicle of American Popular Music*. New York: Frederick Ungar, 1961.

> Includes introduction by George Gershwin, and supplement "From Sweet and Swing to Rock 'n' Roll" by Edward Jablonski.

Hamm, Charles. *Yesterdays: Popular Song in America*. New York: Norton, 1979.

> This well-documented work has chapters relevant to nearly every aspect of the present chapter.

Heaps, Willard A., and Porter W. *The Singing Sixties: The Spirit of Civil War Days Drawn from the Music of the Times*. Norman: University of Oklahoma Press, 1960.

> A copious source of information on the songs in their context.

Levy, Lester S. *Grace Notes in American History: Popular Sheet Music from 1820 to 1900*. Norman: University of Oklahoma Press, 1967.

> Arranged by topic, with background for each of the songs. Includes single-line tunes and photo reprints of covers.

Levy, Lester S. *Give Me Yesterday: American History in Song, 1890–1920.* Norman: University of Oklahoma Press, 1975.

Sanjek, Russell. *From Print to Plastic: Publishing and Promoting America's Popular Music (1900–1980).* I.S.A.M. Monograph no. 20. Brooklyn: Institute for Studies in American Music. 1983.

Schwartz, H. W. *Bands of America.* Garden City, NY: Doubleday, 1957. Reprint. New York: Da Capo, 1975.

Tawa, Nicholas. *Sweet Songs for Gentle Americans: The Parlor Song in America, 1790–1860.* Bowling Green, OH: Bowling Green University Popular Press, 1980.

        Includes music to many songs.

————. *A Music for Millions: Antebellum Democratic Attitudes and the Birth of American Popular Music.* New York: Pendragon, 1984.

————. *The Way to Tin Pan Alley: American Popular Song, 1866–1910.* New York: Schirmer Books, 1990.

Wilder, Alec. *American Popular Song: The Great Innovators 1900–1950.* New York: Oxford University Press, 1972.

        This subjective but highly respected book by a songwriter-author treats in considerable detail a great number of songs by all of the significant songwriters of the period.

Articles

Moseley, Caroline. " 'When Will Dis Cruel War Be Ober?' Attitudes Toward Blacks in Popular Song of the Civil War." *American Music* 2, no. 3 (Fall 1984): 1–26.

Pessen, Edward. "The Great Songwriters of Tin Pan Alley's Golden Age: A Social, Occupational, and Aesthetic Inquiry." *American Music* 3, no. 2. (Summer 1985): 180–97.

Editions of music

These are collections of facsimile reprints of the original sheet music publications, usually including the covers, with notes by the editors.

Crawford, Richard, ed. *The Civil War Songbook: Complete Original Sheet Music for 37 Songs.* New York: Dover, 1976.

Fremont, Robert A., ed. *Favorite Songs of the Nineties: Complete Original Sheet Music for 89 Songs.* New York: Dover, 1973.

Jackson, Richard, ed. *Popular Songs of Nineteenth-Century America.* New York: Dover, 1976.

        Contains sixty-four songs.

————. *Stephen Foster Song Book.* New York: Dover, 1974.

        Contains forty songs.

Projects

1. Sigmund Spaeth wrote that our popular song "captures the civilization of each period far more accurately than do many of the supposedly more important arts." Taking any decade in our history, make a survey of its popular songs, and assess the extent to which this statement applies, and how it applies.

2. Are there any folk or rock groups to which you could compare the Hutchinson Singers, in terms of their use of topical, political, or protest material? Research the question, and do a brief but well-documented paper on it, bringing out contrasts as well as any similarities you might see, in terms both of the groups and of the times.

3. Nicholas Tawa has referred to the "unillusioned song" of pre–Civil War days. Taking the songs from *any* given period, discuss the nature of *illusion* in popular song and the reasons for its presence.

4. Songs about separation by death were common in the nineteenth century. They have always been a staple of country music (which inherited some of its songs from the sentimental repertory of the nineteenth century), and made a brief appearance in the teenage death songs of early rock 'n' roll. But

such songs were almost totally absent from the output of Tin Pan Alley during its "golden years." Putting together what you know, write a paper discussing possible reasons for this.

5. If you come from a relatively small community in which a town or city band has been an important entity, assemble some recollections (either your own, or those of relatives or acquaintances) of the band's activities and significance in the life of the community.

Notes

1. Sigmund Spaeth, *A History of Popular Music in America* (New York: Random House, 1948), 3.

2. Tawa, *A Music for the Millions* (New York: Pendragon, 1984), 1.

3. Charles Hamm, in *Yesterdays: Popular Song in America* (New York: Norton, 1979), delineates the Italian influence in chapter 4.

4. Scottish influence on the American parlor song was significant—probably second only to that of Ireland.

5. The fascinating story of "The Yellow Rose of Texas," a durable song that apparently originated during the Mexican War, is told in the monograph *The Yellow Rose of Texas: The Story of a Song* by Martha Anne Turner (El Paso: Texas Western Press of the University of Texas Press at El Paso, 1971).

6. An excellent capsule history of "The Battle Hymn of the Republic," including excerpts from several different texts, is found in *The Singing Sixties*, 50–54. A facsimile of the first published version is in *Popular Songs of Nineteenth-Century America*.

7. Caroline Moseley has written: "One would expect that antislavery songs would present a positive view of black people. There is, in fact, little in any abolitionist song which relates meaningfully to blacks." See "'When Will Dis Cruel War Be Ober?' Attitudes Toward Blacks in Popular Song of the Civil War" (*American Music* 2, no. 3 [Fall 1984]: 1–26).

8. "The Song of the Red Man" is included, with text and notes, in New World 267, *The Hand that Holds the Bread: Progress and Protest in the Gilded Age*. I am indebted to William Brooks, the annotator of this album, for the reference to these two songs, and for pointing out their interesting juxtaposition.

9. Alec Wilder has documented this extensively in *American Popular Song* (New York: Oxford University Press, 1972), which is organized along the lines of this stratification. George Gershwin noted the same thing early in his career; of his first acquaintance with the songs of Jerome Kern he wrote: "Kern was the first composer who made me conscious that most popular music was of inferior quality, and that musical-comedy music was made of better material."

10. Sanjek, *From Print to Plastic*, 7–8.

11. Arnold Shaw, *Black Popular Music in America*, 42.

12. A lively and sympathetic description of the town bands of the period is given by Schwartz in *Bands of America*, 170–76. Schwartz quotes ads placed in music papers and business magazines, for the purpose of attracting musicians to small communities that could offer them steady employment as well as a position in the local band. Of the twenty-three ads quoted, all but five are from towns in the Midwest.

13. Sanjek, *From Print to Plastic*, 19.

14. Hamm, *Yesterdays*, Appendix 5, 487–88. Any list is apt to have its own self-contained bias, of course; a list of recorded songs may reflect the popularity of a particular dance band or of their particular version of a song, as well as the inherent popularity of the song itself.

15. Wilder, *American Popular Song*, 254–74.

Part Five

Jazz and Its Forerunners

Photo from the Frank Driggs Collection

Jazz occupies a unique and not easily classifiable position in the panorama of American music. It has been widely considered to be popular music, which in a strict sense it has hardly, if ever, been. The terms "folk" and "classical" have also been used in trying to place it in the larger picture of American music. It does not fit well under any of these verbal umbrellas. Jazz is thought by many to be the single most distinctive American music—indeed, by some, *the* American music. This perception, even if exaggerated, is all the more remarkable in that of the six streams we have chosen to identify, jazz, though approaching its century mark, is still the newest.

Beginning, like the blues, as unmistakably the music of African-American musicians, jazz has long since transcended any exclusive racial identity. Jazz and classical music have come to be our two most "serious" forms of music-making—serious in terms of their sophistication, in terms of the intellectual as well as musical qualifications demanded in their practice, and in terms of the low priority that their most dedicated practitioners assign to the profit motive—hence the survival of both genres largely independent of mass appeal, and their inherent resistance to being commercialized. Virgil Thomson's characterization of jazz as a "persecuted chamber music" makes the point deftly.

If jazz and classical music have this much in common, it is natural that there should have been many serious attempts to fuse them—attempts that have yielded interesting if not ultimately satisfactory results. For the ways in which they differ are also fundamental. Although there have been classical improvisers and jazz composers, the most basic difference is that classical music is a comprehensive manifestation of the art of the composer, and jazz a stylistically unique manifestation of the art of the improvising performer.

Chapter 13

Ragtime and Pre-Jazz

The Context of Ragtime from Its Origins to Its Zenith

In the early years of this century the terms *ragtime* and *jazz* both had broader and looser definitions than the more purist ones we find applied today. Our idea of ragtime as exclusively solo piano music is at variance with its contemporary perception. The dominant form of American popular music has always been the song, and as Edward Berlin has pointed out, it was the ragtime songs—songs such as "You've Been a Good Old Wagon But You've Done Broke Down" (1895), "A Hot Time in the Old Town" (1896), "Mister Johnson, Turn Me Loose" (1896), "All Coons Look Alike to Me" (1896), "At a Georgia Camp-meeting" (in its version as a song, 1899), "Hello! Ma Baby" (1899), and "Waiting for the Robert E. Lee" (1912)—that were more often recognized as "ragtime" in their day than the now-familiar piano pieces. This even raises the possibility that the piano versions of these ragtime songs played some part in the evolution and popularization of piano ragtime itself.[1]

The Origins of Ragtime

The roots of ragtime in our vernacular music are broad. Its most easily identifiable feature—a syncopated melody against a steady marchlike bass in duple meter—can certainly be found in music published in the 1880s, not in the middle Mississippi Valley (generally considered to be the cradle of ragtime), but in New York. And the distinctive rhythms (including the syncopations) of the banjo tunes of the early minstrel show had appeared in print before the Civil War.[2]

Both the ragtime songs and the dances of the period had their role in the development of ragtime. The earliest known ragtime instruction book, written in 1897 as the ragtime craze was just beginning, gives "Negro Dance time" as an alternative name for "RAG TIME," and for the next two decades the names of specific dances were associated with published rags.[3] The *march* could be used as dance music; many early rags include the terms "march" or "two-step" or both in their titles or subtitles. A specialty dance that also contributed to ragtime was the *cakewalk*. A march involving an exaggerated kind of strutting, it presumably originated on the plantations, with slave couples competing for the prize of a cake. It was taken over into the minstrel show, and was on Broadway by the 1870s; by the 1890s it had become a popular, though strenuous and exacting, dance for the general public.[4] Many early rags also incorporated the term "cakewalk" in their titles.

Caribbean dance rhythms—rhythms of the danza, the habanera, or the seguidilla—have been cited as one of the sources of ragtime rhythms. Louis Moreau Gottschalk (1829–69) incorporated these rhythms into most of his piano pieces with West Indian associations, including his *Danza* (1857), *La Gallina* (copyright 1869), and *Ojos Criollos* (no copyright date), the latter two of which carry the subtitle "Danse cubaine." The earliest collections of Creole songs from Louisiana also contain syncopations identical to those found in ragtime.[5] The actual extent to which this music could have influenced ragtime itself is debatable, however. The whole question of Latin American influence (principally rhythmic) on the origins of both ragtime and jazz is often overlooked and is in need of more investigation—investigation that might convince us, for example, that a piece like Joplin's **"Solace"** (1909, subtitled "A Mexican Serenade"), an exquisite example of a rag with a habanera bass, is not the isolated anomaly that it may appear to be.

Ragtime as Piano Music and the Work of Scott Joplin

Despite the breadth of interpretations given the term "ragtime," it was as music for solo piano that it ultimately achieved significance and endured. The dissemination of piano ragtime is widely thought to have been given considerable impetus by the gathering of ragtime pianists (before the term had been applied to the genre) at the World's Columbian Exposition in Chicago in 1893. There, according to Blesh and Janis, "hundreds of the itinerant piano clan had gathered" (including Scott Joplin, 1868–1917, and Ben Harney, 1871–1938), presumably to be heard on the "Midway" and in the red-light district, but more informative documentation as to what music was played will probably never come to light.[6] Not long afterward—in the same year (1896) in which Ben Harney moved to New York from his native Louisville, and began introducing ragtime through his highly successful playing and singing—Scott Joplin moved to Sedalia, Missouri, where for the next five years he composed, played, and published the first of the approximately three dozen piano pieces that he and his publisher referred to as "classic rags." Thus Ben Harney, the white Brooklynite Joseph Lamb (1877–1960), and others in New York, and Scott Joplin, Tom Turpin

(1873–1922), Arthur Marshall (1881–1968), Scott Hayden (1882–1915), James Scott (1886—1938), and others in the Midwest, helped to launch ragtime as we know it into what became, in the next two decades, a national craze.

Ragtime for the piano assumed in its initial stages three forms: piano renditions of ragtime songs; the "ragging" of unsyncopated music; and original compositions for the piano. The latter began to be published in 1897—William Krell's "The Mississippi Rag" was possibly the first, with "Harlem Rag" by the St. Louis composer Tom Turpin coming out the same year. It is probable that at least three thousand rags were published between 1897 and 1920; estimates have run as high as ten thousand. As could be expected most of these were mediocre musically, and were simplified in their published versions to be more suited to the modest pianistic abilities of the many who bought them and attempted to play them at home. What are today regarded as the masterpieces of piano ragtime were not necessarily best-sellers; Scott Joplin's most famous work, "Maple Leaf Rag" (1899), was virtually the only one of his works to become widely popular in his lifetime, and it was the work that justified his being heralded on sheet music covers as "the king of ragtime writers."

Scott Joplin has emerged as the single most important ragtime composer of the period. A versatile musician (he played the cornet and piano and led a band) with high musical standards and determined ambition, he lavished a great deal of effort and resources on composing and producing large-scale works for the stage, none of which were successful in his lifetime. But his most enduring and influential works are his rags, whose musical inventiveness and craftsmanship set a standard against which others are measured.

The association of the piano with the ragtime era is no coincidence; figures show that the sales of pianos rose sharply after 1890, and declined just as steeply in the 1920s. But a modified form of the piano, the mechanical player piano, was also an important feature of the era; after 1900, player piano sales also rose steeply, reaching a peak before the ragtime era was completely over.[7] Thus a great deal of ragtime (as did its successor, "novelty" piano music) came into American homes in the form of piano rolls. These rolls could be either "hand-played," often by the composer himself, or "arranged" by the calculated punching of the paper rolls. In fact, many rags, including one by Joplin himself, appeared only in piano rolls and were never published in sheet music form.[8]

Those who bought the sheet music, however, intent on playing it at home, soon discovered that ragtime is not easy to play. To aid the learner and cash in on the boom, instruction books in ragtime began to appear—the earliest by Harney himself in 1897. One truly valuable document is an all-too-brief set of six exercises by Scott Joplin himself, published as *School of Ragtime* in 1908, with accompanying explanations and admonitions. (Joplin concentrates most on accurate rendering of the rhythm, and warns the performer, as he was to do over and over again in his published rags, "Never play ragtime fast at any time.") To provide personal instruction, studios were opened to accept pupils—and, yes, the first advertisement for "Ragtime Taught in Ten Lessons" appeared in Chicago in 1903.

In its heyday the creation and publication of ragtime was not, like Tin Pan Alley and the popular song industry, concentrated in New York City. The mid-Mississippi Valley and the Ohio Valley were strong areas for ragtime, and an examination of sheet music shows that rags were published not only in St. Louis, Kansas City, Columbia, and Sedalia, Missouri, but also in Indianapolis, Cincinnati, Memphis, Nashville, Chicago, Detroit, New Orleans, Dallas, and San Francisco, and even in such places as Temple, Texas (for early Joplin pieces); Moline, Illinois; New Albany, Indiana; Kiowa, Kansas; and Oskaloosa, Iowa. John Hasse has termed the ragtime era "the golden age of local and regional music publishing." Piano ragtime was also a genre to which women composers contributed significantly; May Aufderheide (1890–1972), of Indianapolis, was only the best known among many.[9]

Ensemble Ragtime

The performance of ragtime was not limited either to the solo piano version or the song; as soon as it became popular, this music began to be played by many different kinds of ensembles, including brass bands, concert bands, dance bands and orchestras, and smaller groups that included mandolins, guitars, and banjos. "**St. Louis Tickle**," recorded in 1904 with a banjo, mandolin, and guitar trio, is illustrative. "Stock" arrangements for bands and orchestras (mostly for dancing) were issued by publishers; and sheet music publications of rags for piano often advertised versions of the same piece "published for band, orchestra, mandolin, guitar, etc." John Philip Sousa was quick to recognize the popularity of ragtime. He began to program it in the 1890s, and on his first tour of Europe in 1900 he gave most of his audiences there their first taste of ragtime, with arrangements of such pieces as "Smoky Mokes" and "Bunch o' Blackberries."[10] Sousa's band recorded in 1908 an instrumental version of Kerry Mills's well-known ragtime song "At a Georgia Camp Meeting."

The Musical Characteristics of Ragtime
Ragtime Rhythm

Syncopation is so basic to the rhythmic life of much American music that we shall devote some space to an examination of it as it occurs in ragtime, as a basis for understanding it as encountered elsewhere. Syncopation is the displacing of accents from their normal position in the musical measure, so that they contradict the underlying meter.[11] Syncopation assumes a steady beat, stated or implied, and cannot be said to exist without it. This is normally supplied in ragtime by the "oom-pa" of the left hand, while the right hand has the melody, with its characteristically displaced accents. This displacement is done simply by arranging the succession of long and short notes to make *some* of the longer notes begin at rhythmically weak spots in the metric continuum, so that the accent they create at the moment of their attack serves to contradict rather than reinforce the prevailing background meter.

Some examples will illustrate how this works. Example 13-1 is the rhythm of the first two measures of the fiddler's tune "Turkey in the Straw."

Example 13–1. Rhythmic excerpt from "Turkey in the Straw"

Here all the notes except the last are the same length, so that there can be no accents by virtue of note length, and hence no syncopation. The running notes constitute a continuous background made up of what might be called the "lowest common denominator" of durations, since they are the shortest notes used. They occur in groups of four to a beat. This is the same metric background that is used in ragtime.

Let us observe the ways in which longer notes can be superimposed on this background. If we want a longer note to reinforce the meter, it will do this most strongly if its beginning coincides with the first note of a rhythmic subdivision.

(Background)

Example 13-2. Syncopation I

This is the normal position of the lowest, and hence the "'heaviest," of the left-hand bass notes. Somewhat weaker, and creating a mild contradiction, or syncopation, would be a note beginning on the third of the sixteenth notes of our background (Ex. 13-3).

Example 13–3. Syncopation II

This mild syncopation, called by Berlin "augmented syncopation,"[12] had been in wide use in American popular song since the earliest days of the minstrel show. It is the only type of syncopation found in "Dixie," for example, and it is found in a number of other songs of the same genre, such as "Camptown Races" and "The Yellow Rose of Texas." It persisted to the end of the nineteenth century, and was a feature of many of the ragtime songs described above (including "A Hot Time in the Old Town" and "Hello! Ma Baby"). It flavored some Sousa marches of the 1890s, such as "High School Cadets" and "Manhattan Beach," and in the early years of the twentieth century it was characteristic of some of the peppier songs of George M. Cohan, including "Yankee Doodle Boy" and "Over There."

But this mild form of syncopation was never an important feature of ragtime itself, which characteristically used the still jauntier kind of syncopation created by having longer notes begin on either the second or the fourth of the background sixteenths (Ex. 13-4).

Example 13–4. Syncopation III

These, or variants of these, are the typical syncopations that may be found on every page of ragtime.*

If we now observe the way these syncopations are placed in genuine ragtime, we get an idea of the fine balance the best composers achieved between contradiction and affirmation of the meter within the phrase. In Example 13-5 from the first strain of Scott Joplin's "The Entertainer" (1902), the contradictions, or syncopations, are marked with an S. This well-known rag shows a typical number and distribution of syncopations. Rags of what might be called the classic period usually have between two and four to a phrase, fairly evenly distributed.

Example 13–5. Rhthmic excerpt from "The Entertainer"

It will be readily apparent that given the subdivision of the beat into four parts, the variety of syncopated figures available to the composer is rather limited, and that rhythmically ragtime can all too easily take on the character of a series of clichés. As ragtime strove to evolve, there was a tendency in some works of the middle and late periods to crowd more syncopations into the phrase. Some of Joseph Lamb's compositions reveal this, such as Example 13-6, from

*Edward Berlin makes a distinction between the two forms in Example 13-4. The first he calls "untied" syncopation, and he notes that it was more typical of earlier ragtime; the second, which he calls "tied" syncopation, seems to appear with greater frequency in the more mature phase of ragtime.

the first strain of his "American Beauty Rag" (1913). Here there are seven syncopations in the first phrase—six of them within the first two measures, including four in immediate succession. When we listen to the actual music, it is apparent that Lamb uses these syncopations with ease and grace, but there is a certain air of ripeness about it that suggests a genre that has almost reached the limits of its refinement.

Example 13–6. Rhthmic excerpt from "American Beauty Rag"

A rhythmic feature to appear in late ragtime (Berlin places it about 1911) is the dotted rhythm in Example 13-7; in performance, the first of each pair is longer than the second but not three times as long, as a strict interpretation of the rhythm as written would indicate.

Example 13–7. Rhthmic feature of late ragtime

This unevenness was a performance practice that would later, after the advent of jazz, be applied to the performance of earlier ragtime. A comparison between Scott Joplin's performance, on a piano roll, of his "Maple Leaf Rag" in 1916 with an interpretation of the same piece by Jelly Roll Morton in 1938 shows this clearly.* The relation of the uneven performance of background notes to the "swung" eighths of swing jazz is evident; the appearance of dotted rhythms in ragtime pieces of the teens may be an indication that the practice of swing had earlier precedents than has been generally assumed.

Ragtime Form

It is in its standardized form that ragtime shows most clearly its relation to the march, which is based on a succession of musically independent "strains" of uniform length (16 measures), most of which are repeated. An introduction is optional; Joplin, except in his most famous rag, almost invariably uses one. In the most typical pattern for ragtime, after the introduction two or three strains in the main key are followed by two strains (called the "trio" in the march) in the related key of the subdominant. Often the first strain, unrepeated, is brought

*Both are in the Smithsonian Collection of Classic Jazz.

back just before the trio. There are variants, but a typical rag would have the form *aabb a ccdd*, with each letter representing a 16-bar strain. Sometimes the final strain returns to the principal key; more often (as in the march) the rag ends in a different key from that in which it began. Joplin, in his late rags, tried a somewhat more expanded form.[13]

The Mingling of African-American and European-American Traits in Ragtime

Ragtime represents an interesting intersection of musical traits that can be identified as European and African in origin and approach. Its rhythm is derived from African-American sources. On the other hand, ragtime form, melody (except for syncopation), and harmony are clearly related to those of the American popular song and dance music of the time—European-derived, by way of Tin Pan Alley. The harmonies, where they depart from the basic three chords, employ for the most part the familiar "barbershop" type of chromaticism. A rare intersection of African-Americanism and European-Americanism is found in the first trio (subdominant) strain of Joplin's "Pine Apple Rag" (Ex. 13-8), where the quintessential blues harmony (the subdominant chord with a flatted seventh) appears in the same phrase with a conventional modulation to the mediant key (this rag was copyrighted in 1908, four years before the first published blues appeared).

Example 13–8. Excerpt from "Pine Apple Rag"

The Decline and Dispersion of Ragtime

Ragtime's original heyday was brief, in retrospect; scarcely a generation had elapsed between its full-fledged appearance in the 1890s and its decline and

Jelly Roll Morton. *Courtesy Frank Driggs Collection.*

metamorphosis into other styles. Recognizing the dual forms, vocal and instrumental, that ragtime assumed, Berlin has noted that by the mid-1910s vocal ragtime (as the ragtime song) "merged with the mainstream of popular music, while piano ragtime inclined toward what became known as jazz."[14] Piano ragtime, in its dispersion, assumed several forms, and affected several distinct genres. Foremost, of course, was its merging with jazz. For a time, the two terms were used almost interchangeably.

Jelly Roll Morton

Ferdinand Joseph ("Jelly Roll") Morton (1890–1941), a New Orleans-born pianist and bandleader, was a key figure in this transition. His own works (variously titled "rags," "blues," and "stomps," among other designations) date mostly from the post-ragtime era. In these we can see that Morton's own style had superseded classic ragtime, while reinterpreting some of its elements. Morton's identity as a bandleader is also evident; not only did many of the pieces exist as band numbers, but Morton often wanted his piano itself to "sound as much like a band as possible." Nevertheless, he drew a clear distinction between the new jazz and older ragtime, which he had grown up with and knew thoroughly. His historic recordings, with commentary, made for Alan Lomax at the Library of Congress in the late 1930s, illustrate these distinctions, and are a valuable source of information about the transition from ragtime to jazz.[15] Though Morton makes his first appearance in our panoramic survey in connection with ragtime, it is really for his work in the formative stages of jazz that he is most important. After extensive traveling from 1904 to 1922, he went to Chicago, where he recorded, both as piano soloist and bandleader, the works by which he is known.

Two Offshoots of Ragtime: Stride Piano and Novelty Piano

As classic piano ragtime itself declined, two other offshoots appeared—descendants of the parent form, but not to be confused with it. One was the largely New York phenomenon of "stride piano," also known as "Harlem piano." This genre, cultivated by James Price Johnson (1894–1955) and Fats Waller (1904–43) in the 1920s and 1930s, retains some of ragtime's characteristics, most notably a steady left-hand rhythmic pulse (expanded to wide-reaching "strides" between low bass notes and mid-range offbeat chords), with syncopated right-hand figuration. Basically a virtuoso form developed by pianists with phenomenal facility, stride piano is often faster than ragtime, with a driving beat and very elaborate melodic line. James P. Johnson's ebullient "**If Dreams Come True**," recorded in 1939, is a fine example. The atmosphere and function of the Harlem rent party of the twenties and thirties is succinctly described by Marshall Stearns when he calls it "an unstable social phenomenon that was stimulated by Prohibition and made necessary by the Depression." He continues: "The object of such a party is to raise the rent, and anybody who can pay a quarter admission is cordially invited. The core of the party usually centers around a pianist whose style was shaped by many similar situations: he plays very loud and very rhythmically."[16]

Another offshoot of ragtime was the so-called "novelty piano" music of the early 1920s; anyone familiar with such pieces as "Nola," "Canadian Capers," "Kitten on the Keys," or "Dizzy Fingers" knows the style. A "show-off" kind of piano music (carefully made to sound more difficult than it actually is), it has been described by Ronald Riddle as "a refined, white suburban extension of ragtime."[17] The "novelty" itself was an attraction in tune with the times; such words as "tricky," "sparkling," and "scintillating" were used to describe and sell it. It was ideal for the medium of the player piano during the last few years of that instrument's popularity; before being replaced by the phonograph and the radio, the player piano made this novelty music accessible to people without the technical ability to play it themselves. But the sheet music itself also sold extremely well; Zez Confrey's "Kitten on the Keys" (which first appeared as a piano roll played by the composer) outsold "Maple Leaf Rag" when it was issued as sheet music in 1921. Musically, novelty piano shared the basic underlying features of ragtime, but emphasized greater speed, an obviously exhibitionist kind of virtuosity, and a particular species of syncopation known as "secondary rag," in which the regular quadruple subdivisions of the basic pulse are grouped in threes (Ex. 13-9).

Example 13–9. Secondary rag

The composer most closely associated with the genre was Edward E. "Zez" Confrey (1895–1971). Novelty piano, for all of its short-lived superficiality, had in its technical aspects—especially its secondary rag—an unmistakable influence on certain piano music of the 1920s and 1930s, especially that of George Gershwin. Riddle has mentioned Confrey's influence, via the popular "Kitten on the Keys," on Gershwin's *Rhapsody in Blue*. (Confrey played in the same famous Aeolian Hall concert that introduced the "Rhapsody" in 1924!) He has also pointed out its influence on European composers such as Ravel and Martinů, when they wrote in an obviously "jazzy" style; in fact, some aspects of novelty piano were taken by outsiders to be synonymous with jazz at the time. Riddle's excellent article on the subject closes with the observation that "in the end, the piano novelty suffered a sad but predictable fate: it lost its novelty. While it lasted it was great fun . . . but it was too hot *not* to cool down."

The Ragtime Revival
It was only in revival that ragtime regained its integrity and distinctiveness. This selective revival, focusing almost exclusively on piano rags, which began about mid-century, has now lasted far longer than did the ragtime era itself.

The revival of traditional jazz, under the umbrella name of "Dixieland," began in the 1940s. Working backwards chronologically, the next step was the rediscovery and study of ragtime, which was then generally viewed as a quite dated and old-fashioned precursor of jazz. The writers Rudi Blesh and Harriet Janis, and the performer, entertainer, and scholar Max Morath were among the first to give ragtime serious attention. There were discovered in the best of the piano rags musical excellences that had largely escaped the public in the ragtime era itself. Joshua Rifkin made studio-quality recordings, on a concert grand piano, of the rags of Scott Joplin in 1970; with his first best-selling record he separated ragtime from its association with the tinny, out-of-tune barroom piano and its accompanying stereotypical milieu, and focused on its musical values. In 1972 Gunther Schuller reinstated instrumental ragtime when he refurbished old stock arrangements (notably those found in the famous "Red Back Book") and founded and rehearsed the New England Conservatory Ragtime Ensemble. William Bolcom and John Hasse are among those who have not only continued to perform and record piano ragtime, but composed rags of their own. This renewed attention to the musical aspects of ragtime has made the works of some early composers, especially Scott Joplin, James Scott, and Joseph Lamb, stand out in perspective against the mass of mediocrity perpetrated in the ragtime era itself. Thus a few dozen rags emerge as small gems, illustrative of the potential for investing miniature and highly circumscribed forms such as the rag with refinement, craftsmanship, and vitality.

Pre-Jazz

Minstrelsy, ragtime, and the blues were only the most public and audible forms of black (or black-derived) music that came before jazz. Behind them, mostly unheard and unheeded by white Americans, were all the varied musical manifestations of what has been called the "black experience." Where and when, from all this background, did actual jazz begin to emerge? This is a complex question, the first part of which cannot be adequately answered with the single place name New Orleans. It will be necessary to take a broader look geographically, for there were musical developments in all the cities and towns of the South, and in the larger cities of the North (in other words, wherever there was a sizable population of African Americans) that set the stage for the emergence of jazz.

James Reese Europe and African-American Bands at Home and Abroad

An important forerunner of jazz in New York was orchestral ragtime, which from the late 1890s until after the first World War was heard both in stage shows and as played by black dance orchestras. In many parts of the country it had long been the role of black musicians to furnish music for dancing. As Eileen Southern has said: "In many places the profession of dance musicians was reserved by custom for Negroes, just as was, for example, the occupation of barber. Consequently, black dance orchestras held widespread monopolies on jobs for a long period in the nation's history—even after World War I."[18]

In the early 1900s New York's Black Bohemia (an area in West Manhattan around 53rd Street) furnished the "syncopated dance orchestras" that were much

James Reese Europe (center, holding baton) and the Clef Club Orchestra.
Courtesy Frank Driggs Collection.

in demand for all occasions. Such an orchestra gave a public concert in 1905, and by 1910 James Reese Europe (1881–1919) had founded the famous Clef Club, whose orchestra gave public concerts, including a famous and highly successful one at Carnegie Hall in 1912. Europe, a pioneer in jazz orchestration, aimed at developing an orchestra that "is different and distinctive, and that lends itself to the playing of the peculiar compositions of our race." Two features that distinguished this orchestra from the standard white orchestra of the time were (1) the increased importance, and often dominance, of drums and other percussion, and (2) the presence of proportionately large numbers of banjos and mandolins, which, as Europe explained, took the place of the second violins, and gave "that peculiar steady strumming accompaniment to our music . . . ." James Weldon Johnson, the well-known black poet, wrote of the Carnegie Hall concert: "New York had not yet become accustomed to jazz; so when the Clef Club opened its concert with a syncopated march, playing it with a biting attack and an infectious rhythm, and on the finale bursting into singing, the effect can be imagined.

The applause became a tumult!" Europe's 1914 recording of his "Castle House Rag"* with his Society Orchestra is illustrative of what New Yorkers were hearing, especially the surprising and famous final strain, which Lawrence Gushee describes as "ferociously raggy."[19]

With the entry of the United States into World War I in 1917, African Americans joined the armed forces in large numbers, and bands were formed of black musicians whose services were much in demand. The most famous of these bands was formed and led by James Reese Europe himself.** In France the band was enormously popular, not only with the American troops but with the French as well.[20] Was Europe's band playing jazz? Perhaps not in the strictest sense, since he laid great stress on the musicians' reading the music accurately. (Eubie Blake, who had played with Europe in 1916, described "that Europe gang" as "absolute reading sharks. They could read a moving snake, and if a fly lit on that paper he got played.") Europe's own description of the band's playing is illuminating: "We accent strongly . . . the notes which originally would be without accent. It is natural for us to do this; it is, indeed, a racial musical characteristic. I have to call a daily rehearsal of my band to prevent the musicians from adding to their music more than I wish them to. Whenever possible they all embroider their parts in order to produce new, peculiar sounds."[21]

James Reese Europe and the band had a triumphant return to the States in 1919, and almost immediately embarked on a world tour. Had he not been killed in May of that year (stabbed by a mentally ill band member during a concert in Boston), he surely would have played a still more prominent role in the evolution of the nascent jazz. More formally educated and more commercially successful than most early jazz musicians, he has tended to be dismissed as a mere popularizer. Yet, as J. Reid Badger has pointed out, "by recognizing the achievements of Jim Europe, we can better understand the musical and historical context that eventually produced such major jazz orchestrators as Fletcher Henderson and Duke Ellington."[22]

Brass Bands

Better known as precursors of jazz were the smaller, more informal black brass bands that took part in the nationwide flourishing of bands noted in the preceding chapter. New Orleans, possibly owing to French influence, had an exceptional number of bands, as well as dance orchestras. The French interest in the military,

---

*The "Castle House Rag" is on *Steppin' on the Gas: Rags to Jazz 1913–1927*, New World 269.
**Europe was commissioned as a line officer, and he and the members of his band fought as combat soldiers in the all-black 369th Infantry Regiment (the "Hellfighters"), one of the most highly decorated units of the war.

or brass, band goes back to Napoleonic times. There were also trained musicians playing in the French Opera House who regularly taught the instruments.

The bands were not large by present standards, consisting of only ten or twelve pieces, including trumpets or cornets, alto and baritone horns, trombones, tuba, clarinets, and drums. They could furnish music for concerts as well as parades; in addition, there was often a smaller group affiliated with the band that played for dances, as many of the men doubled on stringed instruments. The repertoire of both groups had of necessity to be broad, and by no means consisted entirely of the new ragtime, but included quadrilles, polkas, waltzes, and mazurkas.

It was for their parade music that black bandsmen in the South ultimately became most famous, and not the least important job of these bands was playing for funerals. The lodge or secret society (often more than one) to which the deceased belonged would engage the band. In the legendary and often-described scene, the band would march solemnly to the graveyard, playing hymns such as "Nearer My God to Thee" or "Come Ye Disconsolate," or "any 4/4 played very slow." After the burial the band would re-form outside the cemetery and march away to the beat of the snare drum only. After it was a block or two away from the graveyard, it would burst into ragtime—"Didn't He Ramble," or a "ragged" version of a hymn or spiritual. It was then that the "second line" of fans and enthusiastic dancing bystanders would fall in behind the band.[23]

The Excelsior and the Onward were the most famous bands. No recordings exist of these bands. But recordings by the surviving Eureka Brass Band (an organization dating from the 1920s), which were made in the 1950s, give some idea of the sound. The juxtaposition of "**Eternity**," the kind of piece that would have been played in the solemn march to the graveyard, and "**Just a Little While to Stay Here**," the kind of jazzed version of a hymn tune that would have been played on the way back, furnish a kind of aural synthesis of this experience.

There was keen competition among the bands, and "cutting" or "bucking" contests were common. A few legendary names emerge from this period—none larger than that of Charles "Buddy" Bolden (1877–1931), the New Orleans trumpet player. He was a versatile musician, reading music when necessary but preferring to play by ear. Bolden played "sweet" music for the general public and "hot" music for the "district" and its patrons. It was for the latter that he became most famous, introducing his "hot blues" about 1894. Was Buddy playing jazz, that far back? Earwitnesses like Bunk Johnson (1889–1949) say that he was. It is certain that he was heavily imbued with the blues. The New Orleans bass player "Pops" Foster has written of him: "He played nothing but blues, and all that stink music, and he played it very loud."[24] Here was ample evidence at an early date of the perennial and symbiotic relationship between blues and jazz.

FURTHER READING

Books

Berlin, Edward A. *Ragtime: A Musical and Cultural History*. Berkeley: University of California Press, 1980.

        An excellent study, with probably the best analysis of the musical elements of ragtime.

Blesh, Rudi, and Harriett Janis. *They All Played Ragtime*. 4th ed. New York: Oak, 1971.

        The first book on the subject, and still the source of a wealth of information.

Hasse, John, ed. *Ragtime: Its History, Composers, and Music*. New York: Schirmer Books, 1985.

        A valuable collection of articles on various aspects, including some by Hasse himself. Extensive bibliography and discography, well organized.

Lomax, Alan. *Mister Jelly Roll: The Fortunes of Jelly Roll Morton, New Orleans Creole and "Inventor of Jazz."* 2d ed. Berkeley: University of California Press, 1973.

        Morton's memoirs as told in the famous Library of Congress sessions in 1938, with some interludes by Lomax.

Schafer, William J. *Brass Bands and New Orleans Jazz*. Baton Rouge: Louisiana State University Press, c.1977.

Schuller, Gunther. *Early Jazz: Its Roots and Musical Development*. New York: Oxford University Press, 1968.

        See chapter 2, "The Beginnings."

Shaw, Arnold. *Black Popular Music in America*. New York: Schirmer Books, 1986.

        See especially chapter 3, "My Ragtime Baby."

Southern, Eileen. *The Music of Black Americans: A History*. 2d ed. New York: Norton, 1983.

        See chapter 9.

————, ed. *Readings in Black American Music*. 2d ed. New York. Norton, 1983.

Stearns, Marshall. *The Story of Jazz*. New York: Oxford University Press, 1956. Reprint, 1974.

        This standard work has excellent chapters on "Ragtime," "The New Orleans Background," and "The Transition to Jazz."

Articles in American Music

Badger, J. Reid. "James Reese Europe and the Prehistory of Jazz," 7, no. 1 (Spring 1989): 48–67.

Berlin, Edward A. "Scott Joplin's *Tremonisha* Years," 9, no. 3 (Fall 1991).

Kenney, William H. "James Scott and the Culture of Classic Ragtime," 9, no. 2 (Summer 1991): 149–82.

Tallmadge, William H. "Ben Harney: The Middlesborough Years, 1890–93," 13, no. 2 (Summer 1995): 167–94.

Projects

1. Write a paragraph, a page, or several pages, giving your own personal perception of the contribution of black music to American popular music. After you have written this, read Arnold Shaw's introduction to his *Black Popular Music in America*. Add another paragraph, or page, commenting on the extent to which Shaw's assessment of the situation confirms or contradicts your own. Does Shaw seem to present a reasonable, well-documented, balanced view? Does his introduction support the rejection of extremist views on *either* side of the question? How?

2. A broad and general sensitivity to the feelings of any group perceived as a minority (whether defined in terms of race, color, religion, or any other basis) is fairly recent and still imperfect, as our jokes and our songs reveal. The study of popular art is a study not of what later periods may select, but of what is actually popular in contemporary culture, and therefore revealing of its nature. This precept leads a scholar like Vera Brodsky Lawrence to include sheet music covers in her edition of the works of Scott Joplin, and Edward Berlin and Arnold Shaw to discuss the "coon song" in their treatises. If you

were doing an illustrated lecture on American popular culture since the Jacksonian era, think about how you would treat the minstrel skit, the coon song, the Irish (or Jewish, or Chinese) song, the Polish (or Italian, or Catholic, or Mormon) joke. Discuss your views in a paper. Is censorship justifiable, and under what circumstances?

3. Write a paper comparing the role of women in ragtime (you could begin with Max Morath's article "May Aufderheide and the Ragtime Women" in Hasse, *Ragtime: Its History, Composers, and Music*) with the role of women in jazz (consulting such works as *American Women in Jazz, 1900 to the Present: Their Words, Lives, and Music* by S. Placksin [Seaview, 1982] or *Stormy Weather: The Music and Lives of a Century of Jazz Women* by L. Dahl [Pantheon, 1984]).

4. The musical relationship between blues and ragtime was, in the classic period of ragtime, somewhat noticeable but not great. Investigate the relationship between the *texts* of ragtime songs (such as those mentioned in the chapter) and those of early blues. For ragtime songs, consult Edward Berlin's chapter "Ragtime Songs" in Hasse, *Ragtime: Its History, Composers, and Music*; Blesh and Janis's *They All Played Ragtime*; and song collections such as *Favorite Songs of the Nineties* (see the previous chapter). For blues lyrics, see chapter 6, and such sources as the W. C. Handy anthology and Paul Oliver's *The Meaning of the Blues*.

Notes

1. See Edward Berlin, *Ragtime: A Musical and Cultural History* (Berkeley: University of California Press, 1980), 1–7.

2. For reference to a piano piece with ragtime syncopations published in 1886, see Berlin, *Ragtime*, 107–8. For a discussion of the banjo's contribution to piano ragtime, see Lowell H. Schreyer, "The Banjo in Ragtime" in John Edward Hasse, ed., *Ragtime: Its History, Composers, and Music*.

3. From *Ben Harney's Ragtime Instructor*, as quoted in Berlin, *Ragtime*, 115 (see also 13–14).

4. See Shaw, *Black Popular Music*, 43–44.

5. See for example "Miché Bainjo," in Allen, Ware, and Garrison, *Slave Songs of the United States*, 1867 (cited in the Further Reading section to chapter 2).

6. See Rudi Blesh and Harriet Janis, *They All Played Ragtime*, 4th ed., 18 and 41.

7. This is graphically shown on a chart in Hasse, *Ragtime*, 15.

8. See "Ragtime on Piano Rolls" in Hasse, *Ragtime*.

9. See the article "May Aufderheide and the Ragtime Women" by Max Morath in Hasse, *Ragtime*.

10. For an extensive treatment of ragtime arrangements see "Band and Orchestral Ragtime" by Thornton Hagert, in Hasse, *Ragtime*. Archival recordings of instrumental ragtime are rare, but a few examples are found in *The Sousa and Pryor Bands: Original Recordings 1901–1926* (New World 282); *Steppin' on the Gas: Rags to Jazz 1913–1927* (New World 269); *Ragtime*, I: *The City* (Smithsonian-Folkways RF 017); and *Ragtime* II: *The Country* (Smithsonian-Folkways RF 018). Some reconstructions by modern orchestras are heard on *Come and Trip It: Instrumental Dance Music 1780's–1920's* (New World 293).

11. A more genetic explanation of the syncopation of ragtime and jazz as survivals of the genuine polyrhythms of African music is put forward in Gunther Schuller's *Early Jazz: Its Roots and Musical Development* (New York: Oxford University Press, 1968), chapter 1, based on the research of A. M. Jones.

12. Berlin, in his *Ragtime*, 82–89, includes a rather thorough treatment of ragtime syncopation that is consistent with the author's explanation.

13. Berlin presents a succinct but fairly comprehensive treatment of ragtime form in his *Ragtime*, 89–91. See also "Joplin's Late Rags: An Analysis" by Guy Waterman, in Hasse, *Ragtime*.

14. Berlin, 61.

15. See *Mister Jelly Roll: The Fortunes of Jelly Roll Morton, New Orleans Creole and "Inventor of Jazz"* by Alan Lomax, 2d ed. (Berkeley: University of California Press, 1973) for the extensive transcription of Morton's reminiscences constituting his personal memoirs. His piano music has been painstakingly transcribed and edited by James Dapogny in *Ferdinand "Jelly Roll" Morton: The Collected Piano Music*

(Washington, DC: Smithsonian Institution Press, 1982), which includes historical and textual annotations. See also "Jelly Roll Morton and Ragtime," also by Dapogny, in Hasse, *Ragtime*.

16. Marshall Stearns, *The Story of Jazz* (New York: Oxford University Press, 1956; reprint, 1974), 122.

17. See Ronald Riddle's article "Novelty Piano Music" in Hasse, *Ragtime*.

18. Eileen Southern, *The Music of Black Americans*, 2d ed. (New York: Norton, 1983), 338.

19. Europe's quotes appear in R. Reid Badger's very informative article "James Reese Europe and the Prehistory of Jazz" in *American Music* 7, no. 1, 51. Also informative are Lawrence Gushee's notes to New World 269, *Steppin' on the Gas: Rags to Jazz 1913–1927*, which begins with Europe's "Castle House Rag."

20. An interesting account of the band's experiences is contained in *From Harlem to the Rhine*, by Arthur Little, who served as a captain in the regiment: excerpts are reprinted in Southern, *Readings in Black American Music*, 2d ed.

21. Quoted in Southern, *The Music of Black Americans*, 352.

22. R. Reid Badger, 60.

23. Much of the foregoing is based on Bunk Johnson's description, as quoted in Marshall Stearns, *The Story of Jazz* (New York: Oxford University Press, 1956), 50–51.

24. From Foster's autobiography, quoted in Bruce Cook, *Listen to the Blues* (New York: Scribner's, 1973), 88.

The New Orleans Style:
The Traditional Jazz of the Early Recordings

The most representative early jazz recordings date from about 1923. By this time the style known as "traditional" or New Orleans jazz was well established, though that city was no longer at the center of its development. Because these early recordings were so important in defining what jazz was and laying the groundwork for what it was to become, we shall begin by examining an early recording in some detail, using this as a point of departure for a brief description of the basic nature and structure of jazz.

Traditional Jazz as Illustrative of Jazz Method and Structure

Our example is the famous "**Dippermouth Blues**." Though recorded by King Oliver's Creole Jazz Band in the north in 1923, it is representative of the New Orleans style in instrumentation, form, and manner of performance.[1]

The essence of jazz has been from the beginning, and remains, a *way* of playing and singing—a style of performance with many intangible features, but whose tangible aspects can be defined in terms of accent, phrasing, tone color, the "bending" of pitch and rhythm, and the freedom of the individual player to improvise within certain limits. The basic procedure of jazz, from the traditional to the most recent, is to produce a series of *variations* on a standard formal harmonic plan, whether that of a popular song (a "standard") or simply the "ground plan" of the blues, as outlined below.

The instrumentation of "**Dippermouth Blues**" is two cornets, one clarinet, one trombone, and a *rhythm section* of piano, banjo, and drums. Except for the addition of a second cornet, innovative for its time, this is a typical makeup for traditional jazz. (The cornets, played by King Oliver and Louis Armstrong, were only later replaced by trumpets, which have a more incisive sound.) In describing the texture we can make an analogy with ragtime. The "front line" instruments (in this case, the cornets, clarinet, and trombone) correspond to the right hand, to which is entrusted the melody, or the simultaneous overlayering of melodies. The rhythm section corresponds to the left hand, which has the job of keeping the beat going and of outlining the harmonies. If we grasp this division of function between front line and rhythm section it will serve us well in understanding jazz texture throughout the decades to follow. The front line will later increase, in the big band, to complete sections of saxophones, trumpets, trombones, and whatever additional melody instruments may be employed. The rhythm section, on the other hand, will remain to a remarkable degree the same as we hear it in these early recordings, only dropping the antiquated banjo and adding the string bass (in place of the tuba which was sometimes used in early jazz). The rhythm section is to remain the most stable and indispensable element of the jazz ensemble.

Ragtime, as a solo piano form, had a single melody (at most lightly harmonized) in the right hand. Traditional jazz, on the other hand, exhibits in its most typical choruses a complex layering of melodic lines, with the cornet(s) in the middle, the trombone below, and the clarinet adding a more ornate and decorative line on top of it all. "**Dippermouth Blues**" shows this texture in all but the solo choruses, in which the clarinet and later the first cornet emerge as soloists.

In its form, this piece is an apt illustration of the fundamental variation technique of jazz. After the 4-bar introduction, each of the nine choruses is an exposition of the 12-bar blues form. It appears in its simplest, most standard form in the sixth chorus (the first solo chorus by King Oliver on cornet):

phrase 1:	—-	—-	—-	I7
phrase 2:	IV7	—-	I	—-
phrase 3:	V7	—-	I	—-

Close listening discloses subtle variations in the harmony from chorus to chorus. The first two choruses of the piece show the kind of embellishing of the harmony that is typical of jazz versions of the blues—embellishments that, in the second and third phrases, show the influence of the European-based harmonies of ragtime:

phrase 1:	I	IV	I	I7
phrase 2:	IV	#ivd7	I	VI7
phrase 3:	II7	V7	I	—-

Countless other blues are variations on some version of this basic blues pattern. But the blues as performed is more than simply a formal and harmonic plan; a manner of performance is implied that includes the inflection of certain notes—the blue notes, as described in chapter 2. It can be heard in King Oliver's lowered thirds of the scale at the beginning of his solos, and clarinetist Johnny Dodds's blues sevenths at the beginning of his.

Another vital ingredient of jazz is improvisation. On a formal and harmonic ground plan such as the one illustrated above the musicians are free to invent, in an appropriate jazz style, their own melodic lines that fit with, and express, that harmony and that form. Ideally, as improvisation, it never sounds exactly the same twice. Depending on the talent and mood of the performer, the improvisation can be fresh, spontaneous, and loaded with new ideas, or it can follow patterns already established in previous performances or by other performers. But jazz improvisation is never a matter of "anything goes." It is a product (as is all good art) of a fine balance between discipline and freedom—in the case of the jazz solo, between the discipline imposed by the preset form and harmony and the freedom to create within these limitations.

Louis Armstrong (1898–1971) has been deemed the first great improvising soloist in jazz. He was one of the performers who defined the "hot" style of playing in the 1920s, and was an early master of "swing." Swing is not easily described, but all of its elements amount to contradictions or dislocations, in one way or another, of a regular metric pattern—playing pairs of shorter notes unequally within a beat so as to give more length and stress to the first, displacing accents, or playing notes slightly behind or ahead of the beat. His solos, with their melodic inventiveness, rhythmic drive, and variety of tonal color, especially during the period from the 1920s through the late 1930s, were models that had a great influence on the course of jazz as it moved out of the traditional period.

Dissemination and Change: The Pre-Swing Era
Chicago

There were two jazz styles in Chicago in the 1920s, black and white, both played by musicians from New Orleans. There were the white bands such as the Original Dixieland Jazz Band, which had begun to record in Chicago in 1917, and the New Orleans Rhythm Kings. Young white musicians in Chicago who began to play jazz had heard the Original Dixieland Jazz Band, but not necessarily King Oliver's Creole Jazz Band, and it was the white bands that were their model. King Oliver and Louis Armstrong and other black musicians were recording and playing on Chicago's South Side—but necessarily playing in places where the young white musicians weren't supposed to go. Mezz Mezzrow, a Jewish jazz player from Chicago who tried his best to *become* black, writes of the white Chicago jazz: "Chicago style is an innocent style. It's the playing of talented

Bix Beiderbecke. *Courtesy New York Public Library.*

youngsters just learning their ABC's, and New Orleans was its source, but you can't expect any derivative to be as good as the source. New Orleans was simple, but not innocent."

One very talented Chicago youngster with a musical family background who grew up knowing his musical ABCs was Bix Beiderbecke (1903–31). He listened to King Oliver and Louis Armstrong as well as the Original Dixieland Jazz Band, played cornet jobs around Chicago as early as 1921, and formed his own band (the Wolverines) in 1923. Bix's cornet solos are unique landmarks, and attest to the talent of the "youngster" who was, in Gunther Schuller's words, "the greatest white jazz musician of the twenties." It is interesting to hear the progression from what Frederic Ramsey Jr. has described as "the fluid, relaxed music of the King Oliver Jazz Band" in "Sweet Lovin' Man" of 1923, through "the variant but nevertheless stimulating New Orleans music played by white musicians from the Crescent City, the New Orleans Rhythm Kings" recording the same piece in the same year, to "the choppy, youthful and provocative jazz played by the mid-western Wolverines," in "Jazz Me Blues" of 1924.[2]

What was the milieu of jazz in the 1920s? Musicians played a great deal for and among themselves, after hours, but for the paying public (a rapidly growing constituency) its home was the nightclub and related establishments. This was to constitute its basic environment, physically and economically, for years to come. One effect of Prohibition was to relegate the public dispensing of liquor to the tough guy—the mobster who could either dictate to the law or take it into his own hands. Consequently, especially in places like Chicago, jazz came under the aegis of the gangster.[3] For a fuller understanding of jazz, its environment must be kept in mind, in terms not only of its effects on the lives of its musicians, but of the whole set of prejudices that grew up around it. The nightclub and its milieu is still basic to the day-by-day support of a sizable core of players who earn wages playing it.

Two New York Developments

New York became the scene of intense jazz activity in the 1920s. But the stage had been set for this long before, as we saw in the preceding chapter. Two important developments began to emerge in New York before 1930. The first was the "Harlem piano" described in chapter 13. The second was the evolution of the big band. This led directly into the period of jazz's greatest stability, popularity, and economic security—an era that lasted until the end of World War II and has been designated the *swing era*. New York can claim no monopoly in the development of the big bands.[4] But it did serve as a magnet to draw talented musicians from New Orleans (often by way of Chicago), from Chicago itself, from Kansas City, and elsewhere—these musicians helped forge the new ensemble that was to carry jazz to every part of the land and, ultimately, of the world.

Early Steps in the Evolution of the Big Band

The term "big band" may be misleading. Compared with a full orchestra, the bands were still small—scarcely more than about fifteen musicians (see Table 14-1). But this was twice the size of a New Orleans-style band, and many players and jazz fans considered the "big" bands a betrayal of the very essence of jazz. We can see the big bands today as a pragmatic solution to the problem of balancing the demand for a fuller, larger, and more varied sound with the need to retain the *sine qua non* of jazz—improvisational freedom, and the elusive hot quality that goes with it.

We have examined **"Dippermouth Blues"** as recorded by King Oliver's Creole Jazz Band, with only seven musicians. Fletcher Henderson (1897–1952), a pianist and leader-arranger from Georgia, recorded the same piece, with slight additions, in New York in 1925, calling it **"Sugar Foot Stomp."** The differences

Table 14-1. The growth and evolution of the jazz band.

Band	RHYTHM	MELODY — Brass	MELODY — Reeds
King Oliver (1923)	Piano, Banjo, Drum set	Cornet, Cornet; Trombone	Clarinet
Duke Ellington (1927)	Piano, Acoustic bass, Banjo, Drum set	Trumpet, Cornet; Trombone	Alto sax, [Soprano sax, Baritone sax] *; Tenor sax [Clarinet]; Baritone sax, Alto sax, Clarinet
Duke Ellington (1940)	Piano, Acoustic bass, Guitar, Drum set	Trumpet, Trumpet, Cornet; Trombone, Valve trombone, Trombone	Alto sax; Tenor sax [Clarinet]; Baritone sax
Stan Kenton (1958)	Piano, Acoustic base, Drum set	Trumpet, Trumpet, Trumpet, Trumpet; French horn, French horn; Trombone, Trombone, Trombone, Bass trombone	Alto sax; Tenor sax; Baritone sax
Gil Evans (1973)	Piano [Electric piano], Electric bass, Guitar, Drum set; Symphonic percussion, Synthesizer	Trumpet, Flugelhorn; French horn, French horn; Trombone, [Tuba], Tuba	Alto sax; Tenor sax [Flute]; Baritone sax
American Jazz Orchestra (1989)	Piano, Acoustic bass, Guitar, Drum set	Trumpet, Trumpet, Trumpet; Trombone, Trombone, Bass trombone	Alto sax [Clarinet, Flute]; Tenor sax [Clarinet]; Baritone sax [Clarinet, Flute, Bass clarinet]

*Reed doublings are common, but not standardized, and will vary over time, from band to band, and even from one piece to another.

constitute an interesting documentation of the beginnings of the big band. There are now eleven musicians, the most significant addition being two saxophones. The individual hot solos are still there, the most memorable being the choruses played by Louis Armstrong himself, who had come from Chicago to join Henderson's band, and who plays essentially the same solos as in the earlier King Oliver version. But the new trend toward *arranged* jazz is apparent in the way the instruments play predetermined figures together at the "breaks" (the fill-in passages at the ends of the phrases), in the tightly disciplined and rehearsed (if not written-down) clarinet ensemble playing, and especially in the almost chorale-like presentation of the blues progression near the end. Another Fletcher Henderson piece, "The Stampede," arranged by Don Redman (1900–64) and recorded in 1926, shows the trend carried further by using a still greater proportion of arranged ensemble effects, while still allowing for individual improvisation.

The Swing Era and the Big Bands

The big band style, as it evolved in the East, drew on the New Orleans archetypal style, either directly or by way of Chicago. The swing era, virtually synonymous with the heyday of the big bands, is usually thought to have begun in the early 1930s, to have come to full flower about 1935, and to have bloomed gloriously for nearly a decade. By this time, after the repeal of Prohibition and partial recovery from the Depression, mob-controlled nightclubs no longer constituted the nearly exclusive support and environment for jazz. Dance halls, which by the mid-thirties grew into large, well-appointed, and well-attended ballrooms, gave jazz a new forum and a broader popular base. The big "name" bands toured these, as well as giving stage shows in theaters. Recordings sold extremely well by this time, and could be heard on phonographs at home, in the jukeboxes that soon provided a ubiquitous accompaniment to nearly all public eating and drinking in the land, or on the new popular mass medium of the day, radio. The disc jockey, with his enormous influence, came into being. There were also weekly broadcasts of live bands. Movies featured jazz bands. This was the period when jazz enjoyed its widest public.

Three Significant Bands

Duke Ellington

Of all the jazz musicians who came into prominence with the big band, none had a more influential career than Edward Kennedy "Duke" Ellington (1899–1974), whose creative activity spanned half a century. He was a pianist, but his medium of expression was the band itself, and as leader, arranger, and composer he made music with a group that held together with exceptional consistency and continuity

Duke Ellington (at piano) and the Cotton Club Orchestra. *Courtesy Frank Driggs Collection.*

throughout the years. A famous early piece is "East St. Louis Toodle-O"* (recorded versions exist from both 1927 and 1937), which already shows the smooth and disciplined playing and the use of instrumental effects and colors typical of Ellington's essentially orchestral approach to jazz.

The Ellington band's unique use of instrumental color is the product of two factors: the imagination of Ellington himself (joined, from 1938 on, by his arranger, Billy Strayhorn), and a succession of remarkable players that Ellington had in his band. Trumpet players Bubber Miley, Cootie Williams, and Ray Nance (who was also a violinist); trombonists Joe Nanton and Juan Tizol; clarinetist Barney Bigard; and saxophonists Johnny Hodges (soprano and alto), Ben Webster (tenor), and Harry Carney (baritone) are a few whose expansion of the tonal possibilities of their instruments, together with Ellington's use of these new possibilities, contributed to the Ellington sound. As a sampling of works from the crucial period of the 1940s, the slow "Blue Serge" with its use of color (1941), the moderate-paced "Ko-ko" (1940) and "Concerto for Cootie" (1940, later becoming the basis for the song "Do Nothing Till You Hear from Me"), and the up-tempo "Main Stem" (1942, a hard-driving piece with a remarkable variety of color in the Kansas City style) are suggested. Especially noteworthy among the shorter works for its pictorial sense and use of color is a train piece that also incorporates the blues, "Happy Go Lucky Local" (1946).

*There are many jazz anthologies, among them *Smithsonian Collection of Classic Jazz*, the *Smithsonian Collection of Big Band Jazz*, the Smithsonian/Folkways series, and many issues in the New World series. Together they constitute a comprehensive source for all but the most recent jazz, including most of the pieces mentioned in this chapter.

As a composer, Duke Ellington had a broad range. He was primarily an instrumental composer, writing for his band, but he also was responsible for a fairly large output of songs—some of which began as such, and some of which resulted from words being put to his band numbers. He pioneered in writing more extended works for jazz ensemble, beginning as early as 1931 with *Creole Rhapsody* (which filled two sides of a ten-inch 78-rpm record), and including *Black, Brown and Beige* (1943, a multimovement commentary on the history of black people in America) and many suites, from the *Deep South Suite* of 1946 to the *Togo Brava Suite* of 1971. He also wrote musicals, film scores, a ballet, incidental music to a Shakespeare play, and, in the late 1960s and early 1970s, a series of *Sacred Concerts*.

The Midwest and Count Basie

Ellington came from Washington, DC, and was based in New York for most of his career. There was another part of the country to be heard from in the 1930s. This was "the West" to easterners, but it was actually the heartland—specifically Kansas City. In the days before mass media threatened to blanket the whole country and induce a homogenized culture suffocating to regional artistic identity, it was possible for different areas to develop artistic dialects as distinctive as their speech. What we are calling attention to here may seem like a fine distinction to the beginning listener to jazz, but listen to the hard-driving beat—"jump," it was called, or "four heavy beats to a bar, and no cheating" (to quote Count Basie)—of "**Taxi War Dance**" of 1939, with its steady, insistent 4-beat under the tenor saxophone solo of Lester Young. You will then get a notion of that Kansas City ingredient that went into big band jazz after the arrival in the East of Bennie Moten (1894–1935), William "Count" Basie (1904–84), Lester Young (1909–59), and a host of other players from "the West." It was closely akin to the drive of boogie-woogie, which had come from the same part of the country.

Benny Goodman

Anyone born before 1925 has lived through this most opulent period in the history of jazz, and can call up a litany of the big bands and their star players. To name a few is to leave out many, but for the purposes of our brief survey the bands of Duke Ellington, Count Basie, and Benny Goodman may be taken as at least representative. Benny Goodman (1909–86), clarinetist and bandleader, was an important white musician of the swing era. His highly skilled band of fourteen to sixteen musicians played an essentially hot style closely derived from that of black jazz artists of the time. Goodman acknowledged this heritage, using arrangements written for him by Fletcher Henderson, some of which were based on traditional New Orleans originals by King Oliver or Jelly Roll Morton. In addition, Goodman was one of the first white bandleaders to incorporate black musicians into his ensembles, using them at first as featured performers in his trio, quartet, and sextet. The disciplined but driving swing of his band helped to bring jazz to a new plateau of popularity and acceptance as dance music. Typical of this Goodman swing style are the Fletcher Henderson arrangements of Handy's "St. Louis Blues" or Oliver's "**Sugar Foot Stomp.**" The latter is especially interesting for two reasons: first, because of the comparison it affords with two earlier versions of the work already cited,* and second, because it was one of the Henderson arrangements that helped to accomplish the historic breakthrough for swing in 1935.

Three More Aspects of the Swing Era
Latin Influence

Latin bands were very popular at the time. The rumba craze was no less intense than that of the tango earlier, or the mambo, samba, or chachachá subsequently. What the purely Latin bands played was not jazz, but it illustrates and reminds us of the perennial Latin presence and influence in American music (see chapter 4). Jazz was by no means unaffected by it, and Latin drummers were soon to be incorporated into jazz ensembles (as were those from Africa, which has quite a different tradition, albeit with similar instruments). An interesting example, from somewhat later, of this Latin assimilation is "Jahbero" (1948), with the celebrated Cuban drummer Chano Pozo.

The Small Combo

The second aspect is the simultaneous cultivation of the small ensemble in the era of the big band. This was no longer the old-time jazz ensemble (which did indeed enjoy a revival) but the intimate group of three to seven players that was the vehicle for developing some of the newest ideas in jazz. Its commercial aspect was represented by the "cocktail combo" playing in small bars, but there were important artistic dimensions to the small combo as well. The Benny Goodman Sextet's recording of "**I Found a New Baby**" (1941) furnishes a good example, of additional interest because of the solo for electric guitar by Charlie Christian. Actually the small combo has always been present at every phase in jazz evolution; it was not an invention of the post–World War II "cool" or "progressive" schools. Louis Armstrong had recorded with from two to six musicians

*The Henderson arrangement is adapted to include solos by Benny Goodman. Harry James models his solo closely on Louis Armstrong's original.

in the twenties. The solo pianist also flourished; Earl Hines (1903–83), Art Tatum (1909–56), Bud Powell (1924–66), and Erroll Garner (1921–77) were leading figures.

The Traditional Revival

The traditional, or New Orleans, style of jazz has shown a persistent vitality. An early copy of New Orleans style (mostly white and more or less New York–oriented), known generally as "Dixieland," was translated into big band terms in the work of such white bandleaders Bob Crosby ("South Rampart Street Parade," 1937) and Eddie Condon ("Somebody Loves Me," 1944). But a real revival of the older style was one of the landmarks of the 1940s as well. In an episode in American music replete with both nostalgia and human interest, players who had been active in the very early days of jazz (some of whom had never before been recorded) were located, sometimes with considerable difficulty, and reinstated with honors in the kingdom of jazz, for the purpose of re-creating the authentic traditions and music of the long-gone New Orleans beginnings. How authentic such re-creations can be in an art so basically improvisational, and so dependent on the player's subjective impressions of a *total* environment, may be open to question. But the documents are there now, recorded a generation after the fact, for all time. For examples, listen to Bunk Johnson, legendary symbol of this revival, in "Down by the River" (1942) or "Make Me a Pallet on the Floor" (1945), or Kid Ory, in any number of revival recordings. Younger musicians, including Lu Watters and Turk Murphy, also became interested in the old style.

Wartime and the Seeds of Change

With the entry of the United States into World War II there came a freezing of the status quo. The feeling of security that a repetition of the accustomed can give was what was needed and sought. During the war people flocked to ballrooms to hear the name bands and bought the latest records; and overseas soldiers, sailors, airmen, and marines heard the same bands and the same pieces. (Notwithstanding this, wartime hardships, including shortages of gasoline for touring, took their toll among the bands, some of which disbanded even before the war was over.) Meanwhile, underneath the desperately needed continuity of the surface, changes were being wrought that would profoundly alter the jazz scene once the war was over.

The Emergence of Modern Jazz: Bop as a Turning Point

In the decades since the end of World War II the whole fabric of Occidental music has frayed into many different strands, and jazz has been no exception:

Beginning in the 1940s a combination of factors wrought evolutionary changes in jazz that brought a whole new set of leaders to the fore and made significant alterations, not only in the music itself, but in the function of jazz, in its audience, and in the way it was perceived. From the beginning of the 1930s through the end of World War II, there had been, for most fans, one kind of jazz—that of the big bands. The best-known names were Benny Goodman, Glenn Miller, Artie Shaw, Tommy Dorsey, Harry James, and the like.* Jazz, however attenuated by the popular bands in the minds of its devotees, came as close in this period to being synonymous with America's popular music as it has ever been or is ever likely to be again. After the war, all was different; the place of jazz in our culture changed. It lost its mass following, especially among the young, who have shown repeatedly that what they really like most is music with a strong beat that they can dance to (a need that was soon to be met by black rhythm-and-blues and white rock 'n' roll). At the same time, jazz began to be considered seriously as *art* music, not only by its fans and critics, but by some of its practitioners as well. Jazz became bohemianized.

It began with *bop* (a shortening of "rebop" or "bebop"). The first outstanding exponents of the new style were the trumpeter Dizzy Gillespie (1917–93) and the alto saxophonist Charlie Parker (1920–55), together with pianist Thelonious Monk (1917–82) and drummer Kenny Clarke (1914–85). Gillespie and Parker had keenly creative minds and extremely facile techniques on their respective instruments. Bop developed as the first jazz to demand an entire ensemble of virtuoso performers.** The ensemble was characteristically small—a quintet or sextet made up of a rhythm section (piano, bass, and drums) and a "front line" of just two or three instrumentalists. In addition to an astounding virtuosity, there was an obscuring of the familiar melodies jazz fans had grown accustomed to hearing. Bop continued to use the harmonic basis (the chord "changes") of certain jazz "standards" (Gershwin's "I Got Rhythm" was a favorite), but free, elaborate, and very difficult new melodic variations were invented on the original harmonies, often overlapping phrase endings. Frequently the harmonic plan itself, the very basis of jazz, would be changed through the use of substitute chords. Tempos were usually very fast, and the supporting rhythm section became much lighter. The cymbal, with its bright, insinuating tone, and the string bass, now "walking" at a fast pace, together took over from the drums the job of keeping the beat, and the drums could now be used both less frequently

*Note that these were all white bandleaders. Even then, the bands of Duke Ellington, Count Basie, Billy Eckstine, Lionel Hampton, Jimmie Lunceford, and other black jazzmen, who were regarded by aficionados as playing "real jazz," had a smaller public.

**In this sense, bop bore the same relationship to swing jazz that bluegrass did to country music.

and more effectively for accentuation, or for the superimposing of cross-rhythms that made the rhythmic texture more complex and tended at times to obscure the beat. From then on the jazz rhythm section was permanently transformed, in an evolutionary development that would outlast bop itself. This lightening and obscuring of the beat, together with the fast tempos, discouraged dancing to bebop; it became instead a music for listeners, and this encouraged its being perceived as an art music.

It has been customary to call the advent of bop a revolution in jazz. Bop *can* be seen as a "black backlash" to the "white synthesis,"[5] but it also had evolutionary aspects that should not be ignored. Bop had, in fact, its antecedents across a fairly broad spectrum of the jazz of the 1940s, including some of the innovative playing and arranging going on in a few of the big bands themselves, notably those of Count Basie and Earl Hines. Other big bands that were playing convincingly in bop style before the end of the forties were those of Billy Eckstine, Boyd Raeburn, Claude Thornhill, and Woody Herman.[6] Bebop's musical ingredients had their precedents in the work of individual players as well, and bop certainly could not have assumed the sound it did had it not been for the playing of such important jazz figures as Art Tatum, Lester Young, and Roy Eldridge.

Early bop was not well documented in commercial recordings, which began to pick it up after its influence among jazz players had spread to a considerable extent. Listen to "Shaw 'Nuff" (1945), with Gillespie and Parker performing with just piano, bass, and drums, or "KoKo," of the same year, with four performers (Gillespie himself doubles on piano), for the essence of the style. Note the unison passages used to open and close the pieces. (These passages possibly had their origins in the rigorous practice sessions Parker and Gillespie had in the early days, playing etudes in unison in all keys as fast as they could.) The unisons were new to jazz, and were a contradiction of the old spirit of heterophony and polyphony that underlay the traditional jazz of the twenties and thirties. The unison lines became in turn a tradition that stuck, reappearing in post-bop works.

In due course bop was translated into big-band terms, just as traditional jazz had been before it. In "Things to Come" (1946) Gillespie records with a band of seventeen pieces (large even for the big band era) a work that transfers to the large ensemble the drive and virtuosity of bop. "Oop-Pap-a-Da" (1947) and "Lemon Drop" (1948) show another characteristic, vocalizing on nonsense syllables (which provided titles for many of these pieces). The singing exhibits the same fluidity and virtuosity that we hear in the instrumental solos. ("Scat" singing, as this is called, was not new to jazz; Louis Armstrong was doing it in the 1920s.)

The Progeny of Bop

Cool Jazz

What has become known as "cool" jazz followed so closely on the heels of bop that it can almost be regarded as the other side of the same coin—the same dispassionate objectivity (symbolized by the typical avoidance of instrumental vibrato), the same underlying complexity, the same careful avoidance of the obvious that tends to obscurity. But now these features were exhibited in a music of understatement, of restraint, of leanness. What had been interpreted by some as an attitude of disdain in bop became in cool jazz one of detachment.

Many of the same musicians played both bop and cool, and a lineage can be established. An early example, in a transitional stage, is "Boplicity" (1949), with Miles Davis (trumpet), J. J. Johnson, (trombone), and Kenny Clarke (drums)—all of whom were influential in the development and spread of bop. The tempo has been slowed, but many bop characteristics remain: the light style of drumming, with the emphasis on the cymbal; the important role of the bass in keeping the beat; and, an important trademark of bop, the unison playing at the beginning of the piece (in this case harmonized by the arranger, Gil Evans).

"Criss-Cross" (1951), by Thelonious Monk, reveals more characteristics of the cool trend. The vibraphone appears, here played by Milt Jackson (b. 1923). The tone of the "vibes"—warmed somewhat by its mechanical vibrato, but still restrained and detached—made it almost a symbol of cool jazz.

One of the most influential small combos in this style was the Modern Jazz Quartet, with piano (John Lewis, also a composer), vibes (Milt Jackson, heard in "Criss-Cross"), bass (Percy Heath), and drums (Connie Kay). With no wind instruments (in fact this entire ensemble is really a rhythm section), their small combo epitomized the restrained understatement toward which cool jazz tended.

"Cool" jazz dominated what was *new* in the jazz of the 1950s—not what was popular. Its adherents were to be found mostly in intellectual circles—on college campuses, among both students and professors. There was an intellectual ferment about jazz that affected critics, fans, and some composer-performers themselves. If jazz was art, then there was no reason why it shouldn't appropriate whatever it took a fancy to in fine-art music, learning and borrowing from both the forms and the technical procedures of European or European-derived classical music. For example, John Lewis, whose Modern Jazz Quartet represented the quintessence of "cool" jazz, in the late 1950s became interested in the music of the Italian Renaissance.

Hard Bop and Funk

Evolving directly from bop in the 1950s and 1960s, and often regarded as a reaction to the restraint and intellectualism of cool jazz, was a development known as *hard bop*. It represented a pull back toward the roots of jazz, especially its roots in black gospel music. Pianist and composer Horace Silver (b. 1928) and drummer Art Blakey (1919–90) were leaders in the evolution of hard bop. This is displayed at its most obvious in such pieces as Silver's "The Preacher" (1954). Many of the features of bop are present (the texture of the rhythm section, the unison or homophonic openings and closings). But hard bop tended to relax the frenetic tempos of bop, and the rhythmic basis of the newer *funky* jazz, as it was called, often showed a return to the characteristically black "backbeat." There was a preference for darker, "earthier" tone colors; for this reason the huskier tenor saxophone was preferred over the lighter alto (as had been the case also in rhythm-and-blues). This is illustrated in "Now's the Time," by a quartet that includes Sonny Rollins, tenor sax, and Herbie Hancock, piano.

Modal Jazz

Another successor to bop in which many of the same musicians were involved has been called *modal jazz*. It represented a new venture for jazz both harmonically and structurally, in that it no longer used the chord progressions of standard tunes as the basis for improvisation; what replaced these was simply a succession of scales on which the performer improvised. One very seminal set of pieces that set a precedent for jazz in this direction were those on the 1959 album *Kind of Blue*. The trumpeter Miles Davis (1926–91), who had a hand in influencing new developments and indicating new trends in jazz for more than three decades, beginning in the late 1940s, was the leader and stimulator of the small combo that produced this album, but Bill Evans, piano; John Coltrane, tenor saxophone; and Julian Adderley, alto saxophone, contributed significantly to the realization of its concepts, and went on to develop the style further.

John Coltrane (1926–67) was a crucially important voice in the jazz of the decade 1955–65. A commanding player technically, he was also one of the most serious-minded composer-performers in jazz. The expressive potential of what we have chosen to call *modal jazz* is summed up in the intense earnestness of his "Alabama" of 1963, with its slow, thoughtful opening and closing sections, emphasizing spare, drone-like open fifths.

Free Jazz

A small proportion of Coltrane's later work fell into the category of one of the most extreme, least understood, and least popular movements in jazz history—so-called *free jazz*. The 1960 album *Free Jazz* by Ornette Coleman (b. 1930) gave the concept its name, and was as seminal in this regard as Miles Davis's *Birth of the Cool* (1949–50) had been for that genre, and as his *Kind of Blue* (1959) was for so-called modal jazz. Free jazz exhibits one or more of the following characteristics:

(1) collective improvisation; (2) freedom from preset chord progressions and/or established tonality; (3) extension of the sonorous range of instruments (especially the saxophone) by playing extremely high pitches, or making the instruments squeal, shriek, or groan; (4) playing deliberately "out of tune" in relation to conventional intonation; (5) expansion of form, by creating pieces in which the length of the sections, and hence the overall length, is not predetermined, and which may thus be quite extensive (*Free Jazz* lasts thirty-six minutes, Coltrane's *Ascension* nearly forty, Cecil Taylor's *3 Phasis'* nearly an hour). The Art Ensemble of Chicago's *Certain Blacks* (early 1970s), with its spoken or chanted additions, is typical of the more theatrical, satirical, and racially specific aspects of the genre.

Fitting into the category of free jazz is the work of Cecil Taylor (b. 1933), which in many ways is in a class by itself. A gifted absorber of many musical influences, including the whole range of jazz styles, he has stated a desire to *use* European influences, rather than try futilely to reject them. In collaboration with a small ensemble, known as the Cecil Taylor Unit, he has produced music of exceptionally high intensity, energy, and turbulence, characterized by long periods of unrelieved tension.

The relationship of all the jazz of the 1960s in which black musicians played a leading role (hard bop, modal jazz, free jazz, and so on) to the social turmoil of the times has been emphasized by some writers, who also point out the identification of many of the young black jazz musicians such as Albert Ayler (1936–70) and Archie Shepp (b. 1937) with one aspect or another of the black nationalism movement.[7]

A turning away from extremism and experimentalism, and a reaching out to a larger audience, began to occur in both jazz and classical music in the 1970s. The overtly and even militantly racial overtones that characterized some black jazz of the 1960s abated in the 1970s, and many of its proponents began to adopt (or readopt) more accessible and popular styles such as rhythm-and-blues.

The "Third Stream" and Other Developments Parallel to Bop

Parallel to the lineage of bop to cool to modal to free jazz, there were other related developments. What these developments had in common was the incorporation of musical elements, procedures, and actual instruments that had hitherto been considered foreign to jazz. The term "third stream" was invented and applied by Gunther Schuller (b. 1925) shortly after mid-century to the merging of elements from the jazz and "classical," or European, traditions to form a new "stream" in music.[8]

Small combos playing a species of "cool" jazz began to incorporate materials derived from the European classical tradition. The so-called "West Coast" school of jazz (mostly white performers, including such men as Dave Brubeck [b. 1920], Paul Desmond, Gerry Mulligan, Chet Baker, Bob Brookmeyer, and Shorty Rogers) is illustrative of this.

One aspect of these explorations was rhythmic innovation that took jazz out of the duple or quadruple grouping of pulses (expressed by the meters 2/4 and 4/4) that had characterized it since its earliest associations with the march and two-step. The first change in this direction was the introduction of triple meter, typified by the waltz. Then followed so-called asymmetrical meters in which groupings of two, three, and four pulses were mixed in recurring sequence. "Take Five" by Paul Desmond is illustrative.

Gunther Schuller himself worked toward a synthesis of avant-garde European procedures and sounds (including twelve-tone technique) with jazz styles and improvisation, over a considerable period of time between the late 1940s and the early 1960s; several of his resulting compositions were included in the album *Jazz Abstractions*.

The Pluralism of the Last Quarter Century
Rock Fusion and Electric Jazz in the 1970s and 1980s

As a strategically important point of departure for comprehending the fusions of the 1970s and 1980s, let us return to the bop lineage and examine what was happening in the bands that Miles Davis assembled during the late 1960s. From *Nefertiti* of 1967 to the landmark *Bitches Brew* of 1969, a fairly rapid and direct transition can be observed. ***Bitches Brew*** illustrates the *jazz–rock fusion* that was to be further explored in the 1970s. The piano and guitar have been completely replaced by their electric counterparts. Most significant is the change in the *rhythmic* basis of the music—always an indicator of major developments in jazz. The beat is now distinctly the "square" beat of rock (that is, with evenly spaced subdivisions), ornamented with Latin embellishments; with no swing to it, it has the static effect of both rock and classical minimalism (see chapter 19). After a long two-and-a-half minute introduction, featuring tape-loop-induced echo effects in Davis's trumpet sound, the bass lays down the familiar, insistent, repetitious *bass riff* of rock.

Many of the players on these Davis recordings of the late 1960s became important in further developments in the jazz-rock fusion of the 1970s, including pianists Herbie Hancock, Chick Corea, and Joe Zawinul, guitarist John McLaughlin, and saxophonist Wayne Shorter. The group Weather Report, formed in 1971 by Zawinul (b. 1932), reflected with a high degree of competence a broad range of trends and influences. Indeed, their work can serve as an index of the ingredients of what has been called *electric jazz*, or the fusion music of the 1970s. The sound is mostly electronic, either in its source or in its manipulation; increasingly divorced from live acoustic sound, it is thus alien to the familiar image of "real" performers playing "real" instruments. In 1983 pianist Herbie Hancock (b. 1940), an alumnus of the Miles Davis group of the 1960s, dispensed with horns entirely and with the aid of very complex electronic technology, produced a piece ("**Rockit**") that was No. 1 on the pop chart and represented the extreme of electrification.

The New Virtuosity, the Return to Acoustic Jazz, and the Reconnection with Tradition

One of the most significant developments in the last two decades has been the post-fusion resumption of the acoustic jazz tradition. Like the bebop of fifty years before, this new resurgence has been led by a new generation of virtuosos—highly skilled performers who are also composers, and who in addition have a thorough understanding of jazz traditions. A well-known example is trumpet player Wynton Marsalis (b. 1961), who has demonstrated a remarkable fluency in both jazz and classical music—a flexibility and catholicity not uncommon among today's young musicians.

There has been a resurgence—a reinterpretation—of bebop, to the extent that the term "neo-bop" has been applied to this current stage of jazz. The unison openings and closings are there, and as an occasional alternative to the prevailing small combo, "big bands" (big in sound, at least) have been formed, made up of virtuoso performers throughout, and reminiscent of the Gillespie bands of the 1940s. Tempos that are fast even by the standards of bop in the 1940s and '50s make the term "super-bop" appropriate; perhaps the stretching of the limits of human capacity, so pervasive in athletics, is a characteristic of our times.[9]

But the new post-fusion acoustic jazz is not revivalism; new aspects, new additions, new influences are evident. The palette of instrumental color has been expanded; Jaco Pastorius (b. 1951), for example, in addition to presenting the electric bass as a jazz solo instrument (a confounding exception, perhaps, to labeling this development acoustic jazz), has also introduced virtuoso harmonica (as played by "Toots" Thielemans) and virtuoso steel drum (as played by Othello Molineaux) with his band, Word of Mouth, in *Invitation* (1983). Although players can still find interesting things to do with the chord progression of "I Got Rhythm" (as Marsalis does in "Hesitation," on his first album), the choice of harmonic basis is much wider than it was in the bop of mid-century. Irregular phrase lengths and more sophisticated formal schemes, including the use of a succession of different tempos, meters, and styles in the same piece, have been employed. In the matter of rhythm, the most crucial element of jazz, cross-rhythms are often superimposed that can confound the sense of the prevailing meter for measures at a time. In "**Skain's Domain**," for example, there is a basic relaxed bop beat of about 230 per minute, which, even as the ear tries to follow and grasp its organization, shifts tantalizingly back and forth between groupings of four and three (expressible as 4/4 and 3/4 respectively). Superimposed on these fluctuations are cross-rhythms of a different order, based on a triple grouping of the shorter values (expressible as 3/8, 6/8, 12/8, and so on), as shown in Example 14-1. All of this is done with a fluency that dazzles the ear even as it mystifies it.

Example 14–1. Rhythmic excerpt from "Skain's Domain"

Paying Homage to, and Conserving, the Past

Accompanying the return to acoustic jazz have been a number of albums that pay homage to the composers, performers, and songs of the past. This homage takes the form of reinterpretations of jazz standards by song and show composers such as Gershwin, Rodgers, Kern, Porter, Arlen, and of instrumental compositions by jazz performers such as Charlie Parker, Thelonious Monk, and Ornette Coleman. Along with the reinterpretation on their own terms of jazz "standards" by present-day artists, there is also the actual *conservation* of jazz classics as live music. There are a growing number of *repertory bands*—bands whose function it is to re-create specific pieces, just as a symphony orchestra re-creates a Beethoven symphony. Unlike a Beethoven symphony, however, a jazz piece may have come into being with little or no written notation associated with it, and what little was written out may have been lost. The reconstruction therefore may have to rely largely on transcribing existing recordings—an extremely arduous undertaking. Repertory bands began to develop in the 1970s, as a result of the independent work of Gunther Schuller and Martin Williams, a noted jazz critic. In New York, the Lincoln Center Jazz Orchestra began playing in 1988 and the Carnegie Hall Jazz Band in 1991. Washington's Smithsonian Jazz Masterworks Orchestra was founded in 1990. Also involved in their own way with the conservation of the jazz of the past are the "ghost bands" that continue to tour with the repertory that they played when their leaders were still alive—those of Count Basie, Tommy Dorsey, and Glenn Miller for example. There are also the numerous school workshops and clinics, such as those established by Stan Kenton and Maynard Ferguson, that have helped to make jazz programs in schools and colleges effective conservators of the big band tradition.

Jazz is nearly a century old. It is fitting that we close this chapter on this remarkable music on two notes: the concern for its conservation by serious musicians, and the openness to change and evolution on the part of equally serious musicians. Often they are the same people. This tells us something about the maturity of jazz, as well as that of its devotees. The place where you find jazz records in the typical large record store of today is indicative of its place in our culture. It is not in the main section, with pop and rock. In the store I go to, jazz happens to be in the same room with folk and ethnic music—whose devotees are equally comfortable with their passions in music, and the fact that these have little to do with what is popular. Relatively seldom in its history has jazz actually been popular music. Yet it has endured, and will continue to endure, growing in breadth, excluding nothing that is true to its essence, and thriving in its own way for those who have come to know and love it.

FURTHER READING

Jazz has stimulated the production of an enormous volume of written material, which runs the gamut from sound, well-informed studies by competent musicians and scholars (too few) to the sycophantic writing typical of record-jacket notes. There are biographical and autobiographical works (some of considerable value), there are pictorial studies, and there are works written with a pronounced racial, social, or musical bias. The discerning student will soon find what is most informative and helpful in this vast array of printed matter. The very numerous biographical works on single jazz figures are not included in the following, highly selective list.

Comprehensive general works published since 1975

Gridley, Mark C. *Jazz Styles: History and Analysis*. 6th ed. Englewood Cliffs, NJ: Prentice-Hall, 1996.

Kennington, Donald, and Danny L. Read. *The Literature of Jazz: A Critical Guide*. 2d ed. Chicago: American Library Association, 1981.

> A well-reviewed bibliography, well indexed.

Tirro, Frank. *Jazz: A History*. 2d ed. New York: Norton, 1993.

> Useful in that its examples are keyed to the recordings in the *Smithsonian Collection of Classic Jazz*, it also includes transcriptions of pieces from that collection. A "Synoptic Table" relates jazz developments to other arts and to history.

Respected older works that are still valuable

Hodeir, André. *Jazz: Its Evolution and Essence*. Trans. David Noakes. New York: Da Capo, 1975. (Reprint of 1956 ed.)

Sargeant, Winthrop. *Jazz: A History*. Rev. ed. New York: McGraw-Hill, 1964.

Stearns, Marshall. *The Story of Jazz*. New York: Oxford University Press 1956. Reprint, 1974.

Highly recommended, especially for its treatment of the beginnings of jazz.

Williams, Martin, ed. *The Art of Jazz*. New York: Da Capo, 1981. (Reprint of 1959 ed.)

Collections of essays and interviews

Baker, David N., ed. *New Perspectives on Jazz*. Washington, DC: Smithsonian Institution Press, 1990.

Transcripts of talks at a national conference held in 1986.

Giddins, Gary. *Riding on a Blue Note: Jazz and American Pop*. New York: Oxford University Press, 1981.

Shapiro, Nat, and Nat Hentoff. *Hear Me Talkin' to Ya*. New York: Rinehart, 1955. Reprint, New York: Dover, 1966.

Quotations from more than 150 jazz musicians, arranged to shed light from firsthand sources on nearly every aspect of jazz.

Williams, Martin. *The Jazz Tradition*. Rev. ed. New York: Oxford University Press, 1983.

———. *Jazz Changes*. New York: Oxford University Press, 1992.

Period studies, in approximate chronological order

Lomax, Alan. *Mister Jelly Roll: The Fortunes of Jelly Roll Morton, New Orleans Creole and "Inventor of Jazz."* 2d ed. Berkeley: University of California Press, 1973.

Based on an extensive series of interviews recorded at the Library of Congress.

Schuller, Gunther. *Early Jazz: Its Roots and Musical Development*. New York: Oxford University Press, 1968.

Deals with the beginnings through early Ellington and early big bands, with emphasis on Armstrong, Morton, and Ellington. Important for its attention to and analysis of the music itself.

———. *The Swing Era: The Development of Jazz 1933–1945*. New York: Oxford University Press, 1988.

A valuable sequel to *Early Jazz*. These two works are the most substantial general works on jazz from the beginning to the end of the big band era.

Hadlock, Richard. *Jazz Masters of the Twenties*. New York: Macmillan, 1965.

Stewart, Rex. *Jazz Masters of the Thirties*. New York: Macmillan, 1972.

Gitler, Ira. *Jazz Masters of the Forties*. New York: Macmillan, 1966.

———. *Swing to Bop: An Oral History of the Transition in Jazz in the 1940s*. New York: Oxford University Press, 1985.

Goldberg, Joe. *Jazz Masters in Transition, 1957–1969*. New York: Macmillan, 1970.

Shaw, Arnold. *52nd Street: The Street of Jazz*. New York: Da Capo, 1977.

Budds, Michael J. *Jazz in the Sixties*. Iowa City: University of Iowa Press. 1978.

Giddins, Gary. *Rhythm-a-ning: Jazz Tradition and Innovation in the '80s*. New York: Oxford University Press, 1985.

Davis, Francis. *In the Moment: Jazz in the 1980s*. New York: Oxford University Press, 1986.

Periodicals

Down Beat. Monthly (Chicago).

Popularly written periodical which now includes blues, rock, and popular music.

Journal of Jazz Studies. Semiannual, 1973–81; annual since 1982 as *Annual Review of Jazz Studies* (New Brunswick, NJ).

Devoted to serious studies in jazz.

Projects

1. Make an assessment of jazz in your local area. Is there music being played that is recognizably jazz, as distinct from rock or merely pop music? Where is it being played, and for whom? What styles can one hear—are there bands playing in a revival of the big band style? of traditional (Dixieland) jazz? of cool?

2. Keep a diary of jazz listening for a month, noting pieces and artists heard, and making some general comments on the music and where it fits into the overall panorama of jazz outlined in this chapter. Make it a point to listen to at least 25 pieces during this time, and include as great a variety of styles and periods as you can.

3. If the calendar of musical events in your area allows, or your travel capabilities permit, attend three separate live jazz performances. Try for a variety of experiences. Write a commentary on the music of each, placing it in the general framework of contemporary jazz as outlined in this chapter.

4. Using as references newspapers such as the *New York Times* or the *Christian Science Monitor*, or general magazines such as *The New Republic* or *The Atlantic Monthly*, or music magazines such as *High Fidelity*, compare the coverage of jazz, and the attitude displayed toward it, in two one-year periods spaced fairly far apart.

5. Interview at least five people (you may include yourself) on the subject "Electric vs. Acoustic Jazz: Which Do You Prefer, and Why?" and write up the results in a brief paper.

6. If your area has a radio show devoted to jazz (on a public radio station, for example), interview the commentator or disk jockey on one of the following topics: (a) his or her assessment of the current trends in jazz; (b) what mail or telephone responses tell about local tastes in jazz; (c) his or her own list of the five best new releases of the past year or so, with reasons for the choice; or (d) a topic of your own invention.

7. If there is a retired jazz musician in your community, interview him or her about his or her experiences, recollections of noted jazz figures, working conditions, comparisons of jazz *now* with jazz *then*, etc.

Notes

1. The fact that this New Orleans group made recordings of this piece in Chicago and Richmond, Indiana, shows the state of dissemination and transition that jazz had already entered by 1923.

2. The two versions of "Sweet Lovin Man" and the Wolverines' recording of "Jazz Me Blues" are all on Smithsonian/Folkways 2806, *Chicago* 2). Mezz Mezzrow's quote is from the first appendix of his *Really the Blues* (New York: Random House, 1946; paperback reprint, New York: Anchor, 1972).

3. See Ronald L. Morris, *Wait Until Dark: Jazz and the Underworld 1880–1940* (Bowling Green, OH: Bowling Green University Popular Press, 1980). The subject is also treated in Mezzrow's *Really the Blues* (cited above).

4. For documentation of the development of the big bands elsewhere, notably in Chicago, St. Louis, Kansas City, and San Antonio, see *Big Bands and Territory Bands of the 1920s* and *Sweet and Low Blues: Big Bands and Territory Bands of the 1930s* (New World 256 and 217).

5. Arnold Shaw, *Black Popular Music in America* (New York: Schirmer Books, 1986), 162. For one view of the whole racial situation that prevailed in jazz in the 1930s and 1940s, see pp. 158–63.

6. Both Dan Morgenstern (in the notes to New World 271) and Mark Gridley (*Jazz Styles: History and Analysis*, 6th ed. [Englewood Cliffs, NJ: Prentice-Hall, 1996]) caution against viewing bop as a revolt against the big bands, and stress its evolutionary rather than revolutionary origin.

7. The seminal work in this regard is LeRoi Jones's book *Blues People* (New York: Morrow, 1963). Frank Kofsky, in *Black Nationalism and the Revolution in Music* (New York: Pathfinder, 1970), is concerned with political and social aspects, while John Storm Roberts, in *Black Music of Two Worlds* (New York: Praeger, 1972), explores the relation to Africa.

8. It is useful to consult Schuller's own writings on the subject, especially as in the 1980s he broadened the meaning of the term "third stream" to include the synthesis of "the essential characteristics and techniques of contemporary Western art music and various ethnic or vernacular musics"—in other words, including other musics in addition to jazz. See his notes to New World 216; "Third Stream Revisited" in his *Musings* (New York: Oxford University Press, 1986) and his article "Third Stream" in *The New Grove Dictionary of American Music*.

9. A comparison of tempos is interesting. Using the quarter note, typically defined in bop by the walking bass, as a basis, the up-tempo bop performances of the mid-1940s hovered around 300 to the minute. Gillespie and Parker's famous "Shaw 'Nuff" of 1945 was played at 288; Parker pushed this to 312 in his "KoKo" of the same year. The Gillespie band played "Things to Come," in 1946, at a frenetic 340, which was fast even for the up-tempo bop of the day, and the performance was not uniformly clean. By contrast, Ricky Ford's ensemble played his "One Up, One Down" in 1977 *cleanly* at 344. To set these tempos in context, the standard fast tempo numbers of the swing bands of the late 1930s were considerably slower; Benny Goodman played Fletcher Henderson's "Down South Camp Meeting" at 216 to the minute, and the Basie band performed "Doggin' Around" at 256. But even in the 1930s there were extraordinary precursors of bop tempos in the Midwest bands; Bennie Moten's famous "Toby" was played at an amazing 316 to the minute in 1932—faster than Parker's "KoKo"!

Part Six

Classical Music

Photo by Jim Steere. Courtesy of the Chicago Symphony Orchestra

The pursuit of fine-art music in America had a prehistory marked by European domination (at first British and then German), with now and then a voice in the wilderness protesting the state of affairs but with only a few hints that a distinctive national music was appearing. This prehistory came to an end after the Civil War, with the emergence of serious, well-trained, and capable composers such as those of the Second New England School. Our classical music emerged from a promising adolescence into strong-featured adulthood between the two world wars, finding its own mature voice. In the third quarter of the century it became polarized. The ground broken in the second quarter, especially in the "definitive decade" of the 1930s, continued to be cultivated by some, who showed that it was capable of yielding new and fresh crops. At the hands of others, pursuing technical innovations and new aesthetic concepts, another segment of our cultivated music, largely indifferent to its audience, either struck out in experimental paths or merged its identity with that of international modernism. In the last quarter of this century our fine-art music is characterized by a renewed relationship with its audience, by a transcending of the dogmatisms of modernism, and by the acceptance, and even the enjoyment and celebration, of a new accessibility, eclecticism, and diversity. In the chapters that follow, we shall explore, in stages corresponding roughly with the five developmental stages outlined above, the complex picture of American classical music.

Chapter 15

Laying the Foundation: Accomplishments from the Jacksonian Era to World War I

When in 1828 General Andrew Jackson was swept by a substantial majority into the presidency—the first president from west of the Appalachians—he was riding the combined wave of two related movements that were to bring fundamental changes to American politics and society, and ultimately to American music. These were the rise of political populism, and the increasing importance of the West.

The soldier-politician who has given his name to the era was not himself so much the instrument as the symbol of these related movements of geographical expansion and an increased degree of political democracy.* The relationship of American democracy to American music—a relationship that will have considerable relevance to this chapter—has been commented on by Irving Lowens, who has pointed out that it is the interaction of two tendencies, equalitarianism on the one hand and libertarianism on the other, that defines American democracy. He further writes: "It is my contention that the past history of the United States has demonstrated a certain correlation between the dominance of the equalitarian urge and the vitality of popular music, and a similar correlation between the dominance of the libertarian urge and the vitality of fine-art music."[1]

It is Lowens's general observation that there was a balance between the two up to about 1830, that equalitarianism was dominant from the Jacksonian era to the Civil War (a fact accompanied by the concurrent vitality of popular music), and that libertarianism dominated between the Civil War and World War I (accompanied by a corresponding vitality of classical music). There can be little doubt of the equalitarian urge of the age of Jackson, and we have already observed in chapters 11 and 12 the growth and vigor of our "vernacular" music, represented by developments in popular song and theater. As a counterbalance to

---

*As an indication of how geographical expansion coincided with increased political democracy, between the battle of New Orleans in 1815 (in which Jackson's frontier militia defeated the British regulars) and Jackson's election in 1828, the union admitted six new states, five of which granted the vote to all adult males.

this musical populism (typified for many by the lowbrow "minstrel ditties"), voices had begun to be raised, even earlier in the century, on behalf of reform, of education, of the propagation of "good music" as being morally and spiritually uplifting. Should music (and with it all art) improve, educate, and enlighten us, or is it enough that it merely entertain us? These were fundamental questions that arose in the nineteenth century—and that still arise. It is on these lines that the boundaries of the categories *classical* and *popular* were set.

1830–1865: Education and Reform in a Time of Expansion

The significant endeavors of this antebellum period all had to do with the teaching of music to the broad masses of people, and especially to children. Three men were representative of this movement: Lowell Mason (1792–1872), Artemas Nixon Johnson (1817–92), and George Frederick Root (1820–95, whom we met in chapter 12 as the composer of some enormously popular Civil War songs). What is most important to note is that the teaching of music, the establishing of music schools, the publication of numerous graded collections of music, and the founding of choral societies (all in a way outgrowths of the singing-school movement described in chapter 8) did not cater to a musical elite, but on the contrary sought to bring what were seen as the benefits of music to the broadest possible public. Neither Mason nor Root had exaggerated pretensions as composers, but they wrote songs, hymns, anthems, and cantatas that were accessible to singers of modest abilities, an accomplishment of which they were justly proud. Both became shrewd business men, and by successfully reaching this broad public, became wealthy (both were connected with their own publishing firms), but they never abandoned the ideal of supplying what Root called the "people's song." As Root explained: "It was not, until I . . . went more among the people of the country, that I . . . respected myself, and was thankful when I could write something that all the people would sing."[2]

George Frederick Root composed many works in the then-popular genre of the cantata. *The Haymakers* (1857), a large-scale secular work, deals in a naive and idyllic way with one episode of farm life—a life that Root knew well from his personal background. While Root grew up with the strong opposition to the theater on moral grounds still prevalent in New England in his time, he did call *The Haymakers* "An Operatic Cantata," and included directions for simple staging. Unjustly forgotten, *The Haymakers* shows Root to have been a more accomplished composer than would be evident from his popular songs. His music is expressive, even on occasion dramatic, while remaining well within the capabilities of the amateur singers for whom it was intended (no mean accomplishment!). The work is as authentic as it is unpretentious; Root composed the work on the same farm in Massachusetts where he had labored as a boy. He later wrote that "by stepping to the door, I could see the very fields in which I had swung the scythe and raked the hay, and in which I had many a time hurried to get the last load into the barn before the thunder-storm should burst upon us."[3]

Root's treatment of this very aspect of haymaking can be heard in two excerpts. Before the storm the Spreaders are turning the hay, and we hear a charming bit of text painting in "**Toss it hither, toss it thither**" in which a "tossing" rhythmic figure is bandied back and forth by the women. But as the sultry day wears on, a threatening cloud appears ("**But see!**"), growing into a monstrous thunderhead in a way that could only have been described by someone who had had firsthand experience with New England summer weather (Root wrote his own text). "Yes! to the work!" describes the hurry to get the hay in, while the cloud rises fast and the wind and the rain come on. But the hay will be brought in, and there is old-fashioned optimism in the farmers' assertion that "We shall not lose the day." This "operatic cantata" is from an age far removed in many ways from ours, but its somewhat dated language should not keep us from enjoying it as an attractive and well-wrought bit of authentic Americana.

Outspoken "Nativists" of the Mid-Nineteenth Century

Given the cultural background of the adolescent nation, it was understandable, even inevitable, that most of those concerned with improvement, education, and reform in music should turn for their source to "the courtly muses of Europe" (to use Emerson's 1837 phrase).[4] There was, especially in intellectually and culturally sophisticated circles in Boston, New York, and Philadelphia, an increased regard for Europe as the fount of all art, including music. However, a few voices of the time, in harmony with Emerson's views, were heard in support of the ideal of self-reliance in American music. Anthony Philip Heinrich, William Henry Fry, and George Frederick Bristow, as composers, were among our most outspoken "nativists"—those who wanted to see flourish a distinctive American music, written by American composers and, equally important, actually performed for American audiences.

Anthony Philip Heinrich

Anthony Philip Heinrich (1781–1861) arrived in Philadelphia from his native Bohemia in 1810; for the next fifty years he pursued with fanatical zeal his ideal of making his adopted country a musical nation. His early sojourn in the then "wild west" was crucial. At one point, worn out and ill, he went to live in a log house in Bardstown, Kentucky. Here, in the relative wilderness, at nearly forty years of age, he began to write music. This now became his ruling passion, and for the rest of his life he referred to himself by such titles as "The Wildwood Troubadour," "Minstrel of the Western Wilds," or, more concretely,

Anthony Philip Heinrich. *Courtesy New York Public Library.*

"The Loghouse Composer of Kentucky." A scant two years after his wilderness experience of self-discovery the industrious Heinrich produced his first published work, with the elaborate title *The Dawning of Music in Kentucky, or The Pleasures of Harmony in the Solitudes of Nature* (1820). In the preface he makes one of the earliest pleas for the cause of the "nativist" in his adopted country: "The many and severe animadversions, so long and repeatedly cast on the talent for Music in this Country, has been one of the chief motives of the Author, in the exercise of his abilities; and should he be able, by his effort, to create but one single *Star* in the *West*, no one could ever be more proud than himself, to be called an *American Musician*."[5]

A short supplement to this publication, *The Western Minstrel*, contains a descriptive piece of the type then much in vogue. Depicting the journey Heinrich had made himself, on foot, it is titled **The Minstrel's March, or Road to Kentucky**. There are landmarks identified in the score, which opens "A Tempo Giusto da Filadelfia." After the call of the post horn, a precipitous descending scale depicts the "Market Street Hill," with a pause at the "Toll Gate" before crossing the "Schuylkill Bridge" and proceeding on to the "Turnpike," and to "Lancaster." The Alleghenies are traversed in nine difficult measures. "Passage on the Ohio" begins *dolce*, but "The Rapids" (agitated passage for left hand) are encountered before the welcome "Standing in for Port," "Casting Anchors," "Landing and Cheers," and the final enigmatic "Sign of the Harp" (an inn?).

The "Loghouse Composer of Kentucky" had left Kentucky for good by 1823, settling permanently in New York in 1837. He was an indefatigable and

William Henry Fry. *Courtesy New York Public Library.*

disarmingly ingenuous promoter of his own music,* but his best efforts to secure even barely adequate performances of his works were frustrated by the fact that they were inordinately difficult and complex. Anthony Philip Heinrich's relationship to what might be termed the populist "mainstream" of American culture of his time is poignantly summed up in an account of his playing at the White House for President John Tyler; we see the enraptured, perspiring artist playing one of his most flamboyantly idealistic and patriotic compositions for the practical politician, who ends the session abruptly by saying to the composer: "That may all be very fine, sir, but can't you play us a good old Virginia reel."[6]

William Henry Fry

William Henry Fry (1813–64) was a practicing journalist, from a well-to-do Philadelphia newspaper family, who was also an opera composer. During his six years in Europe as a journalist, he attempted to secure a rehearsal for his opera

---

*Heinrich was a compulsive letter writer. Often, after the manner of composers, he wrote offering to write or dedicate works, or seeking to secure performances. Among letters not answered, as far as we know, were those to Jenny Lind, Paganini, and Queen Victoria.

Leonora in Paris—a rehearsal for which he was willing to pay all expenses himself. This was met with refusal based on an all-too-familiar prejudice: "In Europe we look upon America as an industrial country—excellent for electric telegraphs, but not for art."[7] Upon Fry's return to America in 1852, he found American prejudice against American music no less in evidence, and, in his view, much less tolerable. While working for the *New York Tribune*, he set out to do something about it, through a series of lectures, illustrated by vocal soloists, a large chorus and orchestra, and military band! In the climactic last lecture Fry delivered a deeply felt plea for America's development and acceptance of its own music, and an American "Declaration of Independence" from European domination. Coming a generation after that of Heinrich, it was not to be the last: "Until this Declaration of Independence in Art shall be made—until American composers shall discard their foreign liveries and found an American School—and until the American public shall learn to support American artists, Art will not become indigenous to this country, but will only exist as a feeble exotic, and we shall continue to be provincial in Art."[8]

Though his own music was quite derivative (as Italianate as the music of Heinrich was Germanic), Fry will be remembered for his ringing call for independence on behalf of American music, issued a mere fifteen years after Emerson had sounded a similar call on behalf of American letters in "The American Scholar."

George Frederick Bristow, and Some Glimpses of the New York Scene at Mid-Century

George Frederick Bristow (1825–98)—"serious, industrious, and unassuming"—a competent, versatile, thoroughgoing professional musician, was born in New York, spent his entire life in and around that city, and died there. He was playing violin in a theater orchestra at the age of eleven, and for over sixty years he was involved in every phase of New York's musical life at the period when it was attaining the position of dominance and influence in American music that it holds to this day. As a composer, the work for which he became best known is his full-length opera, *Rip Van Winkle*, the first on an American subject by an American composer. Bristow wrote orchestral music as well, including at least four symphonies. His dissatisfaction with the New York Philharmonic Society's failure to program American music led him stand up for the "nativists" in a letter published in 1853 in which he said:

> During the eleven years the Philharmonic Society has been in operation in this city, it played once, either by mistake or accident, one single American composition, an

George Frederick Bristow. *Courtesy New York Public Library.*

overture of mine. As one exception makes a rule stronger, so this single stray fact shows that the Philharmonic Society has been as anti-American as if it had been located in London during the Revolutionary War, and composed of native-born British tories.[9]

The Debate over Nationality

We have just examined the careers and works of three composers who, different as they were, all espoused a "nativist" view—that there should evolve a distinctively American music, developing a life of its own not in the shadow of European tradition, together with an audience to appreciate and support such music. There were critics, however, who took an opposite view—a view that has been called "expatriate."[10] These critics were imbued with a reverential attitude toward those European masters—mainly Germanic—whose music was just beginning to be performed in the culturally adolescent republic. Theirs was an idealistic dedication to the cosmopolitan, the universal, the expression that seeks to transcend place and time. This competed with an equally idealistic desire to express the national, the specific, the unique sense of *this* place and *this* time.

This is a debate that takes place in all eras, but at this time it was played out against the background of our period of greatest national expansion, between the Louisiana Purchase and the Civil War. It was a time of fierce national pride; "Manifest Destiny" was its appropriate motto.

Louis Moreau Gottschalk and the Virtuoso in Nineteenth-Century America

We have yet to consider the most gifted musician of the era. In 1853 there appeared in New York, just arrived from Europe, a brilliant pianist. He had recently completed a triumphant concert tour of Spain, where the queen had made him a Cavalier of the Order of Isabella the Catholic; Chopin had predicted a great future for him; the great French composer Hector Berlioz was his friend and mentor.

Louis Moreau Gottschalk (1829–69) would have been an outstanding figure whatever his origin, but his importance is all the greater in the present context because he was an American. He was, in fact, the first American musician to rank unquestionably with the greatest in Europe in his time. Born in New Orleans, he had learned all that he could from any musician there by the time he was eleven; at thirteen, his parents sent him to Paris to study. The director of piano classes at the Paris Conservatoire in 1842 rejected him without even hearing him play, because in his opinion "America was nothing but a country of steam engines." That Gottschalk, seven years later at the age of twenty, was invited to sit as a judge at examinations at this same conservatory is a fitting sequel, and suggests how rapidly he took his place among the leading young pianists of the day. His remarkable appearance, stage presence, and charm were universally commented on throughout his life; he was to become, in effect, one of the first "matinee idols."

By the time Gottschalk returned to this country he had already established himself as a composer. Especially popular were three piano pieces he had written when still in his teens in Paris, based on folk tunes of the Louisiana blacks that he remembered from his childhood—*Le Bananier: Chanson nègre*, *La Savane: Ballade créole*, and **Bamboula: Danse des Nègres**. Gottschalk's compositions, in accord with his needs as a concert artist in the nineteenth century, fall into three main categories. First, there are the folk-tune-based ethnic pieces, such as **Bamboula**. (The original song appears as Ex. 21-2 in chapter 21.) A second class of compositions is the virtuoso concert pieces, or "paraphrases," consisting of medleys of operatic airs, or popular tunes that were often patriotic. *The Union*, for example, so popular during the Civil War, includes "The Star-Spangled Banner," "Hail Columbia," and, as a final tour de force, "Hail Columbia" and "Yankee Doodle" played at the same time! A third class is the so-called salon pieces. These

Louis Moreau Gottschalk. *Courtesy New York Public Library.*

Gottschalk liked the least, but as a popular artist and "matinee idol" he had to write, play, and publish them. They are sentimental creations, with titles such as *The Dying Poet*. The most famous of these is *The Last Hope: Religious Meditation*. It became almost an obligatory ritual for him to end his concerts with it, head bowed and eyes closed.*

His years in the United States were twice interrupted by sojourns in the West Indies. The second of these, beginning in 1857, lasted five years—years in which Gottschalk virtually dropped out of sight. He himself describes them as

> years foolishly spent, thrown to the wind, as if life were infinite, and youth eternal; six years, during which I have roamed at random under the blue skies of the tropics, indolently permitting myself to be carried away by chance, giving a

*The main theme from *The Last Hope* lives on in a different guise. Almost two decades after Gottschalk's death, a Congregational minister put sacred words to it, and it has since led an independent existence as the hymn tune "Mercy."

concert wherever I found a piano, sleeping wherever the night overtook me—on the grass of the savanna, or under the palm-leaf roof of a *veguero* (a tobacco-grower) with whom I partook of a tortilla, coffee, and banana, which I paid for on leaving in the morning, with *"Dios se lo pague"* (God repay you); to which he responded with a *"Vaya usted con Dios"* (God go with you)—these two formularies constituting in this savage country, the operation so ingeniously perfected among civilized people, that is called "settling the hotel bill."[11]

The year he embarked upon his long West Indian rambling Gottschalk began a journal, published as *Notes of a Pianist*. They are brilliantly written (in French), and are reminiscent of the essays and memoirs of his older mentor Berlioz in their wit and insight. As valuable descriptions and commentaries on American life of the time, they rank with the journals and writings of Frances Kemble, Frederick Law Olmsted, and Alexis de Tocqueville. Who knew better, or could better have expressed, the American state of mind with regard to the fine arts a century ago than Gottschalk, writing in 1862?

> There is no doubt that there are immense lacunæ in certain details of our civilization. Our appreciation of the *beaux-arts* is not always enlightened, and we treat them like parasites occupying a usurped place. The wheels of our government are, like our managers, too new not to grate upon the ear sometimes. We perhaps worship a little too much the golden calf, and do not kill the fatted calf often enough to feast the elect of thought. Each of us thinks himself as good as (if not better than) any other man—an excellent faith that engenders self-respect but often leads us to wish to reduce to our own level those to whose level we cannot attain. These little faults happily are not national traits; they appertain to all young societies. We are, in a word, like the beautiful children of whom Montaigne speaks, who bite the nurse's breast, and whom the exuberance of health sometimes renders turbulent.[12]

After the Civil War: The Pursuit of Culture in a Time of Industrialization

After the trauma of the Civil War, the patterns of American life changed. The changes were wrought by the westward movement of a substantial portion of the population, by settlement and cultivation of the land, by the building of towns and cities, by the exploitation of natural resources, and by industrialization. The telegraph was quickly followed by the railroad in linking east and west. Great wealth began to accrue to a new class of men—the builders of a new industrial society, entrepreneurs in growing new enterprises: coal and iron mining, steel-making, railroad building, engineering, construction, manufacturing, and the extracting and refining of petroleum.

With this new wealth came the desire to advance education and culture. Educational and cultural enterprises conceived in the earlier part of the century, which hitherto had led a struggling existence, now prospered on a scale impossible before the industrial age. Colleges and universities were founded and endowed, as were libraries and art museums. In the larger cities, the two most expensive forms of music-making—opera and the symphony orchestra—began to flourish conspicuously.

The passage of opera from an unassimilated alien to an indigenous American art form is chronicled in chapter 20. The symphony orchestra became "naturalized" much sooner than did opera. Not just New York and Boston, but Philadelphia, Pittsburgh, Cincinnati, St. Louis, and even Los Angeles had established symphony orchestras by 1900. A reasonably complete account of the growth of the symphony orchestra in America would have to take into account the work of an immigrant boy from a small town in north Germany, who came here as an accomplished violinist at the age of ten, and went on to become the leading founder and conductor of American symphony orchestras. The unremitting pioneering work of Theodore Thomas (1835–1905) is encountered again and again in the story of the American music of his era. Today there are more than a thousand orchestras in cities throughout the United States, including not only major professional orchestras but semiprofessional, community, and college orchestras. Though perenially beset by financial crises, the place of the symphony orchestra in American musical life is secure.

African-American Performers and Composers

Sometime in 1876 in New York there appeared as soloist with Theodore Thomas's orchestra a Cuban violinist of African parentage, José White.[13] White was trained in Paris and was recognized in Europe as a distinguished violinist and composer. While he was not an American, his accomplishments, and those of others of African descent who had succeeded in Europe, could not but have been an inspiration to black musicians here. Not until quite recently has there been a general awareness of the activities of these musicians in American concert life following the Civil War. Among the best known of these musicians was the phenomenal Thomas Greene Bethune, known universally in his lifetime (1849–1908) as "Blind Tom." He was born in slavery on a plantation near Columbus, in Harris County, Georgia; his extraordinary musical abilities were recognized when he was four by the Columbus journalist-politician

James Bethune, who had purchased him in 1850. He began to be taken on tours and "exhibited" as early as 1857. After the Civil War the Bethune family continued to manage and control Tom's professional career, both in America and in Europe. He appeared last on the Keith Circuit, as a vaudeville attraction, in 1905. He had a phenomenal memory for both words and music; he could play long and difficult pieces after a single hearing, and recite lengthy poems and orations. He also composed and played his own works, which numbered at least one hundred, including another in the long line of "battle pieces," *The Battle of Manassas*. John William Boone, known as "Blind Boone" (1864–1927), another outstanding black pianist and composer, was more fortunate than Blind Tom in having a black manager who was also a devoted friend. He wrote a great deal of brilliant and difficult piano music, some of which incorporated African-American themes. The work of many other black concert artists of the nineteenth century is now becoming better known.[14]

The Second New England School*

Boston, the hub of New England life, has always been an important cultural center, but it occupied an especially commanding position of leadership from the mid-nineteenth century to World War I. Including in its orbit Cambridge and nearby Concord, its intellectual life had already, by the time of the Civil War, been marked by the great literary and philosophical tradition that included Emerson, Hawthorne, Longfellow, Whittier, and Thoreau. Musically, the ground had been cultivated by the formation of the Handel and Haydn Society in 1815 and the Boston Academy of Music, founded under the aegis of Lowell Mason in 1833. In 1867 the New England Conservatory (today one of our leading music schools) was founded, and in 1881 the Boston Symphony Orchestra was formed. It was a time of great patrons and patronesses. The two most notable were Henry Lee Higginson, who founded and supported (for long nearly single-handedly) the Boston Symphony and built Symphony Hall for it in 1900, and Mrs. Isabella Stewart Gardner, a colorful and generous patroness who surrounded herself with a large circle of artists and musicians to whom she gave help. She engaged musicians to give chamber music concerts, orchestral concerts, and even operas at her two successive palatial Boston establishments, 152 Beacon Street and the even more sumptuous Fenway Court.[15]

It is not surprising, then, that Boston should have nurtured during this fifty-year period a tradition of musical composition and a group of composers who are often (conveniently, though inaccurately) considered together as a "school."

*The First New England School is considered to be the eighteenth-century singing-school composers, including William Billings, Justin Morgan, Timothy Swan, Supply Belcher, and others. See chapter 8.

What these composers had in common was a dedication to excellence of musical craftsmanship and to the highest ideals of serious composition as they saw them. The musicians of the Second New England School broke ground for the American composer, helped to establish the place of music in our colleges and universities, and left behind an impressive body of music.

Because he came earliest and was gifted with tenacity and a sense of purpose, to John Knowles Paine (1839–1906), competent and dedicated, fell the role of pioneer. At nineteen, Paine, already an accomplished organist, was giving subscription organ concerts to raise money for study in Europe. Important ground was broken for the place of American music in our colleges when Paine received the first full professorship of music at Harvard—and the first in the United States—in 1875. A good introduction to the works of John Knowles Paine is his ten-minute overture *As You Like It*, after Shakespeare.

Another New England pioneer, George Chadwick (1854–1931), was brought up in a typical Yankee musical atmosphere: his father, in his spare time from his varied pursuits, taught singing-schools and organized a community chorus and orchestra. George, after some study at the New England Conservatory, went to Germany at the age of twenty-three for three years of study. In 1897 he became director of the New England Conservatory, a post he occupied until his death. The range of Chadwick's compositions was broad. He wrote a comic opera, *Tabasco*, and a serious opera, *The Padrone* (an operatic precursor of *The Godfather*), which "tells a realistic story of poor Italian immigrants whose lives are ruined by a small-time mafioso figure who controls them."[16] His works exhibit qualities of exuberance, vitality, and humor. Perhaps his best-known work is a suite for orchestra entitled *Symphonic Sketches*, written between 1895 and 1904. A good introduction to the works of Chadwick is the third of these, the six-minute *Hobgoblin*, which the composer designates a "Scherzo Capriccioso," elucidating it with a quote from Shakespeare's *Midsummer Night's Dream*: "That shrewd and knavish sprite called Robin Good-fellow."

Horatio Parker (1863–1919) was at age sixteen a church organist—a calling shared by many New England composers. He studied with Chadwick, and at the age of nineteen went to Germany for three years of further study. On his return he settled in New York as organist and teacher. In 1894 he became professor of music at Yale University, and from then on was active not only in New Haven (where in addition to teaching he formed the New Haven Symphony) but in New York and Philadelphia also. He is noted chiefly today for his choral works and for two operas, the first of which, *Mona*, was produced at the Metropolitan Opera House in 1912. His best-known work is the cantata *Hora Novissima*, a setting of portions of a twelfth-century satirical poem in Latin. *Hora Novissima* is still performed occasionally; it was given a Carnegie Hall performance forty-four years after its premiere, at which time the *New York Times* critic Olin Downes described it as "irretrievably old-fashioned and genuine, glorious music."

One of the most precocious, talented, and energetic composers of this time and place was also our first prominent woman composer, Amy Marcy Beach (1867–1944). She was composing piano pieces at the age of four, playing public recitals at seven, and performing as soloist with the Boston Symphony Orchestra before she was eighteen. Unlike Paine, Chadwick, and Parker, who went to Europe to study, Amy Beach acquired her musical training entirely in Boston. She composed many songs and piano pieces, as well as chamber music, choral music, and larger works that included a piano concerto, an opera, and the splendid thirty-minute "Gaelic" Symphony (1894). Persistent and resourceful in securing performances of her own works, she was also generous in helping young musicians, and assumed leadership in many musical organizations, including the cofounding of the American Association of Women Composers in 1926.

Five Individualists Around the Turn of the Century

Roughly contemporaneous with the Second New England School were five composers, Edward MacDowell, Charles Martin Loeffler, Henry F. Gilbert, Charles Tomlinson Griffes, and Arthur Farwell, who had little in common but the fact that each had a highly individual background and artistic stance.

In terms of producing a composer of truly international recognition, America had its first success story in the career of Edward MacDowell (1860–1908). MacDowell had gone to Europe to study at the age of fifteen. While still in his twenties he had become a successful pianist, teacher, and composer there, and had virtually settled in Germany when he was persuaded to return to the United States and take an active part in our rapidly developing musical life. In 1888 he came back and settled in Boston, then a center of intense cultural activity. For the next eight years he concertized, composed, and had his works widely performed. From this period come many songs; many solo piano pieces, including the famous *Woodland Sketches*; and some of his most important orchestral compositions, including the *Indian Suite*, published in 1897.

MacDowell's use of genuine Indian themes in this suite represents one of the earliest, and perhaps most successful, attempts to use material of this kind in a symphonic composition. Yet despite the fact that the *Indian Suite* is one of MacDowell's strongest works, it was untypical in that he otherwise seldom used indigenous material e was no "nativist." He declared in a lecture that "purely national music ha no place in art," and he disparaged as "childish" what he regarded as artificial "means of 'creating' a national music." MacDowell's range of expression we can now see to have been rather narrow. Perhaps his talent for art gives us a clue to his musical nature; he was fundamentally a pictorialist, and one who was most at home in miniature forms.

Charles Martin Loeffler (1861–1935) was born either in Berlin or in Alsace, and came to America as an accomplished violinist in 1881. Trained in composition in Europe before his arrival, he wrote a large number of works here that reflected his broad interests, especially in literature. His music reveals an awareness of Russian and especially French music of the time. Although overt "Americanism" in his music is practically confined to one movement of his Partita for Violin and Piano, he had a little-known but genuine enthusiasm for jazz.[17] A widely read man who was esteemed in intellectual as well as artistic circles, Loeffler was often a beneficiary of the patronage of Mrs. Isabella Stewart Gardner. Among works of his currently available, the moody and exotic *La Mort de Tintagiles*, completed in 1897, is representative of his forward-looking harmonic language and use of orchestral color.

Henry F. Gilbert (1868–1928), like Loeffler, had a broad range of tastes (they shared an interest in French literature), but Gilbert's leanings were distinctly nativist. He incorporated African-American melodies, Indian melodies, and ragtime into his compositions. Impressed with the work of the photographer Edward S. Curtis and his pioneering studies of American Indians, Gilbert transcribed phonograph recordings Curtis had collected in the field, and wrote a score, performed by an orchestra of twenty-two musicians, to accompany Curtis's photographic presentation "The Story of a Vanishing Race," which opened at Carnegie Hall in 1911. Gilbert gave full rein to his impulsive curiosity, traveling to Chicago to hear exotic music at the Columbian Exposition of 1893. Illustrative of Gilbert's interest in America's vernacular musical sources is his eleven-minute symphonic poem *The Dance in Place Congo,* composed 1906–8.* The setting, the tunes, and the title are taken from George Washington Cable's 1886 articles on African-American music-making in New Orleans during the Reconstruction era. The principal tune is the one Gottschalk had also used a half-century earlier as the basis for one of his best-known piano works, ***Bamboula***.[18] (The original appears as Ex. 21-2, in chapter 21.)

Charles Tomlinson Griffes (1884–1920), in a productive period as a composer that lasted a bare thirteen years, managed to create an amazingly large body of works, many of which have increased in stature and significance with the passage of time. His early works reflected the influence of German Romanticism; later he produced some remarkable pieces that have become the prime American

The Dance in Place Congo is on New World 80228–2 CD.

examples of Impressionism, including *Roman Sketches* and *The White Peacock*. Toward the end of his life Griffes produced a group of "Oriental" works, including his ten-minute *The Pleasure-Dome of Kubla Khan*, based on the poem by Coleridge. Less well known are his *Three Poems of Fiona MacLeod* of 1918. In these songs, which exist in versions for voice and orchestra, Griffes turned his attention, and his penchant for the exotic, to Celtic lore. That his further development as a composer might have taken him into still other realms of expression is shown by his striking Piano Sonata of 1917–18, which is forward-looking in its dissonance and its neoclassical avoidance of any programmatic associations.

Arthur Farwell, Idealistic Promoter of a Native Music

At the same time that MacDowell and the Boston Classicists were at their honorable work of cultivating in America what were basically European musical forms and modes of expression, there were other musical winds stirring in the land. To understand these, it is necessary to recall a few things that had happened meanwhile on the broad musical scene. In the 1870s the Fisk Jubilee Singers (followed soon by other groups) had begun to open up a reservoir of African-American musical culture vastly different from the popular caricatures of the minstrel stage. In the 1880s American Indian music was beginning to be seriously collected and studied. On the popular musical stage at about the same time, Harrigan and Hart were presenting plays with music that dealt with a cross-section of the everyday life of the people of New York. Ragtime arrived from the Midwest in the 1890s. From 1892 to 1895 the great Czech composer Antonin Dvořák (1841–1904) was in America as director of the National Conservatory in New York. His African-American student Harry Thacker Burleigh (1866–1949), later to become a prominent composer, arranger, and concert singer, was a frequent visitor to his New York apartment and repeatedly sang spirituals for him. Dvořák heard the songs of Stephen Foster; he spent summers in Iowa, where he heard Indian music. He issued what was in effect a challenge to American composers, to look to their own native music as a foundation on which to establish in America what he termed "a great and noble school of music." And there were composers of the time who were more than ready to accept this challenge. A spirit of ferment and optimism accompanied the advent of the new century, which seemed to portend a new era. One pioneer composer, writing in 1903, addressed himself to "all composers who feel the pulse of new life that marks the beginning of an era in American music," inviting them to join those workers who had been striving

> to draw out of the dawning, though widely distributed realities and possibilities of American musical life, the elements and forces necessary to form a definite

Arthur Farwell. *Courtesy New York Public Library.*

movement which shall make for the untrammeled growth of a genuine Art of Music. Such an art will not be a mere echo of other lands and times, but shall have a vital meaning for us, in our circumstances, here and now. While it will take the worthier traditions of the past for its point of departure, it will derive its convincing qualities of color, form, and spirit from our nature-world and our humanity.[19]

So wrote Arthur Farwell (1872–1952), a man of his time, whose initiative, enterprise, and integrity of ideals made him a leader and a mover. A native of the Midwest, after a period of study, which included the study of American Indian music, he settled in Newton Center, Massachusetts, and entered upon a significant venture for American music. Having tried unsuccessfully to get his *American Indian Melodies* published, and having met other American composers who suffered similar rejections, he resolved to try to overcome the resistance to American music by founding a composers' press. The Wa-Wan Press came into being late in 1901. (The name "Wa-Wan" is that of an Omaha Indian ceremony of peace and brotherhood.) The emphasis was on quality—quality not only of the music chosen but of design and typography as well. In this Farwell was inspired by the examples of such predecessors as William Blake and William Morris. The press was in existence for ten years, during all of which time it remained Farwell's venture and published the work of thirty-six American composers, including nine women. A glance at the complete output of the Wa-Wan Press shows that it maintained exceptional standards of workmanship and appearance. Like William Morris before him, Farwell eschewed commercialism, aware of the extent to which it could perpetuate and surround people's lives with shabbiness and mediocrity. For this reason, Farwell's work has special meaning for today.

A second aim of the Wa-Wan Press, and of Farwell himself, is less easily stated, but it had to do with developing an American music more in touch with American life. "It must have an American flavor," he wrote. "It must be recognizably American, as Russian music is Russian, and French music, French." Arthur Farwell sounded for American music the same note that Emerson, two generations earlier, had sounded for American literature: first, find your own voice, cultivate your own field; second, do not divorce art from life.

Farwell's concern with making music an active part of the lives of the great mass of the people expressed itself in many novel ideas, which his abilities as a leader and organizer enabled him to bring to fruition. While working in New York, he organized with Harry Barnhart the New York Community Chorus, which eventually grew to 800 singers. In 1916, using this chorus, he collaborated in the production of a Song and Light Festival on the shores of a lake in Central Park. The lighting effects, spectacular for their day, were described in a contemporary account:

> One-half million candle power of illumination shining through hundreds of artistic panels and huge globes gave the lake at the end of the Mall a fantastic aspect of colorful fairyland. No two of the colored panels were alike. The reflections of delicate red, blue, green and gold shades twinkled in the water, which was dotted with gray boats carrying passengers through the festival of song and light.[20]

An orchestra and the 800-voice chorus performed some standard works by Handel, Wagner, and others, but integrated with these were songs such as "Old Black Joe" and "Nearer, My God, to Thee," in which the entire assembled audience of 25,000 gathered on the opposite shore of the lake participated. The total effect must have been impressive.

In California, where Arthur Farwell lived and worked from 1918 to 1927, he was connected with many projects for involving people more directly with music than the conventional concert format would allow, often in an outdoor setting. While teaching at the University of California in Berkeley he wrote *California*, a masque of song, given in the Greek Theater with audience participation; later, in southern California, he was instrumental in the establishment of the Hollywood Bowl, and he wrote music for *La Primavera*, a "Community Music Drama" produced in Santa Barbara in 1920. In 1925 he organized a series of outdoor concerts in a natural amphitheater that he named The Theater of the Stars, near Big Bear Lake, in the mountains of southern California.

Conclusion

The period of nearly a hundred years with which this chapter has been concerned represents a great deal of ground covered. It began in an ebullient age of expansion and democratization, of fierce and sensitive national pride—an age of artistic innocence in which Heinrich, the "Loghouse Composer," could be dubbed "the Beethoven of America." It closed on the eve of a cataclysmic war involving profound changes in the order of a world more tightly bound together—an age of closer ties with Europe, from which American composers felt compelled to seek both guidance and independence. To use Blake's pair of terms, in art we had traversed the ground from "innocence" to "experience"—from Heinrich's idyllic *The Dawning of Music in Kentucky* to the realistic *The Padrone* of Chadwick.

At this point we proceed not simply to a new chapter, but to a series of parallel chapters, depicting the parallel progress of tradition and innovation.

FURTHER READING

Books

Chase, Gilbert, ed. *The American Composer Speaks*. Baton Rouge: Louisiana State University Press, 1966.
> Includes writings by Heinrich, Fry, Gottschalk, John Hill Hewitt, MacDowell, Farwell, and Gilbert.

Crawford, Richard. *The American Musical Landscape*. Berkeley: University of California Press, 1993.
> See chapter 1 on Farwell, among others, and chapter 5 on Root.

Gottschalk, L. M. *Notes of a Pianist*. New ed., translated and with notes by Jeanne Behrend. New York: Knopf, 1964.
> One of the most perceptive and brilliant documents that we have of nineteenth-century American life as seen by a musician.

Keck, George, ed. *Feel the Spirit: Essays in 19th Century Afro-American Music*. Westport, CT: Greenwood, 1988.
> Includes material on Blind Tom and Blind Boone, with musical examples, by Ann Sears.

Lowens, Irving. *Music and Musicians in Early America*. New York: Norton, 1964.
> See chapters on Hewitt, Heinrich, Fry, and Gottschalk.

Tawa, Nicholas. *The Coming of Age of American Art Music: New England's Classical Romanticists*. New York: Schirmer Books, 1991.

Articles

Chmaj, Betty. "Fry versus Dwight: American Music's Debate over Nationality." *American Music* 3, no. 1 (Spring 1985): 63–84.

Levy, Alan Howard. "The Search for Identity in American Music 1890–1920." *American Music* 2, no. 2 (Summer 1984): 70–81.

Projects

1. In this chapter the nineteenth century has been identified as the age in which the cleavage between classical and popular music became most pronounced. Considering the phenomena of "third stream" music, minimalism, and the current concern with "accessibility" in classical music circles, has this cleavage grown less in our time? Has it become irrelevant? Give your considered views in a brief but well-documented paper.

2. Sample the coverage given the arts in a local newspaper for a period of several weeks. Observe the proportion of space given to local artists and local live performances, as compared with space devoted to "name" artists or stars, whose work is accessible mostly through the media of records, films, or television. Write a paper on how your findings relate to the "nativist" versus "expatriate" controversy dealt with in this chapter.

3. Read Louis Moreau Gottschalk's *Notes of a Pianist*, and write a paper on any of a number of subjects suggested by this brilliant diary—e.g., "The Life of a Concert Artist in Mid-Nineteenth-Century America" or "Music in the Mining Towns of the West."

4. Many composers of the Second New England School, composing between 1875 and 1925, wrote programmatic pieces—pieces with extramusical associations, such as John Knowles Paine's *As You Like It* or Arthur Foote's symphonic prologue *Francesca da Rimini*. Make a survey of programmatic works written during this half-century, and summarize the kind and variety of literary influences on composers of this period. Would your results justify its designation as the "American Romantic Period"?

5. Referring to MacDowell's *Critical and Historical Essays* and other sources, summarize his views about the place of music in "liberal culture," and specifically the directions in which he wished to develop the music department at Columbia University. Include his thoughts on the relation of music to the "sister arts."

Notes

1. Irving Lowens, *Music and Musicians in Early America* (New York: Norton, 1964), 267.

2. George F. Root, *The Story of a Musical Life*, 83.

3. Ibid., 113.

4. Ralph Waldo Emerson, "The American Scholar"; though his remarks referred to the activity of the scholar, and hence primarily to literature, his themes of embracing what is common and prizing what is at hand were later applied to music by one of his most fervent admirers, Charles Ives.

5. The complete *The Dawning of Music in Kentucky* has been reprinted in facsimile (New York: Da Capo, 1972). The preface is reprinted in Gilbert Chase, ed., *The American Composer Speaks* (Baton Rouge: Louisiana State University Press, 1966).

6. The account, worth reading in full, is by John Hill Hewitt (son of the James Hewitt encountered in chapter 11); it can be found in Chase, *The American Composer Speaks*, 72–75.

7. As quoted in Irving Lowens's excellent article "William Henry Fry: American Nationalist" in *Music and Musicians in Early America*.

8. Quoted in Lowens, *Music and Musicians in Early America*, 217–18.

9. Quoted (drawing on John Tasker Howard, *Our American Music*, by Gilbert Chase, in *America's Music, From the Pilgrims to the Present*, 3d ed. (Urbana: University of Illinois Press, 1987), 308.

10. See the article by Betty Chmaj in the reading list for this chapter.

11. L. M. Gottschalk, *Notes of a Pianist*, trans. Jeanne Behrend, 39–40.

12. Ibid., 52.

13. Eileen Southern, *The Music of Black Americans: A History*, 2d ed. (New York: Norton, 1983), 250.

14. See the material on both Blind Tom and Blind Boone, with musical examples, by Ann Sears in George Keck, ed., *Feel the Spirit: Essays in 19th Century Afro-American Music* (Westport, CT: Greenwood, 1988). See also Southern, 246–50.

15. See Herbert A. Kenny's notes to New World 268.

16. See the article on Chadwick in *The New Grove Dictionary of American Music*, vol. 1, p. 385, by Steven Ledbetter and Victor Fell Yellin.

17. See Ellen Knight, "Charles Martin Loeffler and George Gershwin: A Forgotten Friendship," *American Music* 3, no. 4 (Winter 1985): 452.

18. *The Dance in Place Congo* is on New World 80228, which includes valuable notes (including a personal memoir of Gilbert) by David Baker. Cable's original articles have been reprinted in Bernard Katz, ed., *The Social Implications of Early Negro Music in the United States* (New York: Arno, 1969).

19. Arthur Farwell, "A Letter to American Composers," *The Wa-Wan Press* (reprint, New York: Arno/New York Times, 1970), vol. 1, xvii.

20. *A Guide to the Music of Arthur Farwell*, ed. Brice Farwell, 85.

Chapter 16

The Evolving Tradition, 1920-1970

To the listener in the adventurous period that began in the 1920s, *all* American art music seemed new, and stirred interest and controversy. It is only from the vantage point of a later time that we can see how tradition and innovation were being cultivated simultaneously. For example, *Intégrales* by Edgard Varèse, the *Symphony for Organ and Orchestra* by Aaron Copland, and *Rhapsody in Blue* by George Gershwin were all premiered in New York in 1924–25; each was perceived as *new* music, yet each bore quite a different relationship to the current state of musical evolution. What was most readily accepted and absorbed during this period was the music that was evolving along traditional lines. It is with this music that this chapter will be concerned. The less readily approachable innovations of the twentieth century will be treated in the two chapters following.

Some Background for the "Fervent Years"

The qualities that unmistakably characterized the period were enthusiasm, energy, and optimism. As David Owens put it, "America was taking stock, really for the first time, of its cultural assets, and it can be said that nothing before or after in the country's aesthetic history has exhilarated it to such a degree."[1] For it was then that an indigenous fine-art music, the coming of which had been prophesied by so many of the pioneers we encountered in the last chapter, began to flourish. The two decades between the wars, especially, were years of ferment and change—"fervent years," as they have been called.

Partly this was the result of the existence of a group of young musicians who fairly early in their lives made the irrevocable decision to become composers, and who dedicated themselves fully and knowledgeably to preparing themselves for productive careers. As Roger Sessions put it:

> The striking fact is that those who aspired to genuine and serious achievement,
> no longer a handful of ambitious individuals who remained essentially isolated,
> were young Americans who had begun to learn what serious accomplishment

involved. They were determined to find their way to it. Such seeking had not occurred before in the United States, but they did not find what they sought within the then existing framework of American music life.[2]

Americans in Paris

Not finding "what they sought within the then existing framework of American music life," most did turn once more to Europe, but a far different Europe than had existed previously. It was not merely that the war and its aftermath weakened German dominance—it was also that more venturesome things were taking place elsewhere in Europe. Arthur Farwell had already noted, two decades earlier, the greater musical inventiveness of France and Russia. By the third decade of this century the Russian Revolution had created a climate that was not inviting to composers, but France was in all ways more hospitable, and France, specifically Paris, fostered an atmosphere of fervent concern for music (and for the arts generally) that was evidenced in a burst of new music being performed and in new artistic movements. Dada, for example, was a rejection of artistic formalism and rationality. This ferment attracted younger composers. The young French group of *Les Six*— Darius Milhaud, Francis Poulenc, Arthur Honegger, Georges Auric, Louis Durey, and Germaine Tailleferre—in the artistic company of the older iconoclast Eric Satie, held together and motivated by the writer Jean Cocteau, was making itself heard. There was also important music by non-French composers: Igor Stravinsky, Arnold Schoenberg, Paul Hindemith, Béla Bartók, Sergei Prokofiev. Serge Koussevitzky (1874–1951), noted Russian conductor, began in 1921 in Paris the "Concerts Koussevitzky," at which many new works were performed.

Among the young émigrés American composers formed a particular contingent. In the same year that Koussevitzky began his celebrated concerts, a music school for Americans was established in the palace at Fontainebleau. Although Paul Vidal of the Paris Conservatory was the composition teacher, it was an exceptional woman in her thirties, Nadia Boulanger (1887–1979)—an organist and a teacher of harmony, counterpoint, and composition—who was destined to have the most influence on a host of American composers who came to her for instruction, guidance, and encouragement throughout the twenties and thirties. These young "Americans in Paris" who studied at least for a time with Mlle. Boulanger, gaining not only perceptive criticism but the confidence to find and strike out on their own paths, included many of our most important composers of the period.

Americans Back Home

American composers returning from Europe in the 1920s found reasons for both pessimism and optimism. Certainly there was as yet no great audience creating a demand for the music of American composers, and many could justifiably join H. L. Mencken in condemning our tendency to shallow materialism and our lack of interest in, or understanding of, the arts. Some of the young émigrés therefore stayed away for good, but many composers did not. As Copland, with characteristic optimism, has pointed out, positive forces (mostly generated by the composers themselves) were at work. The International Composers' Guild and its offshoot, the League of Composers, were active and gave concerts of new music. In 1924 Serge Koussevitzky, whose celebrated concerts in Paris had introduced many new works, was appointed conductor of the Boston Symphony, beginning a long tenure during which he not only played many new American works but was often responsible, through commissions, for their creation. The decade before the crash of 1929 was a time of opulence in American life, and there were patrons of the arts. In the mid-twenties the Guggenheim Memorial Foundation was established. When in 1929 the RCA Victor Company offered an unprecedented award of $25,000 for a symphonic work, the competition was such that the prize had to be split five ways. These were what Claire Reis (1888–1978), an indefatigable and indispensable supporter of new music in this period, called the "crusading days." Virgil Thomson identified five composer "commandos"* (note the use by both Reis and Thomson of military terms!) who were with a camaraderie born of combat that momentarily submerged their differences, fighting to establish a "beachhead" both for American composers and for new music in general.

The Drive Toward an "American" Music

However they might interpret the term, it was natural that composers of the time should be seeking to write music that was "recognizably American." In this they were responding to the same urges that had been expressed two and three decades earlier by Farwell, Gilbert, and others. As Roger Sessions has stated, "The principal concern of music in the twenties was the idea of a national or 'typically American' school or style and, eventually, a tradition which would draw to a focus the musical energies of our country, which, as Rosenfeld once said to Aaron Copland and the author, would 'affirm America.'"[3]

For the new generation of composers it was no longer a matter of simply incorporating folk material into compositions or using it as a basis for symphonic elaborations, although these practices are perfectly valid. As Copland put it, "Our concern was not with the quotable hymn or spiritual: we wanted to find a music that would speak of universal things in a vernacular of American speech rhythms. We wanted to write music on a level that left popular music far

Aaron Copland (1900–90), Roger Sessions (1896–1985), Roy Harris (1898–1979), Walter Piston (1894–1976), and Thomson himself (1896–1989).

behind—music with a largeness of utterance wholly representative of the country that Whitman had envisaged."[4]

There was much experimentation in this search for "a music that would speak of universal things in a vernacular of American speech rhythms." It was natural, for example, that as earlier composers had looked to American Indian music, African-American spirituals, and minstrel tunes, composers in the third decade of the twentieth century should look to jazz, and the attendant popular music influenced by it.

John Alden Carpenter

The generation that preceded the young "commandos" had not all left the scene, and John Alden Carpenter (1876–1951) was one of the older composers who made use of the idioms of the Jazz Age in some of his works. His 13-minute "jazz pantomime" *Krazy Kat*, based on the George Herriman comic-strip character, was first performed as a ballet-pantomime in New York in 1922. Its success led the Russian impresario Diaghilev to commission another work, *Skyscrapers*, subtitled "a ballet of modern American life"; scenes alternate between depictions of "work" and "play." Produced in New York in 1926, it was something of a landmark in its ballet treatment of modern urban life.

Copland composed his jazz-based *Music for the Theater* in 1925, and the next year utilized jazz motifs again in his Concerto for Piano and Orchestra. George Gershwin's *Rhapsody in Blue*, Piano Concerto in F, and *An American in Paris* (the latter two commissioned by Walter Damrosch for the New York Symphony) date from this period also. After the 1920s, the tendency to turn to jazz as a stylistic source for American classical music waned.

The American Composer Finds a Public

With the onset of the Depression decade before World War II, American fine-art music entered a period in which it became noticeably more functional, possibly more so than in any other period before or since. American composers had a public, and there was an actual need for their music. Copland has written:

> In all the arts the Depression had aroused a wave of sympathy for and identification with the plight of the common man. In music this was combined with the heady wine of suddenly feeling ourselves—the composers, that is—needed as never before. Previously our works had been largely self-engendered: no one asked for them; we simply wrote them out of our own need. Now, suddenly, functional music was in demand as never before in the experience of our serious composers. Motion-picture and ballet companies, radio stations and

schools, film and theater producers discovered us. . . . No wonder we were pleased to find ourselves sought after and were ready to compose in a manner that would satisfy both our collaborators and ourselves.[5]

This new practical direction for American classical music tended to take the form of linking music functionally with other arts: film, dance, and poetry. As an introduction to the traditionally evolving classical music after World War I, we shall consider each of these, and then turn to the more "abstract" forms of composition—the sonata, the quartet, the symphony—which also flourished.

Music with Film

The 1930s saw the rise of the symphonic film score, with lush orchestral music mostly by European composers brought up in the European symphonic-operatic tradition. Film scoring rapidly became a very specialized job. Not until 1936 did one of our major composers write film music, and then it was in the field of the documentary, a genre that is somewhat independent to a degree of the pressures of the entertainment industry.

A Realistic Film of the American West

In the middle thirties, the Resettlement Administration, a United States government agency, wanted a documentary film to propagandize on behalf of its program to aid farm families driven out of drought-stricken areas—mainly the Dust Bowl of the Southwest. Pare Lorentz, a film reviewer turned filmmaker, was engaged to make this, his first movie. The result was a powerful documentary called *The Plow That Broke the Plains*. The film still makes a stunning visual impact today, with its expressive footage of prairie grasslands; devastated, dust-blown farms; and hard-hit, long-suffering farm families; and its visual analogies, as for example between military tanks and mammoth harvesters, or between a collapsed tickertape machine and bleached bones on the plowed-over, denuded land.

Virgil Thomson (1896–1989), an individualistic composer and highly influential writer and critic during this entire period of our musical history, was engaged to write music for the film. Both Thomson and Lorentz felt the rightness of "rendering landscape through the music of its people," as the composer has put it. The music therefore integrates material representative of the vastness and variety of American vernacular music, including a Calvinist psalm tune, cowboy songs, African-American blues, and World War I songs. The music is available in the form of a thirteen-minute suite for orchestra in six movements fashioned by the composer himself, and is quite effective apart from the film, in which it is actually covered at times by the narration.

The "Prelude" is an austere evocation of the virgin prairie (which now exists only in the imagination—and in music like this). "Pastorale (Grass)" is a short movement making much of canonic imitation (music in the manner of a round). The two middle movements in this documentary of the Plains landscape are the ones most clearly related to the "music of its people." "Cattle" blends reminiscences of three authentic cowboy tunes. The first one recalled is "I Ride an Old Paint" (Ex. 16-1).

Example 16–1. "I Ride Old an Old Paint"

Thomson's version of the tune is polyrhythmic—that is, it superimposes on the waltz rhythm of the tune itself a broader, augmented waltz rhythm as accompaniment. This treatment is extended to the second tune as well, "The Cowboy's Lament" (Ex. 16-2).

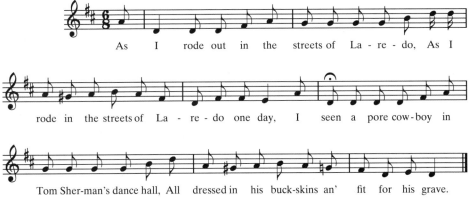

Example 16–2. "The Cowboys Lament"

Virgil Thomson. *Courtesy New York Public Library.*

The third is a brief recollection of "Whoopee Ti Yi Yo, Git Along, Little Dogies." (Ex. 16-3)

As I was a-walk-ing one morn-ing for pleas-ure, I spied a cow-punch-er a-rid-ing a-long:

Example 16–3. "Git Along, Little Dogies"

The fourth movement of the suite is "Blues," appropriately conventionalized and urbanized in the style of 1920s commercial jazz, to underscore the brash and ruinous exploitation of the land. Toward the end the music becomes progressively more dissonant (it is marked "Rough and violent"), and the themes more and more incoherent, climaxed by a final jangling chord that has as its underpinning, appropriately, the diminished triad. "Drought," the fifth movement, is a shorter, more somber version, in the minor mode, of the "Pastorale (Grass)" canon. The sixth and last movement, "Devastation," brings back the material of the first, to complete the archlike structure. It goes on to include a fugue exposition, and ends this documentation of "the most tragic chapter in American agriculture" with a gigantic tango on a stretched-out version of the fugue theme.

Two Films About the Small Town and the Big City

Aaron Copland wrote two film scores for the industry, the second of which was for the film version of *Our Town*, Thornton Wilder's play about life and death, the commonplace and the universal, dramatized in the lives of two families in a small New England town. Much of the music is available in an orchestral piece called simply *Our Town: Music from the Film Score*.

Quite different from the music for *Our Town* is the score Leonard Bernstein created for the Elia Kazan film *On the Waterfront* (1954). This film is about a longshoreman who is possessed of a sensitivity and moral integrity at odds with the harsh, brutal world in which he has always lived. The quiet opening melody, unaccompanied (one of the main themes of the score), has a spacious diatonic simplicity about it, until the introduction of the one "blue note" (a master stroke of inflection and timing) at once affects the whole feel of the music. For all the spareness of its opening, and its references to jazz (appropriate to the urban setting and the theme of alienation), it is soon apparent that this is a "symphonic film score," which has been adapted into a 23-minute symphonic suite.

Music with Dance

The "Americanization" of ballet began about this time, with the search for new material and fresh approaches. A forerunner of this was the aforementioned *Skyscrapers* of 1926. In 1938 Lincoln Kirstein commissioned for his Ballet Caravan a score from Aaron Copland, and brought into being the first "western" ballet.

A Western Ballet: *Billy the Kid*

Kirstein himself devised the scenario for *Billy the Kid*, around the short career of the legendary William Bonney (1859–81). It is given in the score as follows:

> The action begins and closes on the open prairie. The central portion of the ballet concerns itself with significant moments in the life of Billy the Kid. The first scene is a street in a frontier town. Familiar figures amble by. Cowboys saunter into town, some on horseback, others with their lassoes. Some Mexican women do a Jarabe which is interrupted by a fight between two drunks. Attracted by the gathering crowd, Billy is seen for the first time as a boy of twelve with his mother. The brawl turns ugly, guns are drawn, and in some unaccountable way, Billy's mother is killed. Without an instant's hesitation, in cold fury, Billy draws a knife from a cowhand's sheath and stabs his mother's slayers. His short but famous career had begun. In swift succession we see episodes in Billy's later life. At night, under the stars, in a quiet card game with his outlaw friends. Hunted by a posse led by his former friend Pat Garrett, Billy is pursued. A running gun battle ensues. Billy is captured. A drunken celebration takes place. Billy in prison is, of

course, followed by one of Billy's legendary escapes. Tired and worn in the desert, Billy rests with his girl. (Pas de deux.) Starting from a deep sleep, he senses movement in the shadows. The posse has finally caught up with him. It is the end.

The introduction, subtitled "The Open Prairie" in the score, is an evocation of the loneliness of the vast arid plains. When human figures do appear, in the first scene, their smallness is emphasized by the slightness and fragility of the little tune given to the solo piccolo, a tune based on the folk song "Great Granddad" (Ex. 16-4).

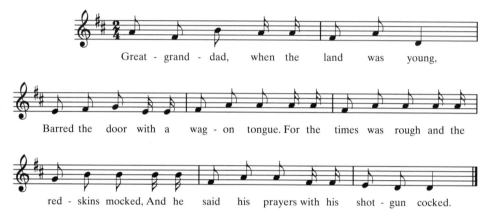

Great - grand - dad, when the land was young,

Barred the door with a wag - on tongue. For the times was rough and the

red - skins mocked, And he said his prayers with his shot - gun cocked.

Example 16–4. "Great Granddad"

The street scene is a collage of derivatives of actual cowboy tunes. There appears presently a distillation of "Git Along, Little Dogies," which alternates with phrases of "Great Granddad." The rough-edged, drunken effect is enhanced by occasional disagreements among the instruments as to what the right notes of the tune are, and by the hiccuping grace notes (Ex. 16-5).

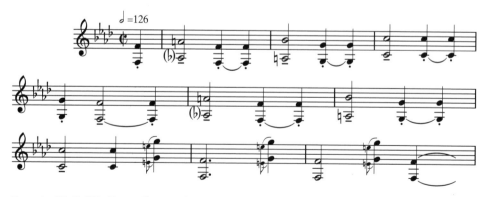

Example 16–5. "Git Along, Little Dogies"

We hear next "The Old Chisholm Trail" (Ex.16-6).

Come a - long, boys, and lis - ten to my tale, I'll

tell you of my troub - les on the old Chis - holm trail.

Example 16–6. "The Old Chisholm Trail"

There follows a long variation on the familiar "Good-bye, Old Paint," beginning with the chorus portion (Ex.16-7).

My foot in the stir - rup, my pon - y won't

stan',___ Good - by, old Paint, I'm a leav - in' Chey -

-enne. I'm a - leav - in' Chey - enne, I'm off for Mon -

-tan',___ Good - by, old Paint, I'm a - leav - in' Chey - enne.

Example 16–7. "Goodbye, Old Paint"

The next section ("at night, under the stars") is a quiet movement based on "Oh, Bury Me Not on the Lone Prairie." Except for an expressive lengthening of the stressed notes, it is very faithful to the original (Ex. 16-8).

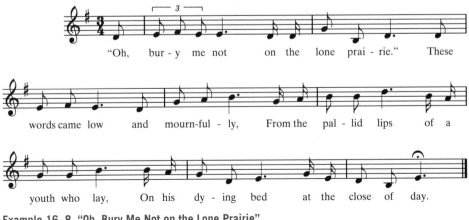

"Oh, bur - y me not on the lone prai - rie." These

words came low and mourn-ful - ly, From the pal - lid lips of a

youth who lay, On his dy - ing bed at the close of day.

Example 16–8. "Oh, Bury Me Not on the Lone Prairie"

There follows in the suite the music for the gun battle, and then the drunken celebration scene after Billy is captured. After this extended sequence, the music of the suite omits the escape scene, the music of the lovers' pas de deux in the desert, and the death of Billy at the hands of the posse, and goes directly to the recapitulation of the impressive "open prairie" music.

Music with Poetry
Music for Solo Voice

The song for a single voice with accompaniment has been an important form of musical expression since the Middle Ages. In America the art song, as it is called, has developed parallel to our vigorous popular song tradition. The distinction is not one of quality, but of the level of sophistication. The art song is not bound by the conventions that have long dictated to popular song its form, its degree of difficulty, its subject matter, and above all its approach to that subject matter. The accompaniment is more independent of the vocal line than in the popular song; it is more developed musically; and, most important, it is fully written out by the composer. Finally, the art-song composer usually works with a text that is more sophisticated and developed as poetry. American composers have set verses by Walt Whitman (one of the most frequently used poets), Sara Teasdale, Vachel Lindsay, Edwin Arlington Robinson, Archibald MacLeish, E. E. Cummings, Emily Dickinson, Tennessee Williams, Mark Van Doren, Wallace Stevens, Paul Goodman, and James Agee.

Five Sets of Songs for Voice and Piano

Songs tend to be composed in groups, most often to poems by the same author. From the wealth of American songs, five such groups for voice and piano are suggested as an introduction; most are settings of poems by significant American poets. The first is ***Four Poems by Edwin Arlington Robinson***, a series of settings by John Duke (1899–1984) of some of the concise and cryptic verse portraits of that American poet (1869–1935). "**Richard Cory**" is from Robinson's *Children of the Night*, written before the turn of the century.* "Richard Cory" and two others of the *Four Poems by Edward Arlington Robinson* are included on New World 80243.

The second is ***Blue Mountain Ballads***, a setting by Paul Bowles (b. 1910) of four poems by Tennessee Williams, of which "**Cabin**" and "**Heavenly Grass**" are suggested as an introduction. The third is *Eight Epitaphs*, settings by Theodore Chanler (1902–61) of extremely concise poems by Walter de la Mare. The fourth

*An interesting reinterpretation of the theme of "Richard Cory," without using the actual text, is Paul Simon's song of the same title. Its lyrics specify a somewhat conventionalized first-person narrator—"I work in his factory"—in a repeated chorus that blurs the sharp focus of Robinson's poem.

Samuel Barber. *Courtesy New York Public Library.*

is *Twelve Poems of Emily Dickinson* by Aaron Copland; and the fifth is *Hermit Songs*, settings of anonymous medieval Irish texts by Samuel Barber.

Solo Voice and Orchestra: *Knoxville: Summer of 1915*

For voice with orchestra, composers will often set a single longer text. This was the case with the sixteen-minute *Knoxville: Summer of 1915* by Samuel Barber, on a text by James Agee. An American masterpiece, it represents a rare coincidence of gifted poet and first-rate composer, each at the height of his powers. The text, a fragment of the prologue to Agee's novel *A Death in the Family*, consists of the wonder-filled observations, through the eyes of childhood, of an uneventful summer evening. Barber, a composer noted for his lyricism, manages to evoke an innocence and nostalgia that perfectly complement the text.

After a brief orchestral opening, a gently rocking, singsong-like theme carries the first portion of the text (Ex. 16-9, p. 320).

The passing of the streetcar becomes a major musical event in this setting, and a descriptive orchestral passage makes much of it. When it is past, the singer calls it forgotten; the orchestra, however, cannot forget it so easily, but mulls over the streetcar theme, ever more faintly, even after the singer has returned to the night that is "one blue dew." Upward-tending figures bring us back to the "rocking" theme once more, as our attention is drawn again to "parents on porches."

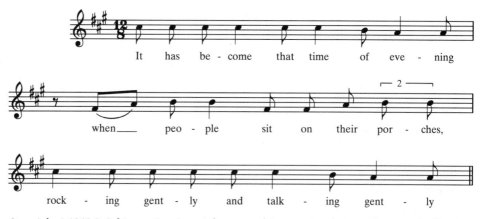

Example 16–9. Excerpt from *Knoxville: Summer of 1915*

The "dry and exalted noise of the locusts" is suggested fleetingly, and then there is a change of scene, to the "rough wet grass of the back yard." The woodwinds anticipate a new theme at this point—one based on a simple three-note motive that has a quality of "nothing in particular" and is repeated over and over, becoming the main building block of this section (Ex. 16-10).

Example 16–10. Excerpt from *Knoxville: Summer of 1915*

This innocent motive, stretched and intensified, carries us to the emotional climax of the work—even as an intensified and purified observation of the simple things around us leads inevitably to a realization of the untellable "sorrow of being on this earth . . . among the sounds of the night."

The benediction "May God bless my people . . ." is accompanied by a return to the music of the opening bars. Finally the rocking theme returns for the third time as the boy is taken in to be put to bed. The boy's unsatisfied quest to find out "who I am" is voiced calmly, in a high, detached *pianissimo*, whereupon the orchestra finishes softly with a final statement of the rocking theme.

Music for Chorus

As a nation we have grown up with choral singing. Psalm tunes were sung by whites and blacks both; the singing-schools early implanted among us a vigorous tradition of part-singing and fostered a native school of choral music; the urban singing societies of the nineteenth century saw to it that the major works of the cultivated tradition were heard; the singing of the Fisk Jubilee Singers and similar groups from other black colleges started the choral singing of spirituals among blacks and whites alike. Large-scale choral works were composed by native composers in the nineteenth century; *The Haymakers* (1857) by George F. Root, and *Hora Novissima* (1891–92) by Horatio Parker are representative.

Two contrasting works are suggested as an introduction to American choral music of the last half-century. The first is *The Peaceable Kingdom* (1936) by Randall Thompson (1899–1984), a sequence of choruses for unaccompanied mixed voices on biblical texts from Isaiah. The title is that of a famous piece of folk art by the American painter and Quaker preacher Edward Hicks (1780–1849), illustrating the millennial text of Isaiah 11:6–9, which begins, "The wolf also shall dwell with the lamb, and the leopard shall lie down with the kid; and the calf and the young lion and the fatling together; and a little child shall lead them." The music shows a mastery of choral writing and exhibits a wide range of textures and devices, including the biting dissonance of "their faces shall be as flames," the quiet desolation of "the paper reeds by the brooks," the delicious word-painting of "the trees of the field shall clap their hands," and the exuberant polyphony of "as when one goeth with a pipe to come into the mountain of the Lord."

A more recent choral work of a different character is a setting by Roger Sessions of Walt Whitman's poem "When Lilacs Last in the Dooryard Bloom'd." It is a 42-minute cantata for soprano, contralto, baritone, mixed chorus, and orchestra, completed in 1970. Whitman's poem is a dirge on the death of Lincoln. The first four stanzas form a kind of prologue, introducing Whitman's "trinity" of "Lilac blooming perennial and drooping star in the west,/ And thought of him I love." It also introduces the symbol of the mourning bird. The second section describes the procession of the coffin, and the tribute of the poet: the sprig of lilac, the perfume ("sea-winds") for the grave, and the pictures— broad Whitmanesque scenes with people—to adorn the burial-house. The third section is the bird's carol of death ("dark mother," "strong deliveress"), Whitman's retrospective view of a Civil War battlefield, and a final passing beyond and leave-taking.

Music Independent of Film, Dance, or Poetry
Three Sets of Short Works for Solo Piano
We begin with three sets of short piano pieces by George Gershwin, Aaron Copland, and Samuel Barber. Each is an *interpretation*, filtered, we might say, through the artistic temperament of each composer, of one or more of the vernacular idioms explored earlier in this book.

George Gershwin composed five piano *Preludes* in 1926. Of the five, three were published the next year—two bright movements flanking a central blues-like "Andante con moto e poco rubato," the best known of the three. The first Prelude uses the jazz-Latin rhythm of the Charleston (very close to a speeded-up tango) with variants. The catchy asymmetry of its rhythms is matched by simultaneous cross-relations in the chords (e.g., A-natural against A-flat), which constitute realizations in piano terms of the blue notes of the scale.

The second of Aaron Copland's *Four Piano Blues,* marked "soft and languid," dates from 1934. A highly attenuated interpretation of the blues, it is an instance of sophisticated play, with piquant poly-harmonies (in the first section) against stylized blues sonorities.

On the flyleaf of Samuel Barber's four *Excursions,* written in 1945, appears the following note: "These are 'Excursions' in small classical forms into regional American idioms. Their rhythmic characteristics, as well as their source in folk material and their scoring, reminiscent of local instruments, are easily recognized." The fourth is an excursion into the realm of the hoedown—a lively evocation of fiddle and banjo figuration. It is interesting to compare this with Louis Moreau Gottschalk's *The Banjo*, a similarly polished "translation" of banjo idioms into a piece for the concert hall a century earlier.

Chamber Music

In this concise edition we can but make a few suggestions for the exploration of American chamber music. For the string quartet, a good beginning might be the pleasantly soporific 11-minute *Lullaby for String Quartet* of George Gershwin (written about 1920). In contrast to this, there is the serious and energetic 23-minute String Quartet No. 3 (1939) by William Schuman (1910–92). For wind chamber music, a good introduction to the medium of the *woodwind quintet* (consisting of flute, oboe, clarinet, bassoon, and one brass instrument, the French horn) would be Samuel Barber's *Summer Music,* of 1956. In contrast to this would be the austere but impressive Concerto for Piano and Woodwind Quintet by Wallingford Riegger, composed in 1953.

The Symphony

The symphony evolved as an important musical form in the eighteenth century, and by the death of Beethoven (1827) it had come to represent the ultimate vehicle for the expression of serious musical thought in terms of "absolute" or "pure" music. American composers who wrote from the 1920s on regarded the symphony in this classical sense, and the typical American symphony since then has been a nonprogrammatic work, generally in several independent movements, and usually regarded as a vehicle for the composer's most serious musical thoughts.

The Third Symphony of Roy Harris

Roy Harris (1898–1979) is the last to be considered here of the five "commandos" active since the 1920s. He tended to be a peripatetic loner, imbued with a sense of his own destiny to express "the American spirit" and, like the poet Robert Frost, caught up in his own legend: that of a man close to the soil (for Frost, New England; for Harris, the Plains).* His undoubted gifts and his authentic contribution are best represented by his Third Symphony (1939), one of the strongest and most compact of American symphonies.

Seventeen minutes in length, it is in one continuous movement, though divided rather clearly into sections, as Harris has outlined for us.

I. Tragic—low string sonorities

II. Lyric—strings, horns, woodwinds (score p. 14, measure 139; ca. 5' in)

III. Pastoral—woodwinds with a polytonal string background (p. 23, measure 209, ca. 7' in)

IV. Fugue—dramatic

   A. Brass and percussion predominating (p. 57, measure 416, ca. 10' in)

   B. Canonic development of materials from Section II constituting background for further development of Fugue (p. 72, measure 505, ca. 12' in)

V. Dramatic—tragic

   A. Restatement of violin theme of Section I: tutti strings in canon with tutti woodwinds against brass and percussion developing rhythmic motif from climax of Section IV (p. 82, measure 567, ca. 13 1/2' in)

   B. Coda—development of materials from Sections I and II over pedal tympani (p. 93, measure 634, ca. 14 1/2' in)

The symphony is not programmatic in a very literal sense, but it will be noted that Harris has attached to each section a word whose significance goes beyond the purely musical. Like Arthur Farwell, who was one of Harris's early teachers and in a sense his "discoverer," Roy Harris has consistently and consciously sought the expression of human states of mind and even cultural values, especially those belonging to what he calls "the American spirit," according to his credo that the "creative impulse is a desire to capture and communicate feeling."

To become receptive to the unique qualities of this symphony, you would do well to purge your ears of complex sounds and sensitize yourself to the drama inherent in the simple but basic conflict between the major and the minor triad.

 **Example 16–11.**

*Roy Harris was indeed born in a log cabin in Lincoln County, Oklahoma, on Lincoln's birthday, but he moved to California at the age of five.

Harris makes much of this tension, changing through the movement of one voice (that entrusted with the third of the chord, the harmonic "coloring agent") the inflection of the entire chord (Ex.16-12),

Example 16–12. Excerpt from Harris, Third Symphony

or else sounding successively two versions of an implied chord third in a melodic line (Ex. 16-13).

Example 16–13. Excerpt from Harris, Third Symphony

Another Harris device is the juxtaposition of distantly related simple chords, as illustrated in Example 16-14, in an extended passage from near the climactic end of the symphony.

Example 16–14. Excerpt from Harris, Third Symphony

Harris in this work is primarily a harmonist; that is, harmony appears to be a prime motivating element of the music. For the most part the melodies themselves appear to grow out of basic chords with a few embellishing tones, as can be seen in the opening tune that the cellos play (Ex. 16-15)

Example 16–15. Excerpt from Harris, Third Symphony

or the melodic idea of the Lyric section, which assumes a number of forms but appears first as in Example 16-16.

Example 16–16. Excerpt from Harris, Third Symphony

Even the energetic fugue subject (Ex. 16-17) has as its skeleton a simple chord with embellishing subordinate harmonies, implying nothing beyond the basic three chords of D major known to every beginning folk guitarist.

Example 16–17. Excerpt from Harris, Third Symphony

The form of the work, according to Harris's own description, is sufficiently clear to allow the listener to follow the unfolding of its essential musical drama, even on first hearing. It has been, and continues to be, widely performed; Virgil Thomson has called it "to this day America's most convincing product in that form."

Two Other Contrasting American Symphonies

For further acquaintance, two other American symphonies are suggested. Here we confront a contrast between two modes of expression within the same broad tradition and in the same general period. The first is a fairly early work, the Symphony No. 2 ("Romantic") by Howard Hanson (1896–1981). Written in 1930, it was a virtual manifesto by its composer, intended in his words to be "lyrical and romantic in temperament," as opposed to what he saw as the tendency toward "cerebral" music. The next work is another Second Symphony—that of Roger Sessions, dating from 1946. The Sessions work is dense, complex, and dissonant; it fits the classic notion of "modern music," and the adjectives called up to describe it might well have been applied more than thirty years earlier to Stravinsky's *The Rite of Spring*. It is "modern music" in the good old-fashioned scandal-creating sense—the kind that used to cause riots among audiences in the days when concertgoers were less inhibited. Yet this four-movement work has strength, expressiveness, moments of fascinating, beguiling sound, and a "difficult" kind of beauty that is more apt to make its greatest impression in retrospect—after the sounds themselves have died away.

In Conclusion

Our survey of traditionally evolving classical music existing independent of the other arts began with the George Gershwin *Preludes for Piano*, and has ended with Roger Sessions's Second Symphony—a considerable journey showing the range of American music in the period 1920–1970 between two extremes of technical difficulty, accessibility, and compositional Americanism. The Gershwin speaks to us with wit, in an urbane and colloquial accent; the Sessions, devoid of any conscious regionalism or nativism, brings us into the rarefied atmosphere of the avant-garde that is our next concern. Backing up somewhat in time so as to follow the developments of our experimental and innovative wing through the twentieth century to date, we enter the restless, challenging arena—sometimes harsh, sometimes quixotic, but nearly always stimulating—of individualism and exploration that is the subject of the next two chapters.

FURTHER READING

General background

Copland, Aaron. *The New Music: 1900–1960*. New York: Norton, 1968.
        A revised and enlarged edition of the 1941 original.

Copland, Aaron, and Vivian Perlis. *Copland: 1900–1942*. New York: St. Martin's, 1984.
———. *Copland Since 1943*. New York: St. Martin's, 1989.
        These two collaborative volumes illuminate the period as well as the composer.

Reis, Claire R. *Composers, Conductors and Critics*. New York, 1955. Reprint (with new introduction by the author and preface by Aaron Copland). Detroit: Detroit Reprints in Music, 1974.

Largely a personal account; the author was director of the influential League of Composers for twenty-five years.

Rosenfeld, Paul. *Musical Impressions: Selections from Paul Rosenfeld's Criticism.* Edited and with an introduction by Herbert Leibowitz. New York: Hill & Wang, 1969.

A reprinting of some important and flamboyantly written essays by this controversial critic and enthusiastic supporter of new music.

Tawa, Nicholas E. *Serenading the Reluctant Eagle.* New York: Schirmer Books, 1984.

Perceptive and detailed overview of the period, including attention to the audiences for American music.

Thomson, Virgil. *American Music Since 1910.* New York: Holt, Rinehart, 1970.

Another essential book by a well-known participant and observer of the period.

Modern Music (1924–46).

This periodical, published by the League of Composers, with contributions from many of the important figures of the period, is an invaluable source; it is available (in a reprint) in many libraries.

Collections of essays by various authors, mostly composers

Boretz, Benjamin, and Edward T. Cone, eds. *Perspectives on American Composers.* New York: Norton, 1971.

Chase, Gilbert, ed. *The American Composer Speaks: A Historical Anthology, 1770–1965.* Baton Rouge: Louisiana State University Press, 1966.

Includes essays relevant to this chapter.

Cowell, Henry, ed. *American Composers on American Music: A Symposium.* Palo Alto, CA, 1933. Paperback reprint (with new introduction), New York: Frederick Ungar, 1962.

An essential collection.

Projects

1. Read Irving Lowens's essay "American Democracy and American Music (1830–1914)" in his *Music and Musicians in Early America* (New York: Norton, 1964). He describes American democracy as having two important components, equalitarianism and libertarianism, and American music as also being made up of two components, a popular music and a fine-art music. He sees, furthermore, "a certain correlation between the dominance of the equalitarian urge and the vitality of popular music, and a similar correlation between the dominance of the libertarian urge and the vitality of fine-art music." He declines, however, to comment on whether this correlation exists past the time of World War I. After careful reading and thought, arrive at your own assessment of the situation in America, either between the World Wars or since World War II. Does such a correlation exist, and if so, how it could be be illustrated? If it does not, what factors make it no longer applicable?

2. Interview a composer in your community who has written music for a film or a ballet, concerning the problems peculiar to the medium and the methods used to solve them.

3. Interview a concert pianist on the subject of American works in the active repertory. Prepare by becoming acquainted with at least three such works. (There are many touring artists, as well as artists-in-residence at colleges and universities. Advance planning, through consulting the offerings of local concert series and contacting the artist's management well ahead of time, will make this go more smoothly and be more productive.)

4. Interview a member of a professional string quartet on the subject of American string quartets in the active repertory. Prepare by becoming acquainted with at least three quartets by different composers. (There are several quartets that tour regularly, and quite a few attached as quartets-in-residence to some of the larger universities and music schools.)

5. Attend a concert that includes the performance of an American symphony. Write a brief essay on any aspect or aspects of it that you wish. Your own observations and impressions are important. As

supporting material, you may find it possible (if it is a local orchestra) to interview the conductor with regard to why he or she chose the particular symphony, some of the problems involved in its preparation, and the place of the American symphony (in general) in the active repertory of our symphony orchestras.

6. If there is a symphony orchestra in your community (a college or university orchestra, an amateur community orchestra, or a professional or semiprofessional orchestra), survey the entire season's programs; report on the percentage of American works included, and their type and vintage. You may want to include an interview with the orchestra's musical director on the subject of programming American music.

Notes

1. David Owens, "American Music's 'Golden Age,'" *The Christian Science Monitor*, May 12, 1982.
2. Roger Sessions, *Reflections on the Music Life in the United States* (New York: Merlin, 1956), 16.
3. Sessions, *Reflections*, 140. Paul Rosenfeld was an influential and controversial writer on the music of the time, enthusiastic about modern American music and active on its behalf. See Further Reading for this chapter.
4. Aaron Copland, *Music and Imagination* (Cambridge, MA: Harvard University Press, 1952), 104.
5. Aaron Copland, *The New Music* (New York: Norton, 1968), 161–62.

Chapter 17

Modernism I: New Ways with Old Tools

"To experiment and to explore has never been revolutionary for an American; he is unaffectedly at home in the unregulated and the untried." So wrote Henry and Sidney Cowell in the first chapter of their influential book on Charles Ives.[1] In this chapter and the next we shall trace this tradition of exploration and experiment from Ives to the present—a span of a century.

Charles Ives (1874–1954)

The Life and Career

For all of what appears to us as his modernity, and the relevance of many of his ideas today, Charles Ives's world was quite a different one from ours. Essentially his world was, and remained for him throughout his life, that of nineteenth-century America, which can be thought of as ending with World War I.* His boyhood in Danbury, Connecticut, a growing manufacturing town in the southwestern corner of the state, was of exceptional significance to his work; he drew on its impressions throughout the whole of his fairly short creative life. Pervading nearly all these impressions, according to Ives himself, was the extraordinary figure of his father. George Ives (1845–94) is somewhat sketchily known to us today, mainly through the recollections of his son Charles, but he was a well-trained musician of broad practical experience who also evidently had an inquiring mind and the spirit of an explorer, especially in musical acoustics. The youngest bandmaster in the Union army during the Civil War,[2] George returned to Danbury to become the versatile town musician. Yet Danbury, a microcosm of growing industrial America, held these musical activities in low esteem. Music, except for the most popular, earthy variety (such as country fiddling), was an effeminate pursuit and no fit profession for a man—this was the

---

*The period 1890 to 1918 has been called the Progressive Era. For an interesting interpretation of Charles Ives as a "progressive," in the tradition of Theodore Roosevelt, John Dewey, and others, see "Charles Ives's Place in American Culture" by Robert M. Crunden in *An Ives Celebration*, University of Illinois Press, 1977.

Charles Ives. *Photo by Frank Gerratana, Bridgeport* Herald. *Courtesy New York Public Library.*

prevailing attitude in nineteenth-century middle-class America. It was the burden of this attitude that Charles had to deal with all his life.[3]

We have Charles's word for many experiments in musical sound made by his father, and for many musical experiences, planned or unplanned, which made a lasting impression on him. There were two complementary sides to Charles Ives's early musical background. On one hand there was the curiosity, the open-mindedness toward tinkering and experimentation. On the other hand there was the solid grounding in musical rudiments that the boy received from his father and from others. Ives, in common with many other New England composers, was a church organist. He got his first permanent job at fourteen, and worked steadily at it for the next fourteen years in Danbury, New Haven, and New York City. Ives, then, was no musical amateur, no dilettante, in no sense any sort of "primitive." His innovative and experimental tendencies showed up early (as in his *Variations on "America"* for organ, which he wrote in 1891), but his father insisted that this sort of thing be supported by an underpinning of solid knowledge and technique.

At twenty Ives entered Yale. He studied with the renowned composer Horatio Parker, a strict taskmaster and academician. Though Ives said that he soon gave up showing Parker his more adventurous essays, it is now clear that Parker's teaching was essential to his growth as a composer.

It is unlikely that Ives ever considered becoming a professional musician. As a product of the Yale of his time, when he graduated in 1898 he went into business. For the next twenty years he was to pursue under full steam two careers at once: that of life insurance executive and that of composer. His creative and humane approach to the former (he pioneered in the field of estate planning and the training of insurance agents) made him and his partnership enormously successful.

Following the entry of the United States into the First World War in 1917 (a significant blow to Ives),* his health broke severely. As early as 1919, sensing and accepting the change in his life, Ives began to make plans for the future of some of his most cherished compositions. He finished the important *Concord* Sonata and had it published at his own expense. To accompany the sonata he wrote a prologue, four essays (on Emerson, Hawthorne, the Alcotts, and Thoreau), and a lengthy epilogue. Called *Essays Before a Sonata*, they constitute an artistic and philosophical manifesto and the single most valuable documentation of Ives's thought. Shortly afterward, he prepared an edition of *114 Songs*, again published at his own expense and distributed free of charge.

Ives was far from idle in his long retirement. He supported attempts to get his work, and that of other composers of new music, before the public. He supervised the editing of his own music by other devoted musicians, and it is thanks to their intensive and exhausting labors that much of Ives's music has reached the public. He disdained the copyrighting of his music, and exclaimed, in connection with the publication of part of his Fourth Symphony, "If anyone wants to copy or reprint these pieces, that's FINE! This music is not to make money but to be known and heard."[4] In later years, royalty checks were returned, or given away. When he received the Pulitzer Prize for his Third Symphony (written mostly in 1904; first performed in 1946), it is said that he told the committee, "Prizes are for boys. I'm grown up," and gave the money away.

The precise chronology of Ives's creative life, including the dating of many of his most important compositions, is still clouded with a degree of uncertainty that may never be dispelled. In the 1920s, when he was "discovered" and his works began to be performed, did he then add more of the dissonances and complexities for which they, and he, became famous? Did he "adjust" the chronology

*Ives was unreservedly opposed to war, but once his country was in, he worked in practical ways for the war effort— selling bonds (he advocated a new small-denomination bond of $50 so that more people could participate, in accord with his philosophy of involving the masses of common people, whether in art, politics, or business), and making a gift to the government of two completely equipped ambulances.

of some of his more adventurous works, assigning them earlier dates so as to validate the role of innovator which his younger contemporaries, especially Henry Cowell, were eager to bestow on him? When his health was still good, did he actually avoid going to concerts, or was he a more normal participant in the musical life of his time? Was he so completely uninfluenced by the then "modernists" such as Wagner, Debussy, Mahler, and Stravinsky of whom he was so contemptuously dismissive in his writings?

These questions only serve to caution us against a naive acceptance at face value of all aspects of the considerable Ives lore—a lore to which Ives himself was evidently willing to contribute. The questions are simply evidence of an understandable desire to know more about the complex and enigmatic man who left such a prodigious legacy of important works. The indisputable reality of Ives for us must be in the works themselves, and it is to these that we now turn.

The Music
Ives's Range as Revealed in the Songs
Ives wrote nearly a hundred and fifty songs, his output spanning his entire creative career. The songs are an excellent introduction to his music. Their range is large—musically, from the simple to the complex and dissonant, and textually, over nearly every aspect of human experience. Six songs, arranged in approximate order of difficulty and dimension, are suggested as a beginning.

"At the River" (1916), one of four songs based on hymn-tune themes published in the *114* collection, shows Ives reworking some of the musical material he likes best. The hymn by Robert Lowry is seen as it passes through the prism of Ives's unique musical imagination; it emerges fractured and colored with unusual harmonies.

"Tom Sails Away" (1917), with a text by Ives himself, is set in Ives's more expansive and dissonant "prose" style. One of three war songs in the *114*, it includes a quote from George M. Cohan's "Over There" in the vocal line, while the piano quotes a tune apparently always in the back of Ives's mind when it turned (as it so often did) to thoughts of his country—David Shaw's "The Red White and Blue" ("O Columbia, the Gem of the Ocean").

Some of the songs make a more philosophical comment on the human condition. In "**The Cage**" (1906) the voice intones Ives's short prose text, using mostly the noncommittal whole-tone scale, while the piano, in a rhythmically independent part, uses severe sonorities based on the interval of the perfect fourth, to depict the restless pacing of the leopard in the cage (Ex. 17-1).

Example 17–1. Opening measures of "The Cage"

A leop-ard went a-round his cage

Several songs reflect Ives's social idealism. The song Ives placed first in the *114* is a startling work, big in conception, which he titled "Majority" or "The Masses" (1914). The text, by Ives, expresses one aspect of his complex and sometimes contradictory idealism—a deep faith in democracy. "Majority" is a thesaurus of Ives's harmonic vocabulary; in addition to a few plain triads it uses extended chords built in thirds, fourths, and fifths, and also—possibly with programmatic connotations—appropriately massive, all-embracing tone "clusters" (chords built in seconds), two octaves in extent, combinations that strike not only the ear but the eye (Ex. 17-2).

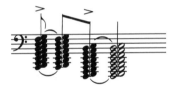

Example 17–2. Excerpt from "Majority"

Many of the recipients of the *114 Songs* were put off, or puzzled, by this opening song, with its strident dissonances. (The album was the butt of many contemporary jokes.) The fact is that Ives felt very strongly about the use of dissonance. It was, in a way, an indication for him of manliness in music. He complained vociferously about the "sissies, that couldn't stand up and take the full force of dissonance like a man." Recalling his boyhood, and the traumatic conflict between his natural bent for music (a form of activity dominated by "nice ladies") and his love of sports and natural honest regard for his peers (among whom music was a "sissy" thing to be spending one's time on), we can begin to understand at least one possible source of Ives's attitudes on the emasculation of art.

There was also a sense for Ives in which dissonance, if used in the service of an art that emphasizes "substance" rather than "manner" (a favorite Ivesian polarity), can be virtuous. In his *Essays Before a Sonata* he wrote, "Beauty in music is too often confused with something that lets the ears lie back in an easy chair." Ives was always contemptuous of any "easy way."

Finally, there are the longer narrative songs, which have their roots in the vernacular. "**Charlie Rutlage**" (1920 or 1921) is a cowboy ballad. The poem, attributed to D. J. "Kid" O'Malley, appeared in John Lomax's *Cowboy Songs*. In the middle three stanzas, the narrative itself, Ives reverts to melodrama; behind the recitation of the singer, the piano works up bits and pieces of "The Old Chisholm Trail" and other cowboy tunes, to a frenzied climax on the words "fell with him."

"General William Booth Enters Into Heaven"* (1914) is Ives's best-known song. The text is a portion of Vachel Lindsay's poem (minus six lines), which Ives read in a review. The drama and imagery of the imaginary scene put into play all of Ives's powers of musical characterization. The opening alliteration, "Booth led boldly with his big bass drum," furnishes Ives with a motive that begins the piece (Ex. 17-3) and also frames it; the ending is a faint dying away of the drumbeats in the distance. (One cannot help remembering here that Ives as a boy had played the drum parts in his father's band on the piano during their practices.)

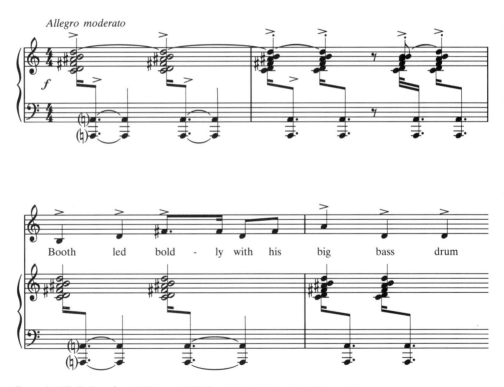

Example 17–3. Opening of "General William Booth Enters Into Heaven"

*General William Booth (1829–1912) was the founder, in England in 1878, of the Salvation Army, a religious philanthropic organization that officially began operations in the United States in 1880. As a means of reaching and helping the poor and downtrodden, the Salvation Army made considerable use of uniformed street bands, which became a familiar sight and sound in American cities.

Vachel Lindsay had noted that his poem was "to be sung to the tune of 'The Blood of the Lamb,'" but Ives chose instead a tune called "Fountain" ("There is a fountain filled with blood"), by Lowell Mason, whose hymn tunes he recalled frequently in his music (Ex. 17-4).

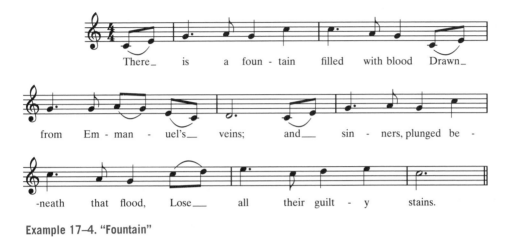

There_ is a foun - tain filled with blood Drawn_

from Em - man - uel's_ veins; and_ sin - ners, plunged be -

-neath that flood, Lose_ all their guilt - y stains.

Example 17–4. "Fountain"

The tune is overtly present only at the very end; prior to this, it is a kind of shadowy presence—Ives's settings of "Are you washed in the blood of the Lamb?" are based on a derivative of the tune, which is also present, unobtrusively, in the piano left hand under the words "Jesus came from the courthouse door." Other touches of text-painting are evident: the "banging banjo" tune, the trumpets, the memorable treatment of "round and round and round and round." "General William Booth" is a vivid musical drama in miniature on the theme of salvation.

Ives and Programmaticism

Ives was fundamentally a composer of program music. Much of his music is "about" something, often with its roots in a vivid impression of a scene. Two sets of orchestral compositions illustrate this particularly well, *Three Places in New England* and *Four New England Holidays*. In the latter, each of the holidays is associated with one of the seasons. For *The Fourth of July* (summer), we have Ives's own description:

> It's a boy's '4th. . . . His festivities start in the quiet of midnight before, and grow raucous with the sun. Everybody knows what it's like—if everybody doesn't—Cannon on the Green, Village Band on Main Street, fire crackers, shanks mixed on cornets, strings around big toes, torpedoes, Church bells, lost finger, fifes, clam-chowder, a prize-fight, drum-corps, burnt shins, parades (in and out

of step), saloons all closed (more drunks than usual), baseball game (Danbury All-Stars vs Beaver Brook Boys), pistols, mobbed umpire, Red, White and Blue, runaway horse—and the day ends with the sky-rocket over the Church-steeple, just after the annual explosion sets the Town-Hall on fire. All this is not in the music—not now.[5]

The multitude of impressions, seemingly random, crowding each other, superimposing themselves—all this is startlingly parallel to Ives's musical composition. Everywhere he looks there is something to record; he cannot get it all down. There is a quiet opening in which the violins and string basses begin "Columbia, the Gem of the Ocean," the tune that is to be the mainstay of the movement. There is a gradual gain of momentum, as bits and pieces of a dozen other tunes are heard; there is an explosion of fireworks; the band finally comes on with a great tumultuous rendition of the main theme, wrong notes, missed beats and all; there is a final explosion—and again quietness. The sound of the band in full swing in this movement is one of the most vividly realized moments in all of Ives's music: the tunes ("Columbia, the Gem of the Ocean," "The Battle Hymn of the Republic," and "Yankee Doodle" all at once), recklessly off key, are heard through the buzz and roar of the crowd noises. Originally thought unplayable, even by Ives himself, these are some of his grandest and most successful pages.

Simultaneity and Perspective

There are many manifestations of simultaneity in Ives's music. His impressionistic bent—his fidelity to his model, which was life itself as experienced—led him to try to render the sense of two or more things going on at the same time. In "Putnam's Camp" (the second of *Three Places in New England*) we hear one march beat established, and presently another—in a different tempo, marked "as a distant drum beat"—is heard superimposed. There are many examples of even more complex simultaneous meters in Ives's music, but this one is particularly clear, and has a direct relationship to his boyhood experience of hearing two bands marching in opposite directions around the park in Danbury, each playing a different tune, in a different key, and at a different tempo.

The concept of *perspective* finds its way into Ives's work as well—a sense of relative nearness and distance. Ives himself wrote: "As the distant hills, in a landscape, row upon row, grow gradually into the horizon, so there may be something corresponding to this in the presentation of music." This spatial sense can be heard in *The Unanswered Question, A Cosmic Landscape*, a work that has philosophical connotations. As Henry Cowell describes it,

The orchestra is divided, the strings playing very softly throughout offstage, representing the silence of the seers who, even if they have an answer, cannot reply; the wind group, on stage, is dominated by the trumpet, which asks the Perennial Question of Existence over and over in the same way, while "the Fighting Answers (flutes and other people)" run about trying in vain to discover the invisible, unattainable reply to the trumpet. When they finally surrender the search they mock the trumpet's reiteration and depart. The Question is then asked again, for the last time, and the "silence" sounds from a distance undisturbed.[6]

Ives's Attitude Toward the Performance of His Music

Charles Ives had as a young man the normal composer's desire to hear his works realized in performance. He occasionally hired individual performers to play with him, and groups of musicians from theater orchestras. But after some bitter and humiliating experiences with performances and readings, his attitude toward performance seemed gradually to change. His music itself became less and less geared to actual realization in sound—less in touch with practical problems. Concerning the music's difficulties and enormous complexities, Ives manifested a curiously dualistic attitude. On one hand, he sometimes freely castigated the laziness, indifference, and lack of ability of performers who would not come to grips with the difficulties of new or hard music. On the other hand, at times he seemed quite ready to acknowledge that some of his music was possibly unplayable. In the postface to the *114 Songs* he wrote: "Some of the songs in this book, particularly among the later ones, cannot be sung, and if they could, might perhaps prefer, if they had a say, to remain as they are; that is, 'in the leaf'—and that they will remain in this peaceful state is more than presumable."

His detachment sometimes dealt with a reality of music that transcended any actual realization in sound, a realization that he seemed actually to disdain at times. His famous "My God! What has sound got to do with music!" is his most succinct and often-quoted statement of this attitude. He continues cogently: "The waiter brings the only fresh egg he has, but the man at breakfast sends it back because it doesn't fit his egg cup. Why can't music go out in the same way it comes in to a man, without having to crawl over a fence of sounds, thoraxes, catguts, wire, wood, and brass?"[7]

Idealism versus Professionalism in Music

One aspect of Ives's idealism regarding art is his attitude toward professionalism, and what it does to an artist's independence and self-reliance. He wrote: "It may be possible that a day in a 'Kansas wheat field' will do more for [the American composer] than three years in Rome. . . . If for every thousand-dollar prize a potato field be substituted, so that these candidates of Clio can dig a little in real life, perhaps dig up a natural inspiration, art's air might be a little clearer."

And again, in a strong statement that summarizes his attitude: "Perhaps the birth of art will take place at the moment in which the last man who is willing to make a living out of art is gone and gone forever."[8]

Ives apparently never regretted his decision to go into business rather than become a professional musician, but saw a relationship between his daily work in the world and his art that tended to develop a "spiritual sturdiness" which showed itself in "a close union between spiritual life and the ordinary business of life." Emerson said: "There is virtue yet in the hoe and the spade, for learned as well as for unlearned hands." Ives said:

> I have experienced a great fulness of life in business. The fabric of existence weaves itself whole. You cannot set an art off in the corner and hope for it to have vitality, reality and substance. There can be nothing *exclusive* about a substantial art. It comes directly out of the heart of experience of life and thinking about life and living life. My work in music helped my business and work in business helped my music.[9]

Ives's Music and the World

Charles Ives's music was not suddenly discovered after his death; the process of bringing it before the public was a protracted one, and the list of hardworking and courageous protagonists in "the Ives case" is long and distinguished. Some recognition came as early as the 1920s. The 1930s was a time when it was mostly composers, and a few critics, who championed Ives's music.

The 1940s was the time when Ives's music began to be championed by important performers. A landmark event, touching off much of the success of the forties, was the first complete public performance of the *Concord* Sonata in 1939 by John Kirkpatrick. This performance marked the beginning of widespread favorable critical acclaim of Ives's music; Lawrence Gilman called the *Concord* Sonata "the greatest music composed by an American." In 1946 Lou Harrison premiered the Third Symphony; the next year it was awarded the Pulitzer Prize. By this time Ives's music was well on its way, and the 1950s saw its acceptance and acclaim by a far greater segment of the general musical public, who now had a chance to hear a fair amount of it.

For Ives the man there is no lack of admiration; his idealism, his grit, his humor, and his generosity have fired the imagination of succeeding generations. For the music there is admiration and love—tempered, for many who know it well, with certain reservations. Copland has pointed out the deleterious effect on

Ives's music of his having worked in virtual isolation—"cut off from the vitalizing contact of an audience." Elliott Carter points to the "large amounts of indifferentiated confusion," and is forced, reluctantly, to the conclusion that Ives's work often "falls short of his intentions." Virgil Thomson has pointed out the need to distinguish purely musical quality from the wealth of not-strictly-musical associations that have grown up around Ives's work: "When time shall have dissolved away his nostalgias and ethical aspirations, as they have largely done for Beethoven and for Bach and even for the descriptive leitmotifs of Wagner, what sheer musical reality will remain in Ives's larger works?"

A good deal, one suspects. Ives's most cogent, most nearly perfect realizations—many of the songs, "The Unanswered Question," "The Housatonic at Stockbridge," practically all the "Holidays"—have been indispensable to our music. Virgil Thomson, speaking for all subsequent composers, hailed Charles Ives as, "whether we knew it or not, the father of us all."

Henry Cowell (1897–1965)

Henry Cowell came into the world gifted with an observant, eagerly absorbing mentality that was able to reap the full benefit of growing up in the richly polyglot atmosphere of the San Francisco Bay area just after the turn of the century—the same milieu that a generation earlier had nurtured Jack London and Gertrude Stein. Unencumbered by even modest means, and free of any predetermined set of cultural values, Cowell was free to accept his musical stimulus where he found it—in Irish folk tunes (from his family), Gregorian chant (from a neighbor), Oriental music, and rural American hymnody (from early sojourns in Kansas and Oklahoma). In San Francisco, young Cowell heard Chinese opera more frequently than Italian. When he got hold of a battered old upright piano, he soon found he had an instrument that would open up new possibilities, and he began experimenting. In 1912, at the age of fifteen, he played in public in San Francisco a piece called *The Tides of Manaunaun*; it was a prelude to an opera he was writing based on Irish mythology. Manaunaun was the maker of great tides that swept through the universe; to convey the sense of this vast motion, Cowell, interestingly enough, hit upon the same device that Ives, on the other side of the continent and at about the same time, was using to convey the sense of the masses in "Majority"—huge groups of tones sounded together that could only be played with the entire forearm. These became known as "tone clusters." Cowell used them in many of his piano works—became notorious for them, in fact—but nowhere more effectively than in this very early piece (Ex. 17-5).

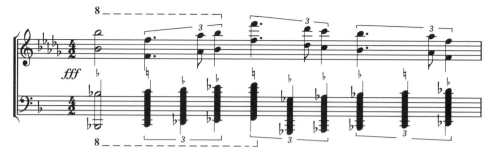

Example 17–5. Opening of *The Tides of Manaunaun*

By the time he was twenty, Cowell had composed 199 pieces, including an opera and a symphony. Convinced of the value of some systematic study, he found an ideal person to supervise it in Charles Seeger, then teaching at the University of California. Cowell's formal education had ended with the third grade, but he was a voracious learner: at the age of twenty he was seeing Seeger for lessons in music every morning in Berkeley, studying English with Samuel Seward every afternoon at Stanford, working at night as a janitor—and writing a book! Cowell went east to New York for further study, and began appearing in concerts playing his own works on the piano. Between 1923 and 1933 he made five important tours of Europe (including a trip in 1928 to the Soviet Union, which he was the first American composer to visit).

There are many sides to Cowell's work. There is Henry Cowell the teacher—one of our best, and an important influence on such composers as Lou Harrison, John Cage, and other free spirits of the musical "left wing."

There is Henry Cowell the tireless worker for new music, and new ideas in music. In 1927 he founded the important periodical *New Music Quarterly*, which published a great many new scores (though not a note of his own). It was through this that he met Charles Ives, becoming his first important discoverer, his lifelong promoter, with his wife, Sidney Cowell, his first biographer, and after Ives's death his musical executor.

There is Henry Cowell the imaginative theorist and inventor, author of the slim but important volume called *New Musical Resources* (1930).

There is Henry Cowell the student of a worldwide range of musical cultures. In 1931–32 he studied comparative musicology in Berlin with Professor Eric Moritz von Hornbostel. Oriental music he had already heard a great deal of in his youth. His works subsequently bore witness to the detailed study of musical cultures as widely separated as those of Japan, Persia, and Iceland.

And finally there is, as our major concern, Henry Cowell the prolific composer. We left him as the fifteen-year-old composer of a remarkable piano piece. His subsequent output was as varied as the interests of the man himself. The experimental works—those that place him in this chapter as one of our innovators—were for the most part early works. Of these, the short works for piano are the most accessible and open up the most interesting possibilities.

About 1923 Cowell began to produce works calling for the performer to play directly on the strings of the piano. In *Aeolian Harp* (1923, named after a harplike instrument whose strings are played upon by the wind) the performer silently depresses the keys of the successive chords, releasing their dampers; the strings are then swept with the other hand, in the manner of the autoharp. They are also plucked. In *The Banshee* (1925) the dampers are all released, and the performer, standing in the crook of the piano, plays directly on the strings—at times sweeping across them in various ways, at times sweeping lengthwise on one or more strings, at times plucking them.

Still other possibilities were explored in a piece written about 1930 called *Sinister Resonance*. It involves further direct manipulation of the strings; playing several pitches on one string by "stopping" the string; "muting" strings with the hand; and playing harmonics by lightly touching the strings at one of the nodes while they are played from the keyboard. The muted, damped, and otherwise manipulated sounds of the piano strings in *Sinister Resonance* led directly into the sounds of the "prepared piano" of John Cage.

Around 1940 Cowell discovered (as had Virgil Thomson before him) the tradition of native religious music, which began with the New England singing-school masters and continued into the rural South and Midwest in shape-note music—the tradition described in chapter 8. This interest resulted in a series of compositions known by the title *Hymn and Fuguing Tune*, written for various combinations.

In 1956–57 Cowell went on a world tour, sponsored in part by the Rockefeller Foundation and the United States government. He spent a considerable amount of time in Iran and in Japan, both studying their music and bringing a knowledge of our music to them. This marked the beginning of a series of works based on Persian music (*Persian Set*, 1957, and *Homage to Iran*, 1959) and Japanese music (*Ongaku* for orchestra, 1957). Later his interest expanded to include the music of Iceland; his Symphony No. 16 (1962) is subtitled *Icelandic*. In these works, as in the works inspired by American and Celtic music, Cowell only rarely uses traditional tunes, but instead writes his *own* Persian, Japanese, or Icelandic music. Always skillfully scored, even to suggesting the timbres of national instruments or the voicing of national choral singing, it nevertheless has a flavor of pleasant musical tourism, of the same type that issued forth in the nineteenth century when Russian and French composers were writing Spanish music.

Henry Cowell's mind was inventive, but quite literal, at times almost child-like. He worked prodigiously at a complicated craft in an uncomplicated way. It was his role to suggest new sound resources without troubling deeper musical waters. But because of his relentless efforts in so many directions (as composer, publisher, editor, impresario, teacher, propagandist, and traveling ambassador), American music and American composers are much in his debt.

Lou Harrison and John Cage

Henry Cowell was the first American composer to remind us that the West Coast of the United States is, culturally as well as geographically, farther from Europe and closer to Asia than is New York. The orientation of our East Coast to Europe continues to survive our Colonial period (which lasted much longer culturally than politically); our West Coast, with more tenuous European ties and a greater variety of influences, has been more open to choices. In music, this openness to a large vocabulary of sounds, which we first noted in Cowell, has been carried further by Lou Harrison and John Cage, both of whom were at one time students of Cowell.

Lou Harrison (b. 1917 in Portland, Oregon) went east in the 1940s to become, for a time, an important part of the New York musical scene. But he has always remained a West Coast man in his independence of "establishment" music and thinking. Harrison has been a dancer, painter, playwright, conductor, and maker of musical instruments.

There have been three main thrusts of Lou Harrison's work, and these are interrelated. The first is his cultivation of percussion instruments, showing up as early as 1941 in his *Fugue* for Percussion, and through the years in a variety of ensemble pieces and concertos. The second is his interest in a return to the pure intonation of just intervals (a topic that will be discussed in connection with Harry Partch), as exemplified in his *Four Strict Songs for Eight Baritones and Orchestra*, on his own text, patterned after the "making-things-right-and-good-again songs of the Navaho." The third is his knowledge of and love for the music of the Pacific Basin, particularly that of the Indonesian *gamelan*, an ensemble of percussion instruments. Lou Harrison and his colleague William Colvig have built and performed on their own gamelans, each with its own unique name and tuning. Harrison has often combined in his works Oriental and Western instruments, as in his *Pacifika Rondo* of 1963, and in many smaller pieces. His ***Threnody for Carlos Chávez*** (1978) for solo viola and gamelan is typical of his wide-ranging musical concerns, since it combines Javanese and European medieval practices with engaging sonorous results. These works stand as unique manifestations of the inclusiveness and breadth of spirit characteristic of Lou Harrison.

Another of Cowell's students, John Cage (1912–92), was a West Coast composer who formed an early attachment to percussion instruments and to the dance. This latter came about partly because some of his earliest jobs consisted of playing for dance classes and partly because in the 1930s, when it was difficult otherwise to find an audience for percussion music, dancers were eager for new sounds to accompany their new choreographic creations. It was in Seattle that Cage first hit on the idea of the "prepared piano." A dancer had requested a score for a new ballet, *Bacchanale*, to emphasize percussion. Since the company could not afford a whole percussion orchestra, Cage (who was the son of an inventor) followed up on some of Cowell's experiments and modified the sound of a grand piano by muting or damping the strings with various objects, thereby in effect creating a percussion orchestra inside the piano, at the control of a single player. This was in 1938, and it was followed by many works for prepared piano, mostly for the dance. In 1946–48, he wrote the well-known *Sonatas and Interludes for Prepared Piano*.

Beginning in the 1950s, electronics, with its new sound sources, engaged him. Also, Oriental teachings, as he understood and interpreted them, were leading him in the direction of indeterminacy as to musical results, and an abdication of the role of composer. These developments belong to the next chapter.

Harry Partch (1901–74)

There was another Westerner, born at the turn of the century, who also struck out on his own—the embodiment, as a musician, of Blake's dictum "I must create a system, or be enslaved by another man's." Harry Partch, working for years alone and virtually unknown, rejected three of the most basic elements of his immediate musical heritage: conventional instruments, a scale of twelve equidistant notes to an octave, and counterpoint. His musical influences, as he himself listed them, are, like Cowell's, varied and typical of the West: "Christian hymns, Chinese lullabyes, Yaqui Indian ritual, Congo puberty ritual, Cantonese music hall, and Okies in California vineyards." Yet Partch did not become a "collector," either of exotic instruments or exotic systems. Instead, he found what he needed as a base for his own music in two ancient ideas that had become eclipsed in Western music: purely tuned intervals and monophony (the singing or reciting of a single voice). And he soon saw that his return to pure intervals would draw him into another endeavor—that of building his own instruments.

Harry Partch, the son of apostate former missionaries to China, was born in Oakland, California, but soon moved with his family into the southwestern desert area of Arizona and New Mexico. His father, who understood Mandarin Chinese, worked for the immigration service, moving frequently from one small railroad-junction town near the Mexican border to another. Thus the boy grew up, lonely and largely self-educated, among the polyglot people of "the declining years of the Old West," as he puts it—including the Yaqui Indians, the Chinese, and the hoboes and prostitutes his father and mother occasionally brought home. He read a great deal, enjoying Greek mythology especially. Musical instruments, obtained by mail order, were in the household. At fourteen Partch began to compose seriously. At twenty-one he found Hermann von Helmholtz's famous book on musical acoustics, *On the Sensations of Tone*, and began writing works using pure, or "just," intonation. At around twenty-six he wrote the first draft of his own treatise and manifesto, *Genesis of a Music*. At twenty-eight he burned, in a big iron stove, all the music he had written up to that time, and set out with determination and (as he describes it) "exhilaration" on new paths.

His first instruments were an Adapted Viola (a viola to which has been attached a longer cello fingerboard, marked so as to facilitate playing the smaller just intervals), an Adapted Guitar, a Chromelodeon (an adapted reed organ), and a Kithara (a lyre-shaped plucked-string instrument with movable bridges, allowing for a sliding tone). With these Partch wrote his first major work, *U.S. Highball*. "A hobo's account of a trip from San Francisco to Chicago," it is to a great extent autobiographical, for Partch's life between 1935 and 1943 consisted in large measure of hoboing, dishwashing, WPA jobs, and wandering. *U.S. Highball* has a Subjective Voice (the protagonist) and several Objective Voices, whose words consist of "fragments of conversations, writings on the sides of boxcars, signs in havens for derelicts, hitchhikers' inscriptions"—all of which Partch had recorded in a notebook he always carried during his wanderings.

In succeeding years Partch built many new instruments, and rebuilt many earlier ones. The percussion instruments feature various marimbas. The Marimba Eroica is the largest; its lowest tone, below any of the notes on the piano, is produced by a Sitka spruce plank more than seven feet long suspended over a resonator eight feet long and four feet high. The smallest and softest is the Mazda Marimba, made of twenty-four light bulbs "with their viscera removed," yielding a sound, according to Partch, like the "bubbling of a coffee percolator." Other percussion include a Gourd Tree, Cone Gongs, and the bell-like Cloud-Chamber Bowls—the tops and bottoms of twelve-gallon glass carboys suspended. Appealing in sound, his instruments, especially as he redesigned them, came to have a great visual appeal as well; they are very much "part of the set" of a Partch performance, which, in accord with the composer's ideas of corporeal music, has always, and increasingly in the later works, a strong element of theater in it. The players themselves (who must be specially trained) are also aware at all times that they are "on stage."

Partch's *Genesis of a Music* (first published, after many drafts, in 1947, with a revised and enlarged second edition completed in 1972) is both manifesto and treatise. Unlike Cowell's earlier and smaller comparable work *New Musical Resources*, it is not a suggestion of what *might* be done but a painstakingly thorough description of what Partch spent a lifetime doing—together with his reasons for doing so. The theoretical portions include, in terms of the *ratios* that Partch used to express intervals, a complete description and derivation of his scale of forty-three tones to the octave.

It takes a bold, energetic, and singularly dedicated and single-minded composer to develop and commit himself to a system of intonation impossible to produce on existing instruments, to build new instruments to the new specifications, and then to create new works exploiting the resources of both the intonation and the instruments. The most poignant limitation in such a lifework is that Partch's music can be performed only by specially trained performers, and only on his own instruments—one of a kind, and difficult and expensive just to maintain, let alone duplicate. Although a few recordings of his works have been made in the late 1990s, most available recordings were made when Partch was still alive. It is not certain what the future of his music—*live*—will be. But it is likely that this was of little concern to Harry Partch. He had done his work. In 1972 he wrote: "I am not trying to institute a movement in any crypto-religious sense. If I were, *idea* would soon turn into something called form, and the world is already plagued with its ephemera. . . . [The pathbreaker's] path cannot be retraced, because each of us is an original being."[10]

Pure Intonation: A Postscript

It is interesting to note that three of the individualists treated in this chapter were concerned with pure, or just, intonation—that is, with the musical intervals resulting from simple and rational mathematical frequency ratios, in contrast with the irrational ratios and the "clouding" of all intervals except the octave that result from the compromise of twelve equal-tempered semitones to the octave. Cowell dealt theoretically with the concept in his *New Musical Resources*. Lou Harrison has written music to be played in pure intonation, and Partch committed himself to it wholly. There are others who have further explored it, including Ben Johnston (b. 1926), who studied with Partch. Johnston's *Sonata for Microtonal Piano* (first performed in 1965) uses a piano specially tuned to a complex scale of eighty-one different pitches, only seven of which appear in octave duplications.

Edgard Varèse (1883–1965)

In the matter of putting genuinely new sounds and sound sources at the disposal of an expressive purpose, Harry Partch and Edgard Varèse have been our two most original composers. Both were dissatisfied with traditional instruments and with the tempered scale of twelve equal half steps to the octave (Partch rejected these instruments outright, while Varèse, whose ties to European tradition were stronger, used both while awaiting the development of technology that would furnish him with new sound sources). Both began composing afresh in their thirties, their earlier output having been destroyed—Partch's deliberately, and Varèse's probably at least partly so. But there were fundamental differences. Partch was committed to a very "corporeal" concept of music; the presence of a musician performing was a vital part of the artistic transaction, which always took place in terms of something staged. Varèse conceived of his music as structures in sound; the human performer was dispensable.

Varèse was born in Paris and studied composition there. He did not come to the United States until the age of thirty-two; at that point he started his career afresh, to such an extent that he is universally considered an American composer. In keeping with this identification, he used the spelling "Edgar" in publishing most of his works, though later he returned to the French form "Edgard."

Varèse himself described some of his conceptions of music. He strongly advocated composers' making use of the latest scientific developments.

> . . . . If you are curious to know what . . . a machine could do that the orchestra with its man-powered instruments cannot do, I shall try briefly to tell you: whatever I write, whatever my message, it will reach the listener unadulterated by "interpretation." . . . after a composer has set down his score on paper by means of a new graphic, similar in principle to a seismographic or oscillographic notation, he will then, with the collaboration of a sound engineer, transfer the score directly to this electric machine. After that anyone will be able to press a button to release the music exactly as the composer wrote it—exactly like opening a book.[11]

This remarkable forecast of electronic music was written in 1939. (Twenty years later, Varèse qualified somewhat his apparent rejection of the performer.)

Varèse conceived of music as spatial, and of musical sounds as analogous to masses in space, with quasi-geometrical characteristics. In a lecture given in 1936 he described his projected "corporealization" of music in a startlingly illustrative paragraph.

When new instruments will allow me to write music as I conceive it, the movement of sound-masses, of shifting planes, will be clearly perceived in my work, taking the place of linear counterpoint. When these sound-masses collide, the phenomena of penetration or repulsion will seem to occur. Certain transmutations taking place on certain planes will seem to be projected onto other planes, moving at different speeds and at different angles. There will no longer be the old conception of melody or interplay of melodies. The entire work will be a melodic totality. The entire work will flow as a river flows.[12]

Four pieces are suggested as illustrative of the music of a composer who has been described as "the first astronaut." *Hyperprism* (1922–23) is the shortest—only four minutes. For this work he arrived at a type of instrumentation he was to use, with various additions, in three more works—an orchestra of eight to a dozen wind instruments and a large percussion section of four to six players playing many different instruments.

In *Intégrales* (1924–25) we find the majority of Varèse's characteristic musical traits most fully exemplified. There are *sustained* sounds, *sliding* sounds, and certain favorite percussion sounds: a snare drummer executing rudimentary flams and rolls (which somehow inject a disturbingly mundane element into the music), little scraping noises, various noises of rattles and ratchets, the sounds of small hollowish wooden objects being hit (castanets, wood blocks, Chinese temple blocks, coconut shells), and of course cymbals and gongs.

In 1928 Varèse went to France for five years, during which time he completed only one work, the famous *Ionisation* (1930–31). For this five-minute work he used nothing but percussion—an orchestra of thirteen percussionists playing thirty-seven instruments (though not all at once).

There followed a hiatus in his composing. He lived in the West for a while, returned to New York for the war years, and did some work on a vast project called *Espace* ("Space"). In theme it was the counterpart of Beethoven's Ninth Symphony, or Ives's "Majority" ("Theme: TODAY, the world awake! Humanity on the march. . . . Millions of feet endlessly tramping, treading, pounding, striding, leaping"). Varèse at one time imagined a performance of it broadcast simultaneously from all the capitals of the world, with a choir in each singing in its own language!

Varèse's eagerly awaited liberation from the limitations of the human performer and traditional acoustical instruments came with the opportunity to create eight minutes of sound to be projected literally *in space* through the medium of 425 loudspeakers in the Philips Pavilion designed by Le Corbusier for the Brussels International Exposition in 1958. (*Poème électronique* was actually the title of the entire concept, which included visual projects designed by Le Corbusier; the pavilion was simply the "vessel" to contain both.) Here the sound masses (a montage made up of a combination of manipulated "real" and synthesized sound carefully assembled by Varèse, who worked for eight months in the Philips laboratory in Eindhoven, Holland) could literally move in space, thanks to a three-track tape and an elaborate "routing" of the sound channels through the maze of speakers installed in the roof of the pavilion.

The technology that finally made *Poème électronique* possible had already, in the post–World War II years, added a lively new electronic wing to the edifice of music, from which much was hoped for by many. It is to these developments, together with some contemporaneous new aesthetic concepts, that we now turn.

FURTHER READING

General

Lederman, Minna. *The Life and Death of a Small Magazine (Modern Music, 1924–1946)*. I.S.A.M. Monograph no. 18. Brooklyn: Institute for Studies in American Music, 1983.

> Valuable record of a periodical important to American music between the wars; the index makes it a useful reference work.

Mead, Rita. *Henry Cowell's New Music 1925–1936: The Society, the Music Editions, and the Recordings*. Ann Arbor: UMI Research Press, 1981.

> An invaluable documentation of the impressive activities of Cowell and others, so crucial to the experimental wing of American music at this time.

Nicholls, David. *American Experimental Music, 1890–1940*. Cambridge: Cambridge University Press, 1990.

Thomson, Virgil. *American Music Since 1910*. New York: Holt, Rinehart, 1970. Paperback ed., 1972.

> In addition to supplying insightful background, this work has summaries and assessments of Ives, Varèse, and Cage.

Yates, Peter. *Twentieth-Century Music: Its Evolution from the End of the Harmonic Era into the Present Era of Sound*. New York: Random House, 1967.

> A readable and perceptive introduction by a Los Angeles author, lecturer, and critic who has produced concerts of new music and wrote regularly for *Arts and Architecture* and other periodicals. Relevant are chapters on Ives and Cage, and two on "The American Experimental Tradition."

Collections of writings by or interviews with composers

Chase, Gilbert, ed. *The American Composer Speaks*. Baton Rouge: Louisiana State University Press, 1966.

> Included are pieces by Ives, Cowell, Cage, Partch, and Varèse.

Cowell, Henry, ed. *American Composers on American Music: A Symposium*. Palo Alto, CA, 1933. Paperback reprint (with new introduction). New York: Frederick Ungar, 1962.

> The prototype of such collections, this excellent "symposium" of the early thirties, focusing on the contemporary scene, includes thirty-one articles on American composers and on general tendencies.

Gagne, Cole, and Tracy Caras, eds. *Soundpieces: Interviews with American Composers*. Metuchen, NJ: Scarecrow, 1982.

Schwartz, Elliott, and Barney Childs, eds. *Contemporary Composers on Contemporary Music*. New York: Holt, Rinehart, 1967.

This collection covers the European scene as well, but Part 2 deals with "Experimental Music and Recent American Developments." There is some inevitable overlap between this collection and Chase, *The American Composer Speaks*.

Charles Ives

Burkholder, J. Peter. *Charles Ives: The Ideas Behind the Music*. New Haven: Yale University Press, 1985.

Cowell, Henry and Sidney. *Charles Ives and His Music*. New York: Oxford University Press, 1955. Rev. ed. (paperback), 1969.

> Always valuable as the first biography (the section written by Sidney Cowell) and the first important study of the music (written by Henry Cowell), this is an excellent introduction to both, by an eminent composer and his wife who knew Ives personally and helped to bring his music before the public over a period of many years.

Hitchcock, H. Wiley. *Ives: A Survey of the Music*. I.S.A.M. Monograph no. 19. Brooklyn: Institute for Studies in American Music, 1977.

> For those interested in the music itself, this brief survey is an excellent place to start.

———, and Vivian Perlis, eds. *An Ives Celebration*. Urbana: University of Illinois Press, 1977.

> A collection of essays growing out of an Ives Festival-Conference in 1974, the year of the Ives centennial.

Ives, Charles, *Essays Before a Sonata and Other Writings*. New York: Norton, 1961; paperback, 1964.

———. *Charles E. Ives: Memos*. Ed. John Kirkpatrick. New York: Norton, 1972.

> These two books are indispensable primary sources for Ives's life, work, and, most important, thought. With some regrettable exceptions (such as the "Conductor's Note" to the Fourth Symphony) they contain nearly everything Ives wrote. The *Memos*, carefully and knowledgeably edited, contain some almost equally valuable appendices including an annotated list of all Ives's compositions.

Perlis, Vivian, ed. *Charles Ives Remembered: An Oral History*. New Haven: Yale University Press, 1974.

> This book consists of transcripts of recorded reminiscences by many who knew Ives: family members, business associates, friends, neighbors, and of course musicians, many of them well known. There are many photos, and reproductions of manuscript pages and programs. The actual voices of some of the contributors may be heard in excerpts from this oral history in the album *Charles Ives: The 100th Anniversary* (Columbia M4–32504).

Rossiter, Frank R. *Charles Ives and His America*. New York: Liveright, 1975.

> A well-researched biography—and more; it also examines the issues faced, and raised, by Ives as an artist in early-twentieth-century America. Rossiter writes: "I became more and more convinced that the Ives Legend which has grown up around him gives a very imperfect picture of the man. I think that the key to an understanding of his place in American culture lies in his extreme artistic isolation."

Henry Cowell

Cowell, Henry. *New Musical Resources*. New York, 1930. New ed. (with preface and notes by Joscelyn Godwin). New York: Something Else Press, 1969.

> The importance of this youthful treatise, at times penetrating and prophetic and at times naive, has been discussed in the chapter.

Lichtenwanger, William. *The Music of Henry Cowell: A Descriptive Catalog*. I.S.A.M. Monograph no. 23. Brooklyn: Institute for Studies in American Music, 1986.

Manion, Martha L. *Writings about Henry Cowell: An Annotated Bibliography*. I.S.A.M. Monograph no. 16. Brooklyn: Institute for Studies in American Music, 1982.

Mead, Rita H. "The Amazing Mr. Cowell." *American Music* 1, no. 4 (Winter 1983).

Saylor, Bruce. *The Writings of Henry Cowell: A Descriptive Bibliography*. I.S.A.M. Monograph no. 7. Brooklyn: Institute for Studies in American Music, 1977.

Other composers (in the order in which they appear in the chapter)

Cage, John. *Silence.* Middletown, CT: Wesleyan University Press, 1961; Paperback. Cambridge, MA: MIT Press, 1966.

> The best single source of Cage's writing and lectures, including material from 1939 to 1961. (For additional material on Cage's later work see chapter 18.)

Partch, Harry. *Genesis of a Music.* 2d ed. New York: Da Capo, 1974.

> In this 500-page volume Partch sets forth the aesthetic and acoustical basis of his work, and describes his instruments (which are illustrated by photographs) and his compositions. Aside from his music and his instruments, this book is Partch's major work. He worked on it for twenty years before the first edition was published in 1947. The second edition is enlarged by a new preface; by chapters on new instruments built after 1947 and on the background of six of his major works; by some important appendices listing all the music; and by a chronology of the instruments.

Ouellette, Fernand. *Edgard Varèse.* Translated by Derek Coltman. New York: Orion, 1968.

> A biography that takes up the works in the context of Varèse's life. With its list of works and very extensive bibliography, which includes a great number of periodical articles and interviews, this "first biography" is informative despite its effusively worshipful tone.

Varèse, Louise. *Varèse: A Looking-Glass Diary.* Vol. 1: *1883–1928.* New York: Norton, 1972.

> Rich in detail as in insight, this account by Varèse's wife is far more objective than the Ouellette biography.

Projects

1. Write a brief paper on Charles Ives as business executive, including an account of his important contributions to the life insurance business. Refer to his innovative concepts and his writings (such as his pamphlet *The Amount to Carry—Measuring the Prospect*).

2. From the approximately 120 songs by Charles Ives, most of which are available in print and many of which are recorded, make up a list of twelve (excluding the ones treated in this chapter) and write program notes for a hypothetical performance of them, "cataloguing" them in some manner similar to that used in this chapter.

3. Review thoughtfully Ives's statements about "idealism versus professionalism in music" in the section so labeled in this chapter, and read Ives more fully in this regard (starting with the complete Epilogue of the *Essays*). In what ways do you agree or disagree with his stance? Is this stance possible today? Make this the subject of a brief talk or paper.

4. Henry Cowell and Harry Partch both began fairly early to write treatises on their conceptions of the directions and resources required of the "new music"—Cowell in *New Musicial Resources*, and Partch in *Genesis of a Music.* Make a brief comparative study of these.

5. John Cage's "Four Statements on the Dance" (four articles written between 1939 and 1957, included in his *Silence*) allude to the correlation of new sounds (especially percussion) with modern dance. If you have the opportunity, attend a performance of "modern dance" (now frequently incorporated into ballet itself) that uses percussive or electronic sounds, and review the program and its impact, including references to the Cage articles.

6. In his *Genesis of a Music*, p. 9, Harry Partch clarifies his distinction between Corporeal and Abstract music, giving instances of each from a broad range of music. Read this and the material leading up to it, ponder this distinction, and think about your own listening habits and preferences. Of which type is the music that most (and least) appeals to you? Make an annotated diary of the music you listen to for a week or a month, describing the degree of Corporeality or Abstractness of each piece, giving your reasons for making the distinction, and describing your reaction to the music in terms of this distinction.

7. Edgar Varèse said: "Science is the poetry of today." Comment on both the truths and fallacies implicit in this, and on the ways in which whatever Varèse meant by this was reflected in his music.

Notes

1. Cowell, Henry and Sidney, *Charles Ives and His Music*, rev. ed. (New York: Oxford University Press, 1969).

2. For a famous and amusing anecdote concerning President Lincoln, General Grant, and George Ives's Brigade Band of the First Connecticut Heavy Artillery, see Cowell and Cowell, *Charles Ives and His Music*, 15.

3. For a rather full treatment of this theme, see Frank Rossiter, *Charles Ives and His America* (New York: Liveright, 1975).

4. Cowell and Cowell, *Charles Ives and His Music*, 121.

5. Ibid., 104.

6. Cowell and Cowell, *Charles Ives and His Music*, 176–77. For an interesting exposition of the way Ives introduced later changes into his works, see H. Wiley Hitchcock and Noel Zahler, "Just What *Is* Ives's Unanswered Question?," *Notes: The Quarterly Journal of the Music Library Association* 44, no. 3 (March 1988): 437–43.

7. Ives, *Essays Before a Sonata*, 84.

8. Ives, *Essays Before a Sonata*, 88, 92–93.

9. Quoted in Cowell and Cowell, *Charles Ives and His Music*, 97.

10. Partch, *Genesis of a Music*, xi.

11. Varèse, "Freedom for Music," in Gilbert Chase, ed. *The American Composer Speaks* (Baton Rouge: Louisiana State University Press, 1966), 190–91.

12. Varèse, from a lecture, reprinted ibid., 197.

Chapter 18

Modernism II: The Impact of Technology
and New Esthetic Concepts

The most direct and ultimately the most enlightening approach to the music of
the modernism that emerged after World War II is through simply listening to
the sounds themselves. Roger Sessions, a composer who long championed the
avant-garde, has written:

> One cannot insist too strongly or too frequently that, in the arts generally and in
> music in particular, it is only productions that really count, and that only in
> these—music, written or performed—are to be found the criteria by which ideas
> about music, as well as music itself, must finally stand or fall: not the converse.[1]

One can observe in the music of mid-century modernism certain pervasive
traits in the sound patterns—a vocabulary of sound types and gestures. This
vocabulary is to a considerable degree independent of the philosophies, systems,
and rationales behind the music, and even how the sounds are produced. Modernism employed live and electronic music in ways that were interchangeable; a
clear example is Milton Babbitt's **Phenomena**, which exists in two versions, one
for soprano and piano (1969–70), the other for soprano and tape (1974).[2] The
styles of modernism, quite apart from either the medium employed or the genetic
procedures used to create the music, asserted an autonomous existence. Much of
the music invites this approach—confining one's attention purely to the aural
surface. If we take John Cage, the genial guru of modernism, at his word, "nothing takes the place but the sounds." Unlike Ives's ideal music, for the listener
what it sounds like *is* what it is.

The Surface Features of Mid-Century Modernism

One consistent characteristic of the sounds is that they tend to avoid the middle
portion of what had previously been the usual range in any parameter. Thus, in
pitch they are often either very high or very low; in volume, either very soft (as in

the case of many of Morton Feldman's compositions throughout) or very loud (George Crumb has specified that the dynamic level of his electrified string instruments in *Black Angels* be "on the threshold of pain"); and in duration either very short or very long indeed, avoiding the medium-length durations upon which traditional music is based.

Rhythmic complexity (engendered by the consistent use of a complicated and nonrepeating series of durations) is a crucial characteristic. This complexity is of the type used by Ives, as shown in the rhythmic pattern from *In the Night* reproduced in Example 18-1—considered unplayable by most performers in his day.

Example 18–1. Rhythmic excerpt from *In the Night*

With the advent of electronic music, it became possible to realize such complexities in the laboratory, so to speak. But there has arisen a new generation of virtuoso performers (challenged, like the John Henry of the ballad, to compete with the machine) who can execute these rhythms manually, and these performers are now given complex series of durations to realize, such as Example 18-2, from Elliott Carter's *Double Concerto*.

Example 18–2. Rhythmic excerpt from *Double Concerto*

It is important to note, as a feature of modernist music, that rhythmic complexity has often obscured, or eliminated, the sense of *pulse*.

New Sounds and New Sound Sources

The search for new sounds was an evident concern in most avant-garde music of the mid-century, and this search has added to the tonal palette sounds that range from extended possibilities with traditional instruments (including the human voice), through electronically generated and/or processed sound, to the admission of any sound whatever (noise) as raw material for composition.*

---

*Amplification has made possible the conversion of ordinary objects into "instruments" that can be played; Miles Anderson, for example, with a degree of whimsy refreshing in the often too-deadly-serious world of contemporary music, adds to his Caravan ensemble the sounds produced by plucking the spines of an amplified cactus.

New modes of simultaneity also produced new sounds. The combining of a few tones in dissonant relationships was extended to the practice of heaping together a great many pitches—often all of the available pitches in a certain range. This is a further development of the "cluster" chords of Ives and Cowell. The perception of dissonance, especially at soft dynamic levels, has been replaced by the perception of *sound mass*.

Another option is *no* sound. Silence is an important element—a more pronounced structural feature than in traditional music. As early as 1952 Cage himself preempted the ultimate position in the use of silence with his famous piece *4´ 33˝*, in which no intended sounds whatever are produced, and which may therefore be performed by "any instrument or combination of instruments."

At the other end of the spectrum from silence are nonmusical sounds— "noise." The selection of noises used is a function of the technology of the age: in the 1920s sirens, typewriters, and airplane propellers were appropriated "live"; as of mid-century, the noises were those rendered accessible by modern amplifying and recording techniques—human brain waves, for example.[3] Moral and ethical concerns are also reflected in the choice of noises. The new compelling environmental awareness found expression in the increased use of the sounds of nature, such as the fascinating "songs" of the humpback whale. Technology is giving us access to worlds of ever-tinier sounds; "plant music," for example, already exists.[4]

Finally, there was a concern with the spatial aspects of sound—specifically, in the musical effects created by separating sound sources and placing them in various ways in the performance space. Ives experimented with this; among many more recent examples of the use of spatial dimension in live performance could be cited Donald Erb's short *Spatial Fanfare for Brass and Percussion* and the final movement of John Corigliano's Concerto for Clarinet and Orchestra (1977)— works of which the spatial dimension cannot be experienced by listening to a conventional recording.

New Approaches to the Ordering of Sounds

Modernism also changed the way in which sounds are organized. There was a discernible tendency away from what was perceived in more traditional music as coherent (and therefore somewhat predictable) structure—away from the perception of a musical passage as some kind of moving line (a melody perhaps) progressing toward some kind of goal or climax. Replacing the sense of movement or progression is the sense either that the music is static—resembling an unchanging field, or a stationary object—or that it consists of a succession of individual *moments*, not perceptibly connected with one another. This discontinuity is congruent with, and was very probably influenced by, two technological media developments: film and tape. In both of these media the *splice* made the instant juxtaposition of discontinuous "moments" possible, and this proved to be a pervasive mode of organization for much of the new music.

The Two Dominant Rationales of Mid-Century Modernism

If the surface of mid-century modern music, as the ear alone perceived it, gave the impression of having simply appropriated more sounds into its vocabulary and devised new ways of relating them to each other, the situation in the 1950s and 1960s was far less simple from the composer's point of view. He or she had, as never before, to *rationalize*. Innocence was no longer possible; the new "advanced" composer had to know too much. There lay in wait for the serious young aspiring composer a maze of ideas, ideologies, methods, dogmas, and intellectual abstractions and justifications. The European intellectual climate had made European composers more prone to rationalization, but American composers had also become involved, despite a certain ineradicable residue of independence and distrust of hierarchical system. Among composers dedicated to advanced music, a fortunate few, such as Morton Feldman, succeeded in extricating themselves and confronting autonomously once more the basic function of the composer—to make music. Feldman himself said in the late 1960s, "Unfortunately for most people who pursue art, ideas become their opium. The sickness that you feel about the situation today is a piling up of multitudinous suggestions and multitudinous misconceptions, each tumbling over the other. There is no security to be one's self."[5]

In terms of rationale and method, the paths that composers took varied in detail with each individual, but two fairly clear general routes were followed—routes that diverged widely. Cage, in an address given in 1957, pointed up the difference rather clearly in terms of the amount of rational control exercised by the composer over the aural result: the production.

> One has a choice. If he does not wish to give up his attempts to control sound, he may complicate his musical technique towards an approximation of the new possibilities and awareness. (I use the word "approximation" because a measuring mind can never finally measure nature.) Or, as before, one may give up the desire to control sound, clear his mind of music, and set about discovering means to let sounds be themselves rather than vehicles for man-made theories or expressions of human sentiments.[6]

The almost diametrically opposed positions represented by the ideal of maximum rational control on the one hand (Milton Babbitt: "I believe in cerebral music, and I never choose a note unless I know why I want it there")[7] and a minimum of such control on the other (John Cage: "Discovering means to let sounds be themselves") polarized the new music in the 1950s and 1960s to the extent that the two approaches were given separate labels: *avant-garde* for the first and *experimental* for the second.

Toward Maximum Rational Control by the Composer

The trend toward ever-greater control over the end result of musical composition was manifested in two distinct but related areas. The first was the control over every aspect of performance, going beyond the historically basic specifications of pitch, rhythm, and tempo (which evolved historically in that order) to include the most detailed instructions regarding tone color and dynamic nuance. The ultimate realization of control, of course, was composition directly on tape (electronic music), which eliminated the performer entirely.

A second, and more fundamentally crucial, area of increased control was that governing the myriad of choices the composer makes in writing the piece to begin with. In this century the greatest degree of predetermined control of choices has been represented by the technique of *serial organization*. "Classical" serial technique, derived from the work of Arnold Schoenberg and other German-Austrian composers beginning in the 1920s, consists of organizing music according to a series, or *set*, consisting of all of the twelve pitches (or *pitch classes*) arranged in a certain invariable order that persists (allowing for permutations) throughout the work. Serial technique applied to pitches alone has been used by many American composers, including Milton Babbitt, Ben Weber, George Perle, Ross Lee Finney, until the late 1960s George Rochberg, and in some works Aaron Copland.

Ultimately, on both sides of the Atlantic, the move was taken toward subjecting the *total* aural result of a composition to the intellectual predetermination of serial procedures. What has become popularly known as *total serialization* involves a procedure by which the ordering of all the other measurable dimensions of sound—duration, intensity, timbre, and register—is serially determined. This procedure results in a composition that has been called "the unpremeditated result of comprehensive premeditation."[8] The idea itself has become well known, although actual pieces in which all the so-called *parameters* of music (a term borrowed, significantly, from mathematics) have been serially predetermined are relatively rare. One such piece is Milton Babbitt's *Three Compositions for Piano*, in which dynamics, rhythm, and pitch are serialized. The early date (1947) is testimony to the independent leadership of American composers in this field.[9]

Around serial music, and the theorizing that went with it, a rarefied atmosphere was created in which the layman was made to feel not only uncomfortable but unwelcome and inferior. The pronouncements of some composers were not calculated to dispel this. Charles Wuorinen said, "Composers have always been 'intellectuals' and this stance is absolutely unavoidable today, for music has grown too rich and complex to be handled by the illiterate."[10] The fact that the universities tended to be the centers for the cultivation of serialism helped to foster the analogy of this type of composition to pure scientific research. This view was cogently expressed by Milton Babbitt himself in a now-famous article, circulated under the title "Who Cares If You Listen?"* Written for a magazine with broad circulation (*High Fidelity*), and in terms any intelligent layman can understand, it is one of the most lucid and unequivocal statements of the viewpoint of the composer-as-research-specialist.[11]

The composer's attempt to achieve total rational control over the compositional process had two acknowledged limitations. The first stemmed from the basic premise of serialism that all the pitches, durations, intensities, and other properties constituting the predetermined series must be heard before any can be repeated. But, as the proverb has it, the more things change, the more they are the same, and the aural result of this constant change was actually a kind of *static* quality. As the German avant-gardist Karlheinz Stockhausen put it, "If from one sound to the next, pitch, duration, timbre and intensity change . . . one is constantly traversing the entire realm of experience in a very short time, and thus one finds oneself in a state of suspended animation, the music 'stands still.'"[12]

A second limitation was the built-in tendency of serialism to defeat the avowed purpose of those adopting it as a means of achieving totally predetermined control; the music comes to resemble, to a remarkable degree, that generated by opposite procedures of deliberate randomness. As the composer Ernst Krenek said of serialism, "It is reasonable to assume that in pursuing this concept beyond certain limits one would reach a point of diminishing returns, for the internal organization of the final product would become so complicated that its outward appearance would be hardly distinguishable from that of organized chaos."[13]

The paradoxical similarity between the results of procedures designed to give the composer maximum control and those designed to give him minimum control has been noted by many observers.** This leads us to the consideration of the other dominant rationale of mid-century modernism.

---

*The title is the source of gross popular misunderstanding, since it was chosen not by Babbitt but by the magazine's editor, who was unwilling to change it at the author's request, and therefore chose to misrepresent, for popular consumption, Babbitt's carefully stated position.

**In explaining the phenomenon of maximum order resembling disorder, George Rochberg has invoked the aid of the physical concept of *entropy*, "the measure of the tendency of nature toward disorder, non-differentiation, and a final state of static equilibrium." See "Indeterminacy in the New Music" in Rochberg, *The Aesthetics of Survival*.

Toward Minimum Rational Control by the Composer

The second path of the new music around mid-century was that of progressive relinquishment of rational control by the composer. Here, as at the opposite extreme of serialism, the musical result cannot be envisioned in full, but for a different reason—the composer has deliberately willed it so. Increasingly, aspects of the whole result are left either to the performer or to the operation, in some form or other, of chance.

Improvisation

A certain degree of planned relinquishment of control to the performer (quite aside from the ever-present element of interpretation) exists in the realm of improvisation. Improvisation was revived in very special instances in avant-garde music of mid-century. Typically it involved wide performer choices within a carefully planned structure, and the interaction of players who were highly skilled, experienced in this type of performance, and used to working together. It was therefore rare.

Limited Indeterminacy

In view of the limitations of true improvisation, composers have sought other related means of applying indeterminacy within controlled limits. Indeterminate notation is one means used, supplying performers with a basic idea of the sound intended and specifying certain guides and limitations to its production. Graph notation, for instance, an early idea that survives in various forms, was used by Morton Feldman in the early 1950s to produce such works as *Projection 4 for Violin and Piano* (1951) and *Intersection 3* (1953), the latter having been realized on both piano and pipe organ. Most indeterminate notation must continue to rely heavily upon explanatory directions, which are sometimes as lengthy as the notation itself.[14]

Another practice was that of giving the performers (including the conductor) certain choices in the performance—choices relating to the order of musical events (including how many of all those possible are to be performed at all) and to the duration of these events. Earle Brown's *Available Forms I* (1961) furnishes an example of this procedure. This is a work for chamber ensemble in which the conductor moves at will from one to another of six "events," the notations for all of which are available to all the performers at all times. To such procedures Brown has given a name: "open form."*

---

*It is significant that Brown was influenced by the work of the sculptor Alexander Calder. There is a certain correspondence between open form in music and the mobile in art; in both, the individual components are predetermined by the artist, but their relationship at any given moment (or in any given performance) is unpredictable.

Unlimited Indeterminacy

The progression toward a minimization of control by the composer may be thought of as a continuum, beginning with improvisation. As we move farther along the continuum in the direction of ever-decreasing control over the realized sound itself, we become involved with significant changes in the aesthetic concepts of what constitutes the essence and function of music, and of art in general. With Cage's "my purpose is to remove purpose," we encounter at once a fundamentally different attitude and aesthetic. If the traditional role of the composer is eliminated, there is no alternative but to leave the artistic results, literally, to *chance*. This is the alternative path that experimental music pursued, in the elevation of chance to a position in which it replaces altogether what has been called imagination, intuition, inspiration. In this we encounter once again (as with indeterminacy's complementary opposite, total organization) the goal of removing artistic decisions from the domain of human memory, experience, and intuition, the effects of which are to be expurgated much as (in another context) would be the consequences of "original sin."

John Cage's *Music of Changes* (a piano piece written in 1951 lasting forty-three minutes) is an early example of this, having been arrived at through an elaborate process of using charts and coin tosses in accord with the Chinese oracular book of wisdom *I Ching* ("Book of Changes"). With this type of new music, the scope of the composer in determining the actual sounds is reduced to that of merely setting up systems, or arranging for the unpredictable to happen. The occupation of the composer *as creative artist* is deliberately eliminated. Cage himself, in a one-man dialogue, asked himself the ultimate question—"Why bother, since, as you have pointed out, sounds are continually happening whether you produce them or not?"[15]—but avoided answering it.

New Technology and the New Music

The sophisticated state of electroacoustic music around mid-century comprised the following capabilities: (1) the ability to record any sound or succession of sounds, (2) the ability to synthesize (to build up from the electronic scratch of the basic sine tone, as it were) any imaginable sound or succession of sounds, and (3) the ability to manipulate sounds obtained from either of these two processes in various ways, including slowing them down or speeding them up, raising or lowering their pitch, reversing their direction in time, changing their timbre by filtering out certain frequencies, combining any number of them simultaneously, introducing echo effects, making them endlessly repeat, and juxtaposing them in any way. *Sampling* constitutes a synthesis of all three of these capabilities, in that a sound from *any* source can be "listened to," analyzed, synthesized, and subjected to any of the aforementioned manipulations.

In the first stages of electroacoustic music (roughly the 1950s) nearly all efforts were directed toward the production of the sound on tape as the sole end product. To attend a "performance," all you did was be in the presence of loud-speakers and listen. The first program of such music in the United States was given at the Museum of Modern Art in New York in 1952, and was the work of two of the pioneers of electroacoustic music, Otto Luening and Vladimir Ussachevsky. Because of the amount and cost of the equipment involved, universities were both the centers and the patrons of the development of electronic music—at first Columbia and Princeton, later joined by the Universities of Michigan and Illinois, and Stanford University.

From the beginning both "live" and synthesized tones were used as raw material. Performerless tape music has continued to be cultivated; *Poème électronique* (1958) by Edgar Varèse, mentioned in the last chapter, was a landmark. Subsequent carefully crafted compositions—some of them large-scale, and by no means inexpressive—by Luening and Ussachevsky, and after them Mario Davidovsky, Mel Powell, Kenneth Gaburo, Charles Wuorinen (whose *Time's Encomium* of 1969 won the Pulitzer Prize), and Morton Subotnick, gave indications of what was possible.*

But by and large the elimination of the performer did not prove to be the altogether worthwhile, liberating advance it was at first thought to be. For one thing, for all the inventiveness that was applied, there seemed to be still a pervasive *sameness* to electronic sounds—the result of what Mel Powell described as tape music's "perilously limited array of options." Probably a more decisive limiting factor was the absence of a human performer—a vital ingredient to the essentially human transaction that is live musical performance. As early as 1953 Luening and Ussachevsky were combining live performers and tape sounds, and they produced two works for orchestra and tape the next year (*Rhapsodic Variations* and *A Poem in Cycles and Bells*).

This proved to be the most prevalent use of electronic music, and works for tape and a single performer or small group of performers are very numerous. The degree to which live performers must synchronize with the tape varies considerably, from situations in which they are completely independent (John Cage's *Aria with Fontana Mix*) to pieces in which the interaction is highly organized, as in Mario Davidovsky's various pieces appropriately called **Synchronisms**.

*Since it soon became evident that the recording, playable at home, and not the public "concert," was the important mode of dissemination for this music, it is not surprising that in the 1960s record companies themselves were commissioning electronic works (e.g., Subotnick's *Silver Apples of the Moon* and *The Wild Bull*, commissioned by Nonesuch).

Other Aspects of Mid-Century Modernism
Toward Theater and the Combination with Other Media

The tendency of many of the endeavors of modernism was toward the involvement of other senses than the auditory, and hence other media. The extension of the new music into the multimedia realm is actually a fairly complex subject, for the heading embraces many essentially different kinds of endeavors. In terms of the combination of live and electronic music, the quasi-dramatic situation inherent in the juxtaposition of performer and inanimate loudspeaker—"man *vs.* the machine"—has been deliberately exploited in some works. Another type of multimedia piece came out of the desire to "theatricalize" the basic concert situation. Making "theater" out of a concert situation makes actors out of the performers. The late works of Harry Partch illustrate this. A more passive kind of theatricalism is represented by a piece such as *Vox balaenae* (*Voice of the Whale*) (1971) by George Crumb, wherein three musicians playing electrified instruments (flute, cello, and piano) and making music "inspired by the singing of the humpback whale" are directed to wear masks and to play in a deep blue light. In this case, the music clearly exists independent of the visual setting, which merely adds an atmospheric dimension to the live performance.

A more recent theatricalism, using a mixture of media, is the "performance art" of the 1980s and 1990s, centered on a solo performer who may play, sing, speak, act, dance, in any combination, aided by a battery of visual displays and props. Laurie Anderson is perhaps the best-known performer in this vein. "Performance art" is apt to verge on pop, its visual aspect related to the video.

Very elaborate attempts were made in the late 1960s and early 1970s to create whole artistic "environments" that would actively involve the audience. A short environmental piece, *Souvenir* (1970) by Donald Erb, presented close coordination of the aural, visual, and tactile components in a "happy" and "non-neurotic" (in the composer's words) piece for dancers, instrumental ensemble of winds and percussion, electronic tape, projections, and "props" that included weather balloons (bounced around in the hall by the audience) and ping-pong balls, which the audience afterwards carried away as "souvenirs."[16]

Once the traditional concert situation was superseded, the temptation to expand multimedia works to gargantuan proportions proved irresistible to some. Robert Moran's *39 Minutes for 39 Autos*, done in San Francisco in 1969, involved a "potential of 100,000 performers, using auto horns, auto lights, skyscrapers, a TV station, dancers, theater groups, spotlights, and airplanes, besides a small synthesizer ensemble." Such mammoth onetime happenings have their counterpart in the visual arts in the works of Boris Christo.

A performance of *HPSCHD* by John Cage and Lejaren Hiller in 1969. *Photo by Bruce Dale, © 1970 National Geographic Society.*

Multimedia works in which there was little or no coordination between the elements were best described in their heyday as "happenings," a large portion of which were the result of chance operations of one kind or another. With John Cage and his followers and collaborators in the 1960s, the combination of multimedia experiments and indeterminacy led to the production of happenings such as *HPSCHD*, a vastly complex work by Cage and Lejaren Hiller. The sound alone was a dense overlaying of fifty-two electronic sound tapes and seven amplified harpsichords played by five live performers. The basic source material for the harpsichordists was *Introduction to the Composition of Waltzes by Means of Dice*, attributed to Mozart (the witty diversion of a genius at play, which has been cited again and again with singular seriousness by theorists of twentieth-century indeterminacy in search of antecedents). The choice of nearly all the sound material, live and electronic, was controlled by chance—in this case, by a computerized version of *I Ching*. The whole performance (which took place in the huge Assembly Hall of the University of Illinois in 1969, and lasted four and a half hours) was accompanied by visual projections from sixty-four slide projectors and eight movie projectors going simultaneously, as well as miscellaneous light beams and the reflected light from spinning mirrored balls—a manufactured "kinetic environment," and the most complex embodiment up to that time of Cage's dictum that "the more things there are, as is said, the merrier."

Anti-Art, and the Confusion of Art with Life

The restlessly experimental fever among the indeterminacy wing of the avant-garde during its most active phase, in the 1960s, led some composers on the fringes to adopt a quasi-philosophical stance, and to direct their energies to exercises whose aim seemed to be to question the nature and function of music itself, and to undermine the assumptions and the *modus operandi* on which it is based. The ideas of John Cage appeared to provide the cues for much of this. Cage himself, while working with craftsmanlike diligence in realizing his own "happenings," as a leader hardly went beyond being a genial, witty, and provocative questioner and storyteller. But there were those in the next generation who took Cage's "purpose . . . to remove purpose" with an intense earnestness that showed itself in a variety of manifestations.

One was the conscious use of human responses normally unrelated to the perception of art as the basis for a "composition." *Danger* was one ingredient (danger to hearing from very loud sounds). *Boredom* (the very thing that all but the most doggedly experimental artists seek to avoid) was studied and exploited by Cage and others. La Monte Young's *Composition 1960 No. 7* consists of two notes forming the interval of a perfect fifth, to be held a "long time"; Philip Corner's *The Barcelona Cathedral* consists of the loud clang of ten metallic percussion instruments being sounded together every few seconds, for half an hour. Minimalism, treated in the next chapter, grew at least partly out of this domain.

"Concept" music consists merely of *ideas* for "pieces," or "happenings," the actual realization of which would be either impossible or, as expressions of the philosophy motivating them, ambiguous or manifestly pointless. Of the first type would be pieces that would take several hundred years to perform, for example. Representative of the second type would be La Monte Young's *Composition 1960 No. 9*, which, in his words, "consists of a straight line drawn on a piece of paper. It is to be performed and comes with no instructions."

The "pieces" often consisted *merely* of instructions ("word-scores"), some of which were gentle invitations to become aware of the beauties of the environment, or to relinquish some of the egotism of the "performer." Pauline Oliveros's *Sonic Meditations* include instructions to "Take a walk at night. Walk so silently that the bottoms of your feet become ears" and "Become performers by not performing." But if everything of which we are aware is to be regarded as art, then art has no distinctive existence, and is meaningless. This anti-art stance was generally related to a confusion of art with life itself. John Cage insisted on the confusion: "Art's obscured the difference between art and life. Now let life obscure the difference between life and art."[17]

The purely musical aspects of modernism—those aspects having to do with sound itself—left their mark on American music and will continue to be adapted and used. But the extremism, the rigid dogmatism, and the contempt for the wider audience and for art itself that characterized the 1950s and the 1960s were doomed to fade in favor of a more inclusive, humane, and richly varied musical art that transcended modernism. It is to that that we turn our attention next.

FURTHER READING

Books
General
Cope, David H. *New Directions in Music*. 6th ed. Madison, WI: Brown and Benchmark, 1993.
>   A most useful book, full of examples and references.
Griffiths, Paul. *Modern Music: The Avant-Garde since 1945*. New York: George Braziller, 1981.
>   Some of the best writing on the subject, especially in conveying the historical perspective. Though much space is devoted to European developments, it is valuable in showing the relationship between the European and American avant-garde.
Rochberg, George. *The Aesthetics of Survival: A Composer's View of Twentieth-Century Music*. Ann Arbor: University of Michigan Press, 1984.
>   A thoughtful critique of modernism.
Rockwell, John. *All American Music: Composition in the Late Twentieth Century*. New York: Knopf, 1983.
>   Includes perceptive individual chapters on Babbitt, Cage, Rzewski, Ashley, Glass, and others.
Tawa, Nicholas. *A Most Wondrous Babble: American Composers, Their Music, and the American Scene, 1950–1985*. Westport, CT: Greenwood, 1987.
Broadly inclusive collections of essays and interviews
Battcock, Gregory, ed. *Breaking the Sound Barrier: A Critical Anthology of the New Music*. New York: Dutton, 1981.
Gagne, Cole, and Tracy Caras, eds. *Soundpieces: Interviews with American Composers*. Metuchen, NJ: Scarecrow, 1982.
———. *Soundpieces 2: Interviews with American Composers*. Metuchen, NJ: Scarecrow, 1993.
Kostelanetz, Richard, and Joseph Darby, eds. *Classic Essays on Twentieth-Century Music: A Continuing Symposium*. New York: Schirmer Books, 1996.
Schwartz, Elliott, and Barney Childs, eds. *Contemporary Composers on Contemporary Music*. New York: Holt, Rinehart, 1967.
The serial wing of the avant-garde
Boretz, Benjamin, and Edward T. Cone, eds. *Perspectives on Contemporary Music Theory*. New York: Norton, 1972.
>   Selections, mostly from the periodical *Perspectives of New Music*; an instructive sampling of writings from the standpoint of the composer-as-research-specialist.
———. *Perspective on American Composers*. New York: Norton, 1971.
>   Broader in scope than the preceding, this takes in Ives, Varèse, Sessions, Copland, Piston, Carter, Berger, and Finney.

John Cage and the experimental wing of the avant-garde

Cage, John. *Silence*. Cambridge, MA: MIT Press, 1966.

>This remains the most important single source of Cage's own expressions of his ideas.

Griffiths, Paul. *Cage*. Oxford: Oxford University Press, 1981.

Husarik, Stephen. "John Cage and Lejaren Hiller: *HPSCHD*, 1969," *American Music* 1, no. 2 (Summer 1983): 1–21.

Montague, Stephen. "John Cage at Seventy: An Interview," *American Music* 3, no. 2 (Summer 1985): 205–16.

Nyman, Michael. *Experimental Music: Cage and Beyond*. New York: Schirmer Books, 1974.

>Good treatment, with many examples, of the indeterminacy-to-minimalism branch of the avant-garde, up to the early 1970s.

Thomson, Virgil. "Cage and the Collage of Noises" in *American Music Since 1910*. New York: Holt, Rinehart, 1970. Paperback ed. 1972.

Electroacoustic and computer music

Much of the writing on this subject is understandably highly technical; the following are relatively accessible to the general reader.

Ernst, D. *The Evolution of Electronic Music*. New York: Schirmer Books, 1977.

Schwartz, Elliott. *Electronic Music: A Listener's Guide*. New York: Praeger, 1975.

>A well-written introduction by a composer, it includes contributed observations by a number of other composers.

Wells, Thomas. *The Technique of Electronic Music*. New York: Schirmer Books, 1981.

>Though highly technical, this book is recommended for its organization, its lucid explanations, and its copious references to sources.

Periodicals

Perspectives of New Music, since 1962 (Seattle, WA).

>More or less the official organ of the academic serial wing, with highly prestigious contributors and editorial board.

Source: Music of the Avant-Garde, 1967–72.

>Published in its brief history a number of scores and articles, mostly of the indeterminacy wing. Available in many libraries.

Ear, since 1973 (New York).

>More or less the organ of the opposition to academic serialism, it has published articles and scores of the Cagean-to-minimalist persuasion, with a growing cross-cultural emphasis.

Projects

1. Write a well-reasoned critique of Milton Babbitt's important essay "Who Cares If You Listen?" (reprinted in Chase, *The American Composer Speaks*; Schwartz and Childs, *Contemporary Composers on Contemporary Music*; and Kostelanetz and Darby, *Classic Essays on Twentieth-Century Music*). Deal with as many of its implications as you can fathom. For example, what do you think would happen if all "advanced" composers of "specialized" music withdrew in isolation from the "public life of unprofessional compromise and exhibitionism"? Or, related to this, what would be the ramifications of the "complete elimination of the public and social aspects of musical composition"?

2. Interview a performer who has worked out a piece written in indeterminate notation: What are the problems, challenges, and rewards? (In addition to touring organizations performing new music, there are new-music groups at most colleges and universities that have a sizable number of music students.) Recapitulate the essence of the interview—with comments, background, and illustrations of the notation, if possible—either orally or in a paper.

3. The most efficient piece of indeterminacy yet designed was a "composition" consisting of one word: "LISTEN." (Its "composer" was Max Neuhaus, and "piece" was "realized" through field trips to sound environments such as power stations; see Nyman, *Experimental Music*, p. 88, for further details.) Write a brief paper discussing this ultimate renunciation of the function of the artist in selecting and transforming his material, and discuss the concept of art as a kind of therapy, to "make us conscious of the life and sounds outside the accepted musical-social environment."

4. Taking a periodical such as *Time* magazine as a source, write a summary of, and commentary on, the pieces and programs of new music reviewed in any twelve-month period between 1950 and 1975.

5. Devise a two-minute piece for a group of performers (not necessarily musicians—perhaps a class) that consists entirely of speech (whispered, spoken, shouted) or other nonsinging vocal sounds (laughing, crying, sustained humming, hissing, clucking, etc.). The piece should have an overall design, and the performance should be directed in some way, but it may involve a good deal of latitude for performer choice (a form of indeterminacy). It may involve two or more things going on at the same time. Have it performed, and get three critiques of the performance—one by yourself, one by a participant, and one by someone who acts as audience.

6. Write a brief essay setting forth your views on the role of any or all of the following in art: chance, boredom, psychological manipulation (e.g., inducing a trancelike state), collage (in the sense of the incorporation or juxtaposition of disparate elements, such as "noise" in music), or the presentation of a "found" or "observed object" as art.

Notes

1. Roger Sessions, "Problems and Issues Facing the Composer Today," in Paul Henry Lang, ed., *Problems of Modern Music* (New York: Norton, 1962), 24. Reprinted in *Roger Sessions on Music: Collected Essays* (Princeton, NJ: Princeton University Press, 1979), 71–87.

2. Both versions can be heard on New World 80466.

3. Alvin Lucier (b. 1931) based his *Music for Solo Performer* (1965, Davis, California) on the amplification of the alpha current, a low-voltage brain signal. David Rosenboom (b. 1947) has gone much further with this, and has produced recordings and edited a publication *Biofeedback and the Arts: Results of Early Experimentation* (Vancouver: A.R.C., 1976).

4. See references in David Cope, *New Directions in Music*, 4th ed. (Dubuque, IA: William C. Brown, 1984), 316–17.

5. Morton Feldman in an interview with Robert Ashley, in Elliott Schwartz and Barney Childs, eds., *Contemporary Composers on Contemporary Music* (New York: Holt, Rinehart, 1967), 365.

6. John Cage, *Silence* (Cambridge, MA: MIT Press, 1966), 10. The notion of "letting sounds be themselves" is strikingly reminiscent of the Polish philosopher Wronsky's definition of music as "the corporealization of the intelligence that is in sounds"—a definition that greatly influenced Varèse.

7. Milton Babbitt, as quoted by Anthony Bruno in "Two American Twelve-Tone Composers" (*Musical America* 71, no. 3 [February 1951]: 22). See Gilbert Chase, *America's Music, From the Pilgrims to the Present*, 2d ed. (New York: McGraw-Hill, 1955), 618.

8. Ernst Krenek, "Serialism," in John Vinton, ed., *Dictionary of Contemporary Music* (New York: Dutton, 1971), 673.

9. Milton Babbitt's *Three Compositions for Piano* (CRI S–461) is cited and analyzed by David Cope in *New Directions in Music*, 4th ed., 42–44. Other available examples of total procedural control by Babbitt, who pioneered in this direction in this country, are *Post-Partitions* (New World 80466) and two works on CRI SD–138, *Composition for Four Instruments* (1948) and *Composition for Viola and Piano* (1950).

10. Charles Wuorinen in an interview with Barney Childs, in *Contemporary Composers on Contemporary Music*, 375.

11. Milton Babbitt, "Who Cares If You Listen?" is reprinted in Schwartz and Childs, *Contemporary Composers on Contemporary Music*, in Gilbert Chase, ed., *The American Composer Speaks* (Baton Rouge: Louisiana State University Press, 1966), and in Kostelanetz and Darby, *Classic Essays on Twentieth-Century Music*.

12. Karlheinz Stockhausen, quoted in Michael Nyman, *Experimental Music: Cage and Beyond* (New York: Schirmer Books, 1974), 23.

13. Krenek, "Serialism" in Vinton, *Dictionary of Contemporary Music*, 673.

14. John Cage, ed., *Notations* (New York: Something Else Press, 1969) reproduces a broad sampling of mid-twentieth-century notation.

15. John Cage, *Silence*, 59.

16. *Souvenir*, by Donald Erb, is admirably described in Cope, *New Directions in Music*, 4th ed., 232–35.

17. John Cage, *A Year from Monday* (Middletown, CT: Wesleyan University Press, 1963), 19.

Chapter 19

Modernism Transcended: Autonomy, Assimilation, and Accessibility

There were some developments as early as the 1960s indicating that modernism was beginning to lose its hegemony—a hegemony sustained by a small but highly influential intellectual elite. By the 1980s, it was clear to the general musical public that it had already reached its outermost limits and receded. Three manifestations attest to this: there was greater *autonomy* for the composer (who no longer felt an outsider if not fully committed to one of two highly exclusive schools, serialism and experimentalism); the music had *assimilated* more from a wide range of sources, including older European music, ethnic musics from around the world, popular and folk musics; and the music was more *accessible*— that is, capable of being enjoyed by a broader audience, an audience that had been left out, and hence turned off, by the excesses of modernist music.

Predictably, new names (such as "postmodern" and "neo-romantic") have been applied to the fine-art music that has emerged with the recession of modernism. But the transcending of modernism is a transcending of categories and "schools" as well. As William Bolcom put it,

> [I]t is generally accepted among most artists that modernism is on the wane. What is happening now is less a new movement—although critics have been quick to name it postmodernism—than it is a movement away from movements, those schools and isms that have bedeviled art and led towards its current sclerotic selfconsciousness.[1]

Thus a label such as "New Romanticism," current in New York and elsewhere during the 1980s, itself connoted a fashion, and at best could characterize only a portion of the phenomenon. The situation is better described as Michael Walsh has done: "The horizons of American music suddenly expanded. . . . The decline of Darmstadtism freed composers once again to give voice to individual modes of expression; while initial reactions were tentative and uncertain, within fifteen years a thousand flowers had bloomed."[2]

Minimalism: A Radical Antidote to Modernism

Towering over the thousand blooms like a colossal sunflower was minimalism, a hardy plant that spread its seeds far and wide. Minimal music is familiar as a kind of musical texture in which short, simple patterns are repeated for long periods of time, either without variation, or subjected to subtle changes that gradually alter the melodic, rhythmic, or timbral content. Minimalist works had their predecessors. Eric Satie's *Vexations*, from the last decade of the nineteenth century, instructed the performer to play a simple 32-bar piece very slowly and softly 840 times—hence it was essentially "concept music." Such pieces involving unrelieved repetition, with no subtle changes, represented experiments in boredom and the hypnotic effects of repetition, and forecast the similar essays of the Cagean experimentalists of mid-century modernism. But minimalism as a way of making music to be taken seriously began to appear prominently in the 1960s. It was associated with two trends of the times: one was an increased interest in Asian and African music, in which repetition plays a very significant role;* the other was the beginnings of a reaction, on the part of some composers born in the 1930s, to mid-century modernism itself, especially the serialism of the dominant academic East Coast/European "establishment."

Minimalism treats music as a gradual, perceptible process, and one that the listener can hear happening throughout the music. Steve Reich explains it by three analogies:

> Performing and listening to a gradual musical process resembles:
>
> pulling back a swing, releasing it, and observing it gradually come to rest;
>
> turning over an hour glass and watching the sand slowly run through to the bottom;
>
> placing your feet in the sand by the ocean's edge and watching, feeling, and listening to the waves gradually bury them.[3]

What minimalism brought back to classical music was tonality, pulsation, and repetition. These elements were certainly not new, but as John Adams has pointed out, "In the context of what had happened in contemporary classical music since the time of Schoenberg [the leading pedagogical proponent of 12-tone serialism], and particularly John Cage's developments, *re-introducing* them was in itself a revolutionary act."[4] This reintroduction propelled minimalist music into an immediate and unanticipated popularity, especially among those

---

*Much Asian and African music that involves repetition exists for a purpose fundamentally different from that of Western music: namely, to produce in its listeners altered states of consciousness. This function of music has, like elements of Eastern philosophy and religion, been adopted by some Western composers.

who had little previous experience with contemporary classical music. It became at once both influential and controversial. Minimalist composers became the new "stars" of classical music.

La Monte Young (b. 1935), in his work with long sustained sounds (either acoustic or electronic) dating from the late 1950s, was an early influence on minimalism.* Composers contemporary with Young who have become better known as proponents of minimalism are Terry Riley (b. 1935), Steve Reich (b. 1936), and Philip Glass (b. 1937). As Ruth Dreier has pointed out, they have many things in common. After a more or less traditional musical education, each rejected serialism; each discovered and studied Asian or African music; each became interested in exploring the physical properties of sound; each was involved with other arts in addition to music; and each founded his own performing group.[5] In addition, each uses or has used electronic means (synthesizers and/or tape).

In addition to African and Asian music, another palpable influence on minimalism, as John Adams has pointed out, is the machine itself. "Composers began to notice that machines, whether old-fashioned mechanical ones, or new electronic ones, tended to operate in interesting and often expressive modes of repetition."

Riley's *In C* (1964) was something of a landmark work. Its relation to modernism is in its indeterminacy; the number and type of instruments is optional, as is the total length (the first performance, in San Francisco, lasted over an hour and a half). There is a single tempo, governed by the steady repetition of a "C" two octaves above middle C on the piano throughout. Each performer plays his or her way through a sequence of fifty-three musical fragments, precisely notated, repeating each as many times as desired before going on to the next. When all the performers have gone through all the fragments, the piece is over. The total aural result is that of a rhythmically active, relatively consonant sound mass, constantly changing in its details.

Two hallmarks of modernism were indeterminacy and the use of tape technology. Most minimalist composers soon abandoned indeterminacy, preferring to give the performers directions in standard notation as to exactly what they want. But tape technology proved to be a more significant resource for minimalism in the beginning, especially the splicing of tapes into loops, so that fragments of speech or music could be recycled in a repeated pattern that could be

---

*The cross-cultural aspect of minimalism, and its curious juxtaposition of mysticism and technology, is projected in the flavor of such titles as La Monte Young's *The Tortoise Recalling the Drone of the Holy Numbers as They Were Revealed in the Dreams of the Whirlwind and the Obsidian Gong and Illuminated by the Sawmill, the Green Sawtooth Ocelot and the High-Tension Line Stepdown Transformer*, of 1964.

played endlessly, or combined with other loops in various ways. Many of the ideas and possibilities of sound manipulation and musical structure were originally suggested by experimentation with tape. Steve Reich tells of an accidental discovery that was to have far-reaching consequences for minimalism. This happened as he was working with the recording he had made of a young black Pentecostal preacher, Brother Walter, in Union Square, San Francisco, that eventually became *It's Gonna Rain* (1965).

> In the process of trying to line up two identical tape loops in some particular relationship, I discovered that the most interesting music of all was made by simply lining the loops up in unison, and letting them slowly shift out of phase with each other. As I listened to this gradual phase shifting process I began to realize that it was an extraordinary form of musical structure. . . . It was a seamless, continuous, uninterrupted musical process.[6]

Thus *phase shifting* came into being. Born of tape technology, the process was soon applied to pieces for human performers, as in Reich's *Piano Phase* (1967) for two pianos and *Violin Phase* (also 1967) for a single violinist playing "against" his or her own prerecorded tape. Reich abandoned this kind of very gradual phase shifting in the early 1970s, when he began the serious study of African and Asian music. But the structural method of having two or more voices repeat patterns in changing relationships—an idea that originated with tape loops—continued to be used in works such as the simple but effective *Clapping Music* (1972) for two people clapping, and the happily jazzy 17-minute *Octet* (1979). John Adams (b. 1947) used this device in his 28-minute *Shaker Loops* (1978), with seven "loops" for seven string players, wherein the shifting phases create what he has called a "congenial friction."

The move away from electronics to live performers in the 1970s was a feature, not only of minimalism, but of all of classical music, as modernism waned. Reich wrote as early as 1970: "In any music which depends on a steady pulse, as my music does, it is actually tiny micro-variations of that pulse created by human beings, playing instruments or singing, that gives life to the music . . . Electronic music as such will gradually die and be absorbed into the ongoing music of people singing and playing instruments."[7]

In the 1980s minimalism began to mellow considerably: the obstinately uncompromising ultra-long stretches of repetition were modified; the harmonic changes were more frequent and the harmonic palette became richer; traces of chromaticism and functional harmony made their appearance (the last movement of Adams's *Grand Pianola Music* of 1982 includes, probably with parodistic

John Adams. *Courtesy New York Public Library.*

intent, a great deal of dominant-to-tonic progression); there was greater variety of instrumental color; and there were settings of English-language texts, especially by American poets, including Walt Whitman, Emily Dickinson, and William Carlos Williams.* Minimalism's great popularity, and the attendant star status of composers like Reich, Glass, and Adams, led to commissions and performances by major orchestras.

Nevertheless, more recent minimalist works manage to retain the quintessentials of pulsation, repetition, and tonality—the latter somewhat expanded. Most clearly a translation into orchestral terms of earlier minimalism's procedures and overall affect are pieces like Adams's 28-minute *Fearful Symmetries* (1988) and Reich's 15-minute *Three Movements for Orchestra* (1986). Reich's work is a pure and almost "classical" re-creation of earlier minimalism. In the remarkable 30-minute *Tehillim* (1981), for four women's voices and small ensemble featuring percussion, Reich, in accommodating the text (four Psalms in Hebrew), departs from the dogged repetition of short fragments, but the often syncopated

*The operatic works of John Adams, Philip Glass, and others are treated in chapter 20.

rhythmic pulse is there, sometimes spelled out with the familiar hand clapping. The voices, though clearly enunciating the rhythm of the text, are treated almost like tuned percussion instruments.

John Adams's orchestral works without text tend to be more "symphonic" and often parodistic. But repetitition (though not tonality or pulsation) is a less prominent feature in Adams's highly expressive and moving works set to English texts, including the 32-minute *Harmonium* (1980–81), for large orchestra and chorus, with texts by John Donne and Emily Dickinson, and his nineteen-minute *The Wound-Dresser* (1988), for baritone and orchestra, a setting of a portion of Walt Whitman's graphic and wrenching poem of the same name from his *Drum Taps*, a memoir of the Civil War.

As we approach the century's end, minimalism remains with us, as a still recognizable but now less abrasive and less segregated part of the whole panorama of American classical music. It is to the rest of this panorama that we now turn.

Modernism Gives Way to Assimilation and Reconnection
Reconnection with Classical Music of the Past

That "the past is dead and must be buried" has been identified as "the chief tenet of modernism."[8] But as modernism has receded, there has emerged a marked tendency for music to reestablish connections with the past. The composer Billy Jim Layton wrote, as long ago as 1965: "The best hope for the world today, the direction, I am fully confident, of the important, vital music to be written, is that of a responsive and enlightened liberalism. . . . Today there is need for a new, rich, meaningful, varied, understandable and vital music which maintains contact with the great central tradition of humanism in the West."[9]

George Rochberg has said, "If it appears that a large part of the music of the twentieth century was a *music of forgetting*, the music of the end of the century and beyond must become a music of remembering."[10] This "remembering" takes many forms.

The first is outright quotation. Quotation in the new music is handled in highly individual ways, and varies greatly in extensiveness. It can be obscure and fragmentary, as in the twelve-minute *Contra Mortem et Tempus* (1965) by George Rochberg. Similarly, in the first movement of his 20-minute *Piano Quartet* (1976), William Bolcom makes a very oblique reference to the music of Chopin. Less obscure is the type of quotation in which recognizable phrases of older music appear. In *Ancient Voices of Children* (1970) by George Crumb, a toy piano plays a portion of a phrase from the eighteenth-century Anna Magdalena Bach Notebook, which slows to a stop before its end, "like clockwork . . . running down." A similar feeling is evoked in Crumb's 20-minute *Black Angels* (also 1970) for

William Bolcom. *Courtesy New York Public Library.*

amplified string quartet, which quotes eleven measures of Schubert's *Death and the Maiden* as "a fragile echo of an ancient music." A somewhat different effect is achieved in the 22-minute **Prism** (1980) by Jacob Druckman, in which recognizable snatches of older music are interrupted or overlaid with dissonant and/or atonal material. This is illustrated in the first movement, which is based on music from a seventeenth-century opera by Marc-Antoine Charpentier.* In the second of the three "acts" of *Music for the Magic Theater* (1967) George Rochberg quotes an entire Adagio of Mozart, reworking it only in terms of instrumental color.

Eclecticism and the Assimilation of Other Musics

Composers have also been influenced by the traditional music of cultures from other continents. We have already noted the influence of African, Indian, and Indonesian music on composers such as Lou Harrison and Steve Reich. But American composers have also incorporated into their works references to various genres of Western popular music, as did Charles Ives nearly a century ago. References

---

*Similar tendencies exist in the other arts. A precisely parallel example of such "quotation" in the visual realm can be seen in the work of Doug and Mike Starn (b. 1961), who, in *The Christ Series*, have produced a great number of pieces based on reworked photographic images of *The Dead Christ*, a painting done by Philippe de Champagne about 1650.

to jazz and blues are not as common nor as overt as they were in the 1920s and 1930s, but are present in very attenuated form in works such as the appropriately titled *Déjà Vu* (1977) of Michael Colgrass, and the final movement of John Harbison's *Symphony #1*. References to other genres of vernacular music are fairly widespread. William Bolcom's 13-minute Quintet for brass (1980) is a tribute to his various ancestors, and in it are snatches of a waltz (rendered momentarily with a Mexican flavor), a march, a gospel hymn, and a bravura cornet solo, as well as a Renaissance *canzona*. It is all done in the spirit of "remembered fathers," as Ives would have done. But references in more recent works have tended to be distinctly parodistic, even satirical, in manner. In this vein could be mentioned *From the Other Side* (1988) by Donald Martino, *Quartetset* (1995) by Sebastian Currier, and, even more extreme, *Carny* (1992) by John Zorn.

Music of Association and the New Accessibility
Music with Associative Connotations

While the term "program music" is not in favor, there has been a marked resurgence of music that has, in one way or another, associations beyond the music itself. As a significant sampling of works, approximately half of the compositions awarded the Pulitzer Prize in the 1970s, 1980s, and 1990s show some extramusical impetus or association. The very use of a title for a work (a practice now increasingly common) suggests the desire to communicate something more than can be done by the generic term "quartet" or "symphony," or clinical titles such as *Synchronism* or *Phonemena*. In an age of sophistication, titles may be indirect in their significance; as George Crumb has said in one case, they are "metaphors chosen more for poetic values rather than for specific meanings."

A text, of course, constitutes a strong associational element. In the new music, there is a notable return to practices of word-setting that are more lyrical than the jagged and fragmented lines of modernism and show attention to natural word rhythms and inflections and a concern to let the words be understood. Composers have shown a deeper concern and commitment both to the poetry and to the poet. Rather than setting a text for a single work and letting it go at that, some composers have developed more profound relationships with the works of particular literary figures, extending over a considerable period of time and encompassing a series of works. This has been the case with George Crumb and the works of Federico García Lorca, with David Del Tredici and the *Alice* books of Lewis Carroll, and with Stephen Albert and the works of James Joyce.[11]

In the case of music without text (the domain of traditional program music) composers have in some instances made public the extramusical associations attached to their works, thereby validating them for the listener. Mysticism in various forms has been the point of departure for many of George Crumb's purely instrumental works: numerology, for example, in the case of *Black Angels* (completed on Friday the 13th, 1970); astrology and the zodiac for *Makrokosmos I* (1974). Christian mysticism is the impetus for *Black Host* (1967) for organ by William Bolcom, based on the occult "black mass." Buddhist concepts of earth, man, and heaven are the stimuli for each of the three movements of the Peter Lieberson's *Piano Concerto* (1983). Dreams, or the state of dreaming, are reflected in the nature and form of George Rochberg's *Music for the Magic Theater* (1966) and William Bolcom's *Whisper Moon* (1971). All of this can be interpreted as evidence of composers seeking, and indeed needing, to relate their music, and art itself, to larger issues of life—neither (in Rochberg's words) "to seal art off from life" nor to confuse art with life, as some of the experimentalists had done. As Rochberg wrote of his *Contra Mortem et Tempus* (1965), composed after the death of his son, "It . . . became clearer than ever before that the only justification for claiming one was engaged in the artistic act was to open one's art completely to life and its entire gamut of terror and joys (real and imagined); and to find, if one could, new ways to transmute these into whatever magic one was capable of."[12]

The New Relationship to the Public

The following statements by two composers of the same generation (John Corigliano, b. 1938; David Del Tredici, b. 1937) represent the new attitude toward the audience, and the reassessed view of the function of the composer:

> I don't understand composers with what I call an eternity complex, people who ignore today's audiences and think of themselves as misunderstood prophets whose masterpieces will be seen as such in a century or so. That, I think, reveals a basic contempt for audiences. . . . I wish to be *understood*, and I think it is the job of every composer to reach out to his audience with all means at his disposal. Communication should always be a primary goal.[13]

> Composers now are beginning to realize that if a piece excites an audience, *that doesn't mean it's terrible.* For my generation, it is considered vulgar to have an audience really, *really* like a piece on a first hearing. But why are we writing music except to move people and to be expressive?[14]

The new accessibility and commitment to communication, however interpreted, have with some composers taken the form of *music as social statement*. Steve Reich's *Come Out* (1966) is a tape composition based on the recorded statement of a black man injured by the police. Christian Wolff, an early associate of John Cage and Morton Feldman, has since his *Changing the System* (1972–73) turned his attention mostly to political subjects, using labor and protest songs as material; examples of his work in this vein are his *Wobbly Music* (1975–76), *The Death of Mother Jones* (1977), and *Peace Marches 1, 2, and 3* (1983–84). An eclectic composer who has turned to social statement is the pianist Frederic Rzewski; *Coming Together* and *Attica* (1972) both had as their source and inspiration a letter from an inmate at the New York state prison in Attica, at the time of the prison uprising there. Best known is his *The People United Will Never Be Defeated!*, a long set of variations for piano on a leftist Chilean song. In this turning to social statement there is an interesting parallel with the folk-protest movement of the 1930s and 1940s. Both movements suffered from the same kind of limitation: that of using (in Rockwell's words) "an idiom that speaks to a far different social and racial group than the victims of the oppression that is being protested."

In Conclusion

The closing years of the twentieth century in American fine-art music are a time of the full blooming of the "thousand flowers"—a time of unprecedented diversity and contrast. In concluding the exploration of this music, the point needs to be made that not all works that have the capacity "to move people and to be expressive," as David Del Tredici puts it, make use of quotation, nor are they all in any overt way referential to the music of the past, or to the music of other cultures. To cite individual works of which this is true is to leave out many more, but as a mere hint of the riches which are there to be explored, there is the dreamlike exoticism of *Aftertones of Infinity* (1978) and *Music of Amber* (1981) by Joseph Schwantner (b. 1943); the often mercurial indulgence of virtuosity of the Concerto for Clarinet and Orchestra (1977) by John Corigliano (b. 1938); the striking and sometimes sudden contrasts of the expressive *Symphony #4* (1986), with its text by Theodore Roethke, by William Bolcom (b.1938); and the sheer musicality and sustained interest, moment by moment, of the 23-minute ***Passages*** (1981), on poems of A. R. Ammons, and the *Symphony #1* (1982) by Ellen Taaffe Zwilich (b. 1939). "**Way to Go**," the sixth and last song of *Passages*, makes a fitting close to our consideration of the transcendance of modernism:[15]

> *West light flat on trees:*
> *bird flying*
> *deep out in blue glass:*
> *uncertain wind*
> *stirring the leaves: this is*
> *the world we have:*
> *take it*

FURTHER READING

Reich, Steve. *Writings about Music*. New York: New York University Press, 1974.

Rochberg, George. *The Aesthetics of Survival: A Composer's View of Twentieth-Century Music*. Ann Arbor: University of Michigan Press, 1984.

Rockwell, John. *All American Music: Composition in the Late Twentieth Century*. New York: Knopf, 1983.

This incisive and readable book by an eminent critic covers many areas; chapters 6 and 7 are especially relevant to this chapter.

Rothstein, Edward. "The Return of Romanticism." *The New Republic* (August 27, 1984): 25–30.

Tawa, Nicholas. *A Most Wondrous Babble: American Composers, Their Music, and the American Scene, 1950–1985*. Westport, CT: Greenwood, 1987.

See especially chapter 8, "Reconciliations," and its many notes and references.

Projects

1. Listen to a fairly extended minimalist piece and write a brief paper examining your own reactions, both as you listen and afterward. Could they best be described in terms of "boredom," "restless annoyance," "trance," or some other? Did they change as you listened? Was there another distinct reaction when the piece was over?

2. If you are acquainted with contemporary developments in one of the other arts, write a brief paper comparing its current state with that of music, as described in this chapter. Has there been a move to transcend modernism?

3. Explore further the use of quotation in twentieth-century classical music. For example, how does obvious quotation (of either substance or style) affect your perception of a piece of music? (George Rochberg's *Music for the Magic Theater*, for substance, or his String Quartet No. 3, for style, might be usable points of departure.) If you were called on to suggest possible reasons *why* quotation has figured significantly in twentieth-century American music, what would you say?

4. Write a brief paper on the use of titles in contemporary music. Include examples of composers who use them, and composers who don't. Does a title alter your expectations of a piece of music? Consider your perception, for example, of George Crumb's *A Haunted Landscape* (New World 80326) if it were simply known as *Piece for Orchestra*; or of George Rochberg's Concerto for Oboe and Orchestra (New World 80335) if it were called *A Haunted Landscape*.

5. Does it bother you to hear a piece by a contemporary composer that might possibly be mistaken for the music of some previous century? Why? Write a brief but well-thought-out essay on this.

6. Does it bother you to hear a number of different styles in a single piece? Why? Think about this, and write a brief essay on it.

7. The composer Carl Ruggles became concerned when audiences at contemporary music concerts in New York earlier in the century actually increased, viewing it as a sign that contemporary music was "selling out." And Milton Babbitt, in his famous (and mistitled) article "Who Cares If You Listen?" of 1958, suggested the "very real possibility of complete elimination of the public and social aspects of musical composition." On the other hand, John Corigliano, as quoted in this chapter, says that he does not "understand composers . . . who ignore today's audiences and think of themselves as misunderstood prophets." Write a brief essay explaining where you stand on this issue, and why.

Notes

1. William Bolcom, in the Introduction to *The Aesthetics of Survival* by George Rochberg (Ann Arbor: University of Michigan Press, 1984).

2. Michael Walsh, in notes to New World 80335, which consists of music by George Rochberg and Jacob Druckman. It will be remembered that Darmstadt, Germany, host to annual summer convocations of the avant-garde after World War II, has been called the "citadel of serialism." In designating

the 1960s as the watershed, Walsh thus assigns a fairly early date to the initial reactions to modernism, which points up the age of this trend, and the increasing overlapping of artistic trends in our time.

3. Steve Reich, *Writings About Music*, 9.

4. The quotes of John Adams in this section on minimalism are from an address "Living on the Edge: The Composer in a Pop Culture" delivered at California State University, Sacramento, November 8, 1996.

5. Ruth Dreier, "Minimalism" in *The New Grove Dictionary of American Music*, vol. 3, 240.

6. Steve Reich, 50.

7. Steve Reich, 25 and 28.

8. William Bolcom, in Rochberg, *The Aesthetics of Survival*, viii.

9. Billy Jim Layton, "The New Liberalism," *Perspectives of New Music* 3, no. 2 (Spring–Summer 1965): 137–42.

10. George Rochberg in a 1981 paper, as quoted in John Rockwell, *All American Music: Composition in the Late Twentieth Century* (New York: Knopf, 1983), 87.

11. Among George Crumb's works using texts of Federico García Lorca are *Night of the Four Moons*; *Songs, Drones and Refrains of Death* (1962–70); *Night Music I* (1963); *Madrigals, Books I–IV, for Soprano and Instrumental Ensemble* (1965–69); and *Ancient Voices of Children* (1970). David Del Tredici's "Alice" works include: *In Memory of a Summer Day (Child Alice, Part I)* (1980); *Virtuoso Alice for Piano* (1984); and *Final Alice*. Works of Stephen Albert on poems of James Joyce are *To Wake the Dead, for Soprano and Chamber Ensemble*, (1977), *Flower of the Mountain*, and *TreeStone* (1983–84).

12. George Rochberg, quoted in notes to CRI 231, which includes *Contra Mortem et Tempus*.

13. John Corigliano, from an interview printed in notes accompanying New World 80309. Emphasis original.

14. David Del Tredici, as quoted in Rockwell, *All American Music*, 83 (emphasis original).

15. "Way to Go" is from A. R. Ammons, *Collected Poems 1951–1971* (New York: Norton, 1972.) It is recorded on Northeastern NR 218.

Chapter 20

Opera Old and New

Opera in America before the 1930s: An Unassimilated Alien

For two hundred years, between the performance of the ballad farce *Flora, or the Hob in the Well* in Charleston in 1735 and the premieres of *Four Saints in Three Acts* (1934) and *Porgy and Bess* (1935), opera was essentially an exotic import—an immigrant form, often performed in a foreign language. *Rip Van Winkle*, by George Frederick Bristow, was an opera on a thoroughly American tale by one of our most competent composers, but its successful run of seventeen performances in New York in 1855 did not set a precedent for American opera in its day. Scott Joplin's *Treemonisha*, a remarkable work based on African-American life and musical idioms, had only a barely noticed performance with piano accompaniment in 1915. (It was lavishly staged and recorded in 1975, and was awarded the Pulitzer Prize in 1976.)

Traditional American Opera Beginning in the 1930s
Some Forerunners

There were some harbingers of change early in the twentieth century. When the Metropolitan Opera of New York, already the nation's leading company, acquired a new general manager in 1908—the Italian Giulio Gatti-Casazza—his enlightened idea of a proper repertory embraced a blend of the old and the new, including new operas by native composers. In 1910 he produced the first American opera that the Metropolitan, already more than a quarter of a century old, had ever performed: *The Pipe of Desire*, by Frederick Converse. Before Gatti-Casazza left in 1935 he had produced a total of sixteen American operas in twenty-seven seasons.* Among these were *Natoma* (1911), on an American Indian theme, by Victor Herbert; *Mona* (1912) by Horatio Parker; *Shanewis* (1918), another Indian opera, by Charles Cadman; and *The King's Henchmen* (1927) and *Peter Ibbetson* (1931), two operas by Deems Taylor that had considerable success. Louis Gruenberg's *The*

---

*In the thirty-eight years following, under the next three managers, the number of American operas produced fell to a mere nine!

Emperor Jones (1933), as appropriate to its subject (it is based on the play by Eugene O'Neill), uses African-American musical elements. *Merry Mount* (1934), an opera by Howard Hanson after a story by Hawthorne, was the last American opera of the Gatti-Casazza regime. Some of these operas were worthy forerunners of what was to come in the "definitive decade" of the 1930s.

Three Landmarks of the 1930s

The innovations of the 1930s were decidedly not happening at the Metropolitan or at any other major opera house. Of the three very different operas we will now examine, one was premiered in Hartford, Connecticut, one in Boston, and the other in a small theater in New York.

The first two, despite their vast differences, were both designated by their authors as "folk operas." The one-act opera *The Devil and Daniel Webster* (1938) by Douglas Moore (1893–1969) is an operatic version of the fanciful short story of the same title by the Americanist writer Stephen Vincent Benét. Though there are no actual folk tunes used, the musical language of New England fiddle tunes and folk hymns is reflected in the lively rhythms and simple triadic harmonies. There are solo "arias" in the operatic tradition; "**I've Got a Ram Goliath**" is Daniel Webster's boasting assurance to the frightened Jabez Stone and his wife, Mary, that the devil (to whom Jabez has sold his soul) is no match for him. "**Now May There Be a Blessing . . . ,**" with its quotation from the book of Ruth, is Mary's prayer for her husband and for Daniel Webster's success. Dramatically and musically effective is the devil's selection of a "jury of the damned" to rule on the case. *The Devil and Daniel Webster* was the first of many such "Americanist" operas.

It is quite a different American world that we enter in George Gershwin's folk opera, *Porgy and Bess* (1935). In Charleston, South Carolina, in the early part of this century there was a crippled black beggar named Samuel Smalls who got himself around by means of a cart pulled by a goat, and thus acquired the name of Goat-Sammy. A white Charleston writer, Du Bose Heyward, wrote a short novel—his first—based on this character, whom he renamed Porgy. He set the story in Catfish Row (originally Cabbage Row), a large ancient mansion with a courtyard that had become a black tenement. Through his knowledge of his city and its black people, he surrounded Porgy with thoroughly believable characters and spun a tale of humor, foreboding, violence, brief joy, and desolation. The novel appeared in 1926. George Gershwin read it, liked it, and wrote to the author proposing that they collaborate in making an opera out of it.* Gershwin had many commitments at this time; after many delays, there was a period of

---

*Heyward was at the time working with his wife on a play adaptation, which was staged in 1927. The play, in turn, nearly became a musical produced by Al Jolson, with music by Jerome Kern.

intensive effort. Gershwin went to Charleston during the winter of 1934, and spent the summer of that year on one of the sea islands off its coast—composing, observing, and absorbing all he could of the atmosphere and the black people's music, with which he felt a great affinity.

For those acquainted only with some of the superb songs of the opera (and who does not know "I Got Plenty o' Nothin'"; "Bess, You Is My Woman Now"; "It Ain't Necessarily So"; and above all, "Summertime"?) the experience of the opera as a whole must come as something of a revelation. *Porgy and Bess* is a full-fledged, full-scale opera, in the realistic tradition. The story has been transformed into a tightly knit tragedy, though not without elements of joy, optimism, and especially (a thing Gershwin insisted upon) humor. The volatile central figure is Bess, around whom the action revolves.

Although Gershwin used no actual African-American folk music, there are touches of unmistakable realism and authenticity in the music. The dramatic situation in which more than one thing is going on at the same time onstage is reflected musically in "Summer time/Seven come, seven come to pappy!" In the opening street scene, Clara is singing ("Summertime") to quiet her baby, while the men are shooting craps. In the second scene, after Robbins's murder by Crown, his widow and her friends are mourning, and hoping that enough money will be put into the saucer to pay for his burial. The call-and-response of "Come on, sister . . ." establishes the atmosphere of an impromptu church service, in which Porgy chants the exhortations of a preacher. The cries of the Strawberry Woman, the Honey Man, and the Crab Man in Act II, scene 3 are colorful bits of authentic street lore. The hurricane bell and the fervent prayers of the terrified people awaiting the storm—a passage for voices alone in which six solo singers chant freely over a background of continuous humming—were inspired by what Gershwin heard while standing outside a black church in Hendersonville, South Carolina. Gershwin thoroughly immersed himself in the musical ambience of the South Carolina blacks. Du Bose Heyward has described how, at a meeting of the Gullah blacks on a remote Carolina sea island, Gershwin joined wholeheartedly in the "shouting." Of his whole South Carolina experience Heyward said, "To George it was more like a homecoming than an exploration."

In 1934 an opera was premiered in Hartford, Connecticut, that broke new ground for the American lyrical stage and forecast, in interesting ways, the non-narrative musical theater that was to come into being more than forty years later. *Four Saints in Three Acts* with music by Virgil Thomson was described by its scenarist Maurice Grosser as "both an opera and a choreographic spectacle." The text is by Gertrude Stein, a formidable talent of forceful originality in the use of language. The opera dispenses with plot in the conventional sense in favor of atmosphere, achieved through a series of "imaginary but characteristic incidents." It is set in Spain, and its principal characters are Saint Teresa and Saint Ignatius. Literal expectations must be laid aside; there are actually fifteen saints in all, in four acts, and one of the saints is represented by two singers identically dressed. The text is simply and beautifully set by Thomson to a light and transparent orchestral accompaniment so that every word can be heard and understood. It was Thomson's idea, daring in its day, that an all-black cast of singers could best interpret the words and music. The memorable sets for the first production were of draped cellophane. Act I takes place at Avila; Act II is a garden party in the country near Barcelona; Act III is set in the garden of a monastery on a sea coast. Act IV takes place in heaven. Two excerpts from Act III are "**Pigeons on the grass, alas,**" which is, according to Stein, St. Ignatius's Vision of the Holy Ghost, and "**Between thirty-five and forty-five . . .,**" which precedes the exit procession of the saints.

Virgil Thomson had this advice to the listeners:

> Please do not try to construe the words of this opera literally or to seek in it any abstruse symbolism. If, by means of the poet's liberties with logic and the composer's constant use of the simplest elements in our musical vernacular, something is here evoked of the childlike gaiety and mystical strength of lives devoted in common to non-materialistic end, the authors will consider their message to have been communicated.[1]

American Opera vis-à-vis American Culture after the 1930s

Two of the three operas selected for attention from the 1930s had American subjects and settings. This is noted, not as an incitement to chauvinism, but because any dramatic form takes root and flourishes best in the soil of its native culture. Composer and writer Charles Hamm, in a 1961 essay critical of American opera composers up to that time, made that point with regard to Italy, Germany, and Russia—countries that developed strong operatic traditions *and indigenous repertoire*. He wrote: "The history of opera tells us, clearly and repeatedly, that the popularity of opera in those countries can be traced back to successful attempts by composers to create operas completely comprehensible to audiences in those countries, comprehensible not merely because they are written in the vernacular but because *they have something to do with the culture of the country*."[2]

Earlier operas had dealt with American subjects (recall *The Indian Princess* of 1808, based on the story of Pocahontas, and Bristow's *Rip Van Winkle* of 1855), but the derivative nature of their musical idioms (English in the first case, Italian in the second) mitigated their validity as authentic expressions of American culture.

Given the state of American musical development when they were composed, one could hardly have expected otherwise. By the 1930s, however, America was developing its own diverse musical voices. In the years that followed, a number of operas were composed that had a valid and palpable relation to the culture of the country. None fits this description better than Virgil Thomson's *The Mother of Us All* (1947), with libretto by Gertrude Stein, who had written the text of *Four Saints in Three Acts*, and who, despite her self-exile, continued to feel a strong identification with her native land. Thomson explains in his preface to the score, "*The Mother of Us All* is a pageant. Its theme is the winning in the United States of political rights for women. Its story is the life and career of Susan B. Anthony (1820–1906). Some of the characters are historical, others imaginary. They include figures as widely separated in time as John Quincy Adams and Lillian Russell . . ."[3] As in the earlier *Four Saints in Three Acts* the vocal writing is exceptionally true to the rhythms of speech; and the music, of a self-effacing simplicity, reinforces its relevance through the use of nineteenth-century-style waltzes, marches, and hymnlike tunes.

After *The Mother of Us All*, the floodgates were opened for a multitude of works having "something to do with the culture of the country." Actual historical figures were the basis for two more operas by Douglas Moore. The first was *The Ballad of Baby Doe* (1956), set in Colorado's fabulous mining era. The second was *Carrie Nation* (1966), based on events in the life of the turn-of-the-century Prohibitionist that led her to launch her crusade. Marc Blitzstein, who had written a famous leftist opera, *The Cradle Will Rock* in 1937, was at work on *Sacco and Vanzetti*, an opera based on that famous case when he died in 1964. Operas based on novels included *Regina* (1949) by Marc Blitzstein, on Lillian Hellman's *The Little Foxes*, and *Of Mice and Men* (1970) by Carlisle Floyd, on John Steinbeck's novel of the same name. A shorter work by Lukas Foss is *The Jumping Frog of Calaveras County* (1950) on the Mark Twain story. Robert Ward's *The Crucible* (1961) is based on the Arthur Miller play about the Salem witch hunts. Carlisle Floyd's best-known work is *Susannah* (1954), which transfers the Apocryphal story of Susannah and the Elders to rural Tennessee; it is thus played out in a setting of rural and primitive Southern orthodoxy—stern, intolerant, and hypocritical. Floyd's more recent *Willie Stark* (1981) is an adaptation of the novel *All the King's Men* by Robert Penn Warren, based on the career of the legendary Louisiana politician Huey Long. Thomas Pasatieri made an opera out of *The Trial of Mary Lincoln* (1972), and Jack Beeson used a famous American murder as the basis for *Lizzie Borden* (1965).

A scene from *Einstein on the Beach*. *Photo © Beatriz Schiller.*

New Opera in the Last Quarter of the Century

Beginning in the 1970s, new approaches to the combining of music and drama began to be tried out, resulting in new genres of serious musical theater. The chapter on opera is the place to consider them in all their variety, first because there is no other place for them, and second, because explorers as diverse as Merideth Monk (with her wordless dramas of music and gesture for which a live audience is a vital ingredient) and Robert Ashley (with his word-laden dramas for television and no live audience) have elected to *call* their productions operas.

Remaking Traditional Genres in Traditional Venues

A public symposium in 1994 involving four opera composers had as its title "Remaking American Opera."[4] The verb is an apt one. It became clear by the 1990s that "grand opera," meaning opera given with lavish staging and full orchestras in major opera houses, was not to be written off after all by innovative American composers, but had been "remade." New American operas in the old tradition of opulent production, while they constitute a minute proportion of the repertoire, do appear from time to time in the major opera theaters. They are not commissioned and produced altogether out of a sense of artistic altruism; the amazing rise in popularity (referred to in the preceding chapter) of minimalist composers such as Philip Glass and John Adams led the big houses to produce, for sellout crowds, Glass's *Satyagraha* (1980), *Akhnaten* (1984), and *The Voyage* (1992); and Adams's *Nixon in China* (1987) and *The Death of Klinghoffer* (1991). All are full-scale "grand operas."

Einstein on the Beach (1976), ultimately responsible for Glass's sudden fame, was written as a mixed-media theater piece to be accompanied by Glass's small amplified ensemble, which played onstage. Musically, *Einstein* is thoroughly minimalist; Andrew Porter, in reviewing the first U.S. performance, described the music as "in essence a series of extended moto perpetuos, each of them lasting longer than Ravel's 'Bolero.'"[5]* *Einstein* is a four-act opera lasting nearly five hours, without intermission. (Members of the audience come and go during the performance.) The orchestra was the Philip Glass Ensemble of five instrumentalists, the solo violinist who plays the role of Einstein (all heavily amplified), and a sound engineer. Like Thomson's *Four Saints in Three Acts*, a seminal opera of forty years earlier, *Einstein* has no plot in the conventional sense. Glass has designated the genre as "non-literary theater"; the "libretto" consists largely of numerals sung or spoken, and sol-fa syllables. The staging, décor, and direction of Robert Wilson were as responsible for its memorability as was the music. According to Porter, there were "three basic images: a train, a courtroom that dissolves into a prison, and a field of dancers with a spaceship in the sky above them."

John Adams went directly into full-scale opera with a commission from the Houston Grand Opera for *Nixon in China* (1987), with a libretto by Alice Goodman. The first act fulfills all of the expectations of grand opera. President Nixon and Chairman Mao have bestowed on them, in late-twentieth-century musical and stage terms, all the operatic ceremony associated in eighteenth- and nineteenth-century operas with kings and pharaohs. The spectacle everyone remembers, the landing onstage of Air Force One and the emergence of Nixon and his wife, Pat, is the equivalent, as Adams has wittily observed, of the onstage elephants in *Aida*, or the burning of Valhalla in *Die Götterdämmerung*—"the things people pay big bucks to see." The second act is, as Adams says, devoted to the women. One of the most expressive moments in the opera comes as something of a surprise in the opera's context; it is Pat's Whitmanesque soliloquy "This is prophetic!" The repetitiousness of the music becomes gentler as the better time she foresees appears as a vision realized in homely terms of everyday life in her own country. In act three statecraft is forgotten, and the leading couples commu-

---

Bolero is an orchestral piece written by the French composer Maurice Ravel in 1929. In a sense an early minimalist piece, it lasts about fourteen minutes, its melodic material consisting of just two tunes each of which is played nine times.

nicate only with each other in private reflections of the past. The opera ends with a soliloquy by Chou En-lai.

Repetitive music works well in *Nixon in China*. Here the music, without notable climaxes, stays in the background (as in traditional Chinese opera), changing harmony and color at appropriate times, and letting the vocal lines, which fit the inflections of the text, stand out in relief.

Other grand operas in recent years have also had as their subjects present-day people and events. Adams treated a notorious assassination in the Middle East in *The Death of Klinghoffer* (1991), an opera he sees as "creating a dramatic experience that found a location on the globe within a stone's throw of the birthplace of the three great Western religions, with an incredible historical expanse between the almost biblical timeless past and the painful and invasive present." Anthony Davis's opera *X: The Life and Times of Malcolm X*, on the assassinated black leader, was produced in 1986. It is in a nonminimalist, dissonant idiom. Davis subsequently composed an opera on the Patty Hearst saga. Another opera having to do with assassination is *Harvey Milk* (1995), by Stewart Wallace, which deals with the fatal shooting of San Francisco mayor George Moscone and supervisor Harvey Milk, San Francisco's first openly gay elected official, in 1978. Thus new American operas on American subjects have found themselves a niche, however narrow, in those prestigious halls devoted to the cultivation of that most expensive of all musical genres, "grand opera." But a place in this niche comes at the price of adherence to grand opera's strict traditions and priorities. And operas on current figures and events, however much attention they may attract, are not without their problems, legal, financial, and political.* These factors have caused innovative composers to look to other venues, and to create other genres. It is to these that we now direct our attention.

Creating New Operatic Genres

Meredith Monk (b. 1943) is a multifaceted artist who is composer, singer, dancer, choreographer, and filmmaker, but who practices none of these in conventional ways, preferring to work "between the cracks," as she has said, and in the process creating new genres. Though she sparingly uses *spoken* text, she has almost never set words to music, preferring to make use instead of what she calls the "abstract" property of the human voice. Freed from language, which is always specific to a particular culture, she seeks a more direct expression of emotion through wordless

---

*John Adams's *The Death of Klinghoffer* was picketed in San Francisco, and sold-out performances in Los Angeles were cancelled, owing to management's fear of losing support from large and powerful contributors. This was at least partly responsible for Adams's turning to a new and more intimate venue, and hence a new style, in his smaller-scale opera *I Was Looking at the Ceiling and then I Saw the Sky* (1995).

vocal sounds. She has mastered and taught to the members of her Meredith Monk Vocal Ensemble a wide variety of what have been called "extended vocal techniques." Asserting that "the body doesn't lie," she bypasses words in dealing with the narrative elements in her pieces, using situations that are simple enough so that their emotional aspect is dealt with through gesture, dance, and textless voice. Her music (especially the accompaniments, which are usually done with piano or organ) is minimalist, so that the vocal parts stand out in relief. A recent long work is *Atlas* (1991). It was inspired by the travels of Alexandra David Neel, the explorer who was the first woman to go into Tibet. The basic "poem," as she expresses it, is about exploration, as a metaphor for following our inner voices no matter what the outside world is saying. "**Choosing Companions**" is an early section of the work in which the young heroine is "auditioning" applicants to accompany her on her journey. Although Meredith Monk uses film, she stresses the importance of live performance, valuing the "energy" that flows between audience and live performers. In combining different mediums, she seeks "ways of integrating all human resources into one life affirmative form—a healing ritual."

Meredith Monk has said that when sound was added to film, something was lost. Philip Glass, an admirer of Meredith Monk's work, has *removed* the sound track from a 1946 film by Jean Cocteau, *Le Belle et la Bête* (Beauty and the Beast), and added his own music performed by his seven-piece ensemble and four singers who are placed in the stage in front of the large screen on which the film is projected. The music is composed so that the voices are synchronized as closely as possible to the images on the screen.

Perfect Lives (1979–84) is an opera for television in seven half-hour episodes by Robert Ashley (b. 1930). There are characters and a scenario, though the "story" is difficult to find and follow through the maze of continuous monochromatic stream-of-consciousness narration by Ashley himself. As to the actual "events" of the scenario, Ashley has said, "[T]here's very little of that in *Private Lives*, of people actually doing things." There is a sense of *place* (the Midwest) in the work, which is expressed in the language, the visual images, and the music. Ashley describes the episodes as ". . . songs about the Corn Belt . . . ." The music is continuous and minimalist. The term "cocktail" has been applied (or misapplied) to it; its ingredients derive from pop-rock, boogie-woogie, and jazz. Ashley himself did not write all of the music; he put great emphasis on the work as collaborative effort. Visually the work is a rapidly shifting collage, its chief ingredients being Ashley himself as narrator, the pianist "Blue" Gene Tyranny (Robert Sheff) performing, the *dramatis personae*, and location shots, all manipulated with the techniques available to the video craft of its time.

In view of what has been touched on in the foregoing brief summary, it should be clear that American opera, as we prepare to enter the twenty-first century, is *work in progress*.

FURTHER READING

Dizikes, John. *Opera in America: A Cultural History*. New Haven and London: Yale University Press, 1993.

> There is a distinction between "opera in America" and "American opera." Although this book devotes a good deal of space to singers, managers, and buildings (opera in America), there is also good coverage of American opera composers and their music.

Gagne, Cole, and Tracy Caras. *Soundpieces: Interviews with American Composers*. Metuchen, NJ, & London: Scarecrow, 1982.

> Includes interviews with Robert Ashley and Philip Glass.

Rockwell, John. *All American Music: Composition in the Late Twentieth Century*. New York: Knopf, 1983.

> Though the period covered is no longer so "late," this is a collection of still interesting essays, including material on Glass, Reich, Monk, Ashley, and Laurie Anderson.

Articles

Lassetter, Leslie. "Opera from Elsewhere: Meredith Monk's *Atlas*." *Sonneck Society Bulletin* (Fall 1994): 10–14.

Thomson, Virgil, and Philip Glass; Gregory Sandow, moderator. "The Composer and Performer and Other Matters." *American Music* 7, no. 2 (Summer 1989): 181–204.

> Includes Thomson and Glass on opera.

Projects

1. As regards opera composed in a language other than English, the controversy between presenting such operas for English-speaking audiences in English or in the original language still rages. Write a brief paper presenting reasoned arguments in support of either practice. Support your arguments with specific examples in which the language of performance either enhances or detracts from the opera's effectiveness.

2. If there is a producing opera company in a city near you, make a survey of the season's programming in terms of the percentage of American operas produced.

3. Read a story or a play that has been made into an opera by an American composer, comparing the original with the opera. Note the changes that have been made, and try to account for them in terms of the requirements of opera. Examples would be Du Bose Heyward's novel *Porgy*, or the play adapted by the author and his wife, vis-à-vis the opera *Porgy and Bess* (score available in many music libraries, many recorded versions available); Emily Brontë's *Wuthering Heights* vis-à-vis Carlisle Floyd's opera of the same title (score available in many music libraries, no current recording available); or Arthur Miller's play *The Crucible* vis-à-vis the opera of the same title by Robert Ward (score in many music libraries, one recorded version available).

4. Listen to Samuel Barber's short opera *A Hand of Bridge* (available in at least 2 recorded versions). Compare the different musical characterizations of the four players, whose unspoken thoughts are sung as the game goes on perfunctorily.

5. Douglas Moore's opera *The Ballad of Baby Doe* and Meredith Willson's musical *The Unsinkable Molly Brown* both have the same setting (Colorado), and both deal with actual historical figures, women who faced the challenges of the mining-camp era of the West. Compare these two works, as a means of pointing out some of the differences—musical, dramatic, and in overall approach—between opera and popular musical theater.

6. In a brief paper, assess the pros and cons from your point of view of producing operas on current "newsworthy" happenings, especially murders or assassinations. Include a consideration of both the motivations and the dangers involved.

7. Attend a live performance, watch a video, or listen to a recording of an "opera" in a new genre such as those described above. Write a review, giving your own assessment of the work and the genre.

Notes

1. Virgil Thomson, as quoted in the notes to the recording conducted by the composer.

2. Charles Hamm, "Opera and the American Composer" in *The American Composer Speaks*. Emphasis is the present author's.

3. Virgil Thomson, from the preface to the printed score.

4. The symposium "Remaking American Opera" took place under the auspices of the Institute for Studies in American Music at the CUNY Graduate Center in New York in November 1994. John Adams, Anthony Davis, Meredith Monk, and Tania León were the composer participants. The moderator was K. Robert Schwarz.

5. Andrew Porter, *The New Yorker*, December 13, 1976.

Part Seven

Regionalism and Diversity

Photo by Elemore Morgan, Jr.

"Diversity" has become, at century's end, a word as constantly in our ears and before our eyes in print as are the manifestations of it that surround us. We swim in diversity. It is no longer as necessary to point out its presence as it seemed when the second edition of this book was in preparation.

This heterogeneity has much to do with the regional differences inherent in the sheer physical extent of the country, and the complexity of its geography and its history. The mass media of today, fed by the popular music industry with its megamarketing machine, may have submerged regionalism, but they have not succeeded in eradicating it. Look carefully under the veneer of a homogenized and ubiquitous popular culture, and you will find in many places a music that derives its character from a sense of *place*—indigenous music, long rooted in the region, and surviving gradual change. The Cajun music of southern Louisiana, the *norteña* music of the lower Rio Grande Valley, and the Scandinavian dance music of the upper Midwest are examples of this.

In other areas, the heterogeneity consists of the presence of a number of relatively small, self-sufficient communities, whose members continue to cultivate music and customs that in the more recent past originated elsewhere—in Latin America, in Europe, or in Asia. These cultural pockets, often virtually unknown to those of the cultural "mainstream," are found most often in, or on the fringes of, huge urban areas. New York City, with its large ethnic enclaves—villages, towns, and cities within the super-city—is the most outstanding example of this, but these pockets can be found in any of our metropolises. They are also typical of areas that have received substantial refugee populations, or that have drawn workers by virtue of powerful but capricious economic magnets such as mining. These pockets can occur in rural as well as urban areas. California is a well-known example, but a substantial amount of cultural diversity, under the surface, can be found even in states such as Wyoming.

Regions that in the recent past have drawn immigrants in large numbers often do not have a single easily identifiable *indigenous* music (such as might be found in the Appalachians or southwestern Louisiana, for example) but tend, like New York City, to be great meeting grounds for a multitude of cultures.

In the chapter that follows we shall look briefly at three places in the United States that are quite far apart geographically. This is no more than a sampling; its main purpose is to encourage interested observers and students simply to look around, wherever they may be, in order to become aware of the heterogeneity of cultures present in their own region.

Chapter 21

Three Regional Samplings

Louisiana and the French Influence

Louisiana is a land of sultry climate, dominated largely by the complex outflow, through shifting channels and bayous, of one of the largest river systems in the world. It has a complex cultural pattern as well—albeit one that is fairly stable, the main ingredients of its mix having been established for over a century. To an indigenous Indian population was added that of French colonizers and settlers beginning in the early eighteenth century. There was scant Spanish immigration during the period of Spanish rule (1764–1800). An important factor in the cultural mix of Louisiana was the dramatic rise in the African-American population, coming mostly from the West Indies, at the end of the eighteenth century. Black people were brought to Louisiana in significant numbers by planters escaping the revolution in Haiti in the 1790s. The cultural ties of Louisiana with the West Indies, especially Haiti, have been important ever since. After the Louisiana Purchase in 1803, American influence and immigration naturally increased, and the substantial black population made possible, in part, the rapid growth of the sugar plantations. Italians, Hungarians, Slovenians, Germans, and Irish have since been added to the mix in smaller numbers. The dominant cultural (and therefore musical) patterns of Louisiana, however, are the result of a complex interaction between those of French and African descent.

The Louisiana French and the Louisiana Africans

French people began settling Louisiana early in the eighteenth century, some coming directly from France and others arriving after a stopover of a few generations in the West Indies. Many were families of means and belonged to the aristocracy, and they soon constituted a wealthy planter class. Their cultural inclinations were urban and sophisticated; this was manifested in the fact that French opera was established in New Orleans as early as the 1790s.

At the other end of the economic scale was the French-descended refugee population that came to Louisiana from Acadia (now Nova Scotia) in the latter part of the eighteenth century. A few of these Acadians had reached Louisiana before the Expulsion, but the great flow took place after 1755, when the victorious English, in a cruel episode known as the Dérangement, began to expel all Acadians who would not take an oath of allegiance to the British crown. The Acadians began arriving in Louisiana some ten years later, after stopovers in France and in the American colonies. These people, mostly farmers and fishermen whose families had come from Brittany and Normandy, were regarded with contempt by the upper-class French, who excluded them from New Orleans but allowed them to settle upstream, along a stretch of the right bank of the Mississippi that became known as the "Acadian coast." The "Cajuns" were regarded as inferior, but the colony benefited from the presence of these industrious people, in their raising of crops and livestock to feed New Orleans and their ability to construct the all-important dikes to control the rivers and bayous.

The Cajuns suffered a "second expulsion" after the Purchase and the coming of the Americans, when it was found that the land they occupied was ideal for raising sugarcane. They moved farther south and west, into the bayous and swamps of the coastal regions, and the prairies of the West. Thus they came to occupy the "French triangle," with its base along the Gulf Coast, and its apex around Alexandria. Tracing their lineage back two centuries to the first Acadian families (the Moutons, the Arceneaux, the Bernards, the Broussards, the Guidrys), they occupy the largest area of French-derived culture and language in the United States. There are now approximately one million people, roughly a quarter of the population of Louisiana, who identify themselves as Cajuns.

People of African descent have played a major role in Louisiana history and culture. Like the French, they have have been stratified into a complex ranking of caste and lineage. High in the social order were the "gens de couleur libres" ("free persons of color"), of whose presence in Louisiana there are records from the early eighteenth century. From 1725 on they either entered free, were freed in recognition of merit and loyalty, were given their freedom by a white parent or lover, or purchased their own freedom. (American Indians also had the status of "free persons of color.") Many became wealthy and influential, owning land and slaves. At the other end of the social scale (though not as low as the Cajuns!) were the black slaves from Africa and the West Indies.

Cajun Music

In general usage, we find that French-derived white folk songs are designated "Cajun," while French-derived black folk songs are designated "Creole."[1] There are some charming French songs and ballads that have been recovered in versions close to very old ones found in Europe. Among old ballads (possibly medieval) that have been recovered are "Le plus jeune des trois" and "Sept ans sur mer."

The fiddle was the basic Cajun instrument from the earliest times, being used for the enduring pastime of dancing. A dance lasting late into the night, to which the children are brought and bedded down, is known as a *fais do-do* (French: "go beddy-bye"). In the 1920s the accordion (possibly making its way into the area via German settlers) began to be adopted, as it was farther west in the *musica norteña* of the Texas-Mexican border (see chapter 4). By the time (about 1926) that the Cajun accordionist Joseph Falcon and his wife, née Cleoma Breaux, recorded "Allons à Lafayette," the accordion had become an integral part of the Cajun band, which consisted in addition of fiddle, guitar, and, in the early days, triangle, or *'tit fer* ("small iron"). Listening to early recorded sources, we find a music that is lighthearted in mood and theme, with a marked predilection for love songs, and a repertory consisting mostly of waltzes, pieces in duple meter related to hoedown music, and pieces related to the blues. The vocal style is unique and unmistakable, though difficult to describe. Vocal tone is somewhat flat and nasal, at times only approximating the pitch, with frequently interjected yells and wails.

Probably the most widely known of the old Cajun songs, which is also a dance tune, is "Saute crapaud" (Ex. 21-1). The enigmatic words—"Jump, toad, your tail will burn;/ Take courage, another will grow"—suggest that this may once have been a satire of some kind. Nothing seems to be known of its origin.

Example 21–1. "Saute crapaud"

In the late 1930s and the 1940s, with the expansion of the oil industry and the influx of workers from the rural Southeast, Cajun music lost many of its earlier distinctive characteristics, and was nearly swamped in the flood of country-and-western music. It was about this time that the Hawaiian steel guitar, which had recently become popular in country music, joined the Cajun band. And one hears in "Le côté farouche de la vie" a Cajun adaptation of the country music song "It Wasn't God Who Made Honky-Tonk Angels" to the tune of "I'm Dreaming Tonight of My Blue-eyes." Many of the recordings of this period take on the character of hillbilly music sung in patois.

A typical zydeco ensemble: Lawrence "Black" Ardoin and His French Band.
Photo by Chris Strachwitz.

Since the 1950s there has been a resurgence of the older styles; the accordion is back, and so are some of the older songs. With musicians such as Michael Doucet (who has revived Cajun fiddle playing) and his group, Beausoleil, Cajun music has undergone a full-fledged revival and reconnection with its traditions. **"J'ai été au zydeco"** (**I went to the zydeco dance**), a reinterpretation by Doucet and Beausoleil of the traditional Cajun song "Jai été au bal," is representative.

Zydeco: Cajun Rhythm-and-Blues

The presence of black musicians in Cajun territory has resulted in a rhythm-and-blues translation of Cajun music known as *zydeco* (or *zodico* or *zarico*). Zydeco* music retains and features the accordion, but adds to the band the piano, electric guitar, electric bass, drums, and sometimes saxophones, usually leaves out the fiddle, often adds a characteristic "rub-board" (which has the function and sound of the washboard of the early jug and blues bands), and has a strong rhythm-and-blues flavor. Clifton Chenier (1925–87), the "king of zydeco" (he had many publicity photos taken wearing an actual crown), was a versatile musician who in the 1960s and 1970s performed both zydeco, singing in Cajun-French, and out-and-

---

*The term *zydeco* is said to have come from the Creole pronunciation of "les haricots" (beans) in the early Cajun song "Les haricots sont pas salé." On the Louisiana-Texas Gulf Coast the term *zydeco* can also refer to a party (like the term *fais do-do*), or to a gumbo dish.

out Gulf Coast rhythm-and-blues, which he sang in English. Chenier's "**Zydeco sont pas salé**" (The snap beans aren't salty), from around 1965, is representative of early zydeco. Important performers of zydeco in an older style, closer to Cajun music, are the accordionists Freeman Fontenot and Alphonse "Bois-sec" Ardoin, and the fiddler Canray Fontenot. The newer style, closer to rhythm-and-blues, is represented by accordionists John Delafose, Rocking Dopsie, Rocking Sidney, Stanley "Buckwheat" Dural, and Boozoo Chavis. White musicians such as Wayne Toups and Zachary Richard are also performing zydeco.

Creole Music

There is ample evidence of African-based music-making in and around New Orleans in the nineteenth century. Seven "Creole" songs, in dialect French, were included at the end of the famous *Slave Songs of the United States* published in 1867. Place Congo, opposite the Vieux Carré (and on the present-day site of Louis "Satchmo" Armstrong Park), was the scene of weekly black festivities and ceremonies, from which whites were traditionally excluded. As was true in Africa itself, there was (and is) a nearly inseparable association of music and dance. The *bamboula*, the *counjaille*, the *calinda*, the *habanera*—these were types of songs, but they were also dances. The *bamboula* was named for a small drum made from a section of the huge bamboo that grows in the West Indies; the drum accompanied both song and dance. The dance itself was vividly described in a much-quoted article by George Washington Cable, which included the music (Ex. 21-2).[2]

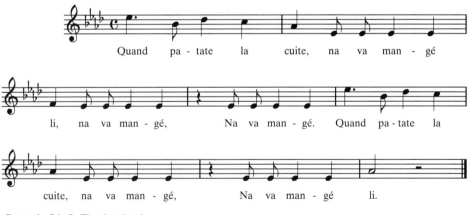

Example 21–2. The *bamboula*

The first measure has a rhythm basic to much Latin American music—and, via New Orleans, presumably, to much American black music as well—that of the *habanera* or *danza*, which could be either song or dance.

A pervading influence among the blacks of French Louisiana—and not unknown among whites, as well—was *voodoo*, known in New Orleans as *hoodoo*. A religion originating principally among the Dahomeans in Africa, voodoo had become intermingled with the liturgy and ritual of Roman Catholicism (despite the general opposition of the Church) among the blacks of the French West Indies, especially San Domingo and Martinique. Hoodoo ceremonies were marked by rhythmic drumming, chanting, and dancing. The bamboula was associated with it. The goal seemed to be a kind of ecstatic possession by one of the hoodoo deities. According to eyewitness accounts, this possession was not unlike that to be seen at primitive revival meetings.

Much of the Creole music we have just described contained some of the important seeds of jazz, the culminating musical form developed by black musicians from the rich variety of influences present in turn-of-the-century New Orleans.[3]

The Upper Midwest and the Scandinavian Influence

We have examined briefly the French-Iberian-African culture at the mouth of the Mississippi. At the source of this great river, and across the upper Midwest, we find a land that in its climate, its topography, and the ethnic background of its people is in utter contrast. In the geological day-before-yesterday the land was scoured by glaciers, which left behind many lakes and a rich glacial soil, supporting vegetation that varied from prairie in the south to dense forest in the north. It lies right in the center of the North American continent, and while its early Scandinavian settlers (especially the Swedes and Finns) found the topography similar to that of their homeland, the Norwegians found the harsh continental climate much more extreme. As a Norwegian immigrant wrote home from Wisconsin in 1857, "The winter here is shorter than in Norway, but it is usually much colder, and when the summer comes, that in turn is much warmer. . . . Many people not adjusted to the climate break down."[4]

The first inhabitants encountered by the Europeans were the Chippewa and the Dakota Sioux. Throughout the seventeenth, eighteenth, and early nineteenth centuries a tenuous white presence was maintained by the successive establishment of forts and trading posts by first the French, then the English, and finally the Americans, all of whom were interested primarily in furs. But the beginning of permanent settlement had taken place well before the Civil War, by which time a series of land-grabbing treaties and military operations had practically driven out the Indians, to make way for a rapid influx of prospective farmers.

Scandinavian immigrants began settling in Wisconsin in the 1840s, and in Minnesota in the 1850s. The Swedes, the most numerous group, began as farmers but later moved to the cities, to be outnumbered in farming by the Norwegians, the next most numerous. The Norwegian immigrant man, bringing with him a strong attachment to the land, would characteristically progress from hired hand to shareman to landowning farmer. Other immigrant peoples, also from northern or central Europe, were the Germans (notably in Wisconsin), the Danes, the Finns, the Poles, and the Czechs. But by the last quarter of the century the Scandinavian presence was decisive in determining the cultural makeup of the upper Midwest.

Scandinavian-American Music in the Upper Midwest

The kind of regional music most in evidence in this area is music for dancing. The music, the instruments, and the dances themselves occur in layers, based on their antiquity. The oldest dances from Norway, such as the *halling* (in which the dancer kicks a hat off of a vertically held pole), the *springer*, or the *gangar*, belong to a bygone era and are encountered only in deliberate and costumed revivals. The same is true of the instruments that were brought direct from Norway and were associated with the old dances. Chief among these was the Hardanger fiddle (*Hardangfele*), an instrument that has, beneath the four strings played with the bow, a set of sympathetic strings that vibrate in resonance with the bowed strings.

As the old dances and the old instruments went out of general use, they were replaced by the three dances most popular among Scandinavian-Americans today—the schottische, the waltz, and the polka. The most popular instruments for dances are now the regular fiddle and the accordion, accompanied by guitar, piano, pump organ, or banjo, as available. In rural areas, dances took place at house parties in homes, or in the cleared-out second-floor lofts of roomy barns. (More recently, barns that have never housed hay or cattle have been built especially for "barn dances.") In the towns and cities, public dances are held in various social halls.

In the first years of this century commercial recordings of Scandinavian music began to be made by professional and semiprofessional bands. As early as 1915 the Swedish immigrant musician and entertainer Hjalmar Peterson (who adopted the stage name "Olle i Skratthult") recorded his love song "**Nikolina**," which became immensely popular in succeeding years, and was performed in many variants both as a song and an instrumental piece (Ex. 21-3). Its use of mixed meter is exceptional in a musical tradition that, being so closely related to the dance, is fundamentally extremely predictable in terms of meter, phrase, length, and form.[5]

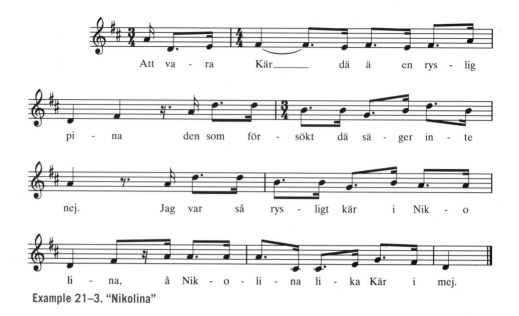

Example 21–3. "Nikolina"

When you're in love you're in an awful torture,
Who ever has tried it will not disagree,
I was so very fond of Nikolina
And Nikolina was as fond of me.

The impact of recordings, radio, the jukebox, traveling vaudeville (Olle i Skratthult himself was "on the road" for years with his band of entertainers), and movies was to force changes in Scandinavian-American music and a decline in home music-making—a familiar pattern everywhere. But it was, ironically, through the very medium of the old recordings that the "old-time" styles of the early twentieth century were ultimately preserved—also a familiar pattern wherever there has been a revival of old-time music. State agencies and programs such as the Folk Arts Program of the Minnesota State Arts Board are engaged in actively encouraging the documentation and preservation of "people's arts."* Closely related to this preservation movement are ethnic gatherings such as the annual Nordic Fest in Decorah, Iowa, and widespread celebrations of Syttende Mai (May 17, Norwegian Independence Day).**

*Most of the fifty states now have such programs, under various titles.
**Practically all ethnic groups everywhere in America have similar gatherings to celebrate their original national holidays—the Mexican "Cinco de Mayo" is another example.

The work of LeRoy Larson, folklorist, scholar, banjo player, and record producer, together with his Minnesota Scandinavian Ensemble, typifies what is being done in the way of contemporary live performance. His work, like that of Michael Doucet in Louisiana, Justin Bishop in California, and many others, is not simply to preserve but to re-create, to reinterpret, and to create anew in traditional styles, and thus to demonstrate their vitality and validity as an effective alternative to the progressive homogenization of American culture. Were it not for them, and people like them in virtually every state, this chapter would have been confined to simply chronicling the decline and death of regional musics in this country.

The Sacramento Valley: A Rich Mix of Cultures

The Sacramento Valley of California is a broad alluvial valley between two mountain ranges—a low coastal range to the west, and the Sierra Nevada to the east. From the high, snow-trapping barrier range of the Sierra flow down into the valley a series of tumultuous rivers that, until barely a century ago, spread wide out of their banks in the spring, flooding the valley, depositing rich alluvial soils and clays, and filling the huge old basins with half a million acres of water from January to May. Tamed now by scores of dams and hundreds of miles of levees, they furnish the water that allows a multitude of crops to grow through the long hot season from May to October, when no rain falls.

Unlike Louisiana and the upper Midwest—longer-settled regions whose cultural identity, bearing the characteristics of a few dominant immigrant groups, has been established for well over a century—the Sacramento Valley presents a picture of a complex "cross-bedding" of successive migrations from many directions, which has left a rich mix of cultures, many of them still distinct and unassimilated. The phase of greatest influx is so recent that the sense of transiency has still not been replaced by one of settled permanency, and there is nothing that can be identified as a single distinctive regional culture. Each wave of newcomers has come with its own culture, in its own time, and for its own reasons. Trappers, mission founders, would-be empire builders, gold seekers, agricultural barons, land speculators, laborers imported en masse for railroad building or harvesting, networks of immigrants bringing relatives from foreign countries, military, defense, and government workers, wealthy entrepreneurs, and refugee populations—all have formed part of the picture.

A Thumbnail Cultural Chronology of the Valley

A peaceful Indian population with a culture singularly well adapted to the unique region were the original inhabitants; they and their way of life have been all but gone for a century. The Spaniards scarcely penetrated the valley to any extent, and the Mexican government, heir to Spain's territorial claim in 1822, could exercise only a tenuous hold on an area where American trappers and adventurers roamed freely. (The significant Mexican influence and presence was destined to come much later.) The discovery of gold in the Sierra foothills in 1848 brought sudden, irreversible, and drastic change. With the rapid influx of easterners (accompanied by significant immigration from Europe, Central and South America, and Asia), acquisition by the United States and statehood (in 1850) were inevitable. The population soared, and when the easily obtainable deposits of gold ran out (about 1853), large corporations took over the mining and individual miners left or went into farming, which was destined to become the fertile valley's major industry. Railroad building in the 1860s brought in the first of the great laborer populations, the Chinese; as an immigrant labor population the Chinese were replaced by the Japanese beginning about 1900.

From 1900 to 1920 was the time of the great land boom, and the period saw further diversification of the Valley's population. Land companies bought up large tracts (many upon the dissolution of the huge holdings that had originally been Mexican land grants) and advertised heavily in the East. Colonization projects brought more immigrants.

As agriculture in the Valley changed from the growing of wheat, which could easily be harvested mechanically, to fruit and vegetable crops, which required handpicking, the need for seasonal labor grew, and this has made a large transient population of farm workers, with the social problems attendant on it, a part of the Sacramento Valley scene since very early in this century. Since as early as 1919, Mexicans have been coming to do this work.

The Depression and drought of the 1930s brought many from the Dust Bowl areas of Texas, Oklahoma, and Kansas (thus adding to the constituency for country music, which became especially strong in the adjoining San Joaquin Valley to the south). World War II brought further shifts in population throughout the nation; many who came to the Valley during the war stayed or returned to it, thus beginning another period of population growth, which is still going on. Significant recent additions are large refugee populations from southeast Asia.

An Incomplete Cultural and Musical Inventory of the Sacramento Valley

Among the American Indians there is, as described in chapter 3, a new movement under way to restore and revitalize their native dance, music, crafts, and culture. This movement is strong in the Sacramento Valley, despite the fact that few of the Indians there may be descended from the original tribes. There are frequent intertribal powwows, often under the auspices of a college or university.

There is considerable mutual cooperation and support between the native American and the Chicano movements.

Many Chinese came to the Valley and worked as miners during the gold rush, until driven out of this occupation by the Americans. Many more were brought in in the ensuing decade to build the railroad. Hardworking, canny, thrifty, keeping to themselves and to their own traditions, they were the object of scorn and persecution. Their numbers in the Valley declined after 1890. In the decades since World War II, many Chinese have become fully integrated into the social, economic, and cultural life of the Valley, and only small groups of mostly elderly Chinese still cling to Chinese culture, language, and music.[6] Beginning in the 1960s the influx of Chinese as refugees from Vietnam and other parts of southeast Asia increased dramatically.

Another early immigrant group was the Portuguese, who were among the first Europeans to settle in the Sacramento area, some arriving with the gold rush. Coming mostly from the Azores, they established small family farms. Following a familiar pattern, the immigrants, once established, encouraged others from the same areas to come and provided for them upon their arrival. The Portuguese tended to form tightly knit communities, their social activities centering around the Church (St. Elizabeth's in Sacramento still celebrates a Portuguese Mass) and its Holy Days. The *festas* are colorful celebrations, including a procession with music, followed by a feast. For years there were radio programs with a live band playing Portuguese music. Portuguese dances and songs are performed in the social halls in the community, accompanied by traditional *violas de arames*, *violãos*, and *guitarras*. A popular folk song from the Azores known and sung by the Portuguese in Sacramento is "Lira" (Ex. 21-4).

> *A shepherd came down from the hills*
> *And knocked on my door.*
> *He brought a sealed letter {with the news}*
> *That my Lira was dead.*

The Japanese began immigrating in significant numbers around the turn of the century, many coming from Hawaii after its annexation by the United States. Replacing the Chinese as a source of labor, they too were targets of persecution and mistrust until after World War II. Members today of a highly visible and well-integrated component of Valley population, a few Americans of Japanese descent are now making conscious efforts to keep alive their own rich traditions of music, dance, and drama. Of special interest is the cultivation of *minyo*, or folk music and dance (as distinct from *buyo*, or the highly cultivated classical dance).

Example 21–4. "Lira"

This costumed dance for multiple dancers is accompanied by a solo singer (either man or woman), one or several *shamisen*s (a plucked stringed instrument of three strings), a *yokobue* (transverse flute), a *kane* (small bell), and a *taiko* (drum). Also accompanying the performance is the *hayashi*, a chorus of women's voices that "responds" to the solo singer's phrases with high-pitched rhythmic vocables that have no literal meaning. Their refrains have been referred to as "cheering calls." These are audible on the recording of "Hokkai bon uta," a folk song from the northern island of Hokkaido highly popular among dance groups in this country. The dance movements of *minyo odori* are largely stylized interpretations of the body motions of *work* performed in the various localities from which the songs come—for example, work in the rice fields, coal mining, fishing, rice pounding, and cattle driving.

The major influx of Mexicans, and their considerable contribution to the cultural mix, is fairly recent, beginning with the harvests of the early 1920s. Their music today is mainly of the *musica norteña* tradition described in chapter 4, with strong Chicano overtones.

Immigrants from Greece, coming primarily from Peloponnesus, began arriving in the early 1900s, and built their first church in Sacramento in 1921. Though the Greeks are thoroughly integrated into the community, they have preserved a good deal of their culture, focused on the Greek Orthodox Church. Since the 1950s and 1960s there has been a renaissance of Byzantine liturgical music in California. This was followed in the 1970s and 1980s by a renewed interest in Greek folk dance and costumes, and consequently in authentic Greek folk music, with regional distinctions preserved. Folk-dance festivals, in which many young people take part, are frequent events. Several Greek bands are active, playing popular American as well as traditional Greek music. The traditional *klarino* (a type of clarinet) is no longer much used in the bands in Sacramento, but the *bouzóuki*, a fretted lutelike instrument with a long neck, has appeared in ensembles with greater frequency since the popularity of the film *Zorba the Greek*. It keeps company in the bands with electric guitar, drums, and electric keyboards. Greek music is flourishing but adapting—or, rather, flourishing *by* adapting.

Immigration from Ukraine to the United States has occurred in five waves, beginning in the 1870s. The latest wave, in the late 1980s and 1990s, followed *glasnost* and the breakup of the Soviet Union, and consisted mostly of Ukrainian Baptists and Pentecostals who were escaping religious persecution. This wave added substantially to the 120 families that previously constituted the population of Ukrainian descent in Sacramento. Today there are in the Sacramento area Ukrainian Catholic, Baptist, Evangelical, and Pentecostal churches, each with a choir and a cantor, and some with a small orchestra. The Ukrainian Heritage Club of Northern California promotes Ukrainian culture, including music, as does the School of Ukrainian Studies, which has a children's choir. Of special interest is the cultivation of the Ukrainian *bandura*, a plucked stringed instrument originally used to accompany the singing of epic folk ballads as early as the seventh century. Enlarged and perfected, it has become, in the hands of accomplished bandurists like Ola Herasymenko Oliynyk of Sacramento, a concert instrument. She performs numerous solo and ensemble works for bandura, and has formed and leads the Bandura Ensemble of Northern California. **Zelenyi Dubochku** ("The Green Oak") and **Chy Ya Tobi Ne Kazala** ("Did I Not Tell You") are Ukrainian folk songs, accompanied by the bandura.

To be complete, this inventory of ethnic cultures of the Sacramento Valley and their musics would have to include many other communities as well. Among those with active organizations devoted to preserving and celebrating their customs and their cultures, in addition to those treated above, are the Filipinos, the Laotians, the Vietnamese, the Koreans, the Sikhs, the Pacific Islanders, the Armenians, the Serbs, the Croats, the Norwegians, the Poles, and the Italians.

Both you and your interests may be far removed from the Sacramento Valley, or Louisiana, or the upper Midwest. The point of this chapter is to encourage you, wherever you may be, to look around your own community, and explore the musical and cultural heterogeneity that exists in your own midst. You may have in store for you some rewarding surprises.

Conclusion

In this final chapter we have concluded our sweeping glance over the panorama of American music by trying to convey a sense of one of its most characteristic attributes—diversity. As this is written, the author senses a renewed concern on the part of many, both in and out of arts councils, commissions, and boards, for the health of our culture. He senses an awareness of the impoverishment that would come with the loss of regional and traditional musics through their complete absorption in mass culture, and he finds generous-minded patrons, producers, scholars, and performers working to see that this does not happen. The economics of the entertainment industry—the great "hit machine"—does indeed depend on the mass production and marketing of a technically perfect, homogenized product devoid of regional eccentricities, and on a public devoted to consumption rather than participation. But what the hit machine cannot do is to reflect, to serve, or to place value on our diversity, our eccentricity—the very things that give us individuality. As Woody Guthrie sang, looking out from the sixty-fifth floor of one of the mass culture machine's chic and insulated bastions,[7]

It's a long ways from here to th' U.S.A.

To lessen this distance and bring "th' U.S.A." and its far-flung and diverse musics into sharper focus has been the goal of this book.

FURTHER READING

Louisiana

Allen, William Francis, Charles Ware, and Lucy McKim Garrison, eds. *Slave Songs of the United States.* New York, 1867. Paperback reprint. New York: Oak, 1969.
> Seven Louisiana songs in patois are included in this famous early collection.

Ancelet, Barry Jean. *The Makers of Cajun Music.* Québec: Presses de l'Université du Québec, 1984.
> A beautifully prepared treatise, in both English and French, with many fine color photos.

Broven, John. *South to Louisiana: The Music of the Cajun Bayous.* Gretna, LA: Pelican, 1983.

Cable, George Washington. "The Dance in Place Congo"; "Creole Slave Songs." Reprinted in Bernard Katz, ed., *The Social Implications of Early Negro Music in the United States.* New York: Arno, 1969.

Krehbiel, Henry Edward. *Afro-American Folksongs: A Study in Racial and National Music.* New York: Frederick Ungar, 1914. Reprint. 1962.
> Krehbiel collaborated with Cable and with Lafcadio Hearn in collecting and studying black folk music in Louisiana in the nineteenth century. Chapters 9, 10, and 11, on Creole music, are the results of this collaboration.

Lomax, John A., and Alan. *Our Singing Country.* New York: Macmillan, 1949.
> The section "French Songs and Ballads from Southwestern Louisiana" contains seven complete songs collected there in 1934, including three of the songs mentioned in this chapter.

Post, Lauren C. *Cajun Sketches.* Baton Rouge: Louisiana State University Press, 1962.
> Deals with the geography, economics, traditions, and music of the region.

Whitfield, Irène Thérèse. *Louisiana French Folk Songs*. Baton Rouge: Lousiana State University Press, 1939. Enlarged paperback ed. New York: Dover, 1969.

> An important collection in this area. Because of its uniqueness, its few weaknesses are all the more unfortunate: the musical transcriptions are not always trustworthy, and there is a lack of uniform documentation as to where, and especially when, the songs were collected. There are translations of the texts into standard French, but not into English.

The Upper Midwest

Bergmann, Leola Nelson. *Americans from Norway*. Philadelphia: Lippincott, 1950.

Larson, Leroy Wilbur. "Scandinavian-American Folk Music of the Norwegians in Minnesota." Ph.D. dissertation, University of Minnesota, 1975.

————, ed. *Scandinavian Old Time Music Book 1 & 2*. Minneapolis: Banjar, ca. 1980, 1984.

Leary, James P. "Old Time Music in Northern Wisconsin." *American Music* 2, no. 1 (Spring 1984): 71–87.

> A valuable documentation of the current state of old-time music in the Chequamegon Bay area, a region of rich ethnic diversity.

The Sacramento Valley

McGowan, Joseph A. *History of the Sacramento Valley*. 2 vols. New York and West Palm Beach: Lewis Historical Publishing, 1961.

> While not up to date, this is an extensive survey of the first century and more of the Valley's history.

Projects

1. Look around in your own community and make an inventory of the various cultures that are not in the "mainstream," that have retained their culture and perhaps their language as well, and that have their own distinctive and identifiable music and musical tradition.

2. Pick one culture in your own community that fits the description in project 1 above, and make a study (through interviews, attendance at social and religious events, etc.) of their music and the way it functions in their culture.

3. Find out about any national holidays that are celebrated by ethnic groups in your community, and attend and report on them. These are usually celebrations of national independence, like the American Fourth of July; Mexicans, for example, celebrate *Cinco de Mayo* (May 5), and Norwegians *Syttende Mai* (May 17).

4. Find out about and report on the support your own state government gives to folk, ethnic, or regional arts, through a state folklorist or a state arts board or arts council.

Notes

1. The term "Creole" can be a source of considerable confusion. It seems to have three distinct applications. The most generally accepted original meaning is that of a person of French, Spanish, or Portuguese descent born in the New World. But a parallel usage of "Creoles" refers to people of African descent born in the Western Hemisphere (as opposed to Africans, who were termed "bozoles"—both terms being derived from the Portuguese, and dating from the first slave importations by the Portuguese in the fifteenth century). A third, and informal, usage simply has the connotation of indigenous or "homemade" as applied to any food, furniture, customs, etc. of the Gulf states region.

2. Two articles by Cable that included music, "The Dance in Place Congo" and "Creole Slave Songs," were printed in *The Century Magazine* in 1886, and are reprinted in Bernard Katz, ed., *The Social Implications of Early Negro Music in The United States* (New York: Arno, 1969).

3. Some of the best treatment of black music in pre–twentieth-century New Orleans and the West Indies is found in Marshall Stearns, *The Story of Jazz* (New York: Oxford University Press, 1956): see

especially chapters 3, 4, and 5. The author also wishes to acknowledge the assistance of the poet and researcher Brenda Marie Osbey of New Orleans.

4. Quoted in Leola Nelson Bergmann, *Americans from Norway* (Philadelphia: Lippincott, 1950), 52.

5. This version of "Nikolina" is transcribed by the author from a 1930s recording reissued on *Early Scandinavian Bandss and Entertainers*, Banjar BR 1840. Another version of it appears in *Scandinavian Old Time Music Book 2*, ed. LeRoy Larson (Minneapolis: Banjar, 1984).

6. Chinese in the Valley seeking to preserve their own musical traditions have been heavily dependent on San Francisco, with its large Chinese population. But Curtis Gaesser, while a graduate student at California State University, Sacramento, witnessed and taped a performance by a group in Sacramento playing traditional Chinese instruments.

7. Woody Guthrie, *Bound for Glory* (New York: Dutton, 1943), 293. Reprinted by kind permission.

INDEX

First New England School, 298n
Fisk Jubilee Singers, 23, 172, 302
Fitzgerald, Ella, 104, 236
Flatt, Lester, 95
Flora, or the Hob in the Well (ballad farce), 380
Florida: blues in, 107; Huguenot psalm singing in, 47, 139; Spaniards in, 53
"Flow Gently, Sweet Afton" (Spilman), 218
Floyd, Carlisle, 384
"Floyd Collins" (folk ballad), 6
Flute: in American Indian music, 45; made of gun barrel, 56; solo instrument in early concerts, 184
"Flying Trapeze, The" (19th-century song), 226
Follies (Sondheim), 212
Fontenot, Canray, 397
Fontenot, Freeman, 397
"Fool in Love, A" (rhythm-and-blues number), 109
Ford, Tennessee Ernie, 90
Fortune Teller, The (Herbert), 204
Forty-five Minutes from Broadway (Cohan), 203
Foss, Lucas, 384
Foster, Stephen Collins, 16, 199, 218–19, 233, 302; Pittsburgh and, 221–23
"Fountain" (Mason), 335
Four Piano Blues (Copland), 321–22
Four Poems by Edwin Arlington Robinson (Duke), 318
4′ 33″ (Cage), 354
Four New England Holidays (Ives), 335, 339
Four Saints in Three Acts (Thomson), 380, 382–84, 386
Four Strict Songs for Eight Baritones and Orchestra (Harrison), 342
Fourth of July, The (Ives), 335–36
Fourth Symphony (Ives), 33
Fox-trot, 236
Franklin, Aretha, 104, 109
Free Jazz (Coleman), 275–76
Freed, Alan (disc jockey), 123
French, in Louisiana, 393–94
French horn, in eighteenth-century bands, 186; as solo instrument in early concerts, 184
Friml, Rudolf, 204–05
From the Other Side (Martino), 375
Fry, William Henry, 289, 291–92

"Fugue for Tinhorns" (Loesser), 209
Fugue for Percussion (Harrison), 342

Gaburo, Kenneth, 360
"Gaelic" Symphony (Beach), 300
Gallina, La (Gottschalk), 244
Gardner, Isabella Stewart, 298, 301
Garner, Erroll, 271
Gatti-Casazza, Giulio, 380–81
"General William Booth Enters Into Heaven" (Ives) 334–35
Genesis of a Music (Partch), 344, 345
"Gens de couleur libre" ("free persons of color") in Louisiana, 394
"Gentle Annie" (Foster), 218
George Washington, Jr. (Cohan), 203
Georgia sea islands, 20
Germans, in upper midwest, 399; stage portrayal of, 195, 202
Germany, influence of music in America, 57
Gershwin, George, 206, 208, 227, 253, 272, 279, 308, 311, 321–22, 326, 380–82
Gershwin, Ira, 207, 208
"Get Off the Track" (Hutchinson Family Singers), 221
"Get Up, Stand Up" (Marley), 132
Gilbert, Henry F., 300–01, 310
Gilbert, W. S., and Arthur Sullivan, 201–02, 208
Gilded Age, 225
Gillespie, Dizzy, 272, 278
Gilmore, Patrick, 230–33
"Girl of the North Country" (Dylan), 15
"Git Along, Little Dogies" (cowboy song), 316
"Give the Fiddler a Dram" (fiddle tune), 10
Glass, Philip, 370, 386, 388
"Glendy Burk, The" (Foster), 222
"Go Down, Moses" (African-American spiritual), 23, 25
"God Moves on the Water" (Blind Willie Johnson), 170
Golden Gate Quartet (gospel group), 172
Goldman, Edwin Franko, 233
Goldman, Richard Franko, 233
"Golondrina, La," 63
González, Andy, 69
"Good Golly, Miss Molly" (Blackwell/Marascalco), 117

New Orleans Rhythm Kings, 263–64

New York City: blues recordings in, 102; blues singers in, 107; Colonial and Federal periods in, 181; jazz in, 265; Latin-American music in, 67–70; nineteenth-century bands in, 231–32; nineteenth-century popular musical stage in, 201–03; rap and, 133; rock radio in, 123. *See also* Theater, popular musical

New York Philharmonic, 292–93

"Nikolina" (Peterson), 399–400

Nixon in China (Adams), 386–87

"No Irish Need Apply" (19th-century song of social comment), 226

"Nobody Knows the Trouble I've Had" (African-American spiritual), 23

"Nola" (novelty piano piece), 252

Nolan, Bob, 88

Nonmusical sounds, use of, 354

"North Country Blues" (Dylan), 14

Norway, dances from, 399

Norwegians, in upper midwest, 398–401

Norwood, Dorothy, 173

Notes of a Pianist (Gottschalk), 295

"Nottamun Town" (folk ballad), 15

Novelty piano, 252–53

"Now's the Time" (funky jazz), 275

Nueva canción, 66–67

"O Columbia, the Gem of the Ocean" (Shaw), 332, 336

"O Tannenbaum," 223

Oakland, Indian music in, 50

Oboe, in eighteenth-century bands, 186

"Ocean Burial, The" (Allen), 218

Octet (Reich), 371

Of Mice and Men (Floyd), 384

Of Thee I Sing (Gershwin), 208

Offenbach, Jacques, 201

"Oh, Bury Me Not on the Lone Prairie" (cowboy song), 218n, 317

"Oh, Dem Golden Slippers" (Bland), 200

"Oh! Susannah" (Foster), 9, 199, 222

Ojos Criollos (Gottschalk), 244

Oklahoma, as Indian Territory, 47–48

Oklahoma!, 210

Oklahoma City, blues in, 100

"Old Arm Chair, The" (Russell), 220

"Old Black Joe" (Foster), 197, 222–23, 304

"Old Chisholm Trail, The" (cowboy song), 317, 334

"Old Dan Tucker" (minstrel song as fiddle tune), 11

"Old Folks at Home" (Foster), 9, 222–23

"Old Hen Cackled and the Rooster's Going to Crow, The" (country-music song), 84

"Old Joe Clark" (fiddle tune), 10

"Old Man at the Mill, The" (play-party song), 79

"Old Rosin the Beau" (19th-century popular song), 12

"Old Rugged Cross, The" (popular sacred song), 165

"Old Time Religion" (Tillman), 167

"Old Uncle Ned" (Foster), 197, 199, 222

"Old Zip Coon," 194–96

Olio (form of musical theater), 194

Oliver, King, 261–67, 270

Oliveros, Pauline, 363

"On Jordan's Stormy Banks I Stand" (revival spiritual), 153–55

On the Town (Bernstein), 210

On the Waterfront (Bernstein), 315

On Your Toes (Rodgers), 210

"Once in a Lifetime" (Byrne), 131

114 Songs (Ives), 331–33, 337

"One Love" (Marley), 118

1000 Fiddle Tunes (Ryan/Cole), 11

O'Neill, Eugene, 381

Ongaku (Cowell), 341

"Only a Bird in a Gilded Cage," 229

"Only a Pawn in Their Game" (Dylan), 14

"Oop-Pap-a-Da" (Gillespie), 273

Operetta, 204–05

Organ, electric: in blues band, 108; in gospel music, 172

Organ, portative, 47, 55

Organ, reed, in gospel hymnody, 163

Original Dixieland Jazz Band, 263

Orpheus (Greek myth), 4

Orquestas típicas, 57

Ory, Kid, 271

Osborne Brothers (bluegrass group), 95

Osbourne, Ozzy, 120, 129

Ostrushko, Peter, 96

Our Town: Music from the Film Score (Copland), 315

"Out of Work" (Winner), 225

"Over the Rainbow" (movie song), 227

Plow That Broke the Plains, The
(Thomson), 312

Poem in Cycles and Bells, A (Luening and
Ussachevsky), 360

Poème électronique (Varèse), 347–48,
360

Poles, in upper midwest, 399

Polka: in "chicken scratch," 49; in Latino
music of Southwest, 57; in Mexican-
American music, 57, 59; in
Scandinavian-American music, 399

Poor Soldier, The (comic opera), 188

Porgy and Bess (Gershwin), 380–82

Porter, Cole, 206, 209, 279

Posadas, Las (Spanish-language
Christmas play), 55

Poulenc, Francis, 309

Powell, Bud, 271

Powell, Mel, 360

Pozo, Chano, 270

"Preacher, The" (Silver), 275

"Preacher and the Slave, The" (Joe Hill,
union song), 12

"Preachin' Blues," 35

"Precious Lord" (Dorsey), 170

Preludes for Piano (Gershwin), 321,
326

Presley, Elvis, 90, 109, 122–24, 128

Primavera, La (Farwell), 305

Prince (Rogers Nelson), 115, 119

Prine, John, 16

Prism (Druckman), 374

"Progress" (Clown Alley), 130

Projection 4 for Violin and Piano
(Feldman), 358

Prokofiev, Sergei, 309

Pryor, Arthur, 232

Psalm tunes: in classical music, 312; in
modern hymnals, 161

Psalm-Singer's Amusement, The (Billings),
144

Psalmody, 139–142; Gaelic, 141;
Regular Singing and, 142; Usual
Way of singing, 141–42

Puccini, Giacomo, 214

Puerto Rico, 68–69

Pulitzer Prize, 331, 338, 360, 375,
380

"Putnam's Camp" (Ives), 336

Quartetset (Currier), 375

Quintet for Brass (Bolcom), 375

"Quittin' Time Song," 28–29

Radio: country music and, 84, 91; the
corrido and, 61; gospel music and,
165, 166; Mexican-American in
southern California, 66; popular
song and, 234; rock and, 123

Rags, as fiddle tunes, 11

Ragtime: 302; blues and, 107; blues harmony in, 250; Chicago and, 252; in
classical music, 301; coon song, 229;
ensemble, 246; form, 249–50; and
gospel music, 172; Latin American
influence in, 244; march and, 249;
novelty piano and, 252–53; origins,
243–44; as piano music, 244–46;
publication, locales of, 246; revival,
253–54; rhythm, 246–49; secondary rag in, 253; song, 229–30,
243; Sousa's band and, 232, 246;
stride piano and, 252

Railroad train: in blues, 82; in country
music, 82–83

Rainey, Gertrude "Ma," 102–04, 170,
172, 199

"Rakes of Mallow, The" (dance tune), 182

Rap, 133–34; African music and, 133;
talking blues and, 133

Ravel, Maurice, 253, 386, 386n

Reaburn, Boyd, 273

Read, Daniel, 147

Red Mill, The (Herbert), 204

Red Moon, The (Cole and Johnson), 203

Redman, Don, 267

Reed, Dock, 27

Reggae, 131–32

Regina (Blitzstein), 384

Reich, Steve, 369–74, 376

Reinagle, Alexander, 183

Reis, Claire, 310

Remain in Light (Talking Heads) 131

Rent (Larson), 211, 213–14

Revivalism, nineteenth century, 151–56

Revivalist, The (19th-century tunebook),
154

Revue (form of musical theater), 199,
205

Rhapsodic Variations (Luening and
Ussachevsky), 360

Rhapsody in Blue (Gershwin), 253, 308,
311

Rhythm Pigs (rock group), 130

Rhythm-and-blues: origins, 108–09;
rock and, 119, 123; Tin Pan Alley
and, 237

Swan, Timothy, 144, 161
Swedes, in upper midwest, 398–401
Sweeney Todd (Sondheim), 211, 212
"Sweet By-and-By" (gospel hymn), 12, 163–64, 167
"Sweet Genevieve" (19th-century song), 226
"Sweet and Hot" (Arlen), 236
"Sweet Little Angel" (King), 109
"Sweet Lovin' Man" (King Oliver), 264
Sweethearts (Herbert), 204
Symphonic Sketches (Chadwick), 299
Symphony for Organ and Orchestra (Copland), 308
Symphony No. 1 (Harbison), 375
Symphony No. 2 ("Romantic") (Hanson), 326
Symphony No. 2 (Sessions), 326
Symphony No. 3 (Harris), 323–25
Symphony No. 3 (Ives), 331, 338
Symphony No. 4 (Bolcom), 377
Symphony No. 16 (*Icelandic*) (Cowell), 341
Symphony orchestras in the nineteenth century, 297
Synchronisms (Davidovsky), 360, 375
Syncopation, in ragtime, 246–49
Syttende mai (May 17, Norwegian Independence Day), 400

"Ta-Ra-Ra-Boom-De-Ay," 229
Tabasco (Chadwick), 299
Tailleferre, Germaine, 309
Taj Mahal, 110
"Take Five" (Desmond), 277
"Take Back Your Gold," 229
Talking Heads (rock group), 131
Tambourine: in gospel music, 27; in minstrel band, 196; in Sanctified church services, 169
Tango, 63, 68
Tatum, Art, 271, 273
"Taxi War Dance" (Basie), 269
Taylor, Cecil, 276
Taylor, Deems, 380
Taylor, KoKo, 110
Taylor, Raynor, 183
Teagarden, Jack, 236
Tehillim (Reich), 372
Telephone, as motive in gospel music, 166
Television evangelism, 165
Terry, Sonny, 107, 126

Texas: blues in, 107; corridos from, 60–61; country music and, 87–89; influence of Cajun music in, 87; influence of Mexican culture on, 87; Lydia Mendoza in, 63; musica norteña in, 58–59
Texas Playboys, 89
Tharpe, Sister Rosetta, 169, 172
"That Old Black Magic" (Arlen), 236
Theater, popular musical: black musicians on Broadway, 203; dance in, 210; in the eighteenth century, 186–89; evolution of dramatic values in, 206–08; foreign importations, 210–02; minstrelsy, 194–200; 1920s through 1950s, 205–10; operetta, 204–05; post–Civil War, 200–03; the revue, 205; since the advent of rock, 210–14; social significance in, 208–09; vaudeville, 201. *See also* individual composers and shows
Thielemans, "Toots," 278
"Things to Come" (Gillespie), 273
Third Symphony (Harris), 323–25
Third Symphony (Ives), 331, 338
39 Minutes for 39 Autos (Moran), 361
Thomas, Theodore, 297
Thompson, Randall, 320
Thomson, Virgil, 150, 234, 310, 312, 339, 341, 380, 382–84, 386; gospel hymns in the works of, 163
Thoreau, Henry David, 298
Thornhill, Claude, 273
Thornton, Willie Mae "Big Mama," 108
Three Compositions for Piano (Babbitt), 356
Three Movements for Orchestra (Reich), 372
Three Musketeers, The (Friml), 204
3 Phasis (Taylor), 276
Three Places in New England (Ives), 335–36, 339
Three Poems of Fiona MacLeod (Griffes), 302
Threnody for Carlos Chávez (Harrison), 342
"Thunderer, The" (Sousa), 233
Tides of Manaunaun, The (Cowell), 339–40
Tillis, Pam, 93
Tillman, Charlie D., 167–68
"Times They Are A-Changin', The" (Dylan), 14, 120

Tin Pan Alley, 226–29; decline of, 237; harmonic language as compared with that of rock, 115–16; gospel music and, 163, 166; marketing compared to that of rock, 124; relation to black vernacular music, 235–36; sheet music as presaging, 190

Tindley, Charles Albert, 15, 170

"'Tis the Gift to Be Simple" (Shaker spiritual), 156–57

Titanic (musical show), 212

"Titanic, The" (folk ballad), 6

"Titanic Man Blues" (Rainey), 103

Tizol, Juan, 268

Togo Brava Suite (Ellington), 269

Tolowa tribe, 42

"Tom Sails Away" (Ives), 332

Tone clusters, 333, 339–40, 354

Train, as motive in country music, 82–83; as motive in gospel music, 166

Travis, Merle, 90

Treemonisha (Joplin), 380

Trial of Mary Lincoln, The (Pasatieri), 384

Triangle ('tit fer) in Cajun music, 395

Trip to Coontown, A (Cole), 203

Trombone: in blues, 104; in gospel music, 27; in nineteenth-century band music, 231; revival meetings and the use of, 165; in Sanctified church services, 169; in traditional jazz, 261–62

Trumpet: in country music, 78; in gospel music, 27; in jazz, 261–62, 266, 268, 272, 274–75, 278; in mariachi music, 57–58; in Sanctified church services, 169

Tuba in traditional jazz, 262

Tubb, Ernest, 88

Tucker, Tanya , 93

Tufts, Rev. John, 142, 149

"Tumbling Tumbleweeds" (Nolan), 88

"Turkey in the Straw," 196, 247

Turner, Ike, 109

Turner, Joe, 108

Turner, Tina, 109

Turpin, Tom, 244

Twain, Mark, 225, 384

Twain, Shania, 93

Twelve Poems of Emily Dickinson (Copland), 319

Two-step (dance), 233n, 243

Tyranny, "Blue" Gene (Robert Sheff), 388

U.S. Highball (Partch), 344

Unanswered Question, The (Ives), 336–37, 339

Uncle Tom's Cabin (novel, Stowe), 222–23

Union Station (bluegrass group), 95

Union, The (Gottschalk), 294

Ussachevsky, Vladimir, 360

Vagabond King, The (Friml), 205

Vamp, in gospel music, 174

Van Halen (heavy metal group), 129

Van Halen, Edward, 130

Varèse, Edgard, 308, 346–48, 360

Variations on "America" (Ives), 330

Vaudeville, 85, 201; blues and, 102

Vaughan, Sarah, 104, 236

Vexations (Satie), 369

Vihuela, in mariachi, 57

"Village Maiden, The" (Foster), 218

Violin: as compared to fiddle, 10n; in country music, as opposed to fiddles, 91; in mariachi music, 57–58; as solo instrument in early concerts, 184

Violin Phase (Reich), 371

Virginia Minstrels, 197

Vocables, in Indian music, 47

"Volunteers" (Jefferson Airplane), 120

Vox balaenae (Voice of the Whale) (Crumb), 361

Voyage, The (Glass), 386

"Wabash Cannon Ball" (traditional country-western song), 79–80

Wagner, Richard, 304, 332

"Wag'ner" (fiddle tune), 10

"Waiting for the Robert E. Lee" (ragtime song) 243

Walker, Albertina, 172

Walker, George, 200

Walker, Joe Lewis, 110

"Wall Street Blues" (Handy), 101

Wallace, Sippie, 104

Wallace, Stewart, 387

Waller, Thomas "Fats," 204, 252

Waltz: in "chicken scratch," 49; as fiddle tune, 11; in Mexican-American music, 57, 59, 63; in Scandinavian-American music, 399

Ward, Clara, 172, 175, 176n

Warren, Robert Penn, 384

Washington, Sister Ernestine, 169

"Washington Post, The" (Sousa), 233, 233n

The following have graciously granted permission to reprint copyrighted material.